The Good Politician

Surveys show a lack of trust in political actors and institutions across much of the democratic world. Populist politicians and parties attempt to capitalise on this political disaffection. Commentators worry about our current 'age of anti-politics'. Focusing on the United Kingdom, using responses to public opinion surveys alongside diaries and letters collected by Mass Observation, this book takes a long view of anti-politics going back to the 1940s. This historical perspective reveals how anti-politics has grown in scope and intensity over the last half-century. Such growth is explained by citizens' changing images of 'the good politician' and changing modes of political interaction between politicians and citizens. Current efforts to reform and improve democracy will benefit greatly from the new evidence and conceptual framework set out in this important study.

Nick Clarke is Associate Professor of Human Geography at the University of Southampton.

Will Jennings is Professor of Political Science and Public Policy at the University of Southampton.

Jonathan Moss is Lecturer in Politics at the University of Sussex.

Gerry Stoker is Centenary Professor of Governance at the University of Canberra and Professor of Governance at the University of Southampton.

The Good Politician

Folk Theories, Political Interaction,
and the Rise of Anti-Politics

Nick Clarke
University of Southampton

Will Jennings
University of Southampton

Jonathan Moss
University of Sussex

Gerry Stoker
University of Southampton and University of Canberra

CAMBRIDGE
UNIVERSITY PRESS

CAMBRIDGE
UNIVERSITY PRESS

University Printing House, Cambridge CB2 8BS, United Kingdom

One Liberty Plaza, 20th Floor, New York, NY 10006, USA

477 Williamstown Road, Port Melbourne, VIC 3207, Australia

314–321, 3rd Floor, Plot 3, Splendor Forum, Jasola District Centre,
New Delhi – 110025, India

79 Anson Road, #06-04/06, Singapore 079906

Cambridge University Press is part of the University of Cambridge.

It furthers the University's mission by disseminating knowledge in the pursuit of
education, learning, and research at the highest international levels of excellence.

www.cambridge.org
Information on this title: www.cambridge.org/9781316516218
DOI: 10.1017/9781108641357

First published 2018

Printed in the United Kingdom by Clays, St Ives plc

A catalogue record for this publication is available from the British Library.

Library of Congress Cataloging-in-Publication Data
Names: Clarke, Nick, 1974– author. | Jennings, Will, author. | Moss,
Jonathan, author. | Stoker, Gerry, author.
Title: The good politician : political interaction and the rise of anti-politics /
Nick Clarke, University of Southampton, Will Jennings, University
of Southampton, Jonathan Moss, University of Southampton,
Gerry Stoker, University of Southampton.
Description: New York : Cambridge University Printing House,
[2018] | Includes bibliographical references and index.
Identifiers: LCCN 2017053784 | ISBN 9781316516218
Subjects: LCSH: Political participation. | Apathy – Political aspects.
Classification: LCC JF799 .C6 2018 | DDC 323/.042–dc23
LC record available at https://lccn.loc.gov/2017053784

ISBN 978-1-316-51621-8 Hardback
ISBN 978-1-108-45981-5 Paperback

Contents

Figures

Tables

Preface: The Long Road to 2016, Brexit, and Trump

We began the research project behind this book in 2014, focused on the period since 1945 – a widely recognised milestone for British politics. We were especially interested in what we call 'anti-politics': citizens' negative sentiment regarding formal politics, with 'formal politics' describing that set of activities and institutions required for collective and binding decision-making in plural societies (i.e. tolerating, canvassing, negotiating, compromising, and their institutionalisation in politicians, parties, elections, parliaments, governments). We were interested in the claim, often made, that political disaffection has grown over time in many democracies, such that – compared to the period following the Second World War – we are now living through an 'age of anti-politics'. We were interested in testing this claim using the case of the United Kingdom (UK), for which good evidence is perhaps uniquely available in the form of public opinion surveys but also letters and diaries collected by Mass Observation (MO), all dating back to the late 1930s.

As our project continued, we realised that another milestone for British politics may have been reached in 2016. Brexit – British exit from the European Union (EU), decided by a referendum in June 2016 – marks a turning point in the process of European institution-building that began soon after the Second World War. Across the Atlantic, a milestone for American politics may also have been reached in 2016. Donald Trump became the first US President with no experience of military service or government, whether elected or appointed. Also worth noting here is the rise of populism across Europe. By 2015, parties aligning themselves with 'the people' against 'the political class' had gained at least 10 per cent of the vote in twenty European countries. In five of these countries – Greece, Hungary, Italy, Slovakia, and Switzerland – such parties had become the largest party. Also worth noting here is the electoral success of Pauline Hanson's One Nation party in Australia, where Hanson and three colleagues became Senators in the federal election of 2016. In short, this book may draw on British evidence, for the most part, but its themes are relevant to the dynamic of democracies across much of the contemporary world.

Let us consider some of these recent events in a little more detail. There are many ways to interpret Brexit, but one way is to view it as a consequence of the long-term increase in citizens' political disaffection we describe and explain in this book. 'Leave' advocates campaigned against the need for politics at the European scale. The campaign against the EU was closely associated with the United Kingdom Independence Party (UKIP), which over the years has campaigned against much of politics at the national scale too. Here is Nigel Farage, then leader of UKIP, speaking on the morning of the referendum result (24 June 2016):

> Dare to dream that the dawn is breaking on an independent United Kingdom ... this will be a victory for real people, a victory for ordinary people, a victory for decent people. We have fought against the multinationals. We have fought against the big merchant banks. We have fought against big politics. We have fought against lies, corruption, and deceit. And today, honesty, decency, and belief in nation, I think now is going to win. And we will have done it without having to fight, without a single bullet being fired.

The anti-politics themes in this extract are clear. Brexit is a 'victory' for the people ('real people', 'ordinary people', 'decent people') against a 'big politics' associated with 'lies, corruption, and deceit'.

The preceding quotation finishes with the line 'without a single bullet being fired'. But a number of bullets *were* fired in June 2016. Jo Cox, Member of Parliament (MP) for Batley and Spen, was stabbed and shot during the EU referendum campaign. Like the result of the referendum, there are many ways to interpret the murder of Jo Cox. It was a particular act: the murder of an MP just prior to a constituency surgery during a referendum campaign. She was a particular politician: a young woman, a Labour MP, a 'Remain' supporter with interests in Syria and Islamophobia – to give just a couple of examples. The attacker was also a particular citizen, of course, to whom the judge said when sentencing him (23 November 2016): 'It is clear from your Internet and other researches that your inspiration is ... an admiration for Nazism and similar anti-democratic white supremacist creeds, where democracy and political persuasion are supplanted by violence towards and intimidation of opponents and those who, in whatever way, are thought to be different and, for that reason, open to persecution.' Our point, here, is that Jo Cox's murder – a particular event – happened against a background of rising anti-political sentiment. In recent years, one expression of this development appears to have been increasing levels of abuse and threat faced by politicians of all parties, and especially women. It was in this context, in July 2017, that Parliament's Committee on Standards in Public Life launched a review of 'Abuse and intimidation experienced by parliamentary candidates during elections'.

Crossing the Atlantic, among the many ways to interpret the election of Trump, one way again is to view it as a consequence of a long-term rise in citizens' political disaffection. Consider this extract from Trump's inauguration speech (20 January 2017):

Every four years, we gather on these steps to carry out the orderly and peaceful transfer of power ... Today's ceremony, however, has very special meaning. Because today, we are not merely transferring power from one Administration to another, or from one party to another – but we are transferring power from Washington DC and giving it back to you, the American People. For too long, a small group in our nation's Capital has reaped the rewards of government, while the people have borne the cost. Washington flourished – but the people did not share in its wealth. Politicians prospered – but the jobs left and the factories closed. The establishment protected itself but not the citizens of our country. Their victories have not been your victories; their triumphs have not been your triumphs; and while they celebrated in our nation's Capital, there was little to celebrate for struggling families all across our land. That all changes – starting right here, and right now, because this moment is your moment: it belongs to you ... What truly matters is not which party controls our government, but whether our government is controlled by the people. January 20th 2017 will be remembered as the day the people became the rulers of this nation again.

Trump campaigned against politics. He campaigned against the institutions of formal politics: 'Washington DC' (as opposed to 'the American people'); 'politicians' (as opposed to 'struggling families'); 'the establishment' (as opposed to 'the citizens of our country'); political parties (as opposed to 'the people'). He also campaigned against the activities of politics, addressed later in the same inauguration speech: 'We will no longer accept politicians who are all talk and no action – constantly complaining but never doing anything about it. The time for empty talk is over. Now arrives the hour of action.' Trump campaigned against the tolerating, canvassing, negotiating, and compromising that may sound like 'empty talk' and may delay or limit 'action' but are necessary for democracy to be more than Alexis de Tocqueville's 'tyranny of the majority'. And, campaigning against politics, Trump won!

As we researched and wrote this book, Trump was elected US President, the UK began the process of leaving the EU, and populism was being discussed across Europe and beyond. There were also two general elections in the UK. We cover the general election of 2015 in the rest of the book. The 2017 election happened just as we completed the manuscript, so we finish this preface with a few comments on that most recent of political events. Anti-political themes were clearly present during much of the 2017 campaign. On 18 April, when Prime Minister Theresa May announced there would be an early election – just two years after the last general election and one year after the EU referendum – a television news reporter asked citizens in Bristol for their reaction. One reaction from a woman called Brenda went viral (as 'Brenda from Bristol') – presumably because of how it resonated with citizens around the UK and, apparently, much of the Anglophone world: 'You're joking! Not another one! Oh for God's sake! I can't, honestly, I can't stand this. There's too much politics going on at the moment.' Once the campaign was under way, Theresa May, Leader of the Conservative Party, sought to present herself as above and beyond politics. Listen to this from a speech she gave when launching her party's manifesto (18 May 2017):

[M]ost important of all, the Government I lead will provide strong and stable leadership to see us through Brexit and beyond: tackling the long-term challenges we face, and ensuring everyone in our country has the chance to get on in life. We need that strong and stable leadership now more than ever. For the next five years will be among the most challenging of our lifetime ... it is why in this election – more than in any before – it is time to put the old, tribal politics behind us and to come together in the national interest: united in our desire to make a success of Brexit. United in our desire to get the right result for Britain. Because every vote for me and my team in this election will strengthen my hand in the negotiations to come.

If May dismissed party politics as 'old, tribal politics' and denied the reality of multiple interests in the UK after the EU referendum (hence, we might say, the continuing need for a vibrant party politics), then Jeremy Corbyn, Leader of the Labour Party, took a different line. Consider this from his first speech after May's initial announcement (20 April 2017):

Much of the media and establishment are saying that this election is a foregone conclusion. They think there are rules in politics, which if you don't follow by doffing your cap to powerful people, accepting that things can't really change, then you can't win. But of course, they do not want us to win. Because when we win it is the people, not the powerful, who win.

And consider this from the speech he used to launch his campaign (9 May 2017): 'We have to convince the sceptical and undecided. They are not sure which way to turn. And who can blame them? People are alienated from politics and politicians. Our Westminster system is broken and our economy is rigged. Both are run in the interests of the few.' This line from Corbyn was different from May's but still incorporated anti-political themes in its own way. 'The people' were positioned against 'the establishment'. A 'Westminster system' that is 'broken' was positioned as responsible for citizens' alienation from 'politics and politicians' (in general). We discuss the relationship between political disaffection and the supply of politics in later chapters of the book. What we can say here is that both leaders of the UK's two main parties campaigned in 2017 *against politics* – against plurality, parties, negotiation, and compromise in the case of May and against 'the Westminster system' in the case of Corbyn – at least as much as they campaigned against each other or (perish the thought!) *for* politics. They did this, presumably, because they sensed the broad scope and high intensity of anti-political feeling in twenty-first-century British society.

As a team, at the time of writing these final words, we are still not quite in agreement about how to interpret the general election of 2017. One conclusion we do share is that our framework developed in the rest of this book brings into sharp focus themes that are central to most if not all contemporary democracies. How is anti-politics to be defined? What explains its growth? What features of politics make it susceptible to anti-political sentiment on the part of citizens? These are questions to which many would say we urgently need answers. In this book, we provide some of these answers in the form of a new analytical framework backed by a unique, rich, long-term view of the issues – drawing on both quantitative and qualitative data.

Since one of us calls geography their disciplinary home, let us finish by mobilising the language of climate science and distinguishing between the political *weather* and the political *climate*. This book is about a long-term change in the political climate. Knowledge of such a change may help us to interpret certain short-term (political) weather events – such as Brexit or Trump or the UK general election of 2017. But just as one cold winter does not undermine the case for climate change in the natural world, so we should be careful of making too much from one campaign or its outcome. The year 2016 may well prove to be another milestone in the history of British politics (and perhaps democratic politics more broadly). But if that is the case, then we are now at the beginning of a new period. Initial signs of this new period are not promising. It looks to be characterised by a resurgent nationalism, populist politicians and parties, the Internet, fake news, social media bubbles, and so on. But actually, as with all periods, the characteristics of this new period are still to be made. By helping us to understand the challenges, this book also aims to shape the future along more desirable paths. Democracy and the politics associated with it were far from perfect in the twentieth century, as our evidence shows, but its changing character, potential, and flaws need to be understood better if we are to avoid a democratic collapse in the twenty-first century.

Acknowledgements

We are very grateful to numerous individuals and organisations for their support over the past three or so years. The research was funded by the Economic and Social Research Council (ESRC) (grant number ES/L007185/1). Ruth Fox from the Hansard Society kindly wrote in support of our funding application to the ESRC. Mike Savage, Andrew Russell, Joe Twyman, and Tristram Hunt kindly agreed to be named reviewers for that application.

The book rests heavily on data collected by Mass Observation (MO) and made available by the Mass Observation Archive (MOA) in Brighton. Archivists Fiona Courage and Jessica Scantlebury were particularly helpful throughout our study – from the project-design stage through the data-collection stage to the final stage of disseminating findings. Quotations from MO panellists are reproduced in the book by kind permission of Curtis Brown Group Ltd on behalf of the Trustees of the MOA (© The Mass Observation Archive).

The book also rests on survey data collected over the years by various research projects and polling organisations. Individual-level survey data from the British Election Study and the British Social Attitudes survey proved invaluable for taking the long view, as did poll data from Gallup, Ipsos MORI, YouGov, and Populus. We are particularly grateful to Joe Twyman and Laurence Janta-Lipinski at YouGov and Laurence Stellings at Populus for their assistance in conducting new survey research used in the book.

We organised three workshops in Southampton to discuss anti-politics with academic and other colleagues from around the country in October 2014, January 2016, and September 2016. We learned a huge amount from these workshops and thank all the participants for their time and critical engagement. We are especially grateful to Florence Sutcliffe-Braithwaite, who, after the second of these workshops, invited us to write a piece on anti-politics for *Renewal* (see Clarke et al. 2016). We also thank Oliver Escobar, Andrew Gamble, and Gavin Shuker MP for thoughtful written responses to that piece in the same journal.

xvi   Acknowledgements

In May 2016, we organised a public event on 'The Rise of Anti-Politics

In May 2016, we organised a public event on 'The Rise of Anti-Politics in the UK' at Portcullis House, Westminster. Again, we are very grateful to all those who participated – especially Isabel Hardman and Tristram Hunt, who participated formally as panellists and contributed their distinct experience and insight to the discussion.

Between 2014 and 2017, we presented the research at numerous conferences, workshops, and seminars organised by others – both in the UK and overseas. We also wrote up elements of the research for papers now published in *Parliamentary Affairs*, *The Political Quarterly*, *Contemporary British History*, *Political Geography*, and *Public Opinion Quarterly*. Through all of these engagements, we think we improved our understanding and refined our arguments. For this, we thank all of those involved: organisers, audience members, reviewers, and editors.

The book is published by Cambridge University Press (CUP) and special thanks must go to publisher John Haslam for seeing worth in the proposal, overseeing the peer-review process, and pushing the book through CUP's Syndicate.

Figure 5.1 is reproduced by kind permission of The Labour Party.

Finally, we have all benefited from the support and critical friendship of brilliant colleagues and students at the University of Southampton (and, in the case of Gerry, the University of Canberra too). And we have all benefited from the support and care of our wonderful – and wonderfully patient! – families.

Introduction

According to the most recent World Values Survey (WVS, 2010–2014), the majority of citizens across the sixty countries surveyed do not have much confidence in government, parliament, or political parties. Just over half reported not very much or no confidence in government, 57 per cent reported not very much or no confidence in parliament, and two-thirds reported such a lack of confidence in political parties. According to the most recent European Social Survey (2014), the majority of citizens across the fifteen countries surveyed think that the political system allows them to have little influence on politics, that politicians don't care about what people think, and that politicians and political parties are not to be trusted.[1] There is potentially a lot at stake. Drawing on WVS data, Foa and Mounk (2016: 6) argue:

Three decades ago, most scholars simply assumed that the Soviet Union would remain stable. This assumption was suddenly proven false. Today, we have even greater confidence in the durability of the world's affluent, consolidated democracies. But do we have good grounds for our democratic self-confidence? At first sight, there would seem to be some reason for concern ... Even in some of the richest and most politically stable regions of the world, it seems as though democracy is in a state of serious disrepair.

Many scholars are not so gloomy about the future, but it would be reasonable to share some concern about the state of democracy in a context where the activity that brings it to life – politics – is viewed with a great deal of negativity and anxiety.

Mainstream politicians have tended to respond to this lack of confidence, trust, and perceived efficacy with 'democratic innovations', e.g. lowering the voting age, devolving power to regions/localities, or participatory decision-making. Other politicians – from Marine Le Pen to Nigel

[1] On a scale running from 10 (completely) to 1 (not at all), just under two-thirds gave a score of 4 or less to the statement 'The political system allows people to have influence on politics', and a similar proportion gave a score of 4 or less to the statement 'Politicians care about what people think'. Fifty-five per cent gave such a low score for trust in politicians and also for trust in political parties.

1

Farage to Donald Trump – have responded with versions of populism, positioning themselves with 'the people' against a system characterised as broken and a political class characterised as uncaring, untrustworthy, and out of touch with ordinary people.

Meanwhile, journalists have tended to respond – both to citizens' disaffection with politics and to populists' denigration of politics – by writing of 'anti-politics'. They sense an 'anti-politics mood' (Rawnsley 2016) or 'anti-politics wave' (Rentoul 2014) or 'anti-politics breeze' (Toynbee 2015). They describe an 'age of anti-politics' (d'Ancona 2016) or 'anti-politics age' (Lichfield 2016). For Rachel Sylvester (2014: 25), writing in *The Times*:

The anti-politics mood is growing all over the world, but manifests itself in different ways. In America, there is a loathing of big government that chimes with the individualism in the land of the free. In France, a distinctive form of nationalism taps into the anti-establishment mood, while in Greece and Spain a left-wing anti-austerity message is winning support. In Britain, intrigued and horrified by its upstairs-downstairs past, UKIP [the United Kingdom Independence Party] is playing on historical class divides.

There is much to unpack here. In this book, we offer our own response to this anti-politics talk and the survey results, democratic innovations, and populist campaigns it brings into focus.

We bring to the debate two connected methodological developments. First, we offer a longer view on the development of anti-politics than is found in most previous analysis. We explore the rise of anti-politics across eight decades. Second, we give a multi-layered voice to citizens' concerns about politics by mixing qualitative data from Mass Observation (MO) studies with quantitative analysis of responses to public opinion surveys. Using these two approaches allows us to conclude that – for the United Kingdom (UK), at least – anti-political sentiment has probably never been absent among citizens but has become more widely held and intensely felt over time. Our explanation for this growth is that citizens' changing images of what makes for a good politician, together with changing patterns of interaction between politicians and citizens, have shaped a more negative folk theory of democratic politics – a more negative popular narrative of how formal politics is *meant* to work and how it *does* work for most people. The increased prevalence of anti-political sentiment among citizens reflects both a heightened set of expectations regarding the qualities and character of a good politician and a reduced set of opportunities for making positive judgements about individual politicians (because of the nature of political exchange on offer in contemporary democracies). Anti-politics is the price that contemporary democracies are paying for developing political systems where citizens expect politicians to be exceptionally competent (capable, trustworthy, strong) and, at the same time, ordinary ('normal', 'in touch'). It is the price paid for political systems where the remoteness and negativity generated by political marketing renders positive judgements about politics unlikely if not impossible.

Anti-Politics

We define anti-politics as citizens' negative sentiment towards the activities and institutions of formal politics (politicians, parties, elections, councils, parliaments, governments). Anti-politics, we argue, should not be confused with healthy scepticism towards formal politics, which most theories see as an essential component of democracy (e.g. Sniderman 1981). Anti-politics goes beyond healthy scepticism to the point of unhealthy cynicism. Nor should it be confused with apathy, where citizens are less disaffected with and more just indifferent to formal politics. Nor should anti-politics be confused with a changing party system. Many citizens around the world are currently shifting their allegiances from older, larger, established parties to newer, smaller, challenger parties. But many others are disengaging completely, having decided that all parties and politicians are just as bad as each other. Finally, anti-politics should not be confused with a crisis of democracy. While there is much evidence of negative sentiment towards the institutions of formal politics, there is little evidence of such feeling towards the idea of democracy itself (Norris 2011).

We argue that anti-politics matters. It is associated with non-participation such as not voting and non-compliance such as not paying taxes (Dalton 2004, Norris 2011). It is associated with support for populism (Ford and Goodwin 2014, Jennings et al. 2016) – a problematic form of politics that misrepresents heterogeneous populations as homogeneous peoples, misrepresents all other politicians as elites opposed to those peoples, and misrepresents the institutions and procedures for negotiation and compromise between competing interests – i.e. politics – as just unnecessary bureaucracy. Anti-politics also makes government more difficult. Government is easier when demands have been aggregated by strong parties (Dalton 2004) and legitimacy has been granted by strong electoral support (Hetherington 2005).

There is a discussion of whether negativity towards formal politics is currently being cancelled out by positivity towards informal politics ('the democratisation thesis' – Dalton 2000). We argue that little empirical support exists for such an optimistic view. In countries like the UK, only minorities participate in alternative activities like signing petitions, buying products for political reasons, or working in voluntary organisations (Whiteley 2012). These numbers are not really growing (ibid.). And, far from being disaffected citizens looking for alternative outlets for their political energies, protesters – whether demonstrators, boycotters, or signers of petitions – are more likely to be members of political parties and voters too (Norris et al. 2006, Saunders 2014). We argue that informal politics is not replacing formal politics but actually depends on a functioning formal politics for its freedoms and achievements. Democracy, if it is to provide government that is not only responsive but also able to make and enforce collective decisions, requires a balance between formal and informal politics. So anti-politics matters in so far as it directly undermines formal politics and indirectly undermines all politics (including informal politics). These issues and some of the conceptual challenges associated with anti-politics are discussed further in Chapter 1.

Taking the Long View

In the rest of the book, we take a longer view of anti-politics than has been taken by most researchers to date. Existing research has mostly taken a relatively short view and considered anti-political sentiment at one particular historical moment or the development of anti-political sentiment over just the past few decades. For example, Steven Fielding (2008) studied popular attitudes to British politics expressed in commercial feature films and public opinion polls in the two decades following the Second World War. He found evidence of anti-party populism. Citizens were viewed as powerless, while politicians were viewed as corrupt. He concluded that 'populism is not a recent phenomenon provoked by social change but something deriving from endemic tensions at the heart of representative democracy' (p128). Another example is the comparative research of Pippa Norris (2011). She studied longitudinal trends and cross-national patterns in political support using data from Eurobarometer (since the early 1970s) and the World Values Survey (since the early 1980s). She found variation by country and object of political support, which led her to conclude that 'confidence in public sector institutions ebbs and flows during these decades' (p12), 'public support for the political system has not eroded consistently in established democracies' (p241), and 'fluctuations over time usually prove far more common than straightforward linear or uniform downward trends' (p241).

Here, we have two different illustrations of the short view. Fielding considers one particular historical moment (the immediate post-war period), finds evidence of anti-politics, and concludes that if anti-politics was prevalent then it is surely a permanent fixture of British political culture. For Norris, the timeframe is recent decades (since the early 1970s). Looking across a range of countries and indicators, she sees only 'trendless fluctuation' (p241). In their own ways, each of these studies challenges common assumptions of declining political support and rising political disaffection. But they do so from particular historical perspectives. We argue that baseline and timeframe are crucial when studying change over time. If a longer period was considered, what would be the pattern of historical continuity and change?

There is a need for longer views of anti-politics. Since popular discussion often assumes a 'golden age' for democratic politics just after the Second World War – when voter turnout in countries like the UK was relatively high (see Chapter 1) – there is a need for views covering both the current so-called 'age of anti-politics' and the immediate post-war period. Some studies do exist going back further than Eurobarometer data from the 1970s. Research on political support in America often takes the late 1950s as its starting point, when the forerunner to the American National Election Study began asking questions about political trust (e.g. Putnam et al. 2000). Other single-country studies have managed to construct datasets going back to 1957 in the case of Norway (Listhaug 2006), 1959 for Italy (Segatti 2006), 1968 for Sweden (Holmberg 1999), and 1969 for Australia (Goot 2002). We are not aware of any existing studies that cover the full period of interest from the present day back to at least the Second World War.[2]

This is hardly surprising. Studies of historical change over more than a few decades are fraught with methodological challenges. We discuss these challenges in Chapter 2. We go on to argue that, for the case of the UK, such challenges can be overcome. Trends for things like approval of government or satisfaction with leaders can be constructed from commercial polling data (first collected by the British Institute of Public Opinion or BIPO in 1937). Historical comparisons for things like the suspected motivations of politicians can be constructed from survey data collected by BIPO, Gallup, Ipsos MORI, YouGov, and other polling organisations. Perhaps most significantly, a long-term index of political disaffection can be constructed from these datasets and others – including

---

[2] Goot's (2002) study of Australia probably comes closest. While he finds data on trust in government and political interest going back only to 1969, he finds more narrowly focused data on political parties – e.g. perceptions of difference between the main parties – going back to 1946.

the British Election Study since 1963 – using James Stimson's (1991) dyad-ratios algorithm. We do this in Chapter 3.

Listening to Citizens' Voices

In addition to taking the long view, in the rest of the book we also listen to citizens' voices more than has been done by most research on anti-politics to date. Existing research in this field has been dominated by large-scale surveys and closed questions. There is a need to listen more to what citizens say about politics when allowed to speak in their own terms on the subject. This has been done to some extent for the current period, where interviews and focus groups have been completed with citizens (e.g. Allen and Birch 2015a, Hibbing and Theiss-Morse 2002, Hörschelmann and El Refaie 2013, Manning and Holmes 2013, McDowell et al. 2014, O'Toole et al. 2003, van Wessel 2010). But it has not really been done for the past, not least because researchers holding twenty-first-century concerns cannot go back in time and discuss them with people from an earlier period. One exception worth mentioning here is Jay Childers' (2012) study of youth in America. He listens to – or reads – their voices in high school newspapers going back to 1965. This longitudinal yet qualitative study is novel and rigorous in its use of high school newspapers to excavate citizens' changing orientations to politics. But the focus is rather narrow – both socially (on American youth) and temporally (going back only to 1965).

In Chapter 2, we argue that listening to a wider range of citizens over a longer period of time is possible for the case of the UK because of a possibly unique dataset: the Mass Observation Archive. Mass Observation (MO) was founded in 1937, the same year BIPO began collecting survey data in the UK. Between 1939 and 1955 and again between 1981 and the present, MO ran a panel of between 400 and 1000 volunteer writers (depending on the year). On numerous occasions during both periods – which happen to correspond to the so-called 'golden age' of democracy and the so-called 'age of anti-politics' – panellists were asked by MO to write about formal politics (politicians, parties, elections, governments). Historians have used MO sources to study the immediate post-war period and to argue that Britain's political culture has long been characterised by anti-political feeling (e.g. Fielding et al. 1995, Jefferys 2007). We build on such research in two main ways. First, instead of taking the short view of just the immediate post-war period, we take the long view by comparing the writing of MO panellists in the earlier period with equivalent writing from the later period. Second, instead of relying on summaries of MO material constructed by MO researchers (known as File Reports and Topic Collections) – as these historians did, at least for the most part – we undertook our own systematic analysis of the 'raw' data.

We discuss this further in Chapter 2, where we also clarify our treatment of the various datasets in the book as a whole. Chapter 3 uses large-scale survey data to establish the changing social scope of anti-politics. This is a topic for which survey data is most appropriate. The original contribution in Chapter 3 is the application of statistical techniques like Stimson's dyad-ratios algorithm. Most of the rest of the book is driven by the MO data. We ask: What can this unusual dataset tell us about anti-politics? What can it tell us about existing claims and theories of anti-politics? What new claims and theories – new patterns and explanations – are suggested by the MO material? What new hypotheses are generated for testing by future research? In the rest of the book, we make some new claims – the original contributions of Chapters 4 to 8 – and begin the process of testing these claims by bringing back the survey data at various points. At some points, we find little available survey data to bring back in (a symptom of the historical development of public opinion research discussed in Chapter 2). But at other points, we can see to what extent our findings from the MO research are supported by available survey data.

One further clarification is worth providing at this early stage. Political support is multi-dimensional (Easton 1965, 1975). Across the chapters, we consider various objects of political support. In Chapter 3, the wide focus covers Members of Parliament, ministers, politicians, parties, Parliament, the government, the system of governing, and citizens (their political efficacy). In Chapter 6, the focus is mostly on parties. In Chapter 8, the focus is mostly on elections, political campaigning, and media coverage of politics. But in much of the book – Chapters 4, 5, and 7 – the focus is mostly on politicians. This emphasis is one reason for the book's title: *The Good Politician*. We focus on politicians above all other objects of political support because the MO material encouraged such a focus. MO panellists wrote much more about politicians than parties, governments, Parliament, or the political system as a whole. We also learned from Hibbing and Theiss-Morse (1995) and Whiteley et al. (2016) that politicians deserve such a central place in research on anti-politics because when citizens think of more abstract objects – such as Congress in the case of Hibbing and Theiss-Morse – they often think of the politicians who make up those institutions. They use politicians as a heuristic to judge the activities and institutions of formal politics in general (Whiteley et al. 2016).

The Rise of Anti-Politics

Having taken the long view and listened to citizens' voices, we provide a new analysis of anti-politics in the UK. We argue that no golden age of political support existed. Even in the immediate post-war period, substantial proportions of the population disapproved of governments and prime ministers (whatever their political persuasion). They thought politicians to be out for themselves and their party (as opposed to their country). They associated political campaigning with vote-catching stunts, mud-slinging, and a focus on personalities over policies. They imagined politicians to be self-seeking 'gasbags'. However, we also argue – contrary to narratives of permanent anti-politics or trendless fluctuation – that anti-political sentiment has increased in the UK over the past half-century in at least three respects: social scope, political scope, and intensity.

In Chapter 3, we use survey data to demonstrate how the *social scope* of anti-politics has increased over time. More and more citizens have expressed negativity towards the activities and institutions of formal politics. For example, more and more citizens have disapproved of governments and prime ministers and judged politicians to be out for themselves and their parties. Today, political disaffection is still felt more strongly in certain social groups (e.g. older, poorer, less educated men). But on some measures – such as questions about the competence of politicians – these differences have now shrunk as the vast majority of the UK's population express negativity towards formal politics.

In Chapter 4, we demonstrate how the *political scope* of anti-politics has increased over time. Citizens have expressed more and more grievances regarding the activities and institutions of formal politics. For example, in the first period of data collection by MO (1939–1955), panellists often described politicians as being self-interested (they were 'self-seekers' or 'place-seekers') and not straight-talking (they were 'gasbags' or 'gift of the gabbers'). In the second period (1981–2015), these storylines were still commonly used by panellists, but so were a number of newer ones. Politicians were also described as being out of touch ('toffs' and 'career politicians') and all the same (from similar backgrounds, focused on similar problems, offering similar solutions, and 'all as bad as each other').

Anti-politics has increased in social and political scope but also in the strength by which more and more citizens hold more and more grievances – what we call *intensity*. This claim is demonstrated in Chapter 5, again drawing on MO sources (with support from survey data). Panellists in the 1940s and 1950s were less deferent and more critical of politicians than we might expect – at least given the 'decline of deference' literature (e.g. Nevitte 1996). They were also critical of doctors (seen as incompetent and self-interested) and lawyers (seen as dishonest 'sharks'). Panellists in recent decades were generally no more critical of these other professions than they had been in the earlier period (indeed, they were often less critical in the later period). The exception was negative feeling towards politicians, which had intensified – and beyond what could reasonably be expected as a result of things like citizens' improved education and higher expectations of politics. Many panellists in the 2000s and 2010s reported feeling 'anger', 'outrage', and 'disgust' towards politicians who they described as 'contemptable', 'disgraceful', 'loathsome', and 'shameful'.

Explaining Anti-Politics: Conceptual Tools

Having offered this new account of how anti-politics has developed over time, we turn to the question of what explains the rise of anti-politics. Much existing research on what explains patterns of political support has focused on either 'demand-side' or 'supply-side' factors. Some argue that citizens have changed and now demand different things from politics (e.g. Inglehart 1997, Norris 1999). Citizens are thought to have become more educated, more secure in economic terms, and less deferent to authority figures. They are thought to expect more from formal politics and also to practise their own informal politics, making formal politics less important for them compared to previous generations. Others argue that politics has changed – the supply of politics – and now provides different things to citizens (e.g. Hay 2007, Mouffe 2005). Parties are thought to have converged on the terrain of neoliberalism – a project of the New Right attacking the public domain in the name of free markets and market discipline. Neoliberalism positions civil servants and politicians as self-interested rent-seekers and removes power and responsibility from public actors via deregulation, privatisation, and audit. In turn, citizens are thought to withdraw from formal politics once there seems to be no meaningful choice between parties, and politicians seem to be at the same time both self-interested and powerless.

At the end of his influential book on *Why We Hate Politics*, Colin Hay (2007: 160) called for something beyond this supply-and-demand framework:

[I]t is time that we rejected the overly parsimonious language of supply and demand. Politics is more complicated than that ... [The] task from now on must surely be to analyse rather more effectively the complex relationships between the ideas and assumptions we project on to politics on the one hand, and the practices and processes on to which those ideas and assumptions are projected on the other.

In responding to this call, we focus on citizens' judgements of politics as they relate to understandings of and encounters with politics. We develop an approach to explaining anti-politics focused on citizens' folk theories of politics and how citizens form judgements of politics in relation to these folk theories but also to interactions with politics and especially politicians.

Folk Theories

Our approach to how citizens understand politics has numerous origins. One is well-established research on political culture, defined as people's attitudes and feelings towards the political system but also their knowledge of the political system and especially their expectations regarding the potential of that system to effect change and the role of the self within that system (Almond and Verba 1963). Another is cognitive science of the past few decades (see Holland and Quinn 1987, Lakoff and Johnson 2003). This teaches how behaviour is shaped by understanding, and, in turn, understanding is shaped by cultural knowledge in the form of shared models, schemas, frameworks, scripts, stories, metaphors, and prototypes. A third origin is social theoretical writing on discourses as forms of consciousness (Foucault 1991) made up of concepts, ideas, representations, images, frames, stories, narratives, and subject positions. Such discourses delimit what can be thought and said, inform practices, and so construct social reality. Yet another origin is the interpretive approach to political science, where actions are taken to follow from beliefs and beliefs are taken to be holistic: action within a discourse or tradition (Bevir and Rhodes 2005).

What all these origins or influences point to is that citizens develop orientations – such as negativity towards the activities and institutions of formal politics – by drawing on repertoires of cultural resources. These are generated where expert knowledge, popular wisdom, and personal experience meet. They are communicated and disclosed through talk or writing. Perhaps most importantly, at least for this book, cultural resources vary over time in their prevalence and prominence. They are constructed and deconstructed in relation to changing social conditions (Fairclough 2002). As they come and go or stay and mutate, certain ways of thinking, being, and doing are made available to citizens at certain historical moments.

In Chapter 2, we discuss existing research where these insights have already been mobilised in political studies (e.g. Gamson 1992, Lakoff 2002). In the rest of the book, we seek to apply these insights with a light touch, allowing us also to present the voices of citizens and tell our own story. To this end, we analyse the MO material for cultural resources. We identify categories, storylines, and folk theories about politics that are shared by panellists at particular historical moments. And we track changes in the prevalence and prominence of different cultural resources over time. To demonstrate all this, we use many quotations from the diaries and letters of MO panellists. There is a risk that some readers may get lost in these quotations. Summary tables of cultural resources are provided in each chapter as navigational aids for such readers. But we positively encourage readers to get delayed by the quotations. We encourage readers to listen to these citizens. We found ourselves fascinated by their voices, and we hope that others will be too.

In Chapter 9, we bring together various parts of the argument and situate folk theories more clearly in debates within and about cognitive science. Citizens, it would seem, do not pay much attention to politics (Marcus et al. 2000, Zaller 1992). They are minimally informed about politics (Delli Carpini and Keeter 1996). So they make judgements about politics using System 1 thinking (Stanovich and West 2000) or fast thinking (Kahneman 2011). These modes of thinking require a model of the world, of what is normal, that provides cognitive cues for understanding, justification, and action (ibid.). These models of the world are 'cultural models' (Quinn and Holland 1987) or 'simplifying paradigms' (Keesing 1987) or 'worldviews' (Lakoff 2002) or 'cultural narratives' (Lakoff 2009) or 'folk theories' (Kempton 1986, Holland and Quinn 1987, Lakoff 2002).

For Willett Kempton (1986), folk theories are 'theories' because they are made up of abstractions and so can be used to guide behaviour in multiple situations. They are 'folk' because they are acquired from everyday experience and social interaction (in addition to expert knowledge), and they are shared by social groups. Folk theories can also be defined by their difference from formal theories such as political ideologies. They are less technical (ibid.), looser and less coherent (Lakoff 2002), more – and more happily – contradictory (Keesing 1987). Folk theories exist and get used because they work well enough as shortcuts to understanding, justification, and action (ibid.). They are made up of categories, cases, types, and exemplars (Lakoff 2002) – which form the focus of analysis in Chapters 4 to 7. They are shaped by institutional environments (Lupia and McCubbins 2000) – and the institutional environment of professionalised and mediatised politics forms one focus of analysis in Chapters 7 and 8.

To explain the rise of anti-politics, we need to identify (changes in) the folk theories used by citizens. These folk theories may be similar to existing political theories of democracy (i.e. those models of democracy found in texts like Held 2006). But they may be something quite different. In this book, drawing on citizens' writing for MO, supplemented by survey research, we ask this question for the UK around the middle of the twentieth century and again around the turn of the twenty-first century. What have citizens understood of democracy and politics, how it should work, how it does work, and their role in it? Have such understandings changed over time, and if so, how? Can such understandings – and associated expectations of politics – help to explain historical patterns of anti-political sentiment?

Political Interaction

Like our focus on citizens' understandings, our focus on political inter-action has numerous origins. Much of the cognitive science and social theory referred to earlier notes how repertoires of cultural resources are constructed and used in context and through communicative interaction. A second influence is American pragmatism and especially the writings of John Dewey on how space – from the frontier to the neighbourhood to the classroom (see Forestal 2017) – shapes encounters and experiences, which in turn shape democratic habits and social relationships. A third inspiration is Erving Goffman (1961), for whom encounters are 'activity systems' that make possible different events and roles – 'local resources' – to be realised by participants. A fourth origin is contextual theories of social action associated with Nigel Thrift (1983) and Anthony Giddens (1984). Social action is not only compositionally determined by struc-tural properties – gender, class, ethnicity etc. – but also contextually determined by spatial and temporal settings or locales. A fifth influence is theories of deliberative democracy, where preferences are not just exogenously generated and 'held' by citizens but formed through delib-eration or communicative interaction. Finally, we draw on the argumen-tative turn in policy analysis (Majone 1992, Fischer and Forester 1993), which encouraged a view of politics as persuasion, to be achieved through texts and justifications but also performances and rhetoric, which in turn are dependent on facilitative institutions.

There is much to learn from these literatures and theories about citi-zens' judgements of politics. Such judgements are constructed from understandings or folk theories but also from encounters and interac-tions. Modes of interaction are structured by context (activity systems, locales, institutions). Certain modes of interaction afford certain performances and judgements by participants. In Chapter 8, we discuss recent empirical studies where these lessons have been applied, including Jon Lawrence's (2009) history of political interaction through electioneering, Maarten Hajer (2009) on the performance of political authority in conditions of governance, and Andrew Dobson's (2014) argument that democracy requires contexts of political encounter structured to encourage better listening. We develop our own approach, emphasising: (1) contexts of political encounter (the settings in which citizens encounter politics and politicians), (2) modes of political interaction (the forms of communicative interaction afforded by these contexts), (3) associated performances by politicians, and (4) associated judgements by citizens. As with our focus on citizens' understandings, this approach was shaped by existing literatures and theories but also by the empirical material we analysed. Specifically, descriptions and judgements of political encounters, interactions, and performances make regular appearances in the diaries of MO panellists.

Explaining Anti-Politics: The Argument

We show in Chapter 7 that popular images of 'the good politician' appear to have changed. This can be seen in the criteria MO panellists used to judge politicians in the mid-twentieth century and again in the early twenty-first century. In the earlier period, citizens imagined the good politician to be sincere, hard-working, able, level-headed, strong, and inspirational. In the later period, citizens imagined the good politician to be trustworthy, able, level-headed, and strong but also 'normal' (in their look, voice, and behaviour; and for a variety of situations, from the world stage to the local supermarket) and 'in touch' (with 'reality' as experienced by 'ordinary' people). The popular image of the good politician was multi-faceted and characterised by tensions in the earlier period. But in the later period, these facets and tensions had increased. Why might this be the case? We focus on three processes. Politics has become professionalised, such that politicians and other political professionals have come to form a relatively homogeneous class, seemingly detached from the rest of society. Second, an ideology of intimacy has spread through society, encouraging citizens to expect warmth and authenticity from their engagements with formal politics (and almost everything else). Third, democratic egalitarianism has spread through society, conflating what is common with what is right or good and encouraging citizens to expect what is common from politics. Whereas the image of the good politician was just about possible for at least some politicians to achieve in the 1940s and 1950s, the current image would be difficult to achieve under any circumstances. It is especially difficult to achieve by current forms of political interaction, as we demonstrate in Chapter 8.

The general-election diaries of MO panellists indicate how, in the mid-twentieth century, citizens encountered politicians and formal politics most prominently via long radio speeches and rowdy political meetings. These contexts afforded certain modes of political interaction (listening, hearing, challenging). Politicians could perform virtues (and vices). Citizens could test, know, judge, and distinguish politicians (as good or bad speakers with better or worse material, delivery, and character). In the early twenty-first century, citizens encountered politicians most prominently in media coverage of 'stage-managed' debates, photo opportunities, and soundbites plus associated opinion polls and expert analysis. In these contexts, politicians were no longer oriented to performances of ability, character, and programme for government. Citizens, meanwhile, were no longer oriented to well-calibrated judgements of politicians and politics. If the current image of the good politician would be difficult to achieve under any circumstances – by virtue of tensions between its multiple facets – it is especially difficult to achieve in these circumstances of abundant, competitive media and professionalised, mediatised political campaigning.

These arguments – about the rise of anti-politics, citizens' changing understandings, and changing modes of political interaction – come together in Chapter 9, where we develop a summary account or theory of anti-politics in the UK. We note that many citizens operated with something akin to Hibbing and Theiss-Morse's (2002) 'stealth' model of democracy around the middle of the twentieth century. Hibbing and Theiss-Morse found this model – this set of beliefs about how government should work (this folk theory, we might say) – in research on the process preferences of Americans at the end of the twentieth century. They found that many Americans assumed that citizens have the same basic goals, political debate is therefore unnecessary, and government is therefore technical in character and best carried out by managers. In Chapter 6, we show that many British citizens operated on the basis of a similar model in the decade following the Second World War. They believed democracy to be important. They felt a duty to vote. But they viewed party politics as just unnecessary 'mud-slinging' and yearned for independent candidates, 'statesmen', coalitions, and national governments (working on behalf of a singular local or national interest). Other studies have found evidence of some dimensions of stealth democracy in twenty-first-century Britain, where many citizens prefer action over talk and principles over compromise (e.g. Stoker and Hay 2017). If stealth understandings of democracy have been continually present and prominent since at least the 1940s, what has changed that helps to explain the rise of anti-politics?

We argue that stealth understandings have changed in terms of their content (Chapter 7). In the immediate post-war period, many citizens wanted politicians of competence and independence (politicians *for* the people). In the current period, many citizens want politicians for the people (trustworthy, able, level-headed, strong) but also *of* the people ('normal' and 'in touch'). Furthermore, the most prominent contexts of political encounter in the middle of the last century encouraged judgements of politicians as potential leaders for the people (Chapter 8). Such contexts in the current period encourage more negative judgements. In summary, many citizens in the 1940s and 1950s wanted government by competent and independent leaders and could imagine at least some politicians as those leaders. They heard them give long radio speeches. They saw them handle rowdy political meetings. By contrast, many citizens in the early twenty-first century want government by leaders *for and of* the people and cannot imagine most politicians filling either of these roles. They see the photo opportunities, hear the soundbites, and note the gaffes. We conclude that stealth understandings of politics have mutated over the past half century into 'stealth populist' understandings. Stoker and Hay (2017) use 'stealth populism' to describe the coming together of stealth preferences (action over talk, principles over compromise) and populist assumptions (the pure and sovereign people against the corrupt political elites). We develop this concept in Chapter 9. Many citizens across the decades have imagined one 'people' who largely agree and so just need action from competent, independent representatives. But now they also imagine an incompetent and 'out-of-touch' political elite who act, if at all, against the interests of the people.

A final chapter completes the book by addressing the question: What is to be done? We argue that not much can be done to combat anti-political sentiment – not least because democracy, by its very nature, is always bound to disappoint. But we argue that *something* can be done. Things have not always been thus, as we show in this book. To conclude, we discuss current debates on democratic reform. Citizenship education, as usually conceived, seems to fit poorly with citizens' use of System 1 or fast thinking to form political judgements. Constitutional reform of the kind required seems unlikely, given the competitive pressures faced by institutions like political parties and media organisations. Calls for more participation and deliberation seem to fit poorly with stealth understandings of democracy and politics. We focus on images of the good politician and modes of political interaction. We accept that citizens' images of the good politician are difficult to change because changing the processes driving them – the professionalisation of politics and the spread of democratic egalitarianism and the ideology of intimacy – would be difficult and perhaps not even desirable. We recommend a new programme of trials focused on creating sites for better interaction between citizens and politicians. These need to look back and learn lessons from political interaction in the past. Such an exercise can be nostalgic and radical at the same time, since a radical politics benefits from not only a sense of what might be gained by future change but also a sense of what has been lost in previous change (Bonnett 2009). However, these trials also need to look forward. Political interaction in the past was too often exclusionary, boorish, masculine (Lawrence 2009). Meanwhile, the technologies and models of the twenty-first century offer much that is new and promising to political interaction.

1 The Problem of Anti-Politics

The term 'anti-politics' has been used for at least five decades to describe various phenomena. In the first half of this chapter, we situate anti-politics in relation to associated concepts like political alienation, the crisis of democracy, withdrawal of political support, political disaffection, post-politics, depoliticisation, and populism. We conceptualise anti-politics as negative sentiment towards the activities and institutions of formal politics, arguing that it should not be confused with certain other phenomena: healthy scepticism, on which democracy is founded; apathy, where citizens are not so much disaffected as indifferent; a changing party system, where citizens are simply changing their allegiance from older parties to newer parties; or a crisis for democracy, where negative sentiment is directed at not only formal politics but also the idea of democracy itself.

In the second half of the chapter, we address the question of why anti-politics matters. We show that anti-politics is associated with non-participation, non-compliance, and support for populism. We argue that anti-politics makes government more difficult – at a time when societies face numerous problems appropriate for governmental action. Finally, we defend the lens of anti-politics against some common critiques and alternative lenses. The most important of these is the 'democratisation' lens. We draw on existing studies to demonstrate how little empirical support exists for the position that negativity towards formal politics is currently being compensated for by positivity towards informal politics. Even if this was the case, we argue, some important functions performed by formal politics would still be at risk – from the interest aggregation performed by parties for policy-makers to the political opportunity structures provided by formal politics to social movements.

Situating Anti-Politics

A Short History of the Term 'Anti-Politics'

Negativity towards formal politics is not new, and neither is concern about it. There is a need, therefore, to define anti-politics and to situate it both conceptually and historically. Bernard Crick (1962) was one of the first scholars to use the term 'anti-politics'. Writing from the United Kingdom (UK) when democracy in Europe still seemed to be threatened by fascism and communism, he defined politics as those activities necessary for government in plural societies: tolerating, canvassing, listening, discussing, conciliating. This politics was threatened by anti-politics: negativity towards politics because it is messy, mundane, inconclusive, and so unsatisfactory. For Crick, such negativity came especially from certain groups he sensed at the time. It came from advocates of ideology, for whom the ends of a final, perfect, stable society justify the means of totalitarianism. It came from advocates of direct democracy, for whom the tyranny of the majority is preferable to the mediation and compromise of political democracy. And it came from advocates – or at least practitioners – of scientism, for whom social problems are technical in character and soluble, therefore, by rational and objective engineers.

We return to Crick's definitions later, but first we consider writing on anti-politics and related phenomena since Crick. In the 1960s and 1970s, researchers in the United States (USA) perceived a seemingly new 'political alienation' among American citizens. Drawing on Seeman (1959), Ada Finifter (1970) disaggregated this alienation into four categories. 'Powerlessness' describes the feeling that citizens are unable to influence the actions of government. 'Meaningless' describes the feeling that political choices are illegible and political decisions are unpredictable. 'Normlessness' describes the feeling that politicians violate the norms meant to govern political relations. Last but not least, 'isolation' describes the rejection of those norms by citizens themselves. Other influential studies of the period disaggregated political alienation into 'political efficacy', or the feeling that citizens can have an impact on the political process, and 'political trust', defined as the basic evaluative feeling that citizens have towards government (Miller 1974a). Alternatively, they located political alienation at one end of a continuum, with the other end representing allegiance, or closeness, or attachment to the principles and institutions of the system (Citrin et al. 1975).

By the mid-1970s, some commentators on both sides of the Atlantic were writing of a 'crisis of democracy'. From a British perspective, Anthony King (1975) noted that politicians were no longer thought to be wise.

Parties were no longer thought to be responsible. The administration was no longer thought to be efficient. And all this was because the nature of problems had changed and the business of government had become harder. Governments now held themselves responsible for a greater range of matters (because they believed the electorate would ultimately hold them responsible). This was the problem of 'great expectations'. The other main problem identified by King was 'intractability' – the increasing dependency of government on other actors (from trade unions to oil exporters) that weakened its grasp on complex societal problems. What were the consequences of all this? One consequence was 'governmental overload' – when government becomes over-worked and fails, leading to mass dissatisfaction with politics. What was the solution? It was devolution of power and responsibility to reduce the reach of government and, in turn, to lower citizens' expectations.

Similar arguments were made by American commentators of the New Right (e.g. Crozier et al. 1975). They perceived a situation of rising affluence, welfare, education, and expectations, all translating into more and more demands on government, promises from government, unwieldy state agencies, and costly state programmes. They perceived a 'crisis of democracy'. Such crisis talk, however, gradually dissipated over the next couple of decades as Ronald Reagan set about rolling back the American state (like Margaret Thatcher in the UK), while a third wave of democratisation moved across Southern Europe, Latin America, Asia, and Central and Eastern Europe.

It took the Oklahoma City bombing of 1995 – the bombing of a federal building in downtown Oklahoma City by Timothy McVeigh and Terry Nichols, apparently motivated by hatred of the federal government – to remind some scholars that negative feeling among citizens towards the institutions of formal politics had never really gone away after the 1970s. Research once again began focusing on the problem of such negativity, this time encouraged by the availability of new international datasets. Much work in this field during the late 1990s and early 2000s was comparative in character and drew on the World Values and Eurobarometer surveys. The other notable characteristic of this wave of research was its conceptual focus on 'political support' – or, more accurately, citizens' withdrawal of political support.

Joseph Nye and colleagues (1997) considered support for the various political objects identified by Easton (1965, 1975) and found a growing mistrust across a range of countries regarding leaders, the electoral process, and institutions (Easton's objects of specific support), which they feared may lead down a slippery slope to mistrust of democracy and national community (Easton's objects of diffuse support). Pippa Norris

(1999) expanded Easton's framework or continuum from three main objects – political community, political regime, political authorities – to five: political community, regime principles, regime performance, regime institutions, and actors. With colleagues, across a range of countries, she found continued support for the most diffuse objects (political community and regime principles) but weakening support for the more specific (regime performance, institutions, and actors). She concluded that most countries face no crisis of democracy, in that most citizens continue to support democracy as an ideal form of government. But they do face a problem – or opportunity – of disaffected democrats: citizens dissatisfied with how democracy currently works in practice (and supportive, at least potentially, of democratic reforms). This situation of support for democracy in theory but disaffection with democracy in practice was later described by Norris (2011) as the 'democratic deficit' of our time.

Attempts to conceptualise, describe, and explain citizens' negative orientations to politics have continued and perhaps accelerated over the past decade or so. Under the heading of 'political disaffection', Torcal and Montero (2006) have studied critical attitudes towards politics and representative institutions, estrangement from politics and the public sphere, and critical evaluations of political institutions, their representatives, and the democratic political process. Some have gone so far as to write of 'post-democracy'. For Jacques Rancière (1999), post-democracy describes the present condition, which he sees characterised by consensus and the disavowal of politics (defined as the demand for equality by those without equality). Alongside others who write of 'post-politics' (Slavoj Žižek) or 'the post-political' (Chantel Mouffe), he notes the paradox of 'triumphant democracy' – the spread of representative democracy and the rise of participatory forms of governance – and political apathy for mainstream parties and politics, combined with insurrectional movements and mobilisations. For these authors, this paradox follows from the colonisation of contestation and agonistic engagement by technocratic mechanisms and consensual procedures. It follows from the reduction of political contradictions to policy problems for management by experts (see Wilson and Swyngedouw 2014).

The term 'post-democracy' is also used by Colin Crouch (2004). He describes a move away from the maximal ideal of democracy, where opportunities exist for the mass of ordinary people to participate, discuss, and shape the agenda of public life, to a situation of post-democracy where elections are tightly controlled spectacles, government is shaped in private by elites, and citizens are frustrated and disillusioned. Post-democracy, then, is where politicians continue to be anxious about their relations with citizens (so this is not quite non- or anti-democracy), but citizens have been reduced to the role of manipulated participants (so this is not quite democracy).

Table 1.1 *Three versions of anti-politics*

	Version 1	**Version 2**	**Version 3**
Definitions	Citizens' negativity towards the institutions of formal politics	Denigration of politics by populists	A political strategy of depoliticisation
Other overlapping concepts	Political alienation, withdrawal of political support, political disaffection	Populism	Depoliticisation, post-democracy, post-politics, the post-political
Commonly assumed relationships	A response to depoliticisation (Version 3) that is used to justify further depoliticisation. Fed on by populism (Version 2), which reinforces citizens' negativity by denigrating politics	Feeds on and reinforces citizens' negativity (Version 1). Can feed on depoliticisation (Version 3), where depoliticisation is perceived to produce governance by out-of-touch elites. Can lend its voice to calls for depoliticisation, where depoliticisation is perceived to involve replacement of politics with management in the public interest	A cause of citizens' negativity (Version 1) but also justified by the same. Draws support from populism (Version 2) but can give populism cause too
Treatment in this book	The main focus	A minor character, though populism has a major role in Chapter 9	A minor character, though post-democracy and depoliticisation have major roles in Chapter 6

Three Versions of Anti-Politics

Anti-politics is a term with a history and no settled upon definition. In this book, we focus on one version of anti-politics but also take into account two other usages (Table 1.1). Our major concern is with negativity towards politics among citizens (i.e. political alienation or withdrawal of political support or political disaffection). A second concern is denigration of politics by populists, which may be a strategic political response to citizens' negativity. A third concern is the political strategy of depoliticisation (i.e. post-democracy or post-politics or the post-political – which may explain citizens' negativity).

Sometimes, these multiple uses or versions have been connected by integrated narratives of anti-politics. One example would be Trevor Smith's (1972) *Anti-Politics*, inspired by Crick's writings of the previous decade. In this surprisingly neglected text, Smith notes a number of developments in British politics during the 1960s. There was a decline in conventional politics – defined as the choice between alternatives – which could be one version of anti-politics. Political protest became prevalent as citizens looked elsewhere for idealism, imagination, and fervour – which could be another version of anti-politics. In response, politicians looked to re-engage citizens with political sloganeering, symbolism, and populism – which could be a third version of anti-politics. For Smith, all these developments resulted from 'the prevailing political formula'. 'Consensus' was a first part of this formula and described the eschewal of ideological partisanship. 'Pluralism', a second part, captured the cosy balance of power between Labour and the Conservatives, the trade unions and big business, and the Establishment and newer elites. Finally, 'managerialism' captured the search for efficiency. For Smith, this prevailing political formula resulted, in turn, from factors that circumscribe the policy-making of domestic political parties (e.g. growing interdependence between nation-states), combined with long-term societal developments that leave politicians and citizens less confident and more vulnerable to philosophical vacuity and privatisation (e.g. the Reformation).

If Smith's text represents one approach to anti-politics – the integrated narrative approach – then another approach has been to focus on just one version, often to operationalise it for empirical research. So anti-politics has been used to describe negativity towards politics among citizens, regardless of what explains such negativity or how politicians respond to such negativity. This usage probably began in the 1970s with Suzanne Berger (1979) on the energy crisis, the economic recession, the growing politicisation of everyday life, and the translation of this growing focus on priority, value, choice, and conflict not into support for political parties but into anti-party and anti-state new political movements (that wished less to capture the state and more to dismantle it). It continued in the 1990s with Geoffrey Mulgan (1994) on 'the rise of an anti-political ethic' and 'an anti-political era' characterised by declining voter turnout, declining party membership, the low repute of politics as a profession, and the success of alternative movements connected to religion or group identity. In recent years, scholarly writing on this version of anti-politics appears to have proliferated. For example, Clare Saunders (2014) uses 'anti-politics' to describe disaffection in democracies and disengagement from formal political institutions. Linda McDowell and colleagues (2014) use 'anti-politics' to capture 'an engaged form of disengagement' that is not apathy so much as dissatisfaction and active rejection of traditional politics. Allen and Birch (2015a) use 'anti-politics' to capture mistrust and cynicism towards politicians and political institutions and associated disengagement from various formal political processes. Or take Boswell and Corbett (2015), for whom 'anti-politics' describes negative beliefs about democratic government, whether held by citizens or elites.

The most prominent alternative version – to anti-politics as citizens' negativity towards the activities and institutions of formal politics – has been anti-politics as political strategy of depoliticisation. This usage probably began in the 1990s with James Ferguson (1994) on the development industry in Lesotho, its refusal to allow its role to be formulated as a political one, its reduction of poverty to a technical problem, and its depoliticisation of poverty, land, resources, wages, and the state ('the anti-politics machine'). Another founding text here is Andreas Schedler's (1997) *The End of Politics? Explorations into Modern Antipolitics*. For Schedler, anti-politics describes a mode of thought or discourse or ideology. If politics assumes a community whose members are mutually interdependent, internally different, able to act in concert, and needful of authoritative decisions, then anti-politics works against politics by doing a number of things. It substitutes collective problems for a self-regulating order (e.g. the market). It substitutes plurality for uniformity (e.g. the people). It substitutes contingency for necessity (e.g. global forces). And it substitutes political power for individual liberty. Put differently, again by Schedler, anti-politics seeks to replace the communicative rationality of politics with another rationality from another societal subsystem. This could be the technology of 'instrumental antipolitics', the absolutism of 'moral antipolitics', or the spectacle of 'aesthetic antipolitics'.

This second main version – anti-politics as depoliticising discursive system – has been much studied since the turn of the century. Weltman and Billig (2001) found Third-Way politics to be anti-political. Its technocratic managerialism denigrates ideology while functioning to obscure the irreconcilability of antagonistic interests, to discourage challenges to powerful vested interests, and to maintain relations of inequality. Similarly, William Walters (2004) found governance discourse to be anti-political. Its focus on inclusion, participation, partnership, and stakeholders excludes those who emphasise structural problems and threaten the social order. Ultimately, governance works to displace political conflict and legitimate inaction. Two final examples are Clarke (2012) and Clarke and Cochrane (2013). In the former, urban policy mobility is characterised as anti-political for positioning urban policy as a technical achievement – as opposed to a political achievement – in order to hold stretched networks of policy-making together. In the latter, the localism agendas of recent UK governments are characterised as anti-political. They imagine a nation of autonomous and internally homogeneous localities and thus deny the conditions of politics (interdependence and difference). They also promote expertise, technology, markets, and direct democracy over the content of politics (listening, discussing, compromising).

In this section, we have shown that 'anti-politics' has been used to mean different things by different scholars in different contexts. It also exists in a heavily populated conceptual world – alongside political alienation, democratic crisis, withdrawal of political support, political disaffection, and post-democracy. In this book, we choose to use the term 'anti-politics' for two main reasons. It is good to think with, not least because it encourages the making or interrogation of connections between citizens' negativity towards politics, political strategies of depoliticisation, and political strategies of populism. It is also good to write with, not least because 'anti-politics' travels well – whether across theoretical and empirical research, scholarly and popular discussion, or radical and reformist politics. Of course, any concept that travels well and encourages connections also carries with it the risk of conceptual confusion. We now turn, therefore, to the working definition we used to frame our research and the rest of this book.

Anti-Politics: A Working Definition

Our starting point is a working definition of politics. There are, of course, many definitions of politics (e.g. see Rancière's definition in the preceding discussion). We are drawn to the tradition running from Aristotle to Crick because we perceive a complex moral terrain, a plural society, and a need for collective and binding decisions. As such, we define politics as those activities appropriate to such conditions – tolerating, canvassing, listening, negotiating, compromising – and their institutionalisation in politicians, parties, elections, parliaments, councils, and governments (the institutions of formal politics). This gives us a working definition of anti-politics as negative sentiment towards those activities and institutions. We finish this section with some important clarifications:

- In this book, our primary focus is on citizens' orientations to politics. We do consider anti-politics as strategy of depoliticisation – and potential cause of citizens' negativity towards politics – but under the distinguishing heading of 'depoliticisation' (see Chapter 6). We also consider anti-politics as strategy of populism – and potential effect of citizens' negativity towards politics – but under the distinguishing heading of 'populism'.

- Anti-politics describes negative sentiment towards the activities and institutions of formal politics but not towards the idea of democracy itself. Previously, we noted how research around the turn of the twenty-first century distinguished between withdrawn support for the actors and institutions of democracy and continued support for the principles of democracy. The presence of anti-political sentiment, therefore, should not be confused with a situation of crisis for democracy.

- If anti-politics describes something less than negativity towards democracy itself, it describes something more than negativity towards particular actors or institutions. Negativity of this latter, most specific kind is to be expected in any plural society and partisan system.

- Anti-politics also describes something more active than apathy, which implies detachment, indifference, and passivity – a lack of interest, concern, and passion. We show later in the book how anti-political sentiment can follow from experiences of engagement with formal politics and can be deeply felt by concerned citizens.

- Anti-politics also describes something more than healthy scepticism. Such scepticism is required for democratic oversight (Sniderman 1981). For Claus Offe (2006), democracies need a certain amount of distrust to reduce participation during normal politics (when it just gets in the way) and to increase participation during extraordinary politics (when it is needed). The problem arises when distrust reaches a certain level where it creates opportunities for populists, breeds non-compliance, leads to state impotence, and threatens anti-democratic mobilisation. Similarly, for Ercan and Gagnon (2014), democracy – as a normative and unfinished project – is meant to be in permanent crisis, at least to a certain extent. But the extent of crisis, like the level of distrust for Offe, is what matters. Compared to healthy scepticism, anti-politics describes something more like unhealthy cynicism towards formal politics.

- Finally, where do we see such anti-political sentiment? We see it directly in qualitative data generated from focus groups where citizens get to speak in their own terms about what interests and concerns them (e.g. Stoker et al. 2016). Then we see it more indirectly in survey measures of trust in things like politicians, parties, parliaments, and governments and approval regarding things like leader performance, government performance, decision-making processes, and policy outcomes (e.g. Jennings et al. 2016, 2017a).

Why Anti-Politics Matters

Why should we be concerned by deeply felt cynicism among citizens towards the activities and institutions of formal politics? In this section, we provide three positive grounds for concern before addressing four potential critiques of research framed in terms of anti-politics. The first reason for concern is that previous research has found an association – relatively weak but significant nevertheless – between anti-political sentiment on the one hand and non-participation and non-compliance on the other (Dalton 2004, Marien and Hooghe 2011, Norris 1999, 2011, Torcal and Lago 2006).

Voter turnout is one common indicator of participation. It varies across the globe, not least because of different degrees of compulsion in different countries, but in recent years voter turnout has been notably low in some of the mature democracies. Among members of the Organisation for Economic Co-operation and Development (OECD), turnout was on average 11% lower in national elections held in 2011 compared to elections held three decades earlier (OECD 2011). According to the International Institute for Democracy and Electoral Assistance (International IDEA), turnout in the US presidential election of 2016 was 68% – the second lowest on record (after 2012), having always been above 80% until 2008 and having once been so high as 96% (in 1964). We find a similar story in the UK. Turnout in the general election of 2017 was 69% – relatively high for general elections of the past two decades but low for those of the twentieth century (when turnout was above 70% in every election from 1945, peaking at 84% in 1950). An additional point here is that citizen disengagement as a result of antipathy towards formal politics disproportionately affects already marginalised groups, including youth (Lawless and Fox 2015, Mycock and Tonge 2014) and the working class (Ford and Goodwin 2014). As such, anti-politics threatens to empty the political field of those who may need it most.

Related to these concerns about non-participation and non-compliance, our second main concern is that anti-politics makes government more difficult (at a time when societies face numerous challenges and requirements for governmental action). Coherent public policy is made difficult when demands on government proliferate without being aggregated by parties (Dalton 2004). Governmental action is made difficult when citizens don't trust government to manage programmes efficiently or fairly and withdraw their support for programmes of redistribution that ask citizens to make sacrifices or take risks (Hetherington 2005). Ultimately, politicians themselves may withdraw, mirroring the withdrawal of citizens, either by focusing on society's easier problems or by turning away from popular democracy and towards constitutional democracy (Mair 2013). By popular democracy, Mair means government by the people who participate through parties. This leaves constitutional democracy as government *for* the people by an elite governing class. This latter version is characterised by checks and balances across institutions, transparency, legality, stakeholder access, depoliticised decision-making, and non-majoritarian institutions like the World Trade Organization (WTO) or International Monetary Fund (IMF). For Mair, citizens are destined to find constitutional democracy unsatisfactory. He foresees a vicious cycle of mutual withdrawal by citizens and politicians and a democracy functioning poorly for citizens and politicians alike.

A third reason why anti-politics matters is that where disaffected citizens do not withdraw completely from participation in formal politics, some shift their support to populist politicians and parties. In the UK, for example, support for the United Kingdom Independence Party (UKIP) is partially explained by anti-political sentiment. According to Ford and Goodwin (2014), UKIP supporters are disaffected, distrusting, and angry. They have lost faith in the political system. They reject the politics of both Brussels and Westminster, which they see as remote, elite, bureaucratic, corrupt, and unresponsive to their concerns. We found something similar in survey data from YouGov and Populus (see Jennings et al. 2016). When social group is held constant, political discontent increases the odds of supporting UKIP by more than a half.[1]

The previous paragraph, of course, begs another question: Why should we be concerned by populism? Well, for Schedler (1997), populism denies the reality of internally differentiated and mutually interdependent communities. It substitutes plurality for uniformism ('the people'). For Offe (2006), populists pose as ordinary people with common sensical views and disgust for bureaucracy ('anti-political politicians'). They incite and exploit both fears and hopes, which attracts a few citizens to politics but repels many others. Finally, we have Crick's (2005) evaluation of populism. On the one hand, by imagining a collective will frustrated by institutions and their procedures, populism embodies the spirit of democracy (i.e. lack of deference towards elites). But on the other, populism is not sufficient for democracy. The will of the majority, which is sometimes wrong, cannot be allowed to deprive individuals and minority groups of freedom (Tocqueville's 'tyranny of the majority'). To summarise all this, we might say that populists trade on a series of

---

[1] 'Political discontent' here was measured by whether citizens think politicians are knowledgeable, can make a difference, possess leadership, are focused on the short-term chasing of headlines, and are self-seeking.

misrepresentations. They claim there is just one people ('the silent majority'), they are of that people, and all other politicians are not of that people (but rather are 'out of touch' elites). They claim there is no mutual interdependence between that people and other peoples (whether external peoples or internal minorities). They claim there is little need for negotiation and compromise between multiple competing interests and opinions. Finally, they claim – again wrongly – that procedures and institutions to facilitate such negotiation and compromise are not required (but just constitute 'bureaucracy' and 'red tape').

Anti-politics matters, then, because it is associated with non-participation and non-compliance, it makes government more difficult, and it is associated with support for populism. However, there are four potential critiques of research framed in terms of anti-politics. The first can be represented by Joseph Schumpeter (1942), for whom democracy constitutes a mechanism of selection; an institutional arrangement for placing power in the hands of high-capacity individuals. In this view, non-participation should be of little concern because democracy works better without too much participation anyway. We do not share this view. We do not share Schumpeter's view of an overly weak, emotional, impulsive, irrational, ignorant, manipulable citizenry. Also, as mentioned earlier, we think participation provides input legitimacy, often making government easier and more effective – especially in situations where governmental action rests on risk-taking or sacrifice-making by citizens.

Another potential critique, also focused on the relationship between anti-politics and non-participation, questions the commonly assumed binaries of participation and non-participation, engagement and disengagement, active citizens and disillusioned citizens. Amnå and Ekman (2013) identify a third group of citizens: 'standby citizens' who keep a low profile but are not so much disillusioned and disengaged as interested and willing to participate, but only when absolutely needed. Theoretically, we find standby citizens interesting and therefore quite attractive. But to date, few standby citizens have been found by empirical research. The same cannot be said for anti-political citizens, as we show in the rest of this book.

The final two critiques for consideration start from the same broad position: that research on anti-politics mistakes change and renewal in politics for decline and crisis. The third critique is that we are not seeing citizen withdrawal and support for populism so much as the fragmentation and remaking of party systems. Citizens are turning away from what traditionally have been the main parties, but less because they are disaffected with politics as a whole and more because they prefer the newer and, for now, smaller parties (which they believe to better represent their current interests). From our perspective, it seems true that many party systems are currently experiencing fragmentation and renewal. For example, the UK's two main parties received 97% of the vote in 1951. By 2015, this had declined to 67% (with figures generally in the 90s during the 1950s and 1960s, the 70s during the next three decades, and the 60s since the turn of the century). If we exclude the general election of 2017 – when share of the vote for the two main parties bounced back up to 82% and which we discuss in the Preface – we have a situation in the UK where citizens have gradually been turning away from the Conservative Party and the Labour Party and towards parties like the Liberal Democrats, the Scottish National Party (SNP), Plaid Cymru, UKIP, and the Green Party. Our point is that, alongside this situation, we also have another situation: complete withdrawal from politics by some citizens who are voting for neither the main parties nor the minor parties. These two situations are connected in complex ways. For example, some disaffected citizens may disengage completely while others may shift support to more populist parties. But the two situations do not fully explain or account for each other. Anti-politics, therefore, is left as a discrete problem worthy of study.

This leaves the final and most important critique, at least by quantity of advocates. These advocates focus less on anti-politics and withdrawal from formal politics and more on new and alternative forms of politics and participation. They propose a democratisation thesis (Dalton 2000) – that democracy is not in crisis or decline but rather is being remade, transformed, post-modernised by citizens who are wealthier, better educated, and more capable of doing things for themselves. These commentators see an expansion of the boundary of politics (ibid.), a broadening of the category of the political (Black 2010), and an expansion of what constitutes politics (Hilton et al. 2013). They see a move from liberal democracy to a more participatory democracy. They see negativity towards formal politics being compensated for by positivity towards informal politics: new social movements, transnational policy networks, internet activism. Such change to a more radical and plural democracy should be expected, they argue, in that democracy has been expanding and deepening – through proliferating antagonisms and new forms of political identity – ever since the French Revolution (Laclau and Mouffe 1985). For many scholars, these developments should be celebrated. The old politics was not only passive, high-cost, and exclusive for citizens but also struggled to deal with new governability problems, e.g. environmental destruction (Micheletti 2003). The new politics is active, flexible, and inclusive of traditionally excluded groups like women and the young. It is prefiguring a different politics that makes opportunities from the challenges faced by contemporary societies (Della Porta 2013).

This 'transformationalist case' (Norris 2002) is commonly used to critique research framed in terms of anti-politics and thus demands a full response. Our first reservation is that much of the literature on democratisation is overly sociological, structuralist, and evolutionary in character (e.g. Bang 2005, Beck 1992, Childers 2012, Dalton 2009, Giddens 1991, Inglehart 1997). Arguments tend to begin with modernisation and its two main component parts: industrialisation/economic development and bureaucratisation/expansion of the welfare state. These structural changes in society are thought to result in changes to, or adaptations by, citizens and politics – seen in a decline of deference, individualisation, a rise of post-materialist values, and the emergence of new political issues, identities, and movements (Giddens' 'life politics', Beck's 'sub-politics', Inglehart's 'evolved democracy', Bang's 'everyday makers', or Dalton's 'engaged citizenship').

These arguments are convincing, but only up to a point. They leave little room for political agency; for the construction of citizenship by political projects. Yet from histories of national citizenship, we should expect forms of citizenship to emerge not only from bottom-up demands for rights, as in T. H. Marshall's (1950) influential account of the historical development of citizenship in Britain, but also from top-down attempts to create capitalist markets and loyal populations. We see this in Benedict Anderson's (1983) global account of the creation and naturalisation of national citizenship around the turn of the nineteenth century. Key actors for Anderson were elites concerned to replace the loss of religious community, to replace the automatic legitimacy that was lost with the decline of sacral monarchy, and to establish markets of reading publics for book and newspaper publishing. We see it in Eric Hobsbawm's (1990) account of how national citizenship was mobilised from the late 1800s by elites seeking loyalty and consent via 'ideological engineering' (especially through national education systems). More recently, Clive Barnett and colleagues (2011) have shown how political consumerism, a commonly used example of the new politics of the current period, did not simply follow from structural changes in society (cf. Micheletti 2003) but was actively constructed by social movement organisations looking for new ways to demonstrate support for their values and policy recommendations.

Our second reservation is perhaps more important. There would seem to be little empirical evidence for the claim that positivity towards informal politics is compensating for negativity towards formal politics. Who are these evolved citizens practising an evolved form of politics? In the case of the UK, they are only a minority of the overall population. Paul Whiteley (2012) found this minority to be significant for low-cost activities like signing petitions or buying products for political reasons. He found it to be small for higher-cost activities like working in voluntary organisations. In addition, participation in alternative forms of political action does not seem to be growing. Globally, the evidence suggests that protest is not on the rise (Stoker et al. 2011). Certainly in the UK, this lack of growth applies not only to protesting and demonstrating but also to volunteering, donating, and signing petitions (Whiteley 2012). Finally, and crucially, the minority who do practise these new forms of politics tend also to practise the older forms. Put differently, the new forms should not be seen as alternatives to the old forms but as part of an expanded repertoire of political action for citizens already engaged in traditional ways. This was found by Norris et al. (2006) when studying demonstrations in Belgium. On average, demonstrators were more likely to be supportive of the political system than non-demonstrators. It was also found by Saunders (2014) in her Europe-wide study. Citizens involved in demonstrations, protests, petitions, and boycotts were less likely to express anti-political feeling than other citizens. The broader point – that negativity towards formal politics is not being compensated for by positivity towards informal politics – is also supported by evidence from the newer democracies of Europe and South America. Here, Torcal and Lago (2006) found that political disaffection had a demobilising effect – through the mechanism of lower political information acquisition and processing – not only on 'conventional' modes of participation but also on 'non-conventional' modes (i.e. informal politics).

Our final reservation derives from our normative and functional evaluation of post-modern forms of political action. Let us bracket, for a moment, the question of whether new forms of politics are replacing older forms. If they were, would that be something to celebrate without any need to lament the passing of the old? We think not. 'Governance beyond the state' lacks the socially agreed rules – e.g. one person, one vote – that make formal politics relatively transparent, accountable, and fair (Swyngedouw 2005). New social movements tend to articulate interests without aggregating them, which is what parties traditionally have done and which has traditionally allowed for coherent public policy (Dalton 2004, Pattie et al. 2004). Furthermore, because new social movements focus primarily on interest articulation, they depend on a functioning formal politics to be effective. This is what narratives of transformation often miss: that formal and informal politics are largely interdependent. We see this in research on the political opportunity structures of social movements (e.g. Tarrow 1998, Tilly 2004). These political environments vary historically and sometimes provide democratic opportunities for citizens, with social movements relying on governments as objects of claims, allies, or monitors of contention. We see this interdependence in Frances Fox Piven (2006), for whom change is achieved by ordinary people through the interplay of 'disruptive power' and electoral politics – not least because disruptive power is more potent when the electorate is more inclusive and elections are fairer. We also see it in Amin and Thrift (2013), for whom leadership and institutions – the stuff of old, conventional politics – are needed by any political movement intent on sustaining momentum and cementing gains. We even see this interdependence in one of the key sociological texts of the transformationalist literature. Anthony Giddens (1991) foregrounds the rise of life politics but notes that emancipation is a necessary condition for this politics of choice or lifestyle. He describes life politics as a supplementation rather than a replacement for emancipatory politics.

To summarise this last set of points, one of the reasons why anti-politics matters is because, far from replacing formal politics, much of informal politics depends on a functioning formal politics for its freedoms and achievements. In this view, democracy requires a balance. This balance is between the 'subject' and 'participant' political cultures identified by Almond and Verba (1963). It is between the 'solid old parties' and 'flexible new movements' of Crouch (2004). It is between Russell Dalton's (2009) 'duty citizenship', which allows governments to act but fails to make them responsive to the concerns of citizens, and 'engaged citizenship', which makes governments responsive but can paralyse governments by subjecting them to multiple and contradictory demands. It is between the concerns of radicals – voice and participation – and pragmatists: coordination, collective and binding decision-making, the exercise of rule (Barnett and Bridge 2013). Our concern is that such a balance is now under threat from the rise of anti-politics across much of the world.

2   Taking the Long View and Listening to Citizens' Voices

Most existing research on anti-politics has taken a relatively short view and considered anti-political sentiment at one particular historical moment or the development of anti-political sentiment over just the past few decades. Yet baseline and timeframe are crucial when studying change over time. There is a need for a longer view of negative sentiment regarding formal politics – a view covering both the current so-called 'age of anti-politics' and the so-called 'golden age' of mass democracy in the years following the Second World War. There is also a need to listen more to citizens' voices and what they have said about formal politics when given an opportunity to speak in their own terms. Most existing research in this field has not done this but has instead been dominated by large-scale surveys and closed questions (which, of course, have their own merits). The case of the United Kingdom (UK) allows us to go some way towards meeting both of these needs. On the one hand, public opinion surveys began asking about the activities and institutions of politics as early as 1937 (when the British Institute of Public Opinion or BIPO was established). On the other hand, the case of the UK offers a unique dataset provided by Mass Observation (MO). This latter organisation was also established in 1937 out of the same context as BIPO – a context characterised not least by government demand for information on public morale in the run-up to war. Where MO differed from BIPO and most commercial polling organisations was in the primacy it gave to relatively unstructured and qualitative data.

In this chapter, we begin by reviewing the availability of survey data on anti-politics in the UK since 1937. We argue that different questions have been asked by survey researchers at different times and that different eras of survey research can be identified. In one respect, this presents a problem to researchers taking the long view of anti-politics. The survey data exhibit gaps and discontinuities, making time-series or even historical-comparative analysis difficult. In Chapter 3, we focus on responses to these different survey questions and use a range of statistical techniques allowing these problems and difficulties to be at least partially addressed. In the present chapter, we focus on the questions themselves and note that historical patterns of concerns held by researchers can tell us at least something about historical patterns of concerns held more broadly in society. Over the past eight decades, public opinion research has become more and more focused on anti-politics, presumably as researchers have perceived anti-politics to be an increasingly widespread and significant phenomenon worthy of study. Public opinion research has also become more and more sensitive to the multiple dimensions of anti-politics – the performance of specific governments and leaders but also the performance of political institutions more generally as well as the conduct of politicians in general – presumably as researchers have perceived a growing range of grievances held by citizens regarding formal politics. We return to this changing *political scope* of anti-politics in Chapter 4.

the present chapter, having identified some limits to the availability of survey data for the relatively long period under consideration and keeping in mind the need to listen for when citizens have spoken or written about formal politics in their own terms, we turn to an alternative or supplementary dataset made available by the case of the UK. Among other projects, MO collected citizens' voices in the form of letters and diaries from its panel of volunteer writers. It did this around the middle of the twentieth century and again around the turn of the twenty-first century, allowing for historical-comparative analysis between these two periods. MO data have been underused by researchers working the field of anti-politics to date. Where they have been used in research on British political history more generally, their use has been limited in two respects. First, researchers have tended to take the short view and focus only on the earlier period around the middle of the twentieth century. Second, researchers have tended to rely on summaries of the data provided by MO itself – in what are known as File Reports or Topic Collections – when the 'raw' material is available to scholars if they wish to pursue original systematic analysis themselves. We introduce our own approach to and use of MO data in the second part of this chapter, discussing issues like comparative-static analysis, sampling, representation, validity, and textual analysis. We conclude the chapter by clarifying how the two kinds of data – survey responses and writing for MO – are used together in the rest of the book.

Survey Data: Availability, Discontinuities, and Eras of Research

The question of whether anti-political sentiment has increased over time is confounded by the inconsistent and irregular character of available survey data, in particular before the 1970s. Behavioural measures of political engagement, such as voting or party membership, have obvious limits as substitute indicators of negative sentiment. A decline in voting, for example, could be seen as evidence of satisfaction, a kind of satisfied apathy, or it could be seen as an expression of disaffection. A decline in party membership might reflect not a disengagement from politics but a preference for single-issue engagement. Evidence used on either side of the debate to assess trends in political support is complicated by the limited timeframe of survey data available. Pippa Norris (2011) looks at cross-national trends in satisfaction with democracy back to the 1970s (using data from the Eurobarometer survey between 1973 and 2008).[1] She finds a mixed picture or 'trendless fluctuation'. In contrast, Pharr and Putnam (2000) consider popular confidence in a number of institutions,[2] relying on a small number of time points over just a couple of decades (waves of the World Values Survey – WVS – between 1981 and 1996). These point towards more of a decline in confidence in politicians and political institutions. Still, we cannot be sure the base period here should be considered the 'normal' state of political support. The longest running measure anywhere is the US trust in the federal government series, which shows a dramatic decline in the confidence of American citizens in government to 'do what is right' between 1958 and the present day. This trend is somewhat complicated by the increased connection of trust in government to partisanship over time (Pew Research Center 2015).

While there is plenty of evidence of a withdrawal of support from the institutions of formal politics in the UK and other countries dating to at least the 1960s, our understanding of popular views of politics is fundamentally limited by the questions that have been asked of citizens in representative surveys at different points in time. This matters in two ways. First, it sets the boundaries of what we can know about public opinion in absolute terms, since it is impossible to reconstruct measures of attitudes retrospectively. This means that if no survey asked about the propensity of politicians to lie or take bribes prior to 1990, for example, we simply cannot tell whether there has been a long-term shift that makes the public more or less distrusting. As a consequence, our

---

[1] The question from the Eurobarometer survey asks: 'On the whole, are you very satisfied, fairly satisfied, not very satisfied, or not at all satisfied with the way democracy works in your country?'

[2] The question from the WVS asks: 'I am going to name a number of organizations. For each one, could you tell me how much confidence you have in them: is it a great deal of confidence, quite a lot of confidence, not very much confidence, or none at all?' Responses are recorded for 'the government in your capital', 'the political parties', 'the armed forces', 'the judiciary', 'the police', 'Parliament', and 'the civil service'.

understanding of what the public think about politics and politicians is inevitably constructed through the lens of survey researchers of the day and the set of norms, interests, and expectations that motivated them to put questions into the field at a given moment. To track long-term trends in mass opinion, we therefore need to reflect on the successive eras of survey questions that have been asked of citizens at different points in time.

The agendas of survey organisations tend to reflect the character of the times; the prevailing sorts of concerns and anxieties in the political and social milieu. In doing so, lines of survey research tend to exhibit the particular diagnosis – or at least expectations – of democratic malaise that influenced the question designers. Since over-time comparisons are reliant on repeated observations, these measures are often subsequently carried forward even after the context changes, establishing norms against which the level of disaffection is assessed. This can create discontinuities in data series on political discontent or leave us with anachronistic or narrow survey measures (Jennings et al. 2016). A further issue is that the interests of survey designers for commercial media clients – i.e. 'polling' – are likely to reflect more short-term priorities of the news agenda (such as favouring 'episodic' framing of issues in relation to specific events – see Iyengar 1991), whereas the focus of academic survey research is likely to shift in a rather more glacial way. The former produce a more varied and reactive set of insights into possible expressions of disaffection, but less in the way of repeated measures that allow for tracking longitudinal trends in mass opinion. The latter may be slow to react to the emergence of new issues or alternative perspectives and is also subject to the intellectual proclivities of the leading investigators of election studies and social surveys. While eras of commercial polling and survey research unfold in parallel, they exhibit distinctive priorities and interests. These in turn shape what we know about anti-political sentiment at particular points in time.

In Table 2.1, we summarise eras of commercial polling and survey research between 1937 and 2016.[3] We identify the broader context in

---

[3] These data were collated from a comprehensive review of survey questionnaires of all national election studies and social surveys in the UK over this period, in combination with a review of available data from commercial pollsters (including monthly reports of Gallup, Ipsos MORI, and YouGov). We used additional data on Gallup polling from King and Wybrow (2001) and George Gallup's (1976) *The Gallup International Public Opinion Polls, Great Britain, 1937–1975*. Our characterisation of the eras of polling and survey research also draws on seminal accounts of political change in the UK (Butler and Stokes 1969, Crewe et al. 1977, Särlvik and Crewe 1983, Heath et al. 1985, Heath et al. 1991, Heath et al. 2001, Clarke et al. 2004 and 2009, Whiteley et al. 2013) and historical accounts of the polling industry (e.g. Worcester 1991, Moon 1999).

Table 2.1 *Eras of polling and survey research in the UK, 1937–2016*

	Political context	Polling*	Survey research	Survey questions	Insights on public opinion
1940s–1950s	*Fragile democracy:* war-time research of society; transition to post-war democracy; threat of communism	BIPO (later Gallup)	No national election studies (only local studies)	Approval of government, party leaders, and ministers	'Specific' support
1960s	*Post-war consensus:* stability of the party system; foundations of the UK's civic culture	Gallup	The Civic Culture Survey (Almond and Verba 1963). Butler and Stokes' (1969) study of *Political Change in Britain*	Citizens' perceptions of own efficacy and competence; system support; assessments of government performance. Affective orientation of citizens to parties (identification) and the political system (how it represents citizens)	'Diffuse' support; efficacy of citizens (identification of a 'civic culture')
1970s	*Ungovernability (the first post-war crisis of democracy):* volatility and dealignment of the electorate; waves of civil protest/unrest; widespread doubt about institutional capacity ('overload' thesis)	Gallup	The Political Action Study (British survey 1974). The British Election Study (BES) at the University of Essex (Crewe et al. 1977, Särlvik and Crewe 1983)	Participation in 'conventional' and 'unconventional' politics; trust in government and other political institutions; feelings towards politicians and local government; support for options for reform of the political system (especially in	How we should be governed (support for arrangements of governing institutions); alienation (efficacy and discontent); affective feelings towards political objects

Table 2.1 (*cont.*)

	Political context	Polling	Survey research	Survey questions	Insights on public opinion
				relation to decentralisation and shifting power from London to the regions)	
1980s	*A divided society*: elite polarisation and the rise of distrust	Gallup, Market and Opinion Research International (MORI)	The BES at the University of Oxford (Heath et al. 1985, Heath et al. 1991). British Social Attitudes (BSA) survey (established 1983)	Trust in government and various professions (including ministers and politicians) to place 'needs of the nation' above party interests or to tell the truth. Politicians out for themselves or their party, will tell lies if truth hurts them politically, out of touch with people, only interested in votes. Responsibilities of government (e.g. to provide health care for all, to control prices, to provide jobs). Participation in formal and informal modes of politics; interest in politics	Trust in politicians and institutions Perceptions of the motivation, conduct, and detachment of politicians. Expectations of government
1990s	*Sleaze and declining participation*: John Major's 'back to basics'	Gallup, MORI	The BES at the University of Oxford (Heath et al. 2001).	Trust in government, Parliament, and the European Union (EU)	Trust in politicians and institutions Perceptions of moral

	Context	Polling companies	Data sources	What is measured	Indicators
	campaign; crisis of standards in public life; falling levels of voter turnout		BSA survey. Eurobarometer surveys	Participation in formal and informal modes of politics; interest in politics	standards in formal politics. Politicians as self-seeking and not truth-telling
2000s	*The end of the New Labour honeymoon and a tripartite crisis:* the Iraq war (the 'dodgy dossier'); the global financial crisis of 2007–2008; the parliamentary expenses scandal	YouGov, MORI	The BES at the University of Essex (Clarke et al. 2004 and 2009). The BSA survey. The European Social Survey (ESS). Hansard Society Audit of Political Engagement (established 2004)	Trust in the National Government, Parliament, devolved governments (Scottish Parliament and Welsh Assembly), politicians, Members of Parliament (MPs) in general, local MP, and the EU. Satisfaction with MPs and Parliament. Standards of conduct of public office holders. MPs user power for personal gain. Politicians only care about people with money, don't keep promises, don't give straight answer when questioned. Doesn't matter which party in power. Participation in formal and informal modes of politics; interest in politics	Trust in politicians and institutions Perceptions of performance and conduct of MPs. Politicians seen as serving special interests. Disengagement from formal modes of participation (e.g. voting or party activism)
2010s	*Austerity, bifurcated politics and the road to Brexit:* populist backlash; distrust of elites	YouGov, Ipsos MORI	The BES at the Universities of Essex (Whiteley et al. 2013) and Manchester,	Trust in government, politicians, MPs in general, and the EU Politicians only care about people with	Trust in politicians and institutions Distrust in official statistics. Belief that

Table 2.1 (cont.)

Political context	Polling	Survey research	Survey questions	Insights on public opinion
('experts' and 'the establishment') and official statistics; rise of identity politics		Oxford, and Nottingham (Green et al. 2016) BSA survey ESS. Hansard Society Audit of Political Engagement	money. Trust ordinary people over experts. Things were better in the past; would like to 'turn back the clock' 20–30 years. Satisfaction with MPs and Parliament. Belief in conspiracy theories. Public trust/confidence in official statistics (e.g. crime and immigration statistics); distrust of government use of official figures	government lies and popularity of conspiracy theories. Distinction between elites (i.e. experts, politicians) and ordinary people Nostalgia for lost post-war greatness

* This indicates those pollsters most active in fielding questions on negative sentiment towards the activities and institutions of formal politics in a given time period.

which surveys were conducted, the corresponding polling firms or survey research teams/leaders, the types of survey question that were introduced or were dominant in that era, and the sorts of knowledge about public opinion that were produced. This exercise is instructive about strands of popular opinion about formal politics even before one considers responses to these survey questions. (Table A1 in the Appendix presents a full overview of survey questions fielded in every year.)

Fragile Democracy (and the Birth of Opinion Polling in the UK)

Surveys of public opinion during the immediate post-war years were dominated by BIPO, which was renamed 'Social Surveys (Gallup Poll) Ltd' in 1952 and from 1995 was known as the 'Gallup Organisation'. In the absence of national election studies or social surveys during this period, BIPO's commercial operations – producing polls for news coverage (specifically a daily newspaper, *The News Chronicle*)[4] – are the only source of information about public attitudes towards formal politics. The BIPO and Gallup data throughout the 1940s and 1950s predominantly relate to what David Easton (1975) terms 'specific support' for political authorities: that is, support for the government of the day, its leaders, and its policies. As such, we have quite frequent (aggregate-level) survey data regarding voting intentions; approval of the performance of the Prime Minister, the main opposition party leader(s),[5] the government,[6] and ministers responsible for a range of portfolios;[7] and support for particular

---

[4] See Roodhouse (2012) for a history of the early years of BIPO and the UK Gallup Poll as an affiliate of the US Gallup organisation.

[5] As early as December 1938, BIPO asked: 'Are you satisfied with Mr Neville Chamberlain as Prime Minister?' Survey measures of opposition party leaders were only introduced during the 1950s but have since become an essential feature of the political landscape.

[6] In October 1945, BIPO asked a variant of what would become the standard measure of government approval: 'At the present time, is the government doing its job well or badly?' (the question was later reworded 'Do you approve or disapprove of the government's record to date?').

[7] As revealed in King and Wybrow (2001), Gallup frequently asked about performance of individual ministers, with more than fifty poll questions regarding whether ministers in particular portfolios were doing a good job over the period between 1941 and the mid-1960s. Setting aside the high level of political knowledge this assumed of respondents, it importantly reflects a focus on cabinet government during the period. Later, in the 1970s, Gallup started asking whether particular ministers and backbenchers were seen as an 'asset' or 'liability' to their parties. This in part may have been a reaction to the polarising influences of Enoch Powell for the Conservatives under Heath and Tony Benn for Labour under Wilson and Callaghan.

policy proposals or legislation (see Gallup 1976, King and Wybrow 2001). Few survey questions in this period measured satisfaction with post-war democracy or general attitudes towards the political system and the conduct of politicians.[8] This imbalance of available data might be interpreted as a reaction to the Second World War and a reflection of the broad assumption that democracy was a good thing. Nevertheless, these early survey measures provide insights on long-term trends in 'specific' support for the government, Prime Minister, and opposition party leaders. Figure 2.1 plots the percentage of respondents expressing disapproval of the government, using data from Gallup and Ipsos MORI,[9] between 1946 and 2016. Here, it is evident that there has been a long-term rise in dissatisfaction with government performance – interspersed by spikes at moments of crisis (e.g. the early 1990s when the UK government was forced to withdraw the pound sterling from the European Exchange Rate Mechanism) and honeymoons shortly after the election of new governments (e.g. the late 1990s after the New Labour landslide of 1997). Such a trend is consistent with evidence of the systematic decline in support for parties in government – 'the costs of governing' (Green and Jennings 2017). But little is known about more diffuse forms of support for democracy and the political system in the immediate post-war period.

Post-War Consensus

The 1960s saw publication of two of the most famous academic surveys of political life in the UK. Almond and Verba's (1963) study *The Civic Culture* broke radically new ground as the behavioural method was not well established at the time in British political science. Their survey – as part of a comparative project – was fielded in 1959 and included questions about citizens' perceptions of their own efficacy and civic competence,[10]

---

[8] The most notable exceptions during the 1940s and 1950s were questions fielded by BIPO in 1944 ('Do you think that British politicians are out merely for themselves, for their party, or to do their best for their country?') and after the general election of 1945 ('Did you approve or disapprove of the way the election campaign was conducted by the various parties' – see Cantril 1951: 196).

[9] The Gallup version of the question asked: 'Do you approve or disapprove of the government's record to date?', while the Ipsos MORI question asked: 'Are you satisfied or dissatisfied with the way ... the government is running the country?' The correlation of these series for the overlapping period is equal to 0.98 ($p = 0.000$).

[10] The questions fielded by Almond and Verba asked: 'Suppose a law was being considered by [appropriate national legislature specified for each nation] that you considered to be unjust or harmful. What do you think you could do? If you made an effort to change this law, how likely is it that you would succeed? If such a case arose, how likely is it you *would actually* try to do something about it?'

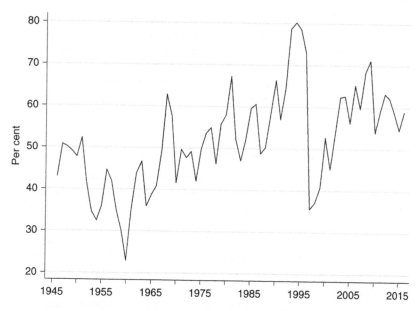

Figure 2.1 Government dissatisfaction in Britain, Gallup/Ipsos MORI, 1946–2016.

pride in the political system,[11] and satisfaction with government performance.[12] This provided insights into 'affective' and 'evaluative' beliefs about politics and government. Soon after, Butler and Stokes (1969) conducted the UK's first national election study, fielding surveys in 1963, 1964, and 1966. The primary focus of their study was affective orientation of citizens to wards parties (partisan identification) rather than considering either regime support or the efficacy of voters. They did, however, ask questions about whether people thought government and Members of Parliament (MPs) paid much attention to voters when deciding what to do – finding a substantial reservoir of cynicism among the public even in the 1960s. In this period, then, there were just these isolated insights from survey research (which anyway was much more focused on the ties between social class and voting behaviour). This

[11] 'Speaking generally, what are the things about this country that you are most proud of?'

[12] 'Thinking about the National Government, about how much effect do you think its activities, the laws passed and so on, have on your day-to-day life? Do they have a great effect, some effect, or none? On the whole, do the activities of the National Government tend to improve conditions in this country, or would we be better off without them?'

limited selection of measures contrasted with the growing corpus of survey questions about political alienation in use in the USA (e.g. Olsen 1969, Finifter 1970) – a product of the acute social and political turbulence of 1960s' America. Meanwhile, the bulk of commercial polling by Gallup and its competitors focused on specific measures of support, asking much the same questions as had been developed in the 1940s and 1950s.

Ungovernability (the First Post-War Crisis of Democracy)

The 1970s has been widely characterised as an era of overload and ungovernability, awash with feelings of disappointment, with 'its problems particularly intractable, its people increasingly bloody-minded' (King 1975: 284). Survey research in this era was increasingly concerned with volatility of the electorate – such as processes of class dealignment (Crewe et al. 1977, Särlvik and Crewe 1983) – and affective orientations towards government and politicians. In 1974, as part of the eight-country *Political Action Study*, a variant of the classic question on trust in government was fielded for the first time (Abrams and Marsh 1981), asking: 'How much do you trust a British Government of either party to place the needs of this country and the people above the interests of their own political party?'[13] Around the same time, the British Election Study (BES) of February 1974 asked: 'Could you tell me the one which best describes how you feel about: politicians in Britain today?', providing a list of options that ranged from 'very happy' to 'very unhappy'. Similar questions were repeated for parties, government, and local government, tapping people's emotive engagement with specific institutions. Together, introduction of these survey measures indicates an increased interest of researchers in affective attitudes towards government and politicians in contrast to previous periods.[14] Alongside this, citizens were being asked their opinions on how the UK should be governed or reformed (such as regarding the distribution of power between London and the regions) and on the quality of its

---

[13] The possible response options were 'just about always', 'most of the time', 'only some of the time', 'almost never', and 'don't know'. As such, there is only a slight difference with the British Social Attitudes survey version of the question, first asked in 1986, which asks about 'the nation' rather than 'the country' and includes the option 'almost always' instead of 'just about always'.

[14] For example, the Crowther-Hunt Commission (1973) fielded this question: 'Which of these statements best describes your opinion on the present system of governing Britain? Works extremely well and could not be improved, could be improved in small ways but mainly works well, could be improved quite a lot, needs a great deal of improvement.'

political system relative to other countries. The idea of opening up politics, breaking up old ways of doing things, was further revealed through survey questions asking whether 'ordinary people' should be given a greater say.[15] Collectively, these new lines of survey research reflected growing scepticism that political institutions were fit for purpose and a recognition that radical reform might be necessary to solve the many intractable problems faced by the UK government. Commercial polls, in contrast, continued to focus on *specific* support for the government of the day and political leaders, as they had done for much of the previous thirty years (in addition to conducting a range of polling on the public's policy preferences, such as on taxation and spending, which is not covered by our review).

A Divided Society?

Following this period of anxiety about whether the UK's political system was in good health, the 1980s left a lasting imprint on the attitudes of generations who lived through the decade (Grasso et al. 2017). The adversarial politics of the time and ideological polarisation of the main parties led researchers to enquire into public trust in politicians and government and the setting aside of narrow partisan interests. Survey measures on trust came into increasing use at this time of ideological battle over the shape of the state and conflict between sectional interests (exacerbated by the policy radicalism of the Thatcher government). Around the same time, both the British Social Attitudes (BSA) survey and pollsters Market and Opinion Research International (MORI, now Ipsos MORI) started to ask people whether government and other groups of political actors could be *trusted* – either 'to place the needs of the nation above the interests of their own political party'[16] or 'to tell the

---

[15] 'Some people think that changing our whole political system is the only way to solve Britain's problems. Some think the system should be changed to give ordinary people much more say in what goes on. But others think the system should be changed so that the country's political leaders have much more power and authority to get on with the job without interference. Which of these statements comes closest to your view? Ordinary people should have much more say in what goes on (very strongly in favour, fairly strongly in favour, mildly in favour). The political system should not be changed much. The Country's political leaders should have much more power (very strongly in favour, fairly strongly in favour, mildly in favour)' (British Election Study 1979).

[16] The BSA question asks: 'How much do you trust British governments of any party to place the needs of the nation above the interests of their own political party?' The response options are 'just about always', 'most of the time', 'only some of the time', and 'almost never'.

truth'[17]. In this regard, the agendas of both social researchers and commercial pollsters were closely aligned, reflecting the salience of political trust in this era. These would reveal, as we show in Chapter 3, rising distrust in politicians and government – though at varying degrees of incline, depending on the survey measure.

Beyond this, commercial pollsters (primarily Gallup and MORI) were starting to field a growing range of survey questions about the motivations and conduct of *politicians* rather than government. These included questions such as whether politicians would tell lies if the truth would hurt them politically, cared more about special interests than ordinary people, or made money through the improper use of public office. The variety of survey measures alone is indicative of the growing newsworthiness of anti-political sentiment – and especially anti-*politician* sentiment – during this period.

Sleaze and Disengagement

The 1990s saw a continued interest of both pollsters and survey researchers in trust in government. Pollsters in particular were influenced by the outbreak of a moral panic surrounding political sleaze and wrongdoing that hit the Major government during the early 1990s. Various scandals and exposés of the private lives of politicians and ministers by the press led to the establishment of the Committee on Standards in Public Life, which, since 1994, has itself commissioned regular surveys monitoring public attitudes towards the conduct of public officeholders. These events of the early 1990s prompted a flurry of polling and survey research into popular opinion regarding the behaviours and practices of politicians. In addition to questions about trust in government and the professions, social surveys, election studies, and commercial pollsters were asking the same sorts of question about the conduct of politicians. During the 1990s, the BSA survey regularly fielded questions asking whether citizens agreed that 'those we elect as MPs lose touch with people pretty quickly' or 'parties are only interested in people's votes, not in their opinions' and whether they would 'trust politicians of any party in Britain to tell the truth when they are in a tight corner'. The 1997 BES asked specifically whether people agreed with the claims that 'moral standards of British politicians have declined in recent years' and that MPs 'don't know much about what ordinary people think'. The notion of a morally decaying and

---

[17] The Ipsos MORI question asks: 'Now I will read out a list of different types of people. For each, would you tell me whether you generally trust them to tell the truth or not?' 'Government' and 'politicians generally' are included as 'different types of people'.

out-of-touch political class had thus taken hold in the formulation of survey questions.

The sleaze scandals also prompted commercial polling on the pathology and conduct of politicians, reflecting much the same interests and concerns as the academic researchers. Numerous poll questions were fielded asking whether people thought politicians put their own interests first, would tell lies, had a high personal moral code, and made money through improper use of office. The volume of polling into politicians as wrongdoers was unprecedented – though many of the survey questions had first been fielded in the 1980s – reflecting the salience of sleaze and scandal during this period.

The End of the New Labour Honeymoon and a Tripartite Crisis

While the landslide victory of the New Labour Government in 1997 appeared to mark the start of a more positive era, this development was short-lived. During the 2000s, trust in formal politics was put under the microscope as a result of a series of crises: the decision to go to war in Iraq (and the Blair government's use of the so-called 'dodgy dossier' to secure that decision from Parliament); the global financial crisis (and its aftermath); and the parliamentary expenses scandal (see Chapter 4 for more on this). There was a sustained focus on trust in government and politics by both survey researchers and pollsters. The BES now also included questions on trust in the newly created Scottish Parliament and Welsh Assembly,[18] while there were surveys of public trust in the European Union (EU) – and in national parliaments and governments – throughout the 2000s as part of the European Commission's Eurobarometer series (which first introduced the trust question in 1999). The BSA and European Social Survey (ESS) also fielded regular questions on trust during this period. Notably, the suite of 'trust' questions in use by survey researchers was expanded beyond 'government' to include Parliament, politicians, MPs in general, and local MPs. This reflected the increasing number of political actors and institutions that were the focus of trust evaluations by citizens and recognition that trust varied depending on the

---

[18] The 2001 BES first asked about *respect* for a range of institutions (e.g. the Parliament at Westminster, the civil service, local government, politicians): 'Now, thinking about institutions like Parliament, please use the 0–10 scale to indicate how much respect you have for each of the following, where 0 means no respect and 10 means a great deal of respect.' In contrast, the 2005 BES asked about trust: 'Now, thinking about institutions like Parliament, please use the scale of 0 to 10 to indicate how much trust you have for each of the following, where 0 is no trust and 10 is a great deal of trust.'

political actor or institution under consideration. Meanwhile, the polling industry maintained its longstanding interest in perceptions of truth-telling by politicians, with Ipsos MORI continuing its annual 'trust tracker' and the newly formed online pollsters YouGov fielding regular questions on trust in politicians – of each of the main parties and local MPs – to tell the truth.[19] Another notable feature of survey research during this era was an increased focus on measuring satisfaction with the performance of political actors and institutions. The Hansard Society's annual Audit of Political Engagement, established in 2003, surveyed the public on their satisfaction with 'the way Parliament works' and 'the way MPs are doing their job', while the Committee for Standards in Public Life fielded a biennial survey that asked about ratings of the standards of conduct of public officeholders.

Beyond this, a sense of political fatalism was recognised in the survey questions being fielded by both academic researchers and pollsters. For example, in 2001 the BSA started to ask whether people agreed that 'it doesn't really matter which party is in power'. Declining political trust, and discontent with 'spin' and dissembling by politicians, was also recognised in questions about whether politicians and parties kept their promises or failed to give straight answers when questioned.[20] The parliamentary expenses scandal, which broke in May 2009, saw a further wave of polling about the conduct of politicians, driven by media interest in the story and widespread public outrage. This led pollsters to revisit a number of questions that had been asked during the 1990s. For example, an Ipsos MORI poll for the British Broadcasting Corporation (BBC) in May 2009 asked about satisfaction with Parliament, whether MPs put their own interests first, trust in local MPs and MPs in general, whether MPs use their power for personal gain or are corrupt, whether MPs make money by using public office improperly, and whether MPs have a high personal moral code.[21] This period thus generated substantial quantities of survey data on the degree to which the public viewed politicians as wrongdoers.

---

[19] 'How much do you trust the following to tell the truth? A great deal, a fair amount, not much, not at all.' Objects of this question included 'Leading Labour politicians', 'Leading Conservative politicians', 'Leading Liberal Democrat politicians', and 'My local MP'.

[20] BBC News Online (2005), 'Voters "don't trust politicians"', 18 March 2005, accessed at http://news.bbc.co.uk/1/hi/uk_politics/4360597.stm.

[21] Ipsos MORI (2009), 'Ipsos MORI Expenses Poll for the BBC', 2 June 2009, accessed at www.ipsos-mori.com/researchpublications/researcharchive/2349/Ipsos-MORI-Expenses-Poll-for-the-BBC.aspx.

Austerity, Bifurcated Politics, and the Road to Brexit

In the period since the general election of 2010, trust and the conduct of politicians have remained a focus for both survey researchers and pollsters. With austerity politics providing a backdrop, this era was distinguished by its prevailing sense of a populist backlash (Ford and Goodwin 2014), increasing polarisation in attitudes (Jennings and Stoker 2016), distrust of elites, and the rise of identity politics. While survey questions about 'trust' – in government, politicians, MPs, and the EU – remained widely used, there was more interest in measuring the degree to which people believed that politicians only cared about people with money, how much people trusted 'ordinary people' over experts, and expressions of nostalgia for halcyon days.[22] These sorts of survey question were, arguably, a reaction to the political response to the economic crisis (i.e. bank bailouts), probing beliefs that politicians were captured by bankers and special interests at a time of falling real wages and cuts to public services.

Distrust in the 'political elite' or the 'political class' (Allen and Cairney 2017) was now being considered through a wider lens than just measures of trust in government or politicians. Survey researchers and pollsters increasingly investigated public distrust in elites as expressed through belief in conspiracy theories,[23] public confidence in official statistics (e.g. crime rates or immigration figures),[24] and distrust of government use of official figures.[25] More broadly, survey measures now embodied the populist distinction between 'elites' (e.g. politicians or experts) and 'ordinary people' (i.e. the general public). Trust – or rather distrust – was thus increasingly understood as constituted in a wider set of social and political relations.

On the one hand, then, we find plenty of survey data on the topic of antipolitics and the case of the UK. But on the other hand, we find gaps and

---

[22] E.g. 'Suppose you could turn the clock back to the way Britain was 20–30 years ago, would you like to do so, or do you, on balance, prefer Britain the way it is today? Turn the clock back; Prefer things as they are today; Not sure' (YouGov); 'How much do you agree or disagree with the following statements? Things in Britain were better in the past / I'd rather put my trust in the wisdom of ordinary people than the opinions of experts' (BES).

[23] YouGov (2016), 'Little British belief in outlandish conspiracy theories', 27 May 2016, accessed at https://yougov.co.uk/news/2016/05/27/conspiracies (e.g. 'Which, if any, of the following statements would you say are true? Even though we live in what's called a democracy, a few people will always run things in this country anyway / Regardless of who is officially in charge of governments and other organisations, there is a single group of people who secretly control events and rule the world together').

[24] Simpson I, Beninger K, and Ormston R (2015), 'Public Confidence in Official Statistics', *NatCen Report for the UK Statistics Authority*, accessed at http://natcen.ac.uk/media/833 802/public-confidence-in-official-statistics_-final.pdf.

[25] Ibid.

discontinuities in these data, making analysis of long-term historical change difficult though not impossible. In Chapter 3, we focus on survey responses and use a variety of techniques to analyse them. Trends for distrust in government and politicians can be constructed from BSA and Ipsos MORI data respectively. Comparisons for a range of dimensions – including perceptions of politicians' motivations, perceptions of citizens' efficacy, judgements of how the system of government is performing, and judgements of politicians' conduct – can be constructed using data from a range of research projects and commercial polling operations (Gallup, YouGov, the Hansard Society, Ipsos MORI, the BSA survey, the BES). Finally, and most importantly, a long-term index of anti-political sentiment can be constructed from these and other datasets using Stimson's dyad-ratios algorithm (see Chapter 3).

Even before we consider the survey responses, however, we can learn something from the questions researchers have asked at different historical moments. The concerns of researchers do not simply mirror the concerns of broader society. But researchers are situated in broader society and often attempt to reflect the concerns of their fellow citizens in their research – especially when research is focused on public opinion. So what did researchers perceive to be significant in British political culture during the period in question? In the 1940s and 1950s, they responded to perceived concerns about the performance of specific governments and leaders. In the 1960s, they responded to those concerns plus concerns about the efficacy of citizens and the performance of parties. In the 1970s, they responded to those concerns plus concerns about the performance of a variety of political institutions. Since the 1980s, they have responded to all these concerns plus newly perceived concerns about the motivations and conduct of a 'political class' now broadly drawn to include politicians but also officials and experts.

Survey data, therefore, help to provide a long view of anti-politics in the UK. But they are limited in terms of availability and thus in terms of the kinds of analysis they support. Survey data, of course, are also limited when it comes to the second aim of our research: to listen to citizens' voices, speaking in their own terms, on formal politics. For these reasons, we now turn to an alternative, supplementary dataset offered by the case of the UK.

Mass Observation: An Alternative Dataset

MO was established in 1937, the same year BIPO began polling British citizens. It was established to record the everyday lives of ordinary people in the UK and, importantly for us, to enable the masses to speak for themselves and to make themselves heard above the noise of the press and politicians claiming to speak in their name (Hinton 2013a). Initially, most of MO's commissions came from the Ministry of Information. Gradually, more and more came from private companies wanting market intelligence (ibid.). MO became a private company itself in 1949 (Mass Observation Ltd) and continued to trade after 1970 as M-O (UK) Ltd – though by that time it was hardly the same organisation in terms of personnel, focus, and activities (ibid.).

In its original incarnation, MO collected material by two general means. A team of 'mass observers' recorded observations, overheard conversations, survey responses, interview responses, and ephemera between 1937 and 1960. Then a panel of volunteer writers, between 400 and 1000 strong (depending on the year), kept monthly diaries (1939–1965), completed day surveys (1937–1938), and replied to quarterly open-ended questions or 'directives' (1939–1955).

In 1969, a deal was struck with the University of Sussex to archive the papers of MO. The Mass Observation Archive was formally opened in 1975. In 1981, the archive founded the Mass Observation Project, reviving the panel of volunteer writers. To this day, directives are still being sent three times a year to approximately 500 respondents.

MO sources have been used by many historians and social scientists who value their richness, frankness, and historical depth (e.g. Hinton 2010, Kushner 2004, Kynaston 2007, Langhamer 2013, Savage 2010). Indeed, a few scholars have used MO to study citizens' orientations towards formal politics around the middle of the twentieth century (Fielding 1992, Fielding et al. 1995, Jefferys 2007). They draw on MO sources to argue against the popular view of a democratic 'golden age' immediately after the Second World War and for a revisionist account of continuity in which Britain's political culture has long been anaemic and characterised by populism, not least because of endemic tensions at the heart of democracy. We have learned a great deal from these studies. But we have also identified two weaknesses or gaps that we seek to address in this book.

MO collected data from 1937 to 1965 and again from 1981 to the present. This offers the possibility of using MO for historical-comparative analysis between the mid-twentieth century and the turn of the twenty-first century. But this is not what has generally been done by existing research, which has tended to take the short view of a decade or two and to evaluate it not against other decades or periods but rather against the often implicit normative standards of the researcher(s). For example, of the 1950 General Election, Steven Fielding and colleagues (Fielding et al. 1995: 193) write:

Only about one-third of the electorate regularly listened to party political broadcasts. A study [by MO] of 600 voters in six London constituencies found that one week before polling day, 86 per cent of the sample had not attended a political meeting and 44 per cent had not read an election leaflet. Over 60 per cent were unable to name all the candidates standing in their area.

Reading this, we might ask: Should we expect more than one-third of the electorate to listen regularly to party political broadcasts? Moreover, should we expect more than two-fifths of the electorate to be able to name all the candidates standing in their area? By what standards should we assess these figures? By the standards of an earlier or later general election, which we are not given in the text? Or by some universal, ahistorical, normative standards, which are implicit in the construction of these sentences – 'only about one-third' – if not made explicit by the authors?

This problem of taking the short view and making judgements on the basis of it, without the comparative perspective a longer view provides, is evident not only in how MO sources are sometimes used and interpreted. For example, here is Kevin Jefferys (2007: 83) on citizens' judgements of politicians in 1944:

When asked to agree with one of three statements about politicians in a BIPO poll in August 1944, as many respondents saw them as out for themselves (35 per cent) as trusting them to do what was best for the country (36 per cent) ... on the basis of this poll – taken shortly after D-Day, when politicians' prestige might be expected to have been high – it seems certain that widespread cynicism about politicians has been endemic throughout the history of British democracy.

There seems to be quite a leap here between the evidence presented and the conclusion drawn. But setting that to one side, we might ask again: Should we expect different proportions for 1944 and on what basis or by what standards? We actually do have historical-comparative figures for this survey question because Gallup asked it again in 1972 and YouGov asked it again in 2014 (commissioned by the project behind this book). While the figure of 35% for 1944 may have seemed high when viewed in isolation, the corresponding figure for 1972 was 38%. For 2014, it was 48%. On the basis of responses to this particular survey question, cynicism – in so far as the question captures generalised distrust (something else to set aside for now) – looks to have become more widespread over time.

If existing uses of MO to study popular understandings of formal politics have tended to take the short view and to lack a means of evaluation by historical comparison, they have also generally relied on summaries of the MO data produced by MO researchers of the time (in the form of File Reports, Topic Collections, and MO publications). Such a reliance is not required of scholars, in that 'raw data' collected by MO are available via the archive for original systematic analysis. Such a reliance is also problematic. Historians such as Jefferys claim to be writing about 'ordinary people' (pxi), providing 'a history of modern British democracy through the eyes of its people' (p3), and providing 'a history of democracy from the "bottom up"' (p5). But often, that is not quite the case. Jefferys relies heavily on the eyes of MO researchers, who were not really 'ordinary people' located at the 'bottom'. He reports that 'Mass Observation investigators were struck in the early part of the [1945 general election] campaign by how many people, in all regions and social groups, took refuge in apathy or cynicism' (pp77–78). '"At no time", Mass Observation concluded [in its study of East Fulham during the 1945 campaign], "could it really be said that the people showed excitement"' (p81). 'Mass Observation reported in May [1947] that "there is a great deal of apathy in Britain today"' (p112). 'In Hendon North, [a] Mass Observation worker, writing up daily observations [in 1950], claimed there was "very little election atmosphere in this constituency"' (p115).

These observations, reports, and conclusions of MO investigators and workers sound plausible. But we should be cautious about relying on such mediated interpretations. MO researchers were 'activators', in David Kynaston's (2007) terms: particularly active post-war citizens, continually disappointed by the relative apathy of their fellow citizens (which may not have been apathy at all, if measured by a different and less-demanding standard). We should also note James Hinton's (2013a) view of MO publications from the 1940s and 1950s. He identifies a theme of popular scepticism regarding the promises of reconstruction. Cynicism and apathy followed recollections of betrayal after the First World War and more recent experiences of delayed implementation of the Beveridge Report. There was a new focus on independence, autonomy, and personal pleasures. This theme in the publications of MO may well have accurately reflected popular understandings at the time. For Hinton, though, it also served an institutional purpose for MO. The theme was that scepticism, cynicism, and apathy would threaten the success of post-war reconstruction unless politicians used MO's research to understand and communicate better with citizens. Through its publications, MO positioned itself as indispensable to the authorities of the time – by claiming that people were apathetic and indifferent yet, at the same time, primed for engagement (if only the authorities could learn how to appeal to them).

In view of the preceding discussion, we did not wish to rely on existing summaries of the MO data, just as we did not wish to compare a short view provided by MO to our own normative standards. Instead, we sought a long view, allowing for comparison between the immediate post-war period and the current period and founded in original systematic analysis of the 'raw data' collected by MO.

Sampling the Archive

As mentioned previously, one means by which MO collected material in the 1940s and 1950s was a team of mass observers who recorded observations and overheard conversations. Anthropologists at the time, including Bronislaw Malinowski, criticised these untrained mass observers for their amateur ethnography that spoke as loudly of their own prejudices as it did of the everyday lives of their intended research subjects (MacClancy 1995). For this reason and our desire for a dataset allowing historical comparison between the mid-twentieth century and the turn of the twenty-first century, we focused our research on the second general means by which MO collected material: the panel of volunteer writers, which Dorothy Sheridan (1994) describes as the most unmediated layer of the archive and which ran originally from 1939 to 1955 and then again from 1981 to the present.

Across both of these periods, we identified thirty-three directives – sets of questions sent to panellists every three or four months – asking panellists to write about formal politics. From these, we selected thirteen directives that asked mostly about the activities and institutions of formal politics in general, did not repeat questions from directives only a year or two previously, and covered the two periods so often compared – whether explicitly or implicitly – in debates about anti-politics: the so-called 'golden age' of British democracy and the so-called 'age of anti-politics'. Dating of the former period was relatively straightforward. The end of the Second World War provided an obvious starting point. The year of 1955, when the original panel ceased to exist, provided a necessary end point. Dating of the latter period was more complicated. Should it start in 1981 when the Mass Observation Project re-established the panel of volunteer writers? This would fit with our argument in Chapter 3 that anti-political sentiment – measured by things like trust in government or politicians – has been on the rise now for more than a couple of decades. But it would pose some practical problems – for example, providing a period of thirty-four years to compare to the early period of only ten years. Or should it start in 2001, when voter turnout in the British General Election – which is associated with anti-political sentiment (see Chapter 1) – dropped to 59%, having previously not fallen below 72%, and the volume of talk about anti-politics rose accordingly? Or should it start in 2015, when the proportion of votes won in the general election by the populist party UKIP – also associated with anti-political sentiment (see Chapter 1) – increased to 13%, having previously not reached higher than 3%, and the volume of anti-politics talk rose still higher? In the end, we chose the period 2001 to 2015. This covered the years when all indications of anti-political sentiment were at their strongest. It also had practical benefits, in that directives on formal politics existed for this period – more so than for the last two decades of the twentieth century – and this period was broadly comparable in length to the earlier, already established period. A final point on the selection of directives is that we commissioned our own directive from the Mass Observation Project in spring 2014, repeating questions from the earlier period that had not yet been asked in the later period. Full details of the selected directives can be found in Table 2.2.

This sample, covering two periods separated by almost half a century, allowed for comparative-static analysis (Hay 2002). We are aware of the strengths and weaknesses of this form of analysis. It makes visible the extent and direction of change over time but not the pace of such change. It also encourages a view of historical oppositions or dualisms ('the golden age' and 'the age of anti-politics', for example). Given these weaknesses, throughout the book we seek to supplement MO data with survey data, allowing for diachronic analysis – the tracing and charting of change over time to establish its temporality – and helping to place MO writing in historical and social perspective. Taken as a whole, the book uses each form of data and analysis to confirm the other.

Placing the MO data in social perspective is especially important because of concerns about the social constitution of the MO panel. For Tom Jeffrey (1978), the original MO was a social movement of the radicalised lower middle class. For Hinton (2013a), while not all the original panellists were lower middle class, that group was certainly over-represented, along with people from London and the South East and people of the Left. To address these concerns, we read the MO writing alongside the survey data. We also sampled within the MO panel, following the example of Andrea Salter (2010). Age, gender, occupation, and place of residence were available for most panellists (either from MO's database of panellists or from the responses themselves). We sampled sixty respondents for

Table 2.2 *Selected Mass Observation directives*

Code	Date	Relevant question/task	Number of responses
SxMOA1/3/84	Feb/Mar 1945	5) What would you say is your normal conversational attitude when talk gets round to each of the following groups of people: a) clergymen; b) politicians; c) doctors; d) advertising agents; e) lawyers; f) scientists.	161
SxMOA1/3/86	May/Jun 1945	1) Please report at intervals on the election campaign in your constituency and people's feelings about it. 4) What is your present attitude to: a) the Conservative Party; b) the Labour Party; c) the Liberal Party; d) the Communist Party; e) the Commonwealth Party. 5) What would you say are the chief points in the Liberal Party policy, and how would you say their policy differed from the Labour and Conservative Party policies respectively?	98
SxMOA1/3/88	Nov 1945	1a) How much interest do you and other people you know take in municipal elections? How important do you think they are? Did you vote in your municipal election last month? If not, why not, and if so, describe your reason for voting as you did. 1b) Do you consider your local council to be a good or bad one? Why?	160
SxMOA/1/3/102	Jun 1947	1) Give in as much detail as you like your views on recent pronouncements of policy by each of the political parties and by Government. Arrange in this order: a) Labour Party; b) Conservative Party; c) Liberal Party; d) Communist Party; e) Government. Write this without referring to any pamphlets etc. you may have about the house, and, if you haven't been following political party policies at all, say so. 2) When you have finished Q1, if you have any recent political party publications in the house which you have already read, please refer to them and describe your reactions to them in detail, saying which parts or points in them especially affect you and how.	420
SxMOA1/3/121	May 1949	3) What is your attitude to the principle of obedience to a 'party line' (regardless of	476

Table 2.2 (*cont.*)

Code	Date	Relevant question/task	Number of responses
		the political colour of the party) in the case of: a) Members of Parliament; and b) rank and file members of a political party.	
SxMOA1/ 3/123	Aug 1949	1) Do you intend at the moment to vote the same way at the next Parliamentary elections as you did at the last? If not, please give reasons in detail. In all cases, please let us know how you voted last time (if you did vote then) and how you intend to vote next time. 2) Regardless of his political beliefs, how effectively do you think the MP for your constituency represents you in Parliament?	351
SxMOA1/ 3/127	Jul 1950	4) How do you feel about: a) Atlee; b) Churchill; c) Bevin; d) Cripps; e) Bevan?	369
SxMOA1/ 3/130	Nov 1950	2) Which political party do you most of all sympathise with at present? Give an account of the development of your feelings about politics and of your political outlook and sympathies.	336
SxMOA2/1/ 62/2	Spr 2001	2) The General Election 2001: If there should be an election in May, please share as much time as you can recording your reactions to the news, to the activities of your local political parties, to election broadcasts, to the debates and discussions you hear all around you, at home, at work, out and about. In effect we would like to receive anything YOU yourself feel is relevant to the present situation ... If you want to keep a diary, or an occasional diary, in the run up to the election, please do. Even if the election is postponed, your views on the current issues would be appreciated.	237★
SxMOA2/1/ 63/3	Sum 2001	3) The General Election 2001: Comments please on the last stages of the run up to the Election and an account of your reaction to the outcome. How did you vote? Were you influenced by the debates about tactical voting? What do you think the key issues were for the voters?	237★

Table 2.2 (*cont.*)

Code	Date	Relevant question/task	Number of responses
SxMOA2/1/ 88/3	Spr 2010	3) The General Election 2010. What do you think? Are you excited by the possibilities of change or are you bored already? Are you actively involved in electioneering or will you let the whole thing pass you by? What does it mean to you?	203
SxMOA2/1/ 99/1	Spr 2014	2) Consider the following people: a) Politicians; b) Doctors; c) Lawyers; d) Scientists. Do you associate any characteristics with each group? If you were in conversation with somebody and these kinds of people were referred to, what would be your attitude? 3) How do you feel about: a) David Cameron; b) Ed Miliband; c) Nick Clegg; d) William Hague; e) George Osborne? Please feel free to share any other comments about any other politicians. 4) How do you feel about: a) The Conservative Party; b) The Labour Party; c) The Liberal Democrats; d) The Scottish National Party; e) The UK Independence Party? We are interested in your immediate reaction to these political parties, but would also like to know more about how your attitude towards them has developed over the years. 5) Turnout at the most recent General Election in 2010 was 65.1%. This is an increase on the previous Election, but still the third lowest figure since 1945. Is it important to vote? Could anything be done to increase the number of people voting? 6) How much interest do you and other people you know take in local elections? How important do you think that they are? Did you vote in your last local election? Do you consider your local council to be an effective/ineffective one? Why?	175
SxMOA2/ 1/102	Spr 2015	2) The General Election 2015. A General Election has been called for Thursday 7th May 2015. What are your thoughts on this election? Are you excited by the	162

Table 2.2 (*cont.*)

Code	Date	Relevant question/task	Number of responses
		possibilities for change, uninterested, or indifferent? Have you been following the news coverage in the run up to the election? Please give details about what media (newspapers, online, radio etc.) you use to keep up to date with the election news. Did you watch the televised leader debates? What did you make of them? Will you vote in the election? Do you feel that your vote counts? If you don't intend to vote, please explain why. In your opinion, what are the key issues for the UK? Are there any policies that are particularly important to you and will affect how you vote? What are your hopes and fears for the next government? On the day, keep an election diary for Thursday 7th May describing your reactions to election issues, newspaper articles, TV or radio programmes, and any conversations you have about the election. When the result is finally announced, describe your reaction. If you come to this directive after the election, please write about your memories of the election day and share your thoughts on the new Government.	

* Responses to the spring and summer 2001 directives were combined in the archive due to delays associated with the foot-and-mouth epidemic of that year.

each directive, seeking to fill quotas for age group, gender, occupational classification, and region. Ultimately, we sought to include a range of people with a range of social and geographical positions in British society. The figure of sixty respondents allowed us to reach descriptive saturation for each directive – the most important consideration when sampling unstructured, qualitative data (Baker and Edwards 2012). In total, we collected 720 responses to thirteen directives, which together made up more than 1500 sides of A4 (typed and single-spaced).

A last point here is that concerns about the social constitution of the MO panel should not be overplayed. Hinton (2013a) compares the panel of the early 1940s to another panel of volunteer writers from the period: the Home Intelligence Panel operated by the Ministry of Information. Members of this panel were invited and vetted by intelligence officers. They were probably on the right of the political spectrum. This was certainly not a social movement of the radicalised lower middle class. While no responses have survived from the Home Intelligence Panel, digests of responses describe findings very similar to MO's summary findings. For Hinton, the panels may have been rivals that competed and accused each other of political bias, but ultimately they served to confirm each other's reliability. Murray Goot (2008) has made a similar argument: MO samples may have been relatively small and unrepresentative, but their findings were largely confirmed by the few larger-scale sample surveys of the time (the Gallup Polls and the Wartime Social Survey).

Concerns about the social constitution of the MO panel should also not be overplayed because they can be addressed, at least in part, by taking an appropriate analytical approach to the writing produced by the panel. Almost by definition, the panellists from both periods constituted a rather strange group of people because they volunteered for a social history project. As such, they were particularly dutiful, engaged, reflexive, and critical (Hinton 2010). For this reason, we did not seek to establish their views and practices as representatives of people in general or of particular social groups. Rather, we sought to establish the cultural resources they used to construct understandings, expectations, and judgements of politics, focusing on the cultural resources they shared with each other, regardless of background, and, plausibly, with other citizens too in their families, friendship networks, workplaces, and audiences for mass cultural products.

Reading for Cultural Resources: Categories, Storylines, Folk Theories

We approached the MO writing from a number of similar directions (see Introduction). Cognitive scientific research taught us how behaviour is shaped by understanding, which in turn is shaped by cultural models, schemas, frameworks, scripts, stories, metaphors, and prototypes. Social theoretical writing on discourse taught us how social reality is constructed from practices, which in turn are shaped by forms of consciousness made up of concepts, ideas, representations, images, frames, stories, narratives, and subject positions. Interpretive social scientific research taught us how actions follow from holistic beliefs, discourses, and traditions.

In recent years, these approaches have been mobilised to good effect in political science. William Gamson (1992) provided an early example. To analyse talk from group discussions on issues like affirmative action and nuclear power, he focused on participants' shared framings of issues and the conversational resources on which those framings drew. In particular, he focused on the cultural resource of media discourse (spotlighted facts, public figures, catchphrases); the personal resource of experiential knowledge (stories or anecdotes about selves, family members, friends, colleagues); and the cultural-cum-personal resource of popular wisdom (rules of thumb like proverbs, maxims, and analogies).

Probably the most influential example was provided by George Lakoff (1996, 2002). To explain the divide between conservatives and liberals in American politics, he focused on worldviews, conceptualisations, and common sense (in the cognitive subconscious), which provide citizens with models, metaphors, and categories for thinking about politics and which arise from a combination of experiential morality and the framings of intellectuals. Lakoff argues that conservatives draw on 'the strict father model', which privileges moral strength, legitimate moral authority, and moral order. Liberals, by contrast, draw on 'the nurturant parent model', privileging empathy, self-nurturance, and self-development. For Lakoff, these moral systems of the family inform political outlooks via the metaphor of the nation-as-family.

A last example is provided by Jay Childers (2012) and is probably the most relevant example for the present study of citizens' changing orientations towards formal politics. To understand how young people view and practise citizenship and how that has changed over time, Childers analysed high school newspapers from the past five decades. In doing so, he focused on different cohorts or generations and their shared collective understandings or worldviews of the political and civic world around them. For Childers, these 'democratic imaginations' were displayed in high school newspapers where young people wrote about themselves, to one another, in ways they believed were acceptable at the time, and in ways they had learned in particular socio-historical contexts.

What have we learned from these examples? The talk or writing of citizens displays their categories, which in turn provide access to their understandings, worldviews, conceptualisations, models, and imaginations. These categories and understandings are often shared by citizens because they derive not only from personal experience but also from popular wisdom and media discourse. These categories and understandings are also often specific to particular historical moments because they evolve with changing societal conditions (Childers) or get changed by the purposeful political projects of cultural actors (Lakoff). We applied these lessons to the writing of MO panellists, reading it not for representative views and opinions but for evidence of cultural resources circulating widely in each period, to be used by citizens in thinking about, talking about, writing about, constructing understandings of, and forming judgements regarding formal politics.

It is worth adding here that we think lessons from research largely focused on the current period can be applied to the writing of MO panellists in the mid-twentieth century. LeMahieu (1988) has argued convincingly that, as early as the 1930s, a 'mass', 'common', 'national' culture had been created in Britain by popular daily newspapers, the cinema, and the gramophone. This 'culture for democracy' largely transcended the boundaries of religion and social class. It provided citizens from divergent groups with a 'shared frame of reference'. LeMahieu found this culture displayed in newspapers, films, and radio programmes from the period. We think it can also be found in the writing of MO panellists from the period.

It is also worth adding that, pushed by the lessons from Lakoff and others and by the MO material itself, we ended up focusing in particular on four sets of cultural resources (and the relationships between them). First, we read the diaries and letters for shared *categories*: words or phrases referring to particular characters, characteristics, practices, events, or objects. Here, we focused especially on *prototypical* categories – a character, for example, used to stand in for people or members of a social group *in general*. Lakoff (2002) includes 'typical cases', 'ideal cases', 'anti-ideal cases' or 'demons', 'social stereotypes', 'salient exemplars', and 'essential prototypes' as prototypical categories. An example from elsewhere in the book is the 'gasbag' politician, who many citizens thought of when asked about politicians in general in the years immediately following the Second World War (see Chapter 4). Second, we read the MO material for shared *storylines*: lines, often populated by (prototypical) categories, about formal politics. An example from elsewhere in the book is the line that 'politicians are not straight-talking' (they are gasbags – again, see Chapter 4). Third, we read the writing of panellists for *subject positions*: shared identities, adopted – if only briefly – in relation to formal politics. An example from Chapter 5 is 'the disgusted citizen' (disgusted with politicians and their conduct or the parties and their offer or the government and its performance). Finally, we read the diaries and letters for evidence of shared *folk theories*:

sets of abstractions, often made up of categories, storylines, and subject positions, used by citizens to guide their judgements of politics. An example from Chapter 6 is 'stealth democracy', made up of categories like 'the common good', storylines like 'political debate is unnecessary and driven by special interests', and subject positions like 'member of the silent majority'.

How does all this fit with existing approaches to MO? Hinton has probably written more than anyone about how to interpret MO material (Hinton 1997, 2010, 2013a, 2013b). He has criticised Fielding for his confident empiricism in the face of suggestive, ambiguous, complex, awkward, contradictory sources. He has criticised Mike Savage for relying on snapshots from the archive, when responses to other directives provide for alternative interpretations. He has criticised Jeffrey for lumping all MO contributors together as progressives from the lower middle class and Savage for lumping them together as members of the technically minded middle class. Constructively, Hinton has argued that panellists, as purposive volunteers, are not representative of broader society but nevertheless are particularly reflective people who provide researchers with access to the cultural world they and others inhabit. This world is populated by newspapers, advice manuals, novels, and films. It is a world of discourse or the raw materials from which people in general construct their own unique selfhoods. Another argument of Hinton's is that MO material is best used to study the life histories or biographies of individuals and, through that, to illuminate historical processes that are molecular and driven by the choices, the self-fashioning, the assertiveness of these historical agents in the face of received cultural norms.

Our approach drew lessons from Hinton. We took more than snapshots by selecting multiple directives. We did not seek representativeness but instead excavated MO writing for the cultural world inhabited by panellists. This brings us to some differences of approach between Hinton and ourselves. Hinton advocates what might be called a vertical approach whereby individual contributors are followed over a series of directives. This provides a window on how individuals construct themselves as unique individuals by interacting with cultural norms and how those norms gradually become remade through such molecular processes. But our starting point was different. We were interested in shared understandings, expectations, and judgements regarding the activities and institutions of formal politics. We wanted to establish these for certain key moments in contemporary British history. This demanded a more horizontal approach focused on as many panellists as possible, from as many social and geographical positions as possible, and the cultural resources they hold in common with each other.

This horizontal approach has been taken successfully by others focused on the public and shared understandings disclosed by MO sources (Salter 2010) or the shared cultural repertoires evident in MO writing (Nettleton and Uprichard 2011) or the 'proverbs, truisms, and everyday episteme' from which MO panellists construct and express their opinions (Gazeley and Langhamer 2013: 161). But the weaknesses of this horizontal approach should also be noted. In seeking commonalities, it is likely to downplay ambiguity and complexity in the MO material. By not following individuals, it is likely to downplay the role of individual agency in social change. We sought to keep these weaknesses in mind during analysis and interpretation. For example, we read MO writing not only for shared cultural resources but also for how panellists interact with such resources as individuals or members of social groups. These weaknesses remain, however, as they do with any study where opening up one pathway closes down another. Our ultimate position is that more than one path is possible through the MO material. Our chosen path was the most appropriate to the broader study, but other paths would no doubt provide additional insights.

In practical terms, we selected the directives, sampled the panellists, and transcribed their responses into Nvivo (a software programme). Each member of the team read the responses independently. Then we met as a team to agree on prominent categories in the responses, how those categories sometimes come together into prominent storylines, and how those storylines sometimes come together into prominent folk theories. Where agreement could be reached, we coded the responses accordingly. Finally, to test and explore these codes further, we subjected them to content analysis using the 'text search', 'word frequency', and 'matrix coding' functions of Nvivo. Note that our sequence here reflected our scepticism about content analysis that fails to account for how meaning arises from interaction between terms (Propp 1968). We sought to establish meaning first by reading the transcripts in full. Then we used content analysis as a supplementary technique to help confirm our initial readings.

In summary, our analysis of the MO material was theoretically informed but not theoretically constraining. We read the letters and diaries of MO panellists looking for specific things: the understandings, expectations, and judgements of citizens regarding formal politics at different historical moments; the shared cultural resources from

which such understandings, expectations, and judgements are constructed; and evidence for existing or new theories of declining political support and rising political disaffection. We did not limit
ourselves to just one form of analysis, not least because writing for
MO is varied in character. Sometimes, panellists write autobiographi-
cal life histories (Sheridan 1993, 1996). Sometimes, they slip between
subjective writing and social reportage (Nettleton and Uprichard
2011). We selected from the toolkit of textual analysis as appropriate
to the particular mode of response. In doing so, we combined formal
analysis with 'natural' or 'intuitive' analysis (Quinn and Holland
1987).

In this chapter, we have considered two kinds of data for taking the
long view of anti-politics and listening to citizens' voices: responses to
public opinion surveys and volunteer writing for MO. Each exhibits
the well-known strengths and weaknesses of their respective data
families. Survey responses allow researchers to establish distributions
and generalise their results. MO diaries and letters allow researchers
to interpret and understand better the content and meaning of citizens' responses. Each kind of data also exhibits weaknesses and
strengths particular to our specific research aims. The survey data
suffer from poor continuous availability across much of the period in
question. They have also been relatively well used in existing research
on anti-politics. By contrast, the MO material has been underused.
It is a strange dataset – for this field of research, at least – in two
respects. Much of it is unstructured and qualitative in character and
so captures citizens' voices using their own terms. Second, much of it
was collected in the 1940s and 1950s, long before many relevant
survey questions were fielded in the UK.
    In the rest of the book, we use both kinds of data. In the next chapter,
we focus on the survey data because, despite their limitations, they are
most appropriate to the questions of *social scope* addressed in that chapter. Who has felt and expressed anti-political sentiment? What proportion of the population? Which social groups? And how has this changed
over time? Also, we show in Chapter 3 how some of the limitations of
discontinuous survey data can be overcome using certain statistical
techniques like trend analysis but also dyadic analysis. Chapters 4 to 8
are then driven by the MO material. These underused data have the
potential to produce new claims, theories, and hypotheses. We ask:
What can this unusual dataset tell us about anti-politics? What can it
tell us about existing knowledge of patterns and explanations? What new

insights can it provide? Finally, where new insights are provided, we use the survey data, where available, to confirm these claims. Such confirmation work is only begun in this book, and we hope that others will take up the task, especially in comparative research focused beyond the case of the UK.

3 Beyond Trendless Fluctuation: The Broadening Social Scope of Anti-Politics

Most research in the field of anti-politics has taken a relatively short view and considered the withdrawal of political support or the rise of political disaffection over just the past few decades. In the Introduction, we noted the influential research of Pippa Norris (2011), who used data from Eurobarometer and the World Values Survey (WVS) to claim that political support since the 1970s has varied by country and object of support and that we are not seeing 'linear or uniform downward trends' so much as 'ebb and flow' or 'trendless fluctuation' (p241). In response to this claim, we argued that baseline and timeframe are crucial when studying change over time. There is a need for longer views of anti-politics covering both the so-called 'golden age' of democratic politics – the middle of the last century in countries like the United Kingdom (UK) – and the current so-called 'age of anti-politics'.

Studies of historical change over more than a few decades are fraught with methodological challenges. In Chapter 2, for the case of the UK, we began to address these challenges by considering what questions have been asked by survey researchers and commercial pollsters over the decades since 1937 (when the British Institute of Public Opinion (BIPO) began operating in the UK). This made clear some of the limits of existing survey data on the topic of anti-politics. But it also made visible the concerns of researchers and pollsters at different historical moments.

In the present chapter, we analyse citizens' responses to the questions asked by survey researchers. We analyse time-series data where available, including for measures of what David Easton (1975) calls 'diffuse support', e.g. trust in governments or politicians of any party, available since the 1980s. We also analyse dyads of survey data, which are much more widely available for a variety of time periods and measures of political support and so are worth considering as supplements to available time-series data. Then we synthesise these two approaches using James Stimson's (1991) dyad-ratios algorithm to construct an index of anti-political sentiment based on thirty-seven survey questions asked 295 times between 1944 and 2016.

Finally, we briefly consider some headline measures of anti-political sentiment in finer detail and wider perspective. We consider the extent to which trust in government has varied by social group (social class, gender, age group, level of educational attainment, preferred newspaper, and region). Then we consider how the experience of the UK compares internationally – using a similar index of trust in the US federal government, again based on Stimson's dyad-ratios algorithm; and using Eurobarometer and European Social Survey (ESS) data to compare trust in the British Parliament and British politicians with trust in corresponding institutions and actors across Europe.

Having completed these different analytical tasks, we find no golden age of political support in the UK around the middle of the last century. And we find no clear pattern of trendless fluctuation in anti-political sentiment for the case of the UK. Rather, in general terms, we find an upward trend over a period of at least five decades. We find growth in the *social scope* of anti-politics, in that more and more citizens from across British society have expressed negativity towards the institutions of formal politics over the past half century.

The Longitudinal Evidence: Trends and Dyads

We have shown how survey data tend to reflect the character of the time in which they are generated (Chapter 2). Because of this, measures of distrust and disaffection regarding formal politics and politicians are often subject to discontinuities and substantial gaps between points in time. Questions are included in surveys in some years and not others. There are often extended time periods in which questions are not fielded at all. And some questions fall out of fashion with survey researchers and pollsters just as others are coming into use. There are different ways of dealing with these challenges. Here, our solution is to derive insights on the long-term trajectory of public opinion from trend data (where sufficient observations are available) and dyadic analysis (by identifying the change in opinion between two points in time where questions have been fielded on more than one occasion).

Trends

We start by considering trends in responses to survey questions that have been fielded at regular intervals over an extended period. Perhaps the best-known measure of political trust in the UK is the question asked in the British Social Attitudes (BSA) survey since 1986: 'How much do you trust British governments of any party to place the needs of the nation

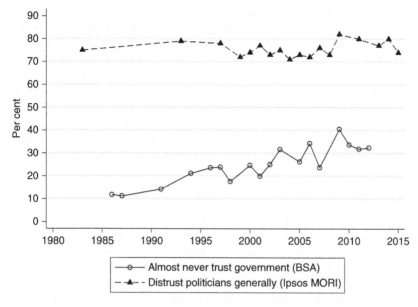

Figure 3.1 Distrust in government and politicians, 1983–2015.

above the interests of their own political party?' This measure reveals a steady decline in the public's trust in government to set partisan interests aside in the wider national interest. The percentage of respondents replying 'almost never' to this question is plotted in Figure 3.1. The trend over the past three decades is unmistakable, revealing rising distrust in government to serve the national interest.

Over roughly the same period, the polling firm Ipsos MORI asked for a range of groups of people, including 'politicians generally', whether respondents 'generally trust them to tell the truth or not?' The percentage of respondents saying they do not trust politicians to tell the truth is also plotted in Figure 3.1. This measure offers a different story about the trajectory of political distrust since the 1980s. The first thing to note is that the level of distrust is much higher when it is measured dichotomously in this way (i.e. whether people do or do not trust politicians to tell the truth). Further – and relatedly, given this higher level – the upward trend in distrust is less pronounced and undergoes a noticeable drop during the honeymoon period of the Blair government that is not fully reversed until 2009, around the time of the MPs' expenses scandal and the height of the global financial crisis.[1] The mixed picture

[1] For more on these events, see Chapter 4.

here highlights how the available measures of political disaffection can shape our understanding of long-term trends. The timeframe also matters. The trend observed looks rather different depending on whether 1992 or 1997 is taken as the starting point for the Ipsos MORI data. Compared to 1992, current levels of distrust of politicians represent a return to roughly where they were after a more optimistic period. If 1997 is taken as the benchmark, the period since exhibits a steady erosion of public trust in politicians. Were the data extended back to the 1940s or 1950s, would they reveal both a long-term increase in public distrust and trendless fluctuation during the more recent time period?

Dyadic Analysis

An alternative to using long-running time-series measures, of which there are few, is to detect long-term shifts in attitudes through *dyadic* comparison of mass opinion at different points in time: assessing the ratio between the proportion of respondents expressing negative attitudes at one moment compared to another. This provides information about *relative* change over time – i.e. whether anti-political sentiment is increasing or decreasing or otherwise has remained stable – drawing on existing survey measures observed at multiple time points. Even this is limited as an approach since, like trend analysis, it depends on the availability of data which cannot be reconstructed retrospectively.[2] Furthermore, in isolation it cannot reveal fluctuations – i.e. random variations around a long-term equilibrium state – in the same way as trend analysis.

In Figure 3.2, we plot the percentage of respondents who expressed dissatisfaction or distrust regarding politicians or government across a selection of survey measures at two points in time (full details of all the survey questions and response options are outlined in Table A2 in the Appendix). By comparing the first and last observation for each measure (or other combinations of time points), it is possible to determine whether there has been a relative change in public opinion – for the observed period at least.[3] Here, for example, it can be shown that the percentage of people believing that Britain's system of governing could be improved (either 'a great deal' or 'quite a lot') increased substantially between 1973

---

[2] A further limitation is the extent to which point estimates derived from surveys using different methodologies are directly comparable, though these can provide important information on both the direction and approximate degree of change.

[3] The twelve cases presented here are selected on the basis that the survey item was first fielded prior to the turn of the current century and the minimum time duration between the pair of observations is one decade. This ensures the dyads provide insights on long(er)-term shifts in opinion.

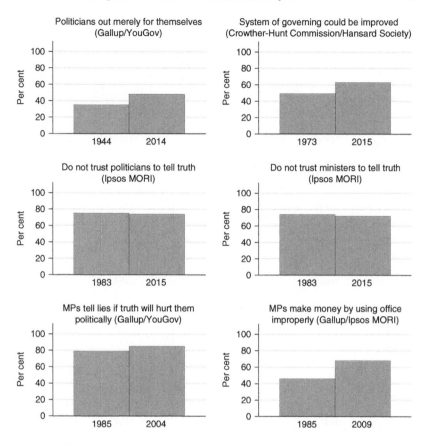

Figure 3.2 Dyads of survey measures of anti-political sentiment.

and 2015 (from 49% to 63%), while there was a similar increase in the proportion agreeing that 'most MPs make a lot of money by using public office improperly' between 1985 and 2009 (from 46% to 68%). Over an even longer period, the percentage thinking 'British politicians are out merely for themselves' increased between the time the question was first asked by BIPO in 1944 and when it was fielded again by YouGov in 2014 seventy years later (from 35% to 48%). While this is just one survey measure, it does suggest that public opinion about the motivations of politicians has become significantly more negative since the 1940s.

Reading across all the survey measures presented here, while a couple do not point to an over-time shift in public opinion (specifically the Ipsos MORI measures discussed previously, which tend to show trendless fluctuation due to the way their question wording produces a high average

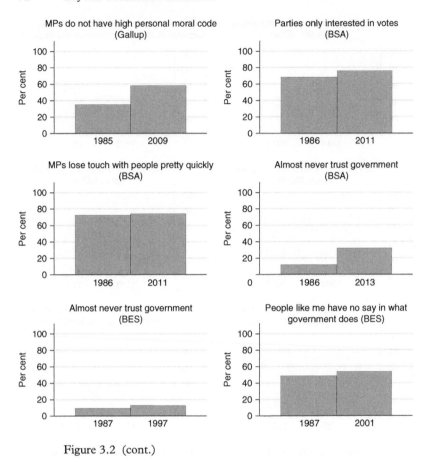

Figure 3.2 (cont.)

level of distrust), the majority of cases – ten out of the twelve – are consistent with the rising social scope of anti-politics over a period of several decades. This offers evidence that an increasing number of people – and an increasing proportion of the population – have expressed negativity towards the institutions of formal politics (politicians but also parties, governments, and the political system).

Constructing a Measure of Anti-Politics

Even though the available survey data are subject to discontinuities, every repeated measure provides *some* useful information about over-time change in public opinion. As discussed earlier, the observation of public attitudes at multiple time points can indicate whether anti-political sentiment has increased, decreased, or remained stable for a defined period. Furthermore, commonalities in the trends that are observed across different survey measures may reveal an underlying mood in affective orientation of the public towards the institutions of formal politics (the 'anti-politics mood' often referred to in recent years by journalists – see the Introduction).

As described in Jennings et al. (2017a), we use Stimson's (1991) dyad-ratios algorithm to construct an index of anti-political sentiment based on thirty-seven survey questions which were asked a total of 295 times over the period between 1944 and 2016. In practice, most of these survey items are drawn from mid-1960s onwards, so estimates of the index are not reliable prior to this point. This method has been used previously to generate aggregate-level measures of public trust in the US federal government (Chanley et al. 2000, Keele 2007, Hetherington and Rudolph 2008), congressional approval (Durr et al. 1997), and support for the Supreme Court (Durr et al. 2000) – as well as measures of public left-right policy preferences, 'public policy mood' (Stimson 1991, Bartle et al. 2011, Stimson et al. 2012), specific policy preferences on criminal justice (Enns 2014, Jennings et al. 2017b) and immigration policy (Ford et al. 2015), and public evaluations of party reputations for competence (Green and Jennings 2012 and 2017).

For the purposes of our study, the dyad-ratios algorithm is used to estimate the latent, underlying dimension of public expressions of discontent about politics, politicians, political institutions, and the political system. In basic terms, it measures the *relative* degree to which the public is more or less disaffected with formal politics at different points in time. Stimson's method offers a solution to the problem of irregular and infrequent availability of poll data. The principle behind the dyad-ratios algorithm is intuitive: it uses the ratio of aggregate-level survey responses ('marginals') to the same question, at different points in time, to derive information about the relative state of public opinion. In doing so, it tells us whether, on average, public attitudes have become more negative or positive towards the institutions of formal politics (see Stimson 1991 and Bartle et al. 2011 for more on the method).[4] The technique extracts the

---

[4] Each survey item can be expressed as the ratio of feelings towards formal politics at two points in time: a 'dyad'. This ratio provides an estimate of relative anti-political sentiment, for a given question, in years $t + i$ and $t + j$.

$$P_{ij} = \frac{X_{t+i}}{X_{t+j}}$$

This enables recursive estimation of the index of anti-politics for each survey item for each time period based on all data available. Because there are multiple estimates of

underlying tendency of all survey items relating to political alienation, withdrawal of political support, and political disaffection, analogous to a principal components approach. We use data from a range of sources, including the BSA survey, the British Election Study (BES), the European Social Survey (ESS), Eurobarometer, the Hansard Society Audit of Political Engagement, and poll data from Gallup, YouGov, and Ipsos MORI.

Table 3.1 reports the factor loading of each survey item and the proportion of variance explained by the underlying factor. This reveals that a substantial proportion of variance loads onto a single underlying dimension, indicating the central tendency in public opinion. This accounts for 50 per cent of all variance in survey questions on disaffection with formal politics. The loading (i.e. correlation with the underlying construct) of a number of survey items is considerable. For instance, the loading of the BSA '(no) trust in government' series is 0.864, while that for the Ipsos MORI '(do not) trust politicians to tell the truth' series is somewhat lower at 0.609 – but still substantial. The loading of the Gallup survey question about whether politicians are out for themselves, discussed earlier, is 0.991. What is striking is that this co-variation of expressions of political disaffection extends across a wide range of measures – relating to, for example, politicians telling the truth, being out of touch with voters, being self-interested, using public office improperly, or lacking integrity. Most of these load to a greater or lesser degree onto the underlying construct. The prevailing sentiment or 'mood' in public opinion (Stimson 1991) – in this case, an 'anti-politics mood' – underlies a range of survey responses. This is consistent with commonality observed in expressions of disaffection at the individual level (Jennings et al. 2016).

The measure is plotted in Figure 3.3 over the period for which there are sufficient data, from 1966 to 2016. This reveals that despite periodic peaks and troughs, there has been a steady rise in anti-political sentiment.[5] Combined with the evidence presented earlier on trends and dyadic analysis, this reveals more than trendless fluctuation in mass opinion. There has been a sustained growth in negative sentiment towards the activities and institutions of formal politics over more than half a century.

political discontent (i.e. there are multiple survey items) and they are not all equivalent indicators of the latent construct, the dyad-ratios algorithm estimates the squared correlation of each series with the underlying dimension and uses this to weight the series (Bartle et al. 2011: 269). This correlation is interpretable as a factor loading and is reported for selected survey items.

[5] The line of best fit for a linear regression of our measure of anti-politics as a function of time indicates that it has been growing at a rate of 0.2 points per year over this fifty-year period.

Table 3.1 *Survey items and the measure of anti-politics*

Survey item (source)	N	Start	End	Factor loading	Standard deviation
Do not trust British governments to place needs of the nation above interests of their own party (BSA)	20	1986	2013	0.864	7.981
Tend not to trust Parliament (Eurobarometer)	17	1999	2015	0.935	7.114
Tent not to trust the National Government (Eurobarometer)	16	1999	2015	0.858	7.005
Do not trust politicians to tell the truth (Ipsos MORI)	18	1983	2015	0.609	3.112
System of governing Britain could be improved (Ipsos MORI, BES, Hansard Society)	19	1973	2015	0.571	7.636
Parties are only interested in people's votes, not their opinions (BSA)	14	1986	2011	0.652	3.775
Do not trust government ministers to tell the truth (Ipsos MORI)	17	1983	2015	0.364	3.465
Low rating of standards of conduct of public office holders (Committee for Standards in Public Life)	6	2004	2014	0.914	8.770
Those we elect as MPs lose touch with people pretty quickly (BSA)	14	1986	2011	0.341	2.245
Most MPs make a lot of money by using public office improperly (Gallup, YouGov, Ipsos MORI)	5	1985	2009	0.913	8.114
Do not trust politicians of any party to tell the truth in a tight corner (BSA)	15	1994	2013	0.302	1.535
It doesn't really matter which party is in power (BSA)	7	2001	2011	0.621	3.016
Dissatisfied with way Parliament works (Hansard Society)	6	2003	2015	0.665	1.886
People like me have no say in what the government does (BES)	4	1987	2001	0.990	5.054
Most MPs will tell lies if they feel the truth will hurt them politically (Gallup, YouGov)	4	1985	2004	0.957	3.832
MPs use power for personal gain (Ipsos MORI)	4	2004	2013	0.948	9.618
Do not trust MPs to tell the truth (Ipsos MORI)	4	2004	2013	0.776	5.853
Dissatisfied with way MPs are doing job (Hansard Society)	5	2003	2015	0.610	3.098
Distrust in MPs in general (BES)	3	2014	2016	0.999	3.120
British politicians out merely for themselves (Gallup, YouGov)	3	1944	2014	0.991	5.558

Table 3.1 (*cont.*)

Survey item (source)	N	Start	End	Factor loading	Standard deviation
Do not trust Parliament (ESS)	7	2002	2014	0.409	2.431
Disagree that most MPs have a high personal moral code (Gallup, YouGov, Ipsos MORI)	4	1985	2009	0.715	11.432
MPs put own interests first (Ipsos MORI)	6	1994	2013	0.420	5.121
People like me do not have enough say in way government runs the country (Gallup)	2	1968	1973	1.000	1.500
Do not trust government to tell the truth (Ipsos MORI)	2	2007	2008	1.000	1.994
Do not trust government to act in best interests of country (Ipsos MORI)	2	2007	2008	1.000	2.500
MPs care more about special interests (Gallup)	2	1985	1994	1.000	5.000
Doesn't really matter which party is in power (BES)	2	2015	2016	1.000	5.119
Do not trust government to put needs of nation above party interests (BES)	2	1987	1997	1.000	1.700
Do not trust Parliament (BES)	2	2005	2010	1.000	5.500
Most politicians are in politics only for what they can get out of it personally (BSA)	2	2004	2014	1.000	2.500
Politicians only care about people with money (BES)	3	2014	2016	0.604	1.033
No trust in British politicians (BES)	3	2005	2015	0.601	6.532
Do not trust national politicians (ESS)	7	2002	2014	0.098	2.344
Do not trust local MP to tell truth (Ipsos MORI)	4	2004	2013	-0.461	4.023
Bribes and abuse of power for personal gain are widespread among politicians (Eurobarometer)	2	2009	2011	-1.000	1.670
Most of the time cannot trust people in government to do what is right (BSA)	3	2004	2014	-0.836	0.713

First dimension: proportion of variance explained = 50.4; N of time series = 37; N of survey items = 295.
Note: Each survey item is coded as the percentage of respondents giving a negative response about politics, politicians, or the political system (i.e. ordinal measures are recoded as a dichotomous measure of disaffection).

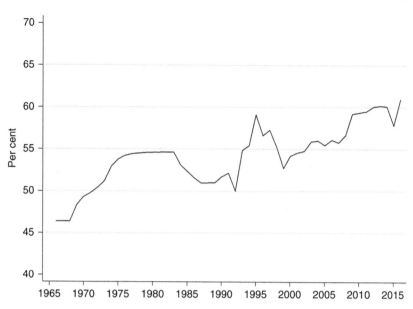

Figure 3.3 Anti-politics in the UK, 1966–2016.

Discussion

In this chapter, we have demonstrated how anti-political sentiment has grown among British citizens over at least the past half century. Our findings show that an increasing number of people have expressed disaffection towards the activities and institutions of formal politics over the period between 1944 and 2016. While there may have been periods of 'trendless fluctuation', depending on the time period or survey measure in question, there has in general been a sustained long-term increase in expressions of political discontentment (across a wide range of survey measures).

Broadening Social Scope

Our argument is that anti-politics has grown in social scope over a period of at least five decades. More and more UK citizens have expressed negative sentiment towards formal politics. The *proportion* of citizens expressing anti-political sentiment has increased. But it is also possible to assess changes in the orientations of particular social groups towards formal politics using waves of the BSA survey between 1986 and 2013, disaggregating responses to its 'trust in government' question. Each of the

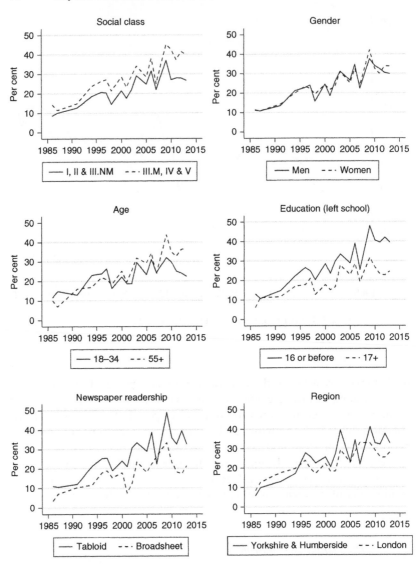

Figure 3.4 Almost never trust government by social group, BSA, 1986–2013.

graphs in Figure 3.4 plots the proportion of respondents indicating they 'almost never' trust governments to place the needs of the nation above the interests of their own party across a range of demographic attributes:

social class,[6] gender, age, education (age left school), newspaper reader-ship (tabloid compared to broadsheet), and region (using London and Yorkshire & Humberside for the purpose of comparison). Each of the graphs reveals an upward trend in distrust (as observed previously for this measure), indicating the growing social scope of anti-politics in recent decades. That is, anti-political sentiment has been on the rise across *a range of social groups.*

A Comparative Perspective

Something else we can do is to compare the experience of the UK to that of other countries. Like the UK, most countries suffer from a shortage of long-term survey data on political disaffection. For example, cross-national surveys like Eurobarometer and the ESS have only been asking questions about political distrust since the late 1990s. This substantially limits possibilities for over-time comparisons. We are able, however, to compare our index of anti-political sentiment with an equivalent measure of trust in the US federal government over a period of almost half a century. This measure again uses Stimson's dyad-ratios algorithm to construct an index of public distrust in government (following Chanley et al. 2000, Keele 2007, Hetherington and Rudolph 2008) based on aggregate-level responses to six survey items which were fielded a total of 382 times over the period between 1958 and 2014 (with data obtained from the Roper Center for Public Opinion Research).[7] Because the measure includes a much narrower subset of survey items, the single underlying dimension accounts for nearly 75 per cent of variance in responses. The strongest loading item (0.990) is the longstanding survey question used by the American National Election Studies and Gallup: 'How much of the time do you think you can trust government in Washington to do what is right – just about always, most of the time, or only some of the time?'

---

[6] For this analysis, we use the Registrar-General's classifications of social class, based on occupation: I (professional), II (managerial and technical), III (skilled non-manual), III. M (skilled manual), IV (partly skilled), and V (unskilled).

[7] The survey questions that are used to construct this measure are: 'How much of the time do you think you can trust the Government in Washington to do what is right'; 'Would you say the government is pretty much run by a few big interests looking out for themselves, or that it is run for the benefit of all the people?'; 'Do you think that quite a few of the people running the government are crooked, not very many are, or do you think hardly any of them are crooked?'; 'Do you think that people in the government waste a lot of the money we pay in taxes, waste some of it, or don't waste very much of it?'; 'How much trust and confidence do you have in our Federal Government when it comes to handling domestic problems?'

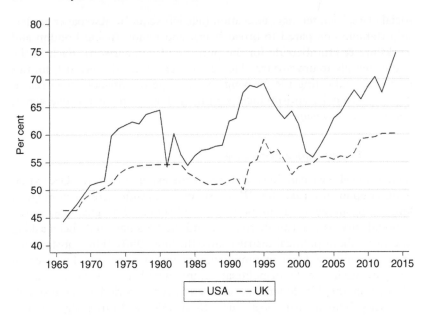

Figure 3.5 Political distrust and anti-politics in the USA and UK, 1966–2014.

Figure 3.5 plots measures for the USA and UK over the period for which there are common data (between 1966 and 2014). Visual inspection of the data reveals quite striking parallels in the trajectory of anti-political sentiment in the two countries given their very distinct political histories, cultures, and institutional contexts. (Note that the correlation between the series is positive and significant: Pearson's $r = 0.826$; $p = 0.000$.) Aside from the obvious commonality of an upward trend in distrust and disaffection in both cases, there would seem to be common ebbs and flows: for instance, rising discontent during the 1960s and 1970s, followed by decline and stabilisation in the 1980s; further rises during the early 1990s, followed by another drop in the late 1990s; and a steady increase since the early 2000s.

In addition to this over-time comparison with the USA, it is possible to compare the current position of the UK – regarding the social scope of anti-political sentiment – in European terms. Both Eurobarometer and the ESS offer cross-national survey measures of political trust that enable comparison across a wide range of political systems and national contexts. In Figure 3.6, we plot the proportion of respondents for each country included in the May 2015 Eurobarometer survey who expressed distrust

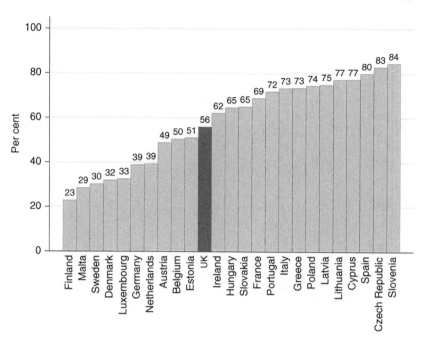

Figure 3.6 Distrust of national parliaments, Eurobarometer, 2015.

of their national parliament. The 56 per cent observed for the UK is just below the median and far from atypical compared to other countries.

A similar pattern is observed using 2014 data from the ESS (this time for a slightly different set of countries) on distrust in national politicians. These are plotted in Figure 3.7. With 64 per cent of respondents expressing distrust of national politicians, the UK again sits just below the median level – and so provides a good case to study, apparently positioned somewhere in the middle of Europe for anti-political mood.

Conclusion

The evidence presented here offers a number of important insights. First, there was no golden age of political support in the UK around the middle of the twentieth century. Even in 1944, 35 per cent of respondents thought politicians were merely out for themselves. Second, if we consider the case of the UK over the past half century, we see less of Norris' 'trendless fluctuation' and more of an upward trend in anti-political sentiment.

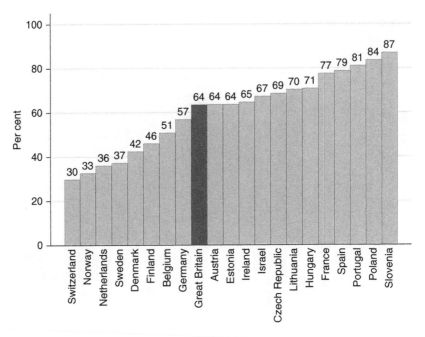

Figure 3.7 Distrust of national politicians, ESS, 2014.

This is the case whether we focus on time-series data on specific support over the long term since the end of the Second World War (Figure 2.1); time-series data on diffuse support over the shorter term since the mid-1980s; dyads of data on diffuse support over both long and shorter terms; or data from a wide range of survey questions synthesised into a measure of anti-political mood using Stimson's dyad-ratios algorithm.

Third, this growth has been in the social scope of anti-politics: more and more citizens from across society – all social classes, men and women, all age groups, all education levels, broadsheet and tabloid readers, all regions of the UK – have expressed negativity towards the activities and institutions of formal politics. Today, the majority of British citizens express disaffection with formal politics (at least by some measures, e.g. disapproval of government performance, distrust of Parliament, or distrust of politicians in general). And British citizens are not outliers when viewed in the context of comparable democracies. There are striking parallels between our index of anti-politics and the index of distrust in the US federal government presented in Figure 3.5. In Europe, the case of the UK ranks near the median for distrust of Parliament (or equivalent) and distrust of politicians (in general).

In the next two chapters, we consider what is added to this picture by analysis of volunteer writing for Mass Observation (MO). The present chapter has argued that anti-politics increased in social scope over at least the past half century. In Chapter 4, we argue that anti-politics has increased in the UK over the long term not only in social scope but also in *political scope* (the range of grievances held by citizens against formal politics). Then in Chapter 5, we go on to argue that anti-politics has also increased in a third way: *intensity*, or the strength by which citizens hold negative sentiment oriented towards formal politics.

4 Beyond Permanent Apathy: The Broadening Political Scope of Anti-Politics

An Unchanging, Anaemic Political Culture?

In Chapter 3, we used survey data to argue that anti-political sentiment has grown in the UK over the past half century in terms of its social scope. More and more people have expressed negativity towards the activities and institutions of formal politics. In this chapter, we draw on volunteer writing for Mass Observation (MO) – supported by survey data where appropriate – to argue that such anti-political sentiment has grown also in terms of its political scope. People have expressed concern regarding more and more aspects of politics, and especially the motivations, backgrounds, and behaviour of politicians.

MO sources have been used previously by others to make claims about Britain's political culture during the immediate post-war period. This existing research provides one starting point for the present chapter. Steven Fielding and colleagues use MO to argue against the popular view of a democratic 'golden age' immediately after the Second World War (Fielding 1992, Fielding et al. 1995). They critique narratives of a 'people's war' that produced a 'spirit of 1945' – a consensus, a national sense of purpose, 'a tidal wave of radicalism' that brought the United Kingdom's (UK's) first majority Labour Government and, ultimately, its welfare state. They argue instead that citizens at this time were preoccupied with personal problems and their own private spheres. They wanted a return to independence and normalcy after years of war. Regarding formal politics, they were ignorant, indifferent, alienated, cynical, apathetic, and disengaged. They voted Labour, if at all, without idealism – but instead because they were hostile to 'the old gang' and Labour campaigned well as a practical party focused on everyday problems.

This argument is well made and has been influential. Kevin Jefferys (2007) builds from it – and Fielding's interpretations of MO sources – the broader argument of his own informative history of popular politics in Britain. He writes: 'Britain has never possessed anything that could be described as a "vibrant" political culture' (p6). 'There has been no decline from an earlier golden age to a contemporary crisis' (p6). Looking back from the current period, he sees that 'much of Britain's political culture has remained unchanged across the generations' (p280). 'Britain's political culture in the early twenty-first century can perhaps best be described', for Jefferys, 'neither as ailing, in terminal decline, nor as healthy and robust, but rather – as it has been since 1918 – as anaemic: lacking in vigour and vitality' (p281).

Fielding has developed his own broader argument in more recent publications. Reflecting on depictions of British politics in fiction, he sees 'firm grounds for believing that populism is not a recent phenomenon provoked by social change but something deriving from endemic tensions at the heart of representative democracy' (Fielding 2008: 128) – 'a process that promises to reflect the people's voice ... a promise that can never be met' (2014: 9). Like Jefferys, he sees 'a basic continuity that ensured the gap between the promise of democracy and its disappointing reality remained unabridged' (ibid.).

We show in this chapter how claims of a political culture that is 'unchanged' and characterised by 'continuity' are called into question once a historical-comparative approach is taken and direct consideration is given to the relatively unmediated writing of MO panellists (as opposed to the relatively mediated summaries of MO researchers from the time). In the rest of this chapter, we provide our own analysis of responses by MO panellists to directives about formal politics. We compare responses between the immediate post-war period and the early years of the twenty-first century, focusing in particular on the cultural resources for thinking and writing about formal politics that are shared across responses from a wide range of panellists – and so, plausibly, were circulating widely in society at each time. We also focus in particular on citizens' judgements of *politicians* in these responses. We consider other activities and institutions of formal politics in later chapters of the book, but we start with politicians – and keep them in the foreground throughout the book – because MO panellists often wrote about politicians when asked to write about politics, just as citizens more broadly often think about politicians when asked to think about formal politics in general (see Introduction).

In doing all this, we develop an argument complementary to that made in Chapter 3. There was no democratic golden age in the UK immediately after the Second World War, but anti-political sentiment has increased over time. This argument challenges the popular narrative of decline from a golden age. Furthermore, it challenges the revisionist narrative that Britain has a permanent, unchanging, anaemic political culture (where alienation, apathy, and cynicism have been continuously present and prominent). In what follows, we draw on volunteer writing for MO to demonstrate how, in the 1940s and 1950s, citizens judged politicians to be self-interested and not straight-talking. In the past couple of decades, they have judged politicians to be these things but also 'out of touch' and 'all the same'. We argue that prominent negative storylines about politicians have increased in number over time. Put differently, the range of grievances held by citizens regarding politicians has expanded. Therefore, not only has anti-politics increased in social scope over the past five decades (Chapter 3). It has also increased in political scope.

1945–1955: Politicians as Self-Seekers and Gasbags

In February 1945, MO asked its panel of volunteer writers the following question: 'What would you say is your normal conversational attitude when talk gets round to each of the following groups of people: a) clergymen; b) politicians; c) doctors; d) advertising agents; e) lawyers; f) scientists?'[1] Britain was still at war in Europe and Asia. It was just beginning to emerge from a period of political co-operation – a prolonged parliament, an electoral truce, a coalition government – unequalled in the country's history (McCallum and Readman 1947). That summer, the first general election for a decade would be fought and won by a Labour Party focused on reconstruction after years of insecurity, against a Conservative Party led by Winston Churchill – who, for many, had recently proved himself to be one of Britain's greatest ever statesmen (ibid.).

In this context, how did panellists respond to MO's question? We compare writing on the different groups – politicians, doctors, lawyers, and scientists – in Chapter 5, where we consider arguments for a generalised 'decline of deference' and rise of 'critical citizens' over the second half of the twentieth century. In the rest of the present chapter, we focus on panellists' judgements of politicians. Something else to note, by way of introduction, is that we should not dwell too much on the specific wording of MO's questions. They presumably do lead panellists a little to certain kinds of response, but generally panellists appear to seize on the most obvious topic of the question, as opposed to its specific wording, and just write in a relatively free way about that topic – at least, that is the impression gained from reading the responses of hundreds of different panellists to tens of different questions asked throughout both periods.

What, then, did panellists write about politicians in February 1945 – and how? The most common form of response was one in which panellists identified a general conception of politicians in society and then

[1] Directive SxMOA1/3/84.

differentiated their own view from that general conception. A farmer and housewife from Campbeltown wrote:

Politicians ... may be of all kinds, varying in their degrees of sincerity as widely as in their position to the right or the left, and I doubt if I should ever generalise about them in conversation ... I should say that the general idea of a politician is unflattering – and depicts a man who is bent first and foremost on making a career for himself out of politics.[2]

A domestic nurse from Leicester wrote: 'I think most people are inclined to think of "politicians" as a whole in a derogatory sense ("a lot of talkers"), forgetting that we ordinary people have chosen them to represent our interests.'[3] These two panellists identified a general conception of politicians – as 'talkers' focused on their own careers – and claimed a more nuanced conception for themselves: politicians 'may be of all kinds', they vary, it is not possible to generalise about them, and they are chosen by citizens to represent their interests (so presumably they *will* vary, *will* 'talk', and should be judged accordingly).

For some panellists, this distinction was between their own sophisticated conception and a general conception held by the relatively 'uneducated' or unintelligent. For this clerk from Scotland: 'In general, a rather large number of people condemn all politicians as twisters, dishonest, and self-serving. Usually the people are rather politically uneducated. For those who have studied politics usually support one side or the other.'[4] Here, the general conception condemns 'all politicians' for being 'self-serving' and 'dishonest' – reasons that will become familiar as we proceed – but the claim is that such a general conception is not held by the politically educated because they understand the differences between politicians from different parties. A similar claim was made by this housewife from Tayvallich: 'I am interested in politicians and often irritated by the conception of them as opportunists and self-seekers, but I should say that is rather the general opinion locally, though perhaps not among my more intelligent friends!'[5] Again, the general conception is described: politicians are viewed locally as 'opportunists' and 'self-seekers'. But this panellist claims to be 'irritated' by such a presumably unfair or simplistic conception, which she thinks would not be held by her 'more intelligent friends'.

Some panellists, irritated or not, described how they would go so far as to defend politicians against this general conception. A civil servant from

[2] Panellist 1534, female, 47, farmer/housewife, Campbeltown.
[3] Panellist 3402, female, 40, domestic nurse, Leicester.
[4] Panellist 1682, male, 25, clerk/forces, Edinburgh/Berwickshire.
[5] Panellist 2490, female, 45, housewife, Tayvallich.

Newcastle wrote that while some politicians are 'mere careerists ...
I always endeavour to defend them as a class from the general public'.[6]
Or consider this from a food packing manager in Belmont:

In conversation, I generally find that people consider politicians as motivated by
ulterior and personal motives, of self-advancement either in pocket or personal
ambition. I don't believe it. I think, and say, that politicians in the majority possess
the best of intentions, but because of the immense criticism they always have to
meet, fall back on compromises in policy with the result that few if any people are
pleased.[7]

These panellists again acknowledge the general conception of politicians
as 'careerists', motivated by 'personal motives' of 'self-advancement'. But
they reject this conception. They adopt a position against 'the general
public' who they seek to educate in the 'intentions' of and constraints
faced by politicians 'as a class'.

   What does this common style of response tell us? Perhaps most
obviously, it tells us something about the panellists themselves.
As Mike Savage (2008) has demonstrated, MO panellists at this time
would often use their writing to distinguish themselves from the culturally inferior working class as part of a process of educated middle class
identity construction. But these responses, we argue, also reveal something of the shared categories and storylines – for thinking and communicating about politicians – that were circulating widely in the mid-
1940s. One common storyline – often to be repeated, sometimes to be
critiqued, from which occasionally politicians were to be defended – was
that politicians are self-interested. They are 'self-serving', 'self-seekers',
driven by 'personal' motivations like 'ambition' and concerns for 'self-
advancement', their 'careers', and their 'pocket'. A second prominent
storyline was that politicians are not straight-talking. They are 'talkers',
'twisters', 'dishonest'.

   These categories and storylines were repeated by panellists who
answered the question more directly, commenting on their own conversational attitude – or, at least, repeating the descriptive terms available to
them when asked about politicians – without self-conscious reference to
some general conception. A teacher from Bingley wrote: 'I think they are
usually out to make a career.'[8] A nurse from Bristol answered the question
most directly: 'I should express a doubt whether any politician is entirely
free from self-interest in one form or another.'[9] This category of 'self-

[6] Panellist 2457, female, 46, civil servant, Newcastle.
[7] Panellist 2684, male, 37, food packing manager, Belmont.
[8] Panellist 3120, female, 79, teacher, Bingley.
[9] Panellist 2466, female, 58, nurse, Bristol.

interest' – alongside related categories like 'self-seeking' and 'place-seeking' – is found regularly in responses to the February 1945 directive. Politicians, it would seem, were often judged to be self-interested at this time.

They were also often judged to be not straight-talking. Of those panellists who answered the question relatively directly, some described their suspicion that politicians speak of one thing while believing another. For this student draughtsman from Wigan: 'Very often they're not sincere in their professed beliefs, but enter politics partly because they don't want to work and haven't the knowledge for a profession and mainly because they desire power.'[10] This commercial traveller from Leamington Spa was particularly blunt in his response: 'Have met many. Like very few. In general, they are hypocritical.'[11] These two quotations demonstrate how the storyline of politicians being not straight-talking was connected to the storyline of politicians being self-interested. If politicians were already suspected of being self-interested, then any talk of 'higher' interests by politicians would be reduced to evidence of insincerity and hypocrisy.

The line that politicians are not straight-talking was also connected to another line: that politicians are not only out for themselves but also for their parties (as opposed to the country). Being a disciplined member of a party meant delivering the party's intentionally clear message, whatever one's own complicated personal views: 'They almost have to be dishonest, squeezing themselves into some party formula.'[12] It also meant attacking the message of other parties, whatever the merits of that message: 'Politicians, by whom I usually mean partymen, is for whom I have no respect. They are usually men whose principal gift is that "of the gab". They always have their own political axe to grind, can say nothing good of their opponents.'[13]

We discuss popular understandings of party politics – including the categories of 'partymen' and 'axe-grinding' – more fully in Chapter 6, where we consider the relationship between depoliticisation, movement to a post-political condition, and citizens' negativity towards formal politics. The main point to note here is that politicians were commonly described in 1945 as 'talkers' (an insult). They have 'the gift of the gab'.[14] They talk to disguise their own personal interests, to advance their party's interests, to cover their own ignorance, or to persuade others

---

[10] Panellist 1478, male, 24, student draughtsman, Wigan.
[11] Panellist 3484, male, 37, commercial traveller, Leamington Spa.
[12] Panellist 1213, male, 28, army/student, Beckenham.
[13] Panellist 3402, female, 40, domestic nurse, Leicester.
[14] Panellist 1165, male, 39, electrical engineer, Ringwood.

of a particular course of action (even if founded on ignorance). A clerk from Glasgow put it like this: 'My normal conversational attitude to politicians is one of distrust and slight contempt; I feel that they often talk glibly of subjects of which they know little and that they are too seldom influenced in their actions by sound judgement.'[15] A factory manager from Lancing put it like this: 'I am suspicious of them all. But I envy some because of their powers of public speech and capacity for turning black into white by a series of logical and indisputable arguments. They also frighten me because of the colossal harm they can do in their ignorance of practical affairs.'[16]

In February 1945, the cultural resources for thinking and communicating about politicians that appear to have been circulating most widely through networks of farmers, nurses, clerks, housewives, civil servants, teachers, commercial travellers, draughtsman, factory managers, electrical engineers – men and women of multiple age groups, writing from many regions of the UK – were largely negative in character and mostly clustered around two prominent storylines. First, politicians are self-interested. They are 'self-seekers' and 'place-seekers'. Second, politicians are not straight-talking. They are 'talkers' and 'twisters'. Importantly, these two storylines were prominent in writing from February 1945 but also from other months in the period 1945–1955 – and so do not appear to have been responses to the particular wording of the February 1945 directive or particular events of early 1945.

Let us consider the November 1945 directive on municipal elections and local councils.[17] A teacher from Accrington explained her participation in municipal elections as follows: '[T]he councillors were mostly a lot of humbugs, who desired the position for their own glory and not because of a genuine interest in the business.'[18] A commercial traveller based in Leamington Spa noted the following in his local election diary:

The Conservative candidate was a young person … He and his party are determined to get this town in the forefront of the country's resorts. More and more visitors are desired. A very powerful section of the local Conservative Party are shopkeepers in the centre of town, or are interested in similar concerns; hotels and the like.[19]

Councillors were described as pursuing personal glory and sectional interests. Or they were accused of being corrupt. A housewife from Bradford bemoaned 'our present state of corruption in local

---

[15] Panellist 3545, female, 28, clerk, Glasgow.
[16] Panellist 2199, male, 40, factory manager, Lancing.   [17] Directive SxMOA1/3/86.
[18] Panellist 3035, female, 52, teacher/housewife, Accrington.
[19] Panellist 3438, male, 37, commercial traveller, Leamington Spa.

government'.[20] A teacher from Bishop Auckland reported how '[t]he "leader" of the Labour Party councillors' had a 'disguised friendship (to the advantages of both) with the German Jewish Factory Owners' and had 'taken up a £1000 a year job as "Personal Advisor" to the ... firm.'[21] The point here is not whether stories like these were true or fair – or anti-Semitic, for that matter – but that local councillors in late 1945, like their national equivalents earlier that year, were commonly described as having suspect motives.

This storyline that politicians are self-interested was also repeated across responses to a question in the July 1950 directive asking panellists about specific national politicians: 'How do you feel about: a) Attlee; b) Churchill; c) Bevin; d) Cripps; e) Bevan?'[22] We consider the responses to this particular question at length in Chapter 7, where we identify images of 'the good politician' revealed by the responses. But here we present a couple of example responses that focused on politicians in general. A chemist from Newquay wrote: 'By and large, people get into the political arena – and, all being well, into the House of Commons – from motives far from altruistic – in other words – from personal motives: a career, leading to jobs, titles, glory, or whatever particular idea they have in mind.'[23] Another response from a transport driver was short and to the point: 'I regard politicians as gas-bags and place-seekers.'[24] Here we have some familiar categories: the 'career', the 'place-seeker', the 'gas-bag'. This latter category alerts us to the presence of that other storyline about politicians from the period: politicians are not straight-talking.

This other storyline was mobilised especially in response to the specific question about Winston Churchill. For a commercial traveller from Leicester, Churchill '[i]s a great man without a doubt, and a great orator too, but sometimes allows his oratorical abilities to overtake his expression of the absolute truth'.[25] A housewife from Birmingham wondered if Churchill could be a 'great man' and, at the same time, use his oratorical abilities to party-political ends: 'He opens his mouth far too wide and then says much about little with constant slurs. A really great man wouldn't act like that and if I was his wife I should feel like blushing for him.'[26] While a food inspector from Chester appeared to dislike or at least dismiss Churchill because '[h]e plays to the gallery',[27] a tax inspector from

---

[20] Panellist 2903, female, 49, housewife, Bradford.
[21] Panellist 1972, female, 42, teacher, Bishop Auckland.   [22] Directive SxMOA1/3/127.
[23] Panellist 2784, male, 65, chemist, Newquay.
[24] Panellist 4493, male, 44, transport driver, place of residence not known.
[25] Panellist 2921, male, 27, commercial traveller, Leicester.
[26] Panellist 2254, female, 48, housewife, Birmingham.
[27] Panellist 4446, male, 53, food inspector, Chester.

Belfast wrote of Clement Attlee: 'I admire his refusal to play to the gallery.'[28] This association between Churchill and oratory, dishonesty, party-political 'slurs', and 'playing to the gallery' – and the contrast to this provided by Attlee – makes sense in the context of 1950. There had been a general election in February. While Attlee had campaigned by touring the UK in his modest family car, with Mrs Attlee driving and just one detective for protection – 'the very stuff of honest, uninvidious, unpretentious, non-queue-jumping, post-war Britain' (Nicholas 1951: 94) – Churchill's tour had been limited by the Conservatives, recalling how badly Churchill's oratory and axe-grinding had played in the 1945 campaign (ibid.).

There are many reasons for thinking of Churchill as an exception to British politicians in general. But his lack of straight-talking is not one of them. If anyone stood out in responses to the July 1950 directive, it was Attlee – who refused to 'play to the gallery' when this was presumably what other politicians generally did. In 'saying much about little', Churchill exhibited the characteristics of what in post-war Britain was commonly termed the 'gasbag'. And this prototypical category is found repeated in responses to directives from across the period. So in February 1945, a film strip producer from London responded to the question about conversational attitudes to politicians by writing: 'Themselves: servants of the people. Critics: out to feather their own nests; gas-bags.'[29] Then in May 1945, a farm worker from Worcester described Howard Williams, a candidate for the Cambridge University seat in the general election of that year, as 'a gas-bag of the Commander Campbell type'.[30] Then in November 1950, a housewife from Gateshead compared the gentleman politician favourably to the gasbag: 'I do like the English gentleman who has come from generations of gentlemen. I mean gentlemen, not gas-bags'.[31] The gentleman politician effectively inherited his position. The gasbag achieved their position by talking, persuading, having 'the gift of the gab'.

These two storylines, then, were prominent in the responses of numerous panellists to numerous directives. Politicians were described as being self-interested: hungry for money, careers, power, and glory; as self-seekers, place-seekers, climbers, and careerists. And they were described as not straight-talking: saying one thing but doing another; saying little

---

[28] Panellist 1066, female, 44, tax inspector, Belfast.

[29] Panellist 1075, female, 55, film strip producer, London.

[30] Panellist 1093, male, 37, farm worker, Worcester. (Commander Campbell, here, probably refers to one of two people: Archibald Campbell, who was a British naval officer during the First World War and, from 1935, a well-known radio broadcaster on the BBC; or Gordon Campbell, who was also a British naval officer during the First World War and was the Member of Parliament for Burnley between 1931 and 1935.)

[31] Panellist 1016, female, 63, housewife, Gateshead.

and allowing parties to discipline their statements; talking to distract and manipulate citizens – as talkers, gasbags, orators, twisters, gift-of-the-gabbers, players to the gallery.

The repetition of these categories and storylines by many different panellists, of different ages and genders, from different parts of the country, with many different occupations, encourages us to claim that for the period in question – 1945 to 1955, the immediate post-war period, the so-called 'golden age' of British democracy – politicians were often thought of using negative terms. They were often thought of as being self-interested and not straight-talking. Such claims are further encouraged by limited polling data from the period. When the British Institute of Public Opinion (BIPO) asked in 1944: 'Do you think that British politicians are out merely for themselves, for their party, or to do their best for their country?', only 36% of respondents chose 'to do their best for their country'. When BIPO asked in 1945: 'In general, did you approve or disapprove of the way the [1945 general] election campaign was conducted by the various parties?', 42% disapproved – compared to 41% who approved – for reasons including 'too much mud-slinging', 'Tory scares, tricks, red herrings obscured the real issues', and '[l]ies and deceit by Labour'.

In turn, these claims encourage us to conclude that, despite high voter turnout and support for the main parties during this period and in keeping with conclusions from Chapter 3, no democratic golden age existed in the UK around the middle of the twentieth century. This conclusion, of course, has been drawn before – not least by Fielding, Jefferys, and colleagues, whose research we discussed at the top of this chapter. But the argument we make in the next section is that, while the immediate post-war period was no golden age for British democracy, we should not build from that conclusion a general account of historical continuity, a permanently anaemic political culture, explained by endemic tensions at the heart of democracy. We argue instead that negative storylines about politicians were present in the 1940s and 1950s, but they were more numerous by the early twenty-first century. Anti-politics had grown in political scope, in that citizens appeared to hold an expanded range of grievances regarding politicians.

2001–2015: An Expanded Range of Grievances

Politicians Are Self-Interested

In spring 2014, MO asked its panel of volunteer writers a similar question to that asked in February 1945: 'Consider the following people: a) politicians; b) doctors; c) lawyers; d) scientists. Do you associate any

characteristics with each group? If you were in conversation with somebody and these kinds of people were referred to, what would be your
attitude?'[32] Reading the responses from 2014, one is quickly struck by
how those prominent storylines from more than half a century ago remain
popular. The line that politicians are self-interested was repeated by
panellists in terms that will be familiar to readers of the previous section.
Consider this from a writer in Watford: 'Most of them seem to be self-
serving and ambitious for power and wealth.'[33] Or this from a local
government officer in Cromer: 'Hot-air, self-importance, power-driven –
these are the words I associate with politicians.'[34] Categories like these –
'self-serving' politicians 'ambitious' for 'power' and 'wealth' – have a long
history as resources for describing and judging politicians in the UK. But
alongside this continuity of terms, three new parts had been added to this
storyline by the early twenty-first century.

First, politicians were described as being 'out for themselves' but
also for their 'cronies'. For this retired banker in Brentwood, politicians are 'only interested in themselves and their cronies'.[35] For this
civil servant from Bath, politicians are 'not adverse to giving backhanders to their mates'.[36] A university administrator from Newcastle
wrote: 'Unfortunately, I do tend to associate politicians at a national
level with vested interests, lying, cheating, and feathering their
friends' nests.' We return to associations of lying and cheating later.
Here, we just note the seemingly new category or set of categories: the
'friends' or 'mates' of politicians; their 'cronies' who benefit from
political power through 'backhanders' – public money channelled by
politicians in a way that lacks transparency.

Second, politicians were described as pursuing self-interest through
politics but also via the later opportunities opened up by a career in
politics. These opportunities were imagined to lie in the diplomatic
corps or, for the most well-known politicians, in lectures, books, and
films:

They are in politics to feather their own nests and increase the family fortune and
gain knighthoods, baronetcies, earldoms, honours, and gongs. That will get them
into the diplomatic corps . . . After that, they start presenting talks on the lecture

---

[32] Directive SxMOA2/1/99/1. (We commissioned this directive from MO. The final wording of the question was a compromise between our desire for something as close as
possible to the 1945 wording, and MO's desire for something meeting the conventions
of MO questions in the current period.)

[33] Panellist A2212, female, 57, writer, Watford.

[34] Panellist C3691, female, 49, local government officer, Cromer.

[35] Panellist R3422, male, 66, retired banker, Brentwood.

[36] Panellist E5014, male, 48, civil servant, Bath.

circuit worldwide and get paid a fortune for it. Then come the books and movies about their lives for which the profits are handsomely large.[37]

Perhaps more realistically, at least for most politicians, these opportunities were imagined to lie in private-sector firms, non-governmental organisations, or international-governmental organisations:

Some people, I am sure, enter politics for personal advantage and power. So many have climbed the greasy pole, gained office and influence, and then left to take up a financially rewarding post with some outside large organisation. No wonder so many of the general public hold them in contempt.[38]

   It was hard going having to watch the workers' party [the Labour Party] evolve into a haven for self-serving professional politicians and would-be millionaires whose over-riding desire was and is for this country to hang on to a corrupt European Union as a means of ensuring continuing top lifestyles for themselves after deservedly being kicked out of office here.[39]

These quotations are substantial and raise many possible themes. We discuss 'professional politicians' later in this chapter and at length in Chapter 7. For now, our emphasis is on categories in the storyline that politicians are self-interested – like 'the greasy pole' of politics that leads up to positions of political power but also *out* to opportunities for personal wealth generation in other arenas.

   A third new part to the storyline 'politicians are self-interested' was provided by 'the expenses scandal' and related categories like 'expense fiddlers'. In 2009, details of the expenses claimed by Members of Parliament (MPs) were leaked to *The Daily Telegraph*. These details, published over subsequent weeks, included a small number of suspected fraudulent claims and a large number of suspect-looking claims, including seemingly petty claims for small items like biscuits, seemingly extravagant claims for luxury items like horse manure, and seemingly cynical claims for home improvements on second homes that appeared to have been designated as second homes primarily for the purposes of claiming (so-called 'flipping').[40] For this retired civil servant from East Boldon, these revelations did not have the expected serious consequences for MPs: 'Jailing a few – a mere handful – of the petty chisellers who fiddled their expenses isn't anything like enough to dispel the view that politicians are a class apart, dedicated to their own advancement and enrichment at the expense of society as

---

[37] Panellist H1470, female, 60, writer/broadcaster, Scotland.
[38] Panellist S2083, male, 83, retired shopkeeper, Lewes.
[39] Panellist R1418, male, 92, decorator, Derby.
[40] Under the rules, MPs who worked between Westminster and their constituencies designated a first home and a second home, with expenses generally covered for the latter but not the former.

a whole.'[41] We will come to politicians as a 'class apart' in due course too (see later and Chapter 7). But while the expenses scandal was perceived to have few consequences for politicians, it was perceived to have important consequences for citizens. As this local government officer from Sale put it: 'I used to vote but since the expenses I see little point because I feel that MPs are only in the job for their own personal gain.'[42]

As we have seen, this feeling that politicians are self-interested predated the expenses scandal of 2009 by more than half a century for many citizens. But the scandal seemed to give the feeling renewed justification. Unsurprisingly, MPs' expenses formed a central character in responses to the spring 2010 directive on the general election of that year.[43] Certain details of the scandal became prototypical categories in their own rights – representing politicians or politics as a whole, or at least what is wrong with formal politics, at least for some panellists. In one election diary from 2010, a carer from Limavady wrote: 'MPs should wise up, as they say here, and remember they are there to promote the good for the country, not for themselves to acquire duck houses on islands and eventual peerages.'[44] In another election diary, a retired sales assistant from Rochester wrote: 'We have all become disenchanted by the expenses scandal ... Jacqui Smith's bath plug and porn films, and the Cons member's duck house and moat-cleaning – moat-cleaning? I know an Englishman's home is his castle but not many of us still have them, and those that do can pay for their own bloody moat-cleaning!!!'[45] Jacqui Smith's claims for a bath plug and films, Peter Viggers' claim for a duck house, Douglas Hogg's claim for moat-cleaning on his country estate – these details stood out for some panellists who used them to stand *in* for the self-interest of politicians they had previously suspected and now had seen confirmed.

We have seen that one familiar storyline from the mid-twentieth cen-tury – that politicians are self-interested – still circulated widely in the early twenty-first century. It was repeated by panellists in a range of positions: young and old, men and women, in a variety of occupational categories, from a variety of regions. It was made up of categories both old and new: 'self-interest', 'ambition', 'power', 'wealth', 'self-serving' politicians 'out for themselves'; but also 'cronies', 'the expenses scandal', and 'expense fiddlers'. Available polling data would appear to confirm and add to this picture. Around the turn of the twenty-first century, politicians were

[41] Panellist M3190, male, 55, retired civil servant, East Boldon.
[42] Panellist T4409, female, 35, local government officer, Sale.
[43] Directive SxMOA2/1/88/3.   [44] Panellist C1191, female, 55, carer, Limavady.
[45] Panellist L1002, female, 63, retired sales assistant, Rochester.

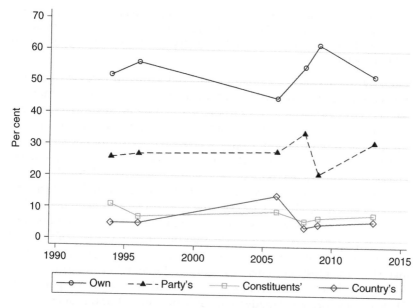

Figure 4.1 In general, whose interests do you think MPs put first: their own, their constituents', their party's, or the country's? (Ipsos MORI, 1994–2013).

commonly judged to put their own interests first, before those of their constituents or country (Figure 4.1). They were *more* commonly judged to be self-interested around the turn of the twenty-first century than around the middle of the twentieth century (as we showed in Figure 3.2).

Politicians Are Not Straight-Talking

Like the storyline that politicians are self-interested, the other most prominent storyline about politicians from the 1940s and 1950s – that politicians are not straight-talking – also remained prominent in the early twenty-first century. Looking at responses to the spring 2014 directive and the question about politicians – their characteristics and panellists' attitudes towards them – we see that categories like 'gasbag' and 'gift of the gab' were no longer repeated by MO panellists, but politicians were still described in similar ways. A retired typesetter from South East England wrote:

I marvel at how they can hog the conversation by avoiding answering questions they are unsure about, by slightly avoiding the subject. It is irritating to watch and it makes me very suspicious about their honesty … I am sure they often do not agree with policies they are promoting, and if they were honest and said so they would find their support and careers would be affected ... Anyone considering taking up this career would need to have a tendency to lie or at least be able to bend the truth.[46]

Similarly, a news agency assistant from Hull wrote: 'If I was in conversation with someone about politicians, I would express the opinion that one can never get a straight answer from them. I have noticed that whenever I hear them on the radio or television, they very rarely answer a question but manage to go round in circles.'[47] Here, the terms of the immediate post-war period may not be used, but the concerns expressed are similar. These concerns are that politicians 'hog the conversation', 'rarely answer a question', 'never give a straight answer', 'go round in circles', 'bend the truth'. They have abilities to talk that are to be marvelled at but that ultimately allow politicians to say little that is honest about their policies.

Some concerns expressed in 2014 are familiar to readers of material from the immediate post-war period. But a newer category in the 2014 material – the most prominent category in this storyline in 2014 – is 'the broken promise'. Such promises were raised repeatedly by panellists. They are false promises made to manipulate voters. For this unemployed woman from Salisbury: '[I]f only there was a way to stop false promises. Then people wouldn't be so cynical.'[48] For this housewife from St Gennys, politicians '[s]ay what they think you want to hear, but do what they want anyway, whether or not it's what they said they would do'.[49] Or promises may have been made with good intentions, but they are broken by politicians who 'when they get in ... change their minds'[50] and 'rarely keep the promises that they make in their manifestos'.[51] Either way, the concern was expressed by many panellists that such broken promises undermine the whole business of representative democracy. When asked about how things would change if Labour won the next general election (due in 2015), responses like this were common: 'If Labour won the next election, it wouldn't change my life particularly. I have little faith in any of the main parties and know that they all backtrack, make promises to break.'[52]

One particular context for the prominence of 'the broken promise' in 2014 was a pledge circulated by the National Union of Students during

---

[46] Panellist H1806, male, 88, retired typesetter, South East.
[47] Panellist J1890, female, 82, news agency assistant, Hull.
[48] Panellist B5342, female, 28, unemployed, Salisbury.
[49] Panellist W3163, female, 56, housewife, St Gennys.
[50] Panellist M3190, male, 55, retired civil servant, East Boldon.
[51] Panellist T4409, female, 35, local government officer, Sale.
[52] Panellist M3190, male, 55, retired civil servant, East Boldon.

the general election campaign of 2010: 'I pledge to vote against any increase in [university tuition] fees in the next parliament and to pressure the government to introduce a fairer alternative.' This pledge was signed by Nick Clegg, leader of the Liberal Democrats, who after the election joined the Conservative Party in Coalition Government. The Coalition Agreement of May 2010 allowed the Liberal Democrats to abstain on the issue but not to vote against. When a vote was held in December 2010, Clegg abstained and the headline annual fee cap was raised from £3,225 to £9,000.

This particular broken promise was referred to repeatedly by panellists in 2014. A twenty-two-year-old panellist from Stone focused on Clegg's relationship to younger citizens: 'He burned his bridges with my age group at the 2010 election, making all sorts of promises he not only didn't deliver on for my age group but reversed and did the complete opposite'.[53] An eighty-seven-year-old panellist from Devon focused on Clegg's broader relationship with citizens in general: 'Nick Clegg has let us all down when he broke his promise regarding the cost of a university education. Clegg should have kept his word.'[54] While these panellists focused on the party leader, others broadened their focus to the Liberal Democrats as a whole: 'The Lib Dems have destroyed any relationship they had with their core voters (young people) by accepting the introduction of university tuition fees, a pledge they agreed they would not do, which contributed to their initial election win.'[55] Or for this artist from Welton: 'They broke their pledge on students' tuition fees and that was the end of the Lib Dems for me.'[56] The focus here on Clegg or the Liberal Democrats is clearly important. But so is the focus on politicians' promises that are expected to be delivered on, words that are expected to be kept, deals that are expected to be respected and not to be 'reneged on',[57] and policies that are expected to remain consistent from manifesto to legislation and not 'to change … which I think is dishonest'.[58]

This last point connects to another: that many responses to the spring 2014 directive focused on broken promises in the specific context of what happened during and after the 2010 general election, but the category of broken promises was actually used frequently across the wider period from 2001 to 2015. For example, in her 2001 general election diary, a communications consultant from London wrote: '[Y]ou can't trust

[53] Panellist B5152, female, 22, teacher, Stone.
[54] Panellist S496, female, 87, cleaner, Devon.
[55] Panellist D5428, male, 40, nurse, Belfast.
[56] Panellist P3209, male, 74, artist, Welton.
[57] Panellist L1002, female, 67, retired sales consultant, Rochester.
[58] Panellist H1806, male, 88, retired typesetter, South East.

them to do what they promise.'[59] Or, in her 2010 general election diary, a housewife from Huntly wrote: '[M]ost of the pre-election promises they make are empty'.[60] Or listen to this from one of the 2015 general election diaries: 'I don't trust any politicians to do what they say they will do ... I don't have very high hopes for the government. Parties promise the earth in their election manifestos but once elected often fall very far short on a lot of their promises.'[61]

For the period 2001 to 2015, 'the broken promise' was one of three newer categories commonly repeated by a range of panellists as part of the storyline that politicians are not straight-talking. The second category was 'spin' or the strong management of political communications (to the benefit of certain parties). During the 2001 general election campaign, spin had been a topic of public discussion among politicians, journalists, and others (Butler and Kavanagh 2002). In this context, it was hardly surprising that a lecturer from Bolton would write in her 2001 general election diary: 'I ... found the Labour Party to be full of spin and no substance, and I can't stand the insincerity of Tony (Tory?) Blair.'[62] This contrast between spin, substance, and sincerity was also present in the 2010 general election diaries:

Several years ago, a man threw an egg at John Prescott, whereupon Prescott launched himself at the man and a scuffle ensued. Obviously this kind of reaction would not have been countenanced by any self-respecting spin doctor, and yet I got the impression it did Prescott some good, probably because it felt authentic. So much of what is said and done during election campaigns feels carefully prepared and less than freshly delivered, and this, more than anything, I think, contributes to the public's feeling of disenchantment with the process.[63]

It was during the 2001 general election campaign that Craig Evans, a farm worker from Denbigh, threw an egg at John Prescott, the Deputy Prime Minister, who retaliated with a punch caught by television cameras. For the quoted panellist, it 'felt authentic' compared to the 'carefully prepared' messaging of the broader campaign. Indeed, at the time, for this very reason, 'the Prescott punch' was precisely the sort of event journalists were starting to look for in their election coverage – incidents that would unmask disciplined politicians and liven up the boring campaign (Butler and Kavanagh 2002). Just as journalists would respond to the spin of the political parties, so the parties would respond to the gaffe-hunting of journalists. Campaigning would become increasingly stage-managed –

---

[59] Panellist G2776, female, 29, communications consultant, London.
[60] Panellist C4562, female, 40, housewife, Huntly.
[61] Panellist H1745, female, 65, researcher, London.
[62] Panellist R2862, female, 42, lecturer, Bolton.
[63] Panellist B3227, male, 43, unemployed, Birmingham.

and the category of 'stage-management' would come to circulate and be repeated in the general election diaries of MO panellists. This from 2010: 'I watched some of [the leaders' debate] online. I thought it was unconvincing. It seemed very staged and fake. I find it hard to believe a word politicians say.'[64] And this from 2015: 'political leaders . . . have spent the campaign hiding in stage-managed 'invited audience only' situations.'[65]

A third part to the storyline that politicians are not straight-talking, not so common in the mid-twentieth century but common in the early twenty-first century, focused on how politicians avoid questions or topics when supposedly speaking with citizens (usually now through journalists). In the 2015 general election diaries, a retired typesetter from Woking was impressed by the abilities of David Cameron in this regard: 'He is very clever at not answering the question by finding another question to answer. The way he can keep talking, not allowing the questioner to stop him so there is not time for him to commit himself, is very skilful'.[66] But generally, panellists were frustrated by such practices, like this retired decorator from Derby: 'This Bank Holiday Monday started off well but any good mood ensuing from the sunshine outdoors was soon dispelled after turning on Radio 4 and listening to Ed Miliband evading questions put to him by John Humphries.'[67]

Politicians don't answer questions, find other questions to answer, evade questions. In doing so, they deny citizens the information required when voting. This idea was especially common in the 2010 and 2015 general election diaries. The UK had suffered a financial crisis in 2007–2008. This had become a fiscal crisis in 2008–2009, when a number of banks were recapitalised and part-nationalised and a fiscal package worth £20 billion was used to stimulate the economy. A key issue for the next two general elections was constraints on public spending and which budgets might be cut by incoming governments (Kavanagh and Cowley 2010, Cowley and Kavanagh 2016). This issue was mentioned regularly by MO panellists during the period. Usually it was mentioned besides a comment on how politicians were avoiding the issue during election campaigns. So in 2010, a science teacher from Belfast wrote: 'Only the Conservatives seem willing to talk about the scale of cuts that must take place to deal with the colossal debt, and even they are hedging about a bit. The other parties are just being plain dishonest (political pragmatism, I suppose you could call it).'[68] For this retired youth and

---

[64] Panellist C4562, female, 40, housewife, Huntly.
[65] Panellist H1541, male, 70, retired film editor, Scotland.
[66] Panellist H1806, male, 89, retired typesetter, Woking.
[67] Panellist R1418, male, 93, retired decorator, Derby.
[68] Panellist R4526, male, 49, science teacher, Belfast.

community officer from Redbourn, the Conservatives were 'hedging' just as much as the other parties:

The most important issue to me at this election is how will a new government deal with the huge fiscal deficit. And on that issue – all three main parties have been exceedingly coy ... They haven't wanted to discuss the cuts that will be required ... I assume that all parties think being honest with the public would be a vote loser. Perhaps it would. Or perhaps, surprisingly, the country would have warmed to a party that was honest with the electorate. We will never know – as the main parties have chosen to withhold significant information about the measures they will actually have to take.[69]

We never will know how citizens would have reacted to more information on each party's plans for cuts to public spending. But we do know that panellists in 2015 were still commenting on the presumed need for additional cuts after the general election of that year and the continued avoidance of questions on this issue by politicians. Early in the campaign, a museum consultant from North Shields wrote: '[T]hey're going to make huge cuts but won't say to what.'[70] As the campaign ended, another

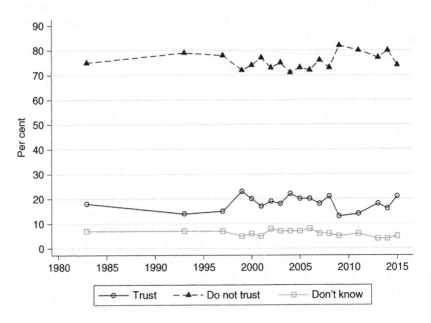

Figure 4.2 Politicians generally ... Would you tell me whether you generally trust them to tell the truth or not? (Ipsos MORI, 1983–2015).

[69] Panellist C3603, male, 66, retired youth and community officer, Redbourn.
[70] Panellist C4131, female, 33, museum consultant, North Shields.

panellist wrote: 'Now we'll see where the cuts will fall – which they wouldn't tell the electorate beforehand.'[71]

We return to evasive politicians and professionalised campaigning more generally in Chapter 8. But here we can say: the storyline that politicians are not straight-talking remained prominent in the early twenty-first century – even if some categories (gasbags, orators, twisters) had been replaced by others (broken promises, spin, stage-management). Available survey data would appear to confirm this claim. Figure 4.2 plots the percentage of people saying they do or do not trust politicians generally to tell the truth, for the survey question asked regularly by Ipsos MORI between 1983 and 2015 ('Would you tell me whether you generally trust them [politicians] to tell the truth or not?'). This reveals that consistently between 70% and 80% of the public do not trust politicians to be truthful. The British Social Attitudes (BSA) survey has asked a similar question regarding how much politicians can be trusted to tell the truth 'when they are in a tight corner'. In Figure 4.3 we plot the percentage of respondents saying 'almost never', 'some of the time', and

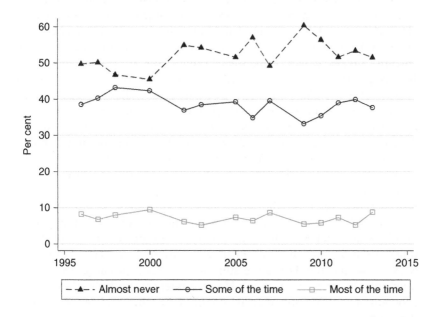

Figure 4.3 How much do you trust politicians of any party in Britain to tell the truth when they are in a tight corner? (BSA, 1996–2013).

---

[71] Panellist C3603, male, 66, retired youth and community officer, Redbourn.

'most of the time'. Consistently around 50% of people say 'almost never', with the number saying 'almost always' being consistently so low that it is not reported in the figure. Notably, in both cases distrust of politicians spiked in 2009 around the time of the parliamentary expenses scandal and following the global financial crisis but appears to have returned to its long-run equilibrium in the years after.

Politicians Are Out of Touch

The account provided by this chapter so far has emphasised historical continuity – the sustained prominence of two storylines about politicians across more than half a century. We now add to this account by demonstrating how, in the early twenty-first century, politicians were described as not only self-interested and not straight-talking but also 'out of touch' and 'all the same'.

The storyline that politicians are out of touch was especially prominent in responses to MO directives from 2014 and 2015. One particular context for this was the perceived family/personal wealth of Prime Minister David Cameron and Chancellor George Osborne and the association between them and 'austerity' (a response to the financial crisis of 2007–2008 and the fiscal crisis that followed, centred on reducing the current budget deficit primarily through cuts to public spending). In spring 2014, panellists were asked by MO to write about politicians in general, particular politicians, and particular political parties. Many described politicians – particularly politicians of the Conservative Party and particularly Cameron and Osborne – as being 'out of touch'. A research manager from Edinburgh described Cameron and Osborne as 'clueless rich boys'.[72] A housewife from Newcastle wrote of the Conservatives: 'I consider them to be a bunch of posh boys, out of touch with common issues and the common man/woman.'[73] For one retired typesetter from the South East, Cameron was 'out of touch' because of his schooling: 'He does seem out of touch with the general public, which I believe is due to his public school education.'[74] A planning officer from Sheffield took a similar view of both Cameron and Osborne, who 'show that the Tories are still public school, privilege-oriented in much of what they say and do'. He continued: 'I think they have a real problem of showing how they are connected to the real lives of many in the country.'[75]

---

[72] Panellist B5258, female, 34, research manager, Edinburgh.
[73] Panellist R5429, female, 39, housewife, Newcastle.
[74] Panellist H1806, male, 88, retired typesetter, South East.
[75] Panellist S3711, male, 38, senior planning officer, Sheffield.

The worlds and lives of these politicians – at independent school, Oxbridge, and Westminster – were frequently contrasted with 'real lives' and 'the real world'. A local government officer from Cromer wrote: 'I can't stand David Cameron as he has no idea what it is like living in the real world.'[76] Of Osborne, an unemployed woman from Salisbury wrote: 'He is out of touch with real life.'[77] What was this 'real life' or 'real world' to which panellists referred? It was hard, expensive, difficult. For this air traffic services assistant from Southampton, the Conservative Party are 'out of touch with ordinary people and have no understanding of how hard life can be for some'.[78] For this broadcaster from Scotland, Cameron 'knows nothing of the life and times of the ordinary working man or woman . . . He does not know what things cost in a superstore'.[79] Also on Cameron, a retired counsellor from the Fylde Coast wrote: 'I do think he is out of touch. He's the sort of person who doesn't realise how difficult it is to get a doctor's appointment.'[80]

Given this focus on Cameron, Osborne, and the Conservatives, we might wonder if some of the storyline that politicians are out of touch – repeated across many responses to directives from 2014 and 2015 – is explained by the particular context of Conservative-led government, led specifically by graduates from independent school and Oxbridge, during a period characterised by austerity. We might wonder this, but we should do so with caution. The same storyline was not prominent in the mid-twentieth century when ministers were often aristocrats and/or from independent school and/or from Oxbridge. Indeed, Clement Attlee's cabinet of 1945 may have lacked aristocrats and been notable for its twelve working-class ministers (Rubinstein 2003), but it was an exception for the time. More typical were the cabinets of Winston Churchill in 1951 (five aristocrats, seven from Eton, nine from Oxbridge) or Anthony Eden in 1955 – himself the son of a landed Baronet, an Etonian, an officer, and a graduate of Oxford (ibid.).

It remains possible, of course, that politicians have become no more 'rich' or 'posh' over time but that citizens' expectations of politicians have nevertheless become more demanding in this regard. We discuss this possibility at length in Chapter 7, where we consider the image of 'the good politician' held by citizens and how that has changed over time. But there is another reason to be cautious about any explanation centred on Cameron, Osborne, and the Conservatives. The storyline that politicians

---

[76] Panellist C3691, female, 49, local government officer, Cromer.
[77] Panellist B5342, female, 28, unemployed, Salisbury.
[78] Panellist D4736, male, 47, air traffic services assistant, Southampton.
[79] Panellist H1470, female, 60, writer/broadcaster, Scotland.
[80] Panellist G226, female, 73, retired counsellor, Fylde Coast.

are 'out of touch' includes more than just these particular individuals and groups. Often, when panellists used the term or expressed the sentiment, they were referring to all politicians. They wrote of politicians being out of touch when asked in the spring 2014 directive about politicians in general. A warehouse worker from Stoke wrote: 'Politicians: a dedicated representative of the people. That's the "Hollywood" version anyway. The reality is somewhat different and looks, maybe, a little like this: a venal and out of touch bureaucrat.'[81] Also on politicians in general, this from a retired nursery worker in Ducklington: '[They] seem to be a bit removed from the "ordinary" people.'[82] And this from a housewife in St Gennys: '[Politicians] live in a world out of touch with the rest of the population's daily experiences. Have no concept of living on a normal wage.'[83]

Some panellists made it clear they were not just describing Conservative politicians in this way. A housewife from Newcastle wrote of '[t]he government (and other parties)' who 'seem to lack a connection with the common voter and critical issues, such as price rises and childcare costs'.[84] Asked about each of the main political parties, a tree inspector from Harpenden replied: 'I have little faith in any of the main parties ... I find so many of today's politicians to be patronising and out of touch and just hope that the next generation are taught to treat voters with more genuine respect and regard for the world away from Westminster.'[85]

Panellists may have described Cameron and Osborne as 'posh boys' and 'rich kids', but they also included Ed Miliband, leader of the Labour Party in spring 2014, in this storyline that politicians are out of touch. For this project manager from Newcastle: 'He does have the image of a toff trying to help the poor. I think this is due to the fact that although he does try and have a commonality with the "people", he is so far removed from the reality of working endless hours for little pay, and having to deal with ever increasing prices.'[86] Or for this teacher from Belfast: 'Like too many politicians, [Miliband] has never worked a day in his life at a "proper job".'[87]

If all or many politicians were seen as being out of touch, then what does 'out of touch' mean for these panellists? It appears to involve being removed from the 'real', 'daily' lives of 'ordinary', 'common' people – which are experienced in terms of low incomes, high prices, and poor

[81] Panellist C3167, male, 42, warehouse worker, Stoke.
[82] Panellist I1610, female, 70, retired nursery nurse, Ducklington.
[83] Panellist W3163, female, 56, housewife, St Gennys.
[84] Panellist R5429, female, 39, housewife, Newcastle.
[85] Panellist M5198, male, 43, tree inspector, Harpenden.
[86] Panellist R5429, female, 39, project manager, Newcastle.
[87] Panellist R4526, male, 53, teacher, Belfast.

service – by virtue of having come from a rich family and having been to independent school and having obtained a 'comfortable' seat in Parliament (with Westminster perceived to be disconnected from the rest of the UK where people do 'proper' jobs). For many panellists, 'out of touch' appears to mean being a 'career politician' – a central category in this storyline. In response to the spring 2014 directive, a student from Newcastle wrote:

I find it hard to stomach that almost all the influential and powerful politicians in our government are privately or Oxbridge-educated, well-off, middle-aged, white men. While as 'career politicians' they have experience in politics and the running of government, they have no idea how most people in this country really live.[88]

Here, for this twenty-five-year-old woman, politicians are out of touch for being well-off, middle-aged, white, and male. But they are also out of touch for being 'career politicians' – for having experience of politics and government but not of life beyond politics and government (beyond Westminster and its training grounds – independent school and Oxbridge).

This category of 'the career politician' appears frequently in the general election diaries of 2015. Career politicians 'reside in Parliament' and 'should be replaced with people with actual life experience of work'.[89] They are 'graduates of political studies with little or no knowledge of real life'.[90] They need 'a real life and real job before, instead of being career politicians starting out as interns in other MPs' offices'.[91] We may dispute whether most politicians are graduates of political studies, or whether being a Member of Parliament (MP) or working for an MP counts as 'actual life experience of work', 'real life', a 'real job'. But something not in dispute is that, while recent parliaments have been more diverse with more women and ethnic minority MPs, they have also been more uniform with more 'professional politicians' who became MPs after graduating from university and working only in Parliament, usually as aides of one kind or another (Criddle 2010, 2016). We consider this professionalisation of politics at length in Chapter 7.

Politicians Are All the Same

Connected to the storyline that politicians are 'out of touch' – and especially the categories of 'the career politician' and 'the professional

---

[88] Panellist C4271, female, 25, student, Newcastle.
[89] Panellist H5557, female, 25, student, North West.
[90] Panellist S3035, male, 66, retired banker, Brentwood.
[91] Panellist 3146, female, 37, publishing manager, Saltaire.

politician' – was another prominent storyline that politicians are 'all the same'. They were described as being all the same because of their similar backgrounds. In spring 2014, a care worker from Leeds wished for 'a wider range of people becoming MPs – they're still mainly white Oxbridge educated straight men'.[92] Also from Leeds, a student noted 'the staggering uniformity of most politicians' backgrounds'.[93]

Politicians were described as being all the same because of their similar backgrounds but also because of their similar, standardised practices in the pursuit of electoral success. In spring 2014, an unemployed woman from Salisbury wrote that politicians 'say whatever pleases the masses . . . Their statements become more bland all the time, more devoid of any sign of real human thought, as though they are androids. That's why anyone who shows real character makes such an impact. Otherwise there isn't much to differentiate them nowadays.'[94] The career politician – trained, socialised, and disciplined at Westminster (and before that at certain schools and universities) – says things formulated through private polling and focus groups; things that have been tested and crafted to avoid offending potential voters. Consequently, their statements appear 'bland'. They themselves appear to lack 'character'. Such politicians are difficult to differentiate between. In spring 2014, a housewife from Newcastle put it like this:

I do find the present collection of MPs a little lacklustre and extremely dull. I grew up under Thatcher and whilst I do not necessarily support the Tory Party politics then (or now), the previous governments and opposition did not lack character . . . Today, with the exception of good old Boris Johnson, blandness seems to win out. Modern day politics is drowning in a sea of greyness.[95]

The 'present collection of MPs' – from similar backgrounds, with similar training, building their careers in politics – are described as 'lacklustre', 'dull', 'bland', 'grey', and lacking in 'character'.

In the 2015 general election diaries, we get more of a sense of why these politicians are perceived in this way. During the campaign, the director of a chamber orchestra wrote: 'It all feels a bit flat. Nobody is trying to sell us a compelling vision of the future; everybody is saying much the same things on the most important issues . . . the two big parties are reduced to bribing various parts of the electorate with silly tweaks to the tax and benefits system.'[96] We return to 'the two big parties' and their offers to

[92] Panellist M4780, female, 30, care worker, Leeds.
[93] Panellist S5202, male, 25, student, Leeds.
[94] Panellist B5342, female, 28, unemployed, Salisbury.
[95] Panellist R5429, female, 39, housewife, Newcastle.
[96] Panellist G4373, male, 49, director of chamber orchestra, South West.

voters later. Here, we note the storyline that politicians are all the same because their professionalised campaigns all focus on the same tested messages and the same inoffensive policy 'tweaks'. It was a common line in 2015. After the campaign, for example, a student from Cheshire wrote: 'I did get a bit bored by much of the coverage, which consisted of the different leaders all basically saying the same thing.'[97]

If the storyline that politicians are 'all the same' connects to the category of 'the career politician', it also connects to the lines that politicians are self-interested and not straight-talking. Once all politicians are thought to be self-interested, they are judged to be 'all as bad as each other'. In her 2010 general election diary, a housewife from Finchingfield wondered 'if the MPs expenses scandal has left people feeling that it was not worth voting because "they're all as bad as each other"'.[98] When asked about politicians as a 'group' in the spring 2014 directive, a podiatrist from Dunblane responded: 'I find them all equally corrupt and disappointing.'[99] The same applies once all politicians are thought of as not straight-talking. Two examples from responses to the same two directives illustrate this point. From the 2010 general election diaries, we have a graphic designer from Rotherham: 'I do find that politicians, no matter what their party, all seem the same. Before the election, they're all nice as pie, then when they're elected, that's when all the cuts and tax increases come.'[100] From the spring 2014 directive, we have a factory worker from Lowestoft: 'I don't like anybody who's in government or anybody who's an MP. They cannot be trusted. I don't care what party they belong to, they are all the same.'[101]

Two categories from this storyline – repeated across many responses to multiple directives from the current period – were that politicians are 'all as bad as each other' and so there should be 'a plague on all their houses'.[102] But sometimes these maxims were phrased a little differently. They referred less to individual politicians or politicians in general, and more to the two main political parties: 'they are both as bad as one another';[103] 'a plague on both their houses'.[104] This brings us to a third part of the storyline that politicians are all the same. Not only are they all career politicians who are bland, self-interested, and not-straight-talking.

[97] Panellist C4271, female, 26, student, Cheshire.
[98] Panellist C3513, female, 50, housewife, Finchingfield.
[99] Panellist E5296, female, 33, podiatrist, Dunblane.
[100] Panellist B4563, female, 42, graphic designer, Rotherham.
[101] Panellist C2579, female, 69, factory worker, Lowestoft.
[102] Panellist S2083, male, 83, retired shopkeeper, Lewes (spring 2014).
[103] Panellist C1939, female, 66, radio programme monitor, Ipswich (spring/summer 2001).
[104] Panellist R1418, male, 79, decorator, Derby (spring/summer 2001).

In addition, they are all the same because their parties have come to believe similar things and so to offer little by way of electoral choice. 'All the parties are the same'[105] and 'there's not much difference in the parties'.[106] More specifically, 'there isn't much difference between the policies of the three main parties'.[107] This means 'there is not a great deal of choice out there'.[108] As a communications consultant from London wrote in his 2001 general election diary: 'I am a disillusioned voter. I do not feel that we have a real choice in this country. The different parties are not very different . . . Labour and the Conservatives seem to have the same policies.'[109] The different parties may not be that different, but the Labour Party was often singled out by panellists as being particularly responsible for this state of affairs. In response to the spring 2014 directive, a broadcaster from Scotland wrote: 'The new Modern Labour Party is so busy chasing the Tories and trying to be like them.'[110] A similar response came from a housewife in St Gennys: 'Over the years, the Labour Party has moved more and more to the right so that generally speaking they are becoming more like the Conservative Party.'[111] Another housewife, writing from Essex, put it like this: 'I think Labour have gone too far towards the "centre" over recent years, so there isn't much to distinguish them from Conservative.'[112]

While panellists on the left bemoaned the 'shades of capitalism'[113] or 'flavour[s] of neo-liberalism'[114] on offer, those not so easily positioned on the left-right spectrum still bemoaned the 'different shades of the same colour'[115] and the 'dancing to the same tune with slight variations'.[116] Ultimately, for many panellists, the similarities of policy between the main parties and the consequent lack of choice on offer had consequences for how elections were perceived. This is especially clear in responses to a question asked by MO in the spring 2014 directive: 'What would a change of government mean to you?' The response of many panellists was that it would mean little because little would change for them as a result. A civil servant from Bath wrote: 'I can't see anything changing much if Labour wins the next

[105] Panellist B1426, male, 65, quality engineer, Bracknell (spring/summer 2001).
[106] Panellist N2058, female, 57, telephonist, Yarmouth (spring/summer 2001).
[107] Panellist D3958, female, 28, secretary, Wallsend (spring 2010).
[108] Panellist S4002, female, 36, administrator, Cardiff (spring 2015).
[109] Panellist G2776, female, 29, communications consultant, London.
[110] Panellist H1470, female, 60, writer/broadcaster, Scotland.
[111] Panellist W3163, female, 56, housewife, St Gennys.
[112] Panellist C3513, female, 55, housewife, Essex.
[113] Panellist C2204, male, 49, labourer, Nottingham.
[114] Panellist S5202, male, 25, student, Leeds.
[115] Panellist G5421, male, 35, data architect, Wigan.
[116] Panellist B5152, female, 22, teacher, Stone.

election.'[117] Also of Labour, a warehouse worker from Stoke wrote: 'If they did win the election ... what do I think would change? Nothing at all, alas.'[118] Labour were described as too similar to the Conservatives. For this student from Newcastle: 'I'm not sure they would do anything differently. I think the current direction of the Labour Party is too similar to the Conservative Party.'[119] For this retired banker from Brentwood: 'The Conservative Party and the Labour Party are now identical, and not in a good way ... A Labour win will make no difference either to me or to the country.'[120] A change of government would make no real difference. It might lead to some 'tinkering around the edges'[121] or some 'token reversal of Conservative actions.'[122] But fundamentally 'they'd just continue the spending cuts in the same way the Tories are doing'.[123] This housewife from Newcastle was 'not under any illusion they will reverse the decisions of the present government, particularly with regards to public spending'.[124]

The storyline, then, is that politicians and their parties are 'all the same'. They are 'all as bad as each other'. 'Career politicians' come from similar backgrounds and head towards similar destinations. They say similar things, carefully crafted to speed them along the way. The main parties offer similar policies with just a few 'tweaks', some 'tinkering' at the edges, a few 'token' differences. But these are just 'variations on the same tune' or 'different shades of the same colour'. They make no fundamental difference to the lives of ordinary people.

As with the storyline that politicians are out of touch, the indications are that such a storyline – politicians are all the same – was circulating widely in the UK at the beginning of the twenty-first century. It and its categories – its prototypes and maxims – were used as cultural resources for thinking and writing about politicians, parties, and governments by MO panellists from numerous positions in society. Again, as with the storyline that politicians are out of touch, this line that politicians are all the same was not commonly used in the earlier period (1945–1955). Our main claim here is that two storylines were circulating widely in the early twenty-first century that were not really prominent in the mid-twentieth century. In addition to being viewed as self-interested and not straight-

---

[117] Panellist E5014, male, 48, civil servant, Bath.
[118] Panellist C3167, male, 42, warehouse worker, Stoke.
[119] Panellist C4271, female, 25, student, Newcastle.
[120] Panellist R3422, male, 66, retired banker, Brentwood.
[121] Panellist K5246, male, 45, railway signal designer, Crewe.
[122] Panellist S5292, male, 63, senior technician, Bagstone.
[123] Panellist B5258, female, 34, research manager, Edinburgh.
[124] Panellist R5429, female, 39, housewife, Newcastle.

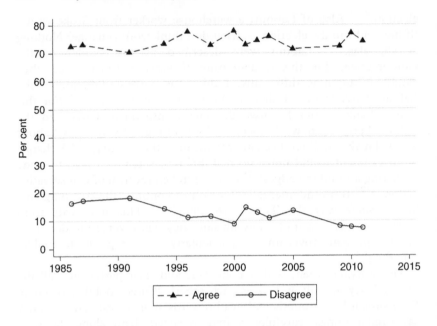

Figure 4.4 How much do you agree or disagree that … generally speaking those we elect as MPs lose touch with people pretty quickly? (BSA, 1986–2011).

talking, politicians were now viewed as being out of touch and all the same.

This claim is also apparently confirmed by available survey data. In Figure 4.4, we plot the percentage of people agreeing or disagreeing with the proposition that those elected as MPs 'lose touch with people pretty quickly' (we combine responses for 'agree' and 'agree strongly' into a single category and do the same for 'disagree' and 'disagree strongly'). Between 1986 and 2011, consistently around 70% to 80% of respondents either agreed or agreed strongly that MPs lose touch, while the percentage disagreeing fell by around a half to below 10%. There is also evidence that citizens generally consider there to be little difference between the parties. Figure 4.5 plots the percentage of people agreeing or disagreeing that 'it doesn't really matter which party is in power, in the end things go on much the same' (again combining the responses for 'agree' and 'agree strongly', and for 'disagree' and 'disagree strongly'). Between 2001 and 2011, the proportion expressing agreement increased by around 10% to over 70%, while the proportion expressing disagreement decreased by around the same amount to 20%.

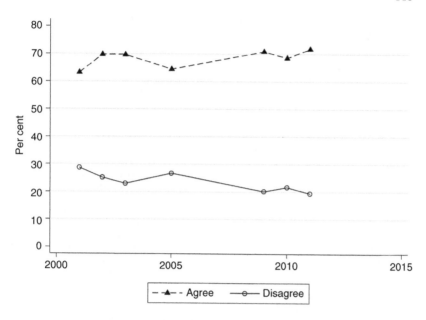

Figure 4.5 How much do you agree or disagree that ... it doesn't really matter which party is in power, in the end things go on much the same? (BSA, 2001–2011).

Conclusions

In this chapter, we have re-analysed the responses of MO panellists to directives on formal politics and compared them for the so-called 'golden age' of mass democracy and the so-called 'age of anti-politics'. We have read them for the categories and storylines repeated by a wide range of panellists in response to multiple questions from multiple directives, which we think provide access to prominent ways of thinking about formal politics in wider society in each historical period. Focusing on judgements of politicians, we have identified the categories and storylines in Table 4.1. In doing so, we have built an argument in three parts. (1) There was no golden age of British democracy, in that prominent story-lines about politicians in the immediate post-war period were negative in character: politicians are self-interested; and politicians are not straight-talking. (2) There has been some historical continuity in judgements of politicians, in that such lines about politicians from the mid-twentieth century were still prominent in the early twenty-first century. (3) There has been some historical change in judgements of politicians over time, in that such lines about politicians have been supplemented in the early

Table 4.1 *Prominent storylines and categories for politicians, 1945–1955 and 2001–2015*

1945–1955		2001–2015	
Storylines	Categories	Storylines	Categories
Politicians are self-interested	Self-interested	Politicians are self-interested	Self-interested
	Ambitious		Ambitious
	Self-serving/the self-server		Self-serving
	Self-seeking/the self-seeker		The feathering of nests
	Place-seeking/the place-seeker		Cronies
			The expenses scandal
	The climber		The careerist
	The feathering of nests		The expense fiddler
			Snouts in the trough
			The duck house
Politicians are not straight-talking	Oratory	Politicians are not straight-talking	The broken promise
	Dishonesty		Spin/the spin doctor
	The gift of the gab		Stage-management
	Playing to the gallery		Avoidance (of topics or questions)
	The talker		
	The twister		
	The gasbag		
		Politicians are out of touch	The rich boy
			The posh boy
			The toff
			Public school
			Eton
			Oxbridge
			Westminster
			The career politician
			The common man or woman
			Ordinary people
			Real life/the real world
			The proper job
		Politicians are all the same	The career politician
			The character
			Different shades of the same colour
			Variations on the same tune
			All as bad as each other
			A plague on all houses

twenty-first century by additional prominent storylines of negative character: politicians are out of touch and politicians are all the same.

This argument complements that of Chapter 3: there was no golden
age, but despite this baseline, anti-political sentiment has grown in social
scope over the past half century. Our argument here is that anti-political

sentiment has also grown in political scope. Not only have more and more people come to feel negatively towards formal politics. Also, people have come to feel negatively regarding more and more aspects of politics. Put differently, citizens have come to hold a broader range of grievances regarding formal politics.

In the next chapter, we identify yet another grievance widely held in the later period but not the earlier period: that politicians are a joke (an embarrassment – not least for the gaffes they make). In the next chapter, we also provide another complementary argument. Anti-political sentiment has grown in social scope (Chapter 3), political scope (the present chapter), and intensity (Chapter 5). People have come to feel negatively towards formal politics with more and more strength. Finally, in the next chapter, we begin to address explicitly the question of explanation. What explains the rise of anti-politics in the UK – its broadening scope and rising intensity? Any explanation, or set of explanations, will need to fit the pattern and temporality of change described in the past couple of chapters. To achieve this, we must look beyond endemic tensions at the heart of representative democracy (foregrounded in the accounts of Fielding, Jefferys, and others). We must also look beyond particular historical context. In the 1940s, Churchill's 'oratory' was but one category in the storyline that politicians are not straight-talking. In the 2010s, the 'expenses scandal' was but one category in the storyline that politicians are self-interested. In Chapter 5, we consider evidence for one theory – influential in current debates about anti-politics – that would appear to meet these criteria: the decline of deference and the rise of critical citizens.

5   Beyond the Decline of Deference: The Rising Intensity of Anti-Politics

The Rise of Critical Citizens?

For the case of the United Kingdom (UK), we have argued that anti-politics has been on the rise for at least the past five decades in terms of its social scope (Chapter 3) and political scope (Chapter 4). In this chapter, we argue that anti-politics has also been on the rise in terms of its intensity – the strength of negative feeling held by citizens towards the activities and institutions of formal politics. We draw on volunteer writing for Mass Observation (MO), alongside relevant survey evidence, to demonstrate how citizens around the middle of the twentieth century commonly viewed politicians as self-interested and not straight-talking (Chapter 4) but also as *difficult to judge* (without more knowledge about what politicians and governments do). By contrast, citizens in the early twenty-first century commonly viewed politicians as self-interested, not straight-talking, out of touch, and all the same (Chapter 4), but also as stimulants – alongside other dimensions of formal politics (parties, governments, elections) – of *strong emotional responses* among citizens: contempt, rage, disgust, depression. A mood of scepticism about politics, tempered by a willingness to give its practitioners the benefit of doubt, appears to have been replaced by a mood of cynicism about politics – that in turn feeds contempt for its practitioners.

In this chapter, we also begin the task of explaining this rise of anti-politics. We consider evidence for existing accounts focused on broad socio-cultural change, which are sometimes labelled 'demand-side' accounts (e.g. Hay 2007, Norris 2011). Two interconnected and overlapping theories have been prominent: that citizens have become less deferent over time and that citizens have become more critical over time. One claim is that citizens have become less passive, less attracted to order, and less acquiescent to elite direction (Nevitte 1996). Another set of claims is that such a 'decline of deference' is explained by modernisation. Connected to modernisation are 'post-materialist values' (Inglehart 1977) emphasising self-expression and quality of life over economic security. Also connected to modernisation is 'cognitive mobilisation' (Dalton 1984) – the process by which education levels and political skills drive both lower trust in government and the emergence of new, less elite-directed forms of political action.

Over the past couple of decades, these claims have been developed at length by Ron Inglehart (e.g. 1997, 1999) and Russell Dalton (e.g. 2000, 2004, 2009). They have also been added to by Pippa Norris (1999), for whom the flip side of the decline of deference is the rise of 'critical citizens'. With colleagues, Norris argues that citizens across much of the world – and especially younger citizens – continue to support regime principles (democracy as an ideal form of government) but have withdrawn support from regime institutions (the performance of parties, parliaments, governments). They have become 'disaffected democrats' or 'critical citizens', questioning traditional sources of authority, withdrawing from conventional forms of political participation, and pursuing new forms of self-expression (e.g. activism in social movements).

We have already discussed certain aspects of these accounts in Chapter 1, where we critiqued the 'democratisation thesis' from both empirical and normative perspectives. The empirical critique is relevant again here. Existing studies of contemporary British citizenship (e.g. Whiteley 2012) have found little evidence of widespread participation in alternative forms of political action like signing petitions, purchasing goods for political reasons, volunteering, or protesting and demonstrating.

In this chapter, we develop this empirical critique further. We ask what evidence is provided by the responses and diaries of MO panellists for a generalised decline of deference and rise of critical citizens. Focusing on the shared cultural resources used by a range of panellists and supplementing the MO material with relevant survey data, we find that citizens in the mid-twentieth century did not commonly *sound like* deferential citizens. They actually sounded quite critical – expressing negative judgements or discriminating judgements between kinds of object or a reluctance to judge without more information – regarding politicians but also comparable figures of authority or high social status like doctors, scientists, and lawyers. Furthermore, citizens in the early twenty-first century did not commonly *sound like* critical citizens. In some situations, they sounded educated, skilled, questioning, self-directed – as we might expect. But in other situations, they sounded more deferent than we might expect (especially regarding lawyers, scientists, and doctors). Moreover, when responding to formal politics, citizens in the later period often sounded contemptuous, angry, sickened, or depressed. The intensity of their disaffection appeared to be much stronger and more specifically directed – towards politicians, parties, government – than might reasonably be expected as a result of broad socio-cultural change.

From Reticence to Ridicule

In Chapter 4, we identified two storylines about politicians circulating widely in British society in the decade following the Second World War: politicians are self-interested (they are self-servers, self-seekers, place-seekers, and climbers); and politicians are not straight-talking (they are talkers, twisters, gasbags, and gift of the gabbers). But there was also a third cultural resource on which MO panellists often drew to write about politicians during the period. This was a common way of responding to questions on the topic of politicians and governments. It involved acknowledging that such questions are 'difficult', 'knowledge' is needed to answer them, such knowledge is lacking, and such questions, therefore, cannot be answered. Its popularity suggests a reticence on the part of many citizens during the period to judge politicians and governments (and especially to do so in strong terms).

This cultural resource – or set of cultural resources, containing both a common way of responding to questions ('that's a difficult question') and a commonly available subject position (the citizen who takes little interest, knows little about the topic, and so cannot answer the question) – was mobilised by a range of panellists in November 1945 when MO asked for views on municipal elections and local councils.[1] A tax inspector from Belfast wrote: 'I don't take enough interest in local government . . . I must confess to knowing little about local politics.'[2] Perhaps unsurprisingly, a statistician from Manchester wanted more reasons on which to base his response: 'I really haven't the slightest idea. Council activities are insufficiently publicised for one to be able to come to a reasonable judgement.'[3] But then we have this from a farm worker in Aberdeen, who – perhaps surprisingly – also wanted more knowledge before passing judgement: 'My knowledge of our Town Council was and is very scrappy. Therefore, I shouldn't like to criticise either the old Town Council, which was predominantly Conservative, or the new one, which for the first time has a Labour majority.'[4]

These panellists confessed to not taking an interest, knowing little, having scrappy knowledge, or not having the slightest idea. They were

---

[1] Directive SxMOA1/3/88.   [2] Panellist 1066, female, 39, tax inspector, Belfast.
[3] Panellist 2514, male, 28, statistician, Manchester.
[4] Panellist 3361, male, 25, farm worker, Aberdeen.

reluctant to criticise. They refused to pass judgement. And these forms of response – these confessions and hesitancies – were also mobilised by a range of panellists in August 1949 when MO asked for views on the effectiveness of 'the MP for your constituency'.[5] 'I confess I do not know how effective he is', admitted a teacher from Enfield.[6] A civil servant from Morecambe wrote: 'not being very politically minded, am afraid I don't know much about my present MP'.[7] A housewife from the West Midlands also claimed she did not know enough to answer the question: 'I don't follow our MP's career in Parliament, so can't answer this as I ought to be able to.'[8]

A lieutenant from Dartford found this question about the MP from his constituency a 'very difficult question to answer adequately or accurately'.[9] The 'difficult question' was a category panellists used repeatedly during this period, seemingly as a means of withholding judgement regarding politicians (and governments). So in July 1950, when MO asked panellists for their views on five leading politicians of the day,[10] responses often began like this from a teacher in Ripon: 'This is a difficult question to answer';[11] or this from the superintendent of a nursery: 'I'm afraid this question is one I find difficult to answer. I am not politically minded.'[12]

Throughout the period, in response to multiple directives, a range of panellists drew on a common set of cultural resources – a standard way of responding to questions, the subject position of the citizen without knowledge and unable to judge, the category of the 'difficult question' – to write about politicians and governments. In doing so, they expressed a reticence to judge that was presumably one popular way of engaging with formal politics at the time, to be set alongside the popular storylines about politicians identified in Chapter 4.

How does this reticence compare with orientations towards formal politics in the period 2001–2015? In Chapter 4, we identified four storylines about politicians that were prominent in the early twenty-first century: politicians are self-interested (they are expense fiddlers), not straight-talking (they break promises), out of touch (they are career politicians), and all the same (they are all as bad as each other). But there is a fifth storyline, almost as prominent in the MO material, demanding of discussion in the present chapter: politics and politicians

---

[5] Directive SxMOA1/3/123.   [6] Panellist 2984, female, 41, teacher, Enfield.
[7] Panellist 2675, female, 57, civil servant, Morecambe.
[8] Panellist 1644, female, 72, housewife, West Midlands.
[9] Panellist 3635, male, 27, lieutenant, Dartford.   [10] Directive SxMOA1/3/127.
[11] Panellist 2984, female, 42, teacher, Ripon.
[12] Panellist 4744, female, 65, superintendent of nursery, place of residence not known.

are a joke (to be ridiculed, to be embarrassed by, and ultimately to be dismissed).

Of course, to some extent, politicians have long been ridiculed – as Fielding (2014) demonstrates in his survey of how British politics has been represented in fiction since the end of the nineteenth century. But the writing of MO panellists, which tells us something of how representations of politics were received (or not) by audiences, suggests that politicians were judged to be appropriate for such treatment far more regularly and widely in the early twenty-first century than the mid-twentieth century.

One category repeated by a range of panellists in the later period was 'the gaffe'. This category was used from 2001, as when a clerical worker from York wrote in her general election diary that William Hague, Leader of the Conservative Party, 'has made so many gaffes'.[13] But use of the category became especially common in 2010 after Prime Minister Gordon Brown was widely reported to have made 'a gaffe' by forgetting to remove his microphone when returned apparently safely to his campaign car and then criticising a woman he had just met on a walkabout in Rochdale. A range of panellists picked up on the reporting of this incident (and the terms in which it was reported). For an unemployed man from Birmingham: 'Gordon Brown made a gaffe yesterday … He had a conversation with a Labour supporter – and then got into his car and criticised her to an aide.'[14] For a clerical assistant from Northern Ireland: 'Gordon Brown made a bit of a gaffe yesterday. After chatting to a pensioner, he got into his car, forgot about his microphone, and called her a "bigot".'[15] Numerous similar descriptions of the incident were provided in the general election diaries of 2010.

We return to the gaffes of politicians – where they come from and what citizens make of them – in Chapter 8. But if the category of the gaffe was one part of the storyline that politicians are a joke, then another part was the description of politicians as embarrassing or excruciating. In 2010, Gordon Brown was described in this way for 'mechanically concluding speeches with a smile – which does not come naturally to him, and which actually looks rather sinister on his face'.[16] In 2014, a woman from Salisbury described at some length how politicians in general are daft, odd, and awkward – in a way that makes one cringe with embarrassment:

Politicians are generally odd in some way, either looks or personality, all too frequently both. It seems that some kind of social alienation has led them into

---

[13] Panellist J2830, female, 43, clerical worker, York.
[14] Panellist B3227, male, 43, unemployed, Birmingham.
[15] Panellist F4125, female, 45, clerical assistant, Northern Ireland.
[16] Panellist B3227, male, 43, unemployed, Birmingham.

politics. Despite achieving much higher levels of education than most, they are known for being a bit daft, out of touch with reality. They tend to see life through the prism of their political ideology. The more normal they try to appear, the more we cringe and become convinced of the opposite. There is something that makes the back crawl about each and every one of them ... If I was talking about politicians, it would invariably descend into sneering, sarcasm, laughing at them for making yet another cock-up.[17]

Here, we see a connection between the storylines that politicians are a joke and politicians are out of touch. It is partly because politicians are seen as being different – uncommon, extraordinary, unreal – that they are also seen as being funny. And they are seen as being funny in two respects: funny as in strange (odd, abnormal) and funny as in ripe for ridicule (for sneering and laughing at – not *with* – and for their gaffes).

This particular respondent went on to describe Ed Miliband, Leader of the Labour Party:

Strange Marxist upbringing. Extremely untrustworthy and unfortunate-looking, with an awful voice. His voice is a major obstacle and I don't think people will ever take him seriously. I can't imagine him on the world stage. It would be so awkward and embarrassing ... Even his name is a problem – that casual diminutive at odds with his serious manner, and a silly-sounding surname that is all too easy to parody. He is just the wrong person for Prime Minister.

For this supporter of Miliband's opponents (the Conservative Party), who may also be drawing on the cultural resources of anti-Semitism here, Miliband could not be taken seriously and was an embarrassment because of his strange background, his unfortunate looks, his awful voice, and his silly name. But this panellist was not the only one to find Ed Miliband laughable and embarrassing. In his general election diary of 2015, an administrator from Birmingham wrote this of Miliband's performance in a televised interview: 'Ed Miliband is nobody's idea of a tough guy, but when asked whether he would be able to stand up to Putin, he said, excruciatingly, "Hell yeah".'[18] Equally excruciating, for this apparently more sympathetic project manager from Newcastle, was Miliband's performance on the British Broadcasting Corporation's (BBC) *Question Time* during the same campaign: 'Ed's tripping up over the *Question Time* set only served to ridicule him in the eyes of the public. People were not talking about his policies and his honesty. They were remarking on the way he tripped over the 'Q'. Very unfortunate!'[19]

---

[17] Panellist B5342, female, 28, unemployed, Salisbury.
[18] Panellist B3227, male, 48, administrator, Birmingham.
[19] Panellist R5429, female, 39, project manager, Newcastle.

Figure 5.1   Campaign poster for the Labour Party, 2001 (© Victoria and Albert Museum, London).

It should be stated that panellists found other politicians to be embarrassing and excruciating too. But Miliband was often used by respondents to stand in for politicians in general – as the prototypical figure in the storyline that politicians are a joke. This brings us to a third part of this storyline. When asked to write about formal politics, panellists often referred to how politicians are ridiculed in society – by other politicians, comedians, family, and friends. We see this in the general election diaries of 2001. A child carer from London reported on 'a dig by Labour' that was a campaign poster depicting William Hague with a 'Margaret Thatcher wig on' (Figure 5.1) and also a cartoon from *The Times* comparing Hague's wife to a guide dog – that 'made me laugh'.[20] Of Labour's campaign posters for the same election, a computer worker from London wrote this: 'It's just a series of cheap jokes – spoof posters for disaster moves featuring William Hague wearing a Maggie Thatcher wig. It treats the whole thing as a joke.'[21]

Whether cheap or not, the jokes came from the political parties seeking to undermine each other but also from a variety of other sources. Jogging past a campaign poster in 2010, an unemployed man from Birmingham 'was reminded of a scene in the political comedy series *The Thick of It*'.[22] Elsewhere in his General Election diary, this panellist reported on a special edition of the BBC's *Newsnight*:

It was a mixture of the public, various comedians, and minor politicians, with Jeremy Paxman in the chair ... A female comedian ... was asked what she thought about Labour co-opting Blair so late. She said: 'It's like England being four-nil down in the World Cup and Fabio Capello bringing on Stephen Hawking as a last minute substitute'. The audience fell about.

[20] Panellist H2870, female, 38, child carer, London.
[21] Panellist W2720, male, 46, computer worker, London.
[22] Panellist B3227, male, 43, unemployed, Birmingham.

Jokes were to be found in the more obvious places like political comedies but also the less obvious places like news and current affairs programmes. In 2010, they were also to be found online, as reported by this radio broadcast assistant from Cardiff: 'My inbox is filling up with various satirical jokes and videos' that 'keep the circus interesting, rather than boring bleatings about promises and manifestos'.[23]

Responding to a special directive about politics in spring 2014,[24] panellists continued to describe how politicians are ridiculed in society. These politicians included William Hague: 'Two things spring to mind about William Hague – the "William Vague" nickname, which I seem to remember hearing on some radio or TV programme years ago; and the image of him when he wore his little baseball cap, which made him look about 12.'[25] They included Nick Clegg, Leader of the Liberal Democrats, who issued a filmed apology in 2012 for breaking a campaign promise on student tuition fees: 'I admire him for issuing an apology ... but cringe at how this left him open to ridicule, especially in a media age when his video apology could so easily be made into a mash-up song.'[26] These politicians also included Michael Gove, then Secretary of State for Education:

How one man can be the butt of so many jokes is beyond me. This guy means well but is totally misguided and must be a spin doctor's nightmare! The general public find him a figure of such amusement there is even a YouTube channel dedicated to his bumbling adventures. My particular favourite is of him attempting to rap whilst on a visit to a primary school.[27]

But more than anyone else, the focus was on Ed Miliband – by 2014, the prototypical figure in this storyline. For one data architect from Wigan: 'He's a joke ... Ed wouldn't need to have a spitting image puppet made of him – he is one.'[28] For many other panellists, however, Miliband was a joke precisely because of the resemblance drawn between him and a well-known animated character of the period.

After Ed Miliband became Leader of the Labour Party, Peter Brookes, a cartoonist for *The Times*, began drawing him as Wallace from Nick Park's *Wallace and Gromit* (Figure 5.2). This cartoon quickly became the cultural resource used by MO panellists – and presumably many citizens in wider society – to think about Miliband. In 2014, a wide range of panellists referred to Ed as Wallace in one way or another. There was the graphic designer from Norfolk: '*Wallace and Gromit* – crazy looks and

---

[23] Panellist G4296, male, 33, radio broadcast assistant, Cardiff.
[24] Directive SxMOA2/1/99/1.   [25] Panellist S3711, male, 38, planning officer, Sheffield.
[26] Panellist P5340, male, 37, marketing manager, Basingstoke.
[27] Panellist R4526, male, 53, science teacher, Belfast.
[28] Panellist G5421, male, 35, data architect, Wigan.

Figure 5.2 Ed Miliband as Wallace (© News Syndication).

ideas to match. Crackin' cheese.'[29] There was the teaching assistant from Bythorn: 'My husband and I think he has a *Wallace and Gromit* type mouth! I know he can't help that and don't mean to be nasty. But even his voice irritates me. He always seems like a right pillock to me.'[30] Then there was the civil servant from Nottingham: 'Slightly handicapped by his odd manner of speaking and not helped by relentless (but very funny) lampooning by the cartoonists who have spotted his unfortunate resemblance to Wallace of the *Wallace and Gromit* animated films.'[31]

A tree inspector from Harpenden wrote of Miliband: 'Ed reminds me of a character from ... *Wallace and Gromit.*'[32] Were Miliband to become Prime Minister in 2015, this panellist worried that he would not be 'taken seriously on the world stage'. In her general election diary of 2015, a blogger from Wiltshire reported the same worry: 'I am dreading the Labour Party getting in ... I can't even imagine how embarrassing it would be to see Miliband on the world stage.'[33] Elsewhere in the same diary, this panellist wrote: 'I do get excited about general elections. It is

[29] Panellist C4102, male, 50, graphic designer, Norfolk.
[30] Panellist D4400, female, 43, teaching assistant, Bythorn.
[31] Panellist F3409, female, 63, civil servant, Nottingham.
[32] Panellist M5198, male, 43, tree inspector, Harpenden.
[33] Panellist B5342, female, 29, blogger, Wiltshire.

Figure 5.3 The 'Ed stone' (© PA Images).

like the World Cup or Eurovision with all the funny stuff on Twitter nowadays.' She also wrote of newspaper coverage during the campaign: 'The Ed-bashing has been mostly silly, jokey stuff, quite childish.' During the 2015 campaign, this 'Ed-bashing' appears to have reached a crescendo in early May when Miliband unveiled an eight-foot limestone tablet inscribed with Labour's six policy pledges (Figure 5.3). It was described by a hostile media as 'the Ed stone', 'the cenotaph', 'the tombstone', and 'the heaviest suicide note in history' (Cowley and Kavanagh 2016). The first of these terms became yet another category for citizens to use – in thinking about Ed Miliband but also the ridiculous, gaffe-prone, embarrassing world of twenty-first-century politics.

Listen to this retired film director from Scotland: 'Ed Miliband has bizarrely unveiled an 8½ ft high limestone edifice (Labour's "Ed stone"), carved with six rather illiterate and incoherent Labour pledges, destined if he wins for the now infamous Rose Garden of 10 Downing Street.'[34] Then listen to this retired nursery nurse from Ducklington: 'On the day before the election, I was at my sewing group and they were in fits about the stone Ed Miliband appeared with. One lady mentioned the cartoons which depicted Ed as Moses with his tablets of stone.'[35] Finally, writing after polling day when Labour lost the election, we have this warehouse worker from Stoke-on-Trent: 'The Ed Stone, as the press rapidly dubbed

[34] Panellist H1541, male, 70, retired film editor, Scotland.
[35] Panellist 1610, female, 71, retired nursery nurse, Ducklington.

it, has become something of a minor obsession for me. Where has it gone? I have this fantasy where some twenty years from now, Red Ed has it installed in the garden of his retirement bungalow as a, literally, concrete reminder of how badly he messed things up.'[36]

This storyline – that politics and politicians are a joke – was repeated by clerical workers, teachers, project managers, carers, planning officers, marketing managers, data architects, graphic designers, civil servants, tree inspectors, film directors, nurses, warehouse workers from York, Birmingham, Belfast, Salisbury, Newcastle, London, Cardiff, Sheffield, Basingstoke, Wigan, Nottingham, Harpenden, Ducklington, Stoke-on-Trent. It was repeated by men and women, young and old, in response to multiple directives, and about multiple politicians. We have demonstrated how the storyline was made up of multiple parts: the category of the gaffe; the subject position of the embarrassed, cringing citizen; the numerous categories produced and circulated by journalists and comedians (e.g. 'Wallace' or 'the Ed Stone'). And there is one final part for us to add. If politicians are a joke, then one conclusion reached by many is that politicians are not for taking seriously. This applied, of course, to Ed Miliband: 'I just cannot take him seriously. He seems to be an Aardman animation with a pulse. I know that I should be looking at policies and the content of the speech but, when it comes from him, I keep expecting Gromit to walk past.'[37] But it also applied to other politicians. Here, we have a writer from Scotland on Nick Clegg:

[He] is like a keen younger brother, desperate to emulate [Prime Minister] David Cameron, but without any means of establishing himself as a powerful presence. He is not capable of being powerful. He is too much like a little schoolboy wanting to get a gold star off teacher for work well done. You can't take him seriously.[38]

And here, to finish, we have an artist from Welton on William Hague:

I grin when I see and hear William Hague. I remember him as a ghastly boy making a precocious speech under Margaret Thatcher's eye. In his brief leadership of the Tories, I remember his frightful attempt at being 'one of us' with his baseball hat, and now I see him as Foreign Secretary trying to sound statesmanlike, representing a country that has little or no effect on world affairs. He looks utterly out of place and sounds like a parody of himself. I just cannot take him seriously. When he 'goes all serious', I start laughing.[39]

---

[36] Panellist C3167, male, 43, warehouse worker, Stoke-on-Trent.
[37] Panellist K5246, male, 45, railway signalling designer, Crewe.
[38] Panellist H1470, female, 60, writer/broadcaster, Scotland.
[39] Panellist P3209, male, 74, artist, Welton.

Anger, Disgust, Depression

Volunteer writing for MO suggests a reticence about judging politics and governments in the mid-twentieth century. It also suggests that such a reticence was no longer popular by the turn of the twenty-first century. Instead, politicians and politics were commonly viewed as a joke – to be ridiculed, embarrassed by, and ultimately dismissed.

MO panellists from neither period sounded particularly deferent. In the earlier period, they either criticised politicians for being self-interested and not straight-talking or else withheld judgement for lack of information (another form of critical response). In the later period, they either criticised politicians – for an expanded range of failings – or else ridiculed them. But do these proliferating criticisms, and does this newly pervasive ridicule, suggest the kind of critical citizens imagined by Norris and others? The panellists writing in the early twenty-first century do not really sound like highly educated, skilled, and active citizens – constantly questioning all forms of authority. Often, they sound like rather passive citizens, easily embarrassed, and directed by an expanded set of elites: politicians, journalists, and comedians. And this set of elites can be quite cruel to (fellow) politicians. And these citizens can often lack the serious-ness one might expect from critical citizens.

This argument is further supported by our focus in the present section on yet another set of cultural resources drawn on repeatedly by a range of panellists in the early twenty-first century (but not the mid-twentieth century). In this later period, a set of subject positions appear to have been circulating widely in society – such that panellists from different situations could mobilise them in their writing – including the citizen angered, outraged, or appalled by formal politics; the citizen disgusted or sickened; and the citizen depressed by their political interaction.

In response to various directives between 2001 and 2015, many panel-lists described themselves as angered by politics. Sometimes this outrage was provoked by parties and politicians they did not support as opposed to formal politics in general. In 2010, this was the new coalition govern-ment for one grants officer from Edinburgh: 'I have now got to the stage where I can't bear to read or watch the news; that every time I see any member of the Government on TV I get so angry I have to turn it off.'[40] In 2014, it was the same coalition government for this library assistant from London: 'I cannot stand this Government with its Eton-raised ethos. I become angry as I write so break off to see to something else.'[41] And in 2015, it was the Conservative Party for this administrator from

---

[40] Panellist C4131, female, 28, grants officer, Edinburgh.
[41] Panellist H2418, female, 62, library assistant, London.

Wales: 'I am outraged by the Tories. As a volunteer for the CAB [Citizens Advice Bureau], I have lost count of the number of food vouchers given out, people seen as fit to work when they are really ill.'[42] On the day after the general election of 2015, the same panellist wrote: 'Waking up this morning was devastating. I am beyond angry and upset, and I cannot begin to say how much I hate the Tories.'

It is perhaps no surprise that specific parties and politicians were sources of such anger. But a range of panellists also described themselves as angry, outraged, appalled, and/or infuriated by politics and politicians more generally. The stated reason for such anger varied. For this housewife from Aberystwyth, responding to MO's request for a general election diary in 2015, it was the 'fuss' associated with elections: 'May I be brutally honest? I hate politics! I have so little interest in the election, politics, party leaders, voting, campaign trails, the election debates. No – not my thing I'm afraid … I shall keep a very low profile. I won't be keeping a diary as the whole day and the 'fuss' of it all infuriates me. Sorry!'[43] For many respondents, however, their main reason was the MPs' expenses scandal (see Chapter 4). 'I was amongst the many who were outraged by the "game" MPS OF ALL PARTIES had been playing – at the public's expense', wrote a retired youth and community officer from Redbourn in his general election diary of 2010. 'They were all at it. "Snouts in the trough".'[44] An artist from Yorkshire also chose upper-case text for much of his diary of the same year: 'ANGER-DISGUST-FRUSTRATION-DISTRUST … I was utterly appalled when I learned about the corruption in Parliament.'[45]

If one subject position circulating in this period was 'the angry citizen', then another was the citizen disgusted or sickened by politics. Again, in some cases, parties and politicians not supported appear to have been responsible for stimulating these visceral reactions. In 2014, it was the coalition government for one respondent: 'The present government and its officials disgust me … They slash and burn their way to victory, money, and success, even if the body count along the way is large.'[46] And it was the Prime Minister for another respondent: 'David Cameron disgusts me – his ignorance (and apparent dislike) of working class people is not acceptable.'[47] In 2015, for a third panellist – writing just after the general election of that year – it was the new Conservative Government:

[42] Panellist J2891, female, 50, administrator, Wales.
[43] Panellist A5197, female, 40, housewife, Aberystwyth.
[44] Panellist C3603, male, 66, retired youth and community officer, Redbourn.
[45] Panellist P3209, male, 71, artist, Yorkshire.
[46] Panellist H1470, female, 60, writer/broadcaster, Scotland.
[47] Panellist V3773, female, 52, pharmacist, Solihull.

'I was not happy with the result ... They really make me sick to the stomach and (if they last) the next five years are not going to be good.'[48]

Disgust was often targeted at specific parties and politicians. But just like anger and outrage, it was also often targeted at politics conceived of in more general terms. And just like anger and outrage, it was often a response to the expenses scandal, especially in the general election diaries of 2010. 'The expenses scandals of last year made me very angry', wrote a child protection officer from Edinburgh. 'It seemed to me to be yet another example of how politicians try to twist things for their own ends and it sickened me in terms of future political interest.' She concluded: 'In summary, I am totally sickened by the whole process and therefore don't feel I have much more to say at this point for the MO.'[49] A similar conclusion was reached by this museum visitor assistant from Dundee: 'Such a scandal as the expenses issue from late last year is a true disgrace and thoroughly sickening.'[50] In focusing on the expenses scandal, however, we should not overlook less narrowly targeted revulsion, like that of one art teacher from Cambridge who 'just can't summon up the effort to be really interested. This may be because of reason within myself, but it is also through a general sense of disgust at politicians and the way they behave'.[51]

A third and final subject position frequently adopted by panellists in the early twenty-first century was the citizen depressed by politics. As we might expect, given previous paragraphs, this depression was often connected to the success of those perceived to be on the other side of the partisan divide. After the general election of 2001, a film editor from Scotland found it 'profoundly depressing to observe "New" Labour walk easily into such a landslide'.[52] In the next set of general election diaries, completed in 2010 between the start of the campaign in April and the formation of a coalition government in May, we have this from a grants officer in Edinburgh: 'I am writing this a while after the election and my main feeling is of disappointment and quite a lot of fear of what is to come. I don't want to write too much as it genuinely depresses me.'[53] A similar response to the results of the 2015 general election, won by the Conservative Party, was recorded by a teaching assistant in Brighton: 'Feeling quite numb, tired, and depressed. Five more years of unnecessary austerity is a total disaster for the country.'[54]

---

[48] Panellist S4002, female, 36, administrator, Cardiff.
[49] Panellist M3469, female, 47, child protection officer, Edinburgh.
[50] Panellist E2977, male, 28, museum visitor assistant, Dundee.
[51] Panellist B4572, female, 29, art teacher, Cambridge.
[52] Panellist H1541, male, 57, film editor, Scotland.
[53] Panellist C4131, female, 28, grants officer, Edinburgh.
[54] Panellist S2207, female, 63, teaching assistant, Brighton.

More important for us, however, given our focus on negative sentiment oriented towards formal politics in general, is depression connected to the perceived failings of the activities and institutions of such politics. This could be depression stimulated by the behaviour of politicians in general, as reported by one farmer from Llandysul in 2010: 'I'm depressed by MPs' expenses. It doesn't seem like enough has changed and I'm appalled to hear that three Labour MPs are claiming legal aid to fund their defence against the investigators. What twats.'[55] Or it could be depression stimulated by a perceived lack of electoral choice and inspiration provided by the main parties. 'I was fairly depressed about the whole process', wrote a retired clergyman from Newcastle in 2015. 'I accepted the general idea about the likely outcome but was enthusiastic about none of the possible alternatives.'[56]

The following extract from the 2015 diary of one panellist, a museum consultant from North Shields, captures the range of strongly held negative feelings towards politics found in the early twenty-first century:

I am fed up with it, depressed by the likely outcomes, uninspired by what politics has to offer me ... In 2010, I said I would leave the country if the Conservatives won ... I was so disgusted that my Lib Dem vote had helped put David Cameron in Downing Street that it didn't feel like it would have been an over-reaction ... Reading this back now, I know I probably sound like a crazy person, but it makes me so angry ... I know that Russell Brand is a ridiculous person but at the root of it, he's right: politics is broken. It is government by the elite for the elite, and I don't know where it will end.[57]

This panellist was fed up and depressed. She was uninspired by the choice she was offered in the general election of 2015. She was disgusted by the events of 2010, when the Liberal Democrats campaigned on ground arguably to the left of Labour, before joining the Conservative Party in coalition government. She was angry to the point where the anti-politics of comedian Russell Brand resonated with her.[58] In all this, she represents many British citizens of the early twenty-first century who felt strongly about formal politics: outraged, sickened, depressed.

We have argued that anti-politics has been on the rise in the UK. Not only has it broadened in social and political scope. Also, it has become

---

[55] Panellist B3757, male, 24, farmer/piano teacher, Llandysul.
[56] Panellist B2710, male, 85, retired clergyman, Newcastle.
[57] Panellist C4131, female, 33, museum consultant, North Shields.
[58] Between 2013 and 2015, Russell Brand used numerous platforms – articles in *The New Statesman*, appearances on the BBC's *Newsnight* and *Question Time*, speeches at various protests, videos on YouTube, his book on *Revolution* – to argue that formal politics is broken and people should not vote (because to do so is to legitimise a broken and corrupt system).

more intense. Negative feeling towards formal politics has become held by more people, regarding more aspects of politics, and has become held more strongly (and communicated in stronger terms). In the mid-twentieth century, citizens commonly expressed negative views about formal politics, but they did so with reticence. In the early twenty-first century, citizens expressed negative views about politics – and more commonly than before. They expressed a broader set of views – that politicians are self-interested and not straight-talking but also out of touch, all the same, and a joke. They also expressed such views in stronger terms. Citizens were now contemptuous, angry, disgusted, and depressed regarding the institutions of formal politics.

This argument has been constructed from volunteer writing for MO. We have little survey research on this question of intensity, especially going back to the mid-twentieth century. Between 2005 and 2015, however, we do have this question from the British Election Study: 'Now, thinking about British political institutions like Parliament, please use the 0 to 10 scale to indicate how much trust you have for each of the following, where 0 means no trust and 10 means a great deal of trust.' A further part of the question asked: 'And how much do you trust British politicians generally?' In Figure 5.4, we plot the percentage of respondents who expressed distrust in politicians (the dotted line, for values between 0 and 4 on the 10-point scale), contrasted with those who expressed *intense* distrust (the black line, for values between 0 and 2) and more moderate distrust (the dashed line, for values between 3 and 4). Consistent with our findings elsewhere in this book, the overall trend of distrust is a steady rise over time – here observed between 2005 and 2015. Moreover, for the purposes of this chapter, the level of moderate distrust declined slightly over the period, with the upward trend being driven by a steady increase in the level of intense distrust. This is counter to what we might expect if the long-term trend was being driven simply by a rise in distrust (from those who previously were trusting of politicians). It is consistent with a shift from low-level distrust to more intense anti-political sentiment.

All of this leads us to question demand-side accounts of broad socio-cultural change as the main explanatory factor in the rise of anti-politics. Citizens in the early twenty-first century may have been more educated and skilled than citizens of previous times – in some respects, at least – but many of them did not sound like the questioning, self-directed, active citizens of such accounts. Rather, they expressed strongly held emotional responses to formal politics – of an intensity that is not readily explained by the outcomes of modernisation (improved economic security and educational attainment).

Before we conclude, however, there is one final empirical test of such theories made possible by the MO material. If the rise of anti-politics was

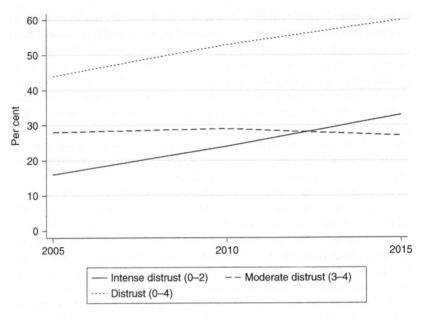

Figure 5.4 Intensity of distrust in politicians, BES, 2005–2015.

to be explained by a generalised decline of deference associated with modernisation, then we would expect to see a generalised deference towards all or most figures of authority and high social status in the period immediately following the Second World War and a generalised lack of deference towards such figures in later decades. To pose the problem slightly differently – from the perspective of scholarship on how feeling and its expression varies historically at the societal level (e.g. Mishra 2017) – we might ask of the change described in the last two sections: Was this not just a reflection of a more generalised shift in the way British citizens wrote, spoke, and thought about others and themselves? Have we not just seen a shift from a hesitant and careful style in the middle of the last century to something more confident and also more self-aware and emotionally literate at the beginning of the current century? In the next section, we consider evidence for such a broadly focused change in citizens' understandings, judgements, and styles of expression.

A Generalised Decline of Deference?

In February 1945, MO asked panellists the following question: 'What would you say is your normal conversational attitude when talk gets round to each of the following groups: a) clergymen; b) politicians; c) doctors; d) advertising agents; e) lawyers; f) scientists?'[59] Almost sixty years later, in 2014, a similar question was asked by MO: 'Consider the following people: a) politicians; b) doctors; c) lawyers; d) scientists. Do you associate any characteristics with each group? If you were in conversation with somebody and these kinds of people were referred to, what would be your attitude?'[60] The responses to these two questions allow us to do three things. First, they allow us to establish the cultural resources available to people for thinking and communicating about politicians at each historical moment. Second, they allow us to compare these cultural resources – and the popular understandings and judgements to which they provide access – to those cultural resources used by people for thinking and communicating about other groups like clergymen or doctors. Third, the responses allow us to compare popular understandings and judgements for some of these groups over time. (Given the requirements of this final task, we focus our discussion in the present section on the four groups common to both questions: politicians, doctors, lawyers, and scientists.)

In February 1945, cultural resources used by panellists to write about politicians included the storylines that politicians are self-interested and not straight-talking (Chapter 4). But they also included a storyline connected to those cultural resources identified in the preceding sections: the subject position of the citizen who knows little about politics and is reluctant to judge politicians and governments; and the category of 'the difficult question'. This was the storyline that politicians vary (so we should be reticent about judging them in general terms). 'Some good, some bad' was how one businessman from Torquay succinctly put it.[61] Other panellists provided more detail and commonly structured their answer using 'but' as a pivot: 'We've got some grand men … but we have some gift-o'-the-gabbers too.'[62] 'A few may be slackers but most are, I imagine, hardworking and industrious'.[63] One panellist wrote at length and classified politicians into 'several kinds':

1. The unscrupulous Machiavellian type. 2. The self-seeking type in the pay of a member of the capitalist class. 3. The lesser lights and party 'yes-men'. 4. The sincere but misguided liberal type. 5. The extreme 'leftists', sincere but oversimplifying. 6. A few far-seeing, courageous, altruistic, honest individuals.[64]

---

[59] Directive SxMOA1/3/84.   [60] Directive SxMOA2/1/99/1.
[61] Panellist 1345, male, 28, businessman, Torquay.
[62] Panellist 1016, female, 58, teacher, Gateshead.
[63] Panellist 1095, male, 69, railway draughtsman, Wilmslow.
[64] Panellist 3650, male, 24, occupation not known, place of residence not known.

We discuss self-seekers in Chapter 4, party 'yes-men' in Chapter 6, and political sincerity in Chapter 7. Here, our focus is on the storyline that politicians are of 'several kinds'. They vary such that, as another panellist put it, what one thinks 'depends on the politician's views ... No general condemnation of politicians but only those with whom I don't agree or don't trust'.[65] This storyline, when placed alongside the cultural resources identified in the sections above, appears to reflect a number of things. First, this was no golden age of political support. Second, this was no age of generalised deference to politicians. Third, it was possible and likely common in this period for citizens to be critical in their judgement of politicians: critical in the sense of passing negative judgements but also critical in the sense of discriminating between members of the category 'politicians'.

How does this treatment of politicians compare with treatment of other groups in the responses from 1945? Many panellists wrote about doctors in similarly discriminating ways. They commonly used a similar structure for their responses, which pivoted on the word 'but'. We see this in the response of a civil servant from Purley: 'I admire a handful that I know personally, but I haven't much respect for most.'[66] And we see it in the response from an electrical engineer from Ringwood:

Here again, one feels that there are those who regard their work as a vocation, for these one has great respect, but others one feels differently about. At the moment too, one has a feeling that too many of them are thinking more about their salaries than making a good medical service.[67]

One context for the latter part of this response was the movement for a National Health Service (NHS), which culminated in the National Health Service Act of 1946, and opposition to this movement by the British Medical Association (BMA) – the main body representing doctors at the time and articulating their concerns regarding the proposed NHS. This context led many panellists to distinguish between individual doctors and doctors as a group (represented by the BMA). One such panellist was this secretary from Earley: 'I think the BMA is reactionary, but I like my own doctor.'[68] Another was this railway draughtsman from Wilmslow: 'In the mass, I loathe and despise them as selfish and unprogressive. But when I come to individuals, they seem kindly and attentive ... I regard the BMA as far too powerful and hope more doctors

---

[65] Panellist 1682, male, 25, clerk, Edinburgh.
[66] Panellist 1066, female, 38, civil servant, Purley.
[67] Panellist 1165, male, 39, electrical engineer, Ringwood.
[68] Panellist 1635, female, 30, secretary, Earley.

will become state servants.'[69] A third such panellist was this farmer from Campbeltown who identified 'kinds' of doctor:

The same applies to doctors – they are of all kinds. On the whole, I was inclined to respect the medical profession and to hold up their standards as an example for businessmen, for instance, to follow. But the BMA's recent agitation against the establishment of the National Health Service has made me wonder ... I incline to class doctors on the whole amongst the reactionary sections of the community, with of course many notable exceptions.[70]

One prominent storyline, then, available to panellists for thinking and communicating about doctors was that doctors vary – between the individual doctor, known personally, admired and respected for their kindness and attentiveness; and doctors in general, represented by the BMA, too concerned about their salaries, reactionary in the face of progress. This storyline suggests a popular orientation towards doctors at the time that was rather mixed. But other storylines found in responses to this question suggest a popular orientation towards doctors that was more straightforwardly negative (and more negative than we might expect, given accounts of the decline of deference). Doctors were described by some panellists as incompetent. 'What have they accomplished?', asked a teacher from Gateshead. 'They cannot cure the common cold or the many forms of rheumatism or the influenza.'[71] Another panellist responded to MO's question as follows: 'A little scornful at their pretence at omniscience. Annoyance at their often arrogant manner. Contempt for their medicines and their inability to cure such things as a common cold, in spite of all their drugs.'[72] Doctors were also described by some panellists as self-interested – not only for opposing the foundation of the NHS but also for seeking a better social position through medicine. Our teacher from Gateshead continued:

They seldom go into the profession for love of it – just an easy life and a better social one. The patients are nothing to them ... Of course, being human, there are good men among them. But most are ignorant and they like their patients to be ignorant too. Mostly they are out for themselves and not for people's health.[73]

Such concerns – that doctors may be good or bad but many are ignorant and self-interested – were also expressed by this factory manager from Lancing:

[69] Panellist 1095, male, 69, railway draughtsman, Wilmslow.
[70] Panellist 1534, female, 47, farmer, Campbeltown.
[71] Panellist 1016, female, 58, teacher, Gateshead.
[72] Panellist 3650, male, 24, occupation not known, place of residence not known.
[73] Panellist 1016, female, 58, teacher, Gateshead.

Doctors . . . are divided into two groups about equal. Half are good, hard-working, reliable, and admirable men. The rest are bogus and use medicine as a means of climbing the social ladder. I think really that doctors have too much power in England. Their word is accepted as definite in too many quarters and mostly they don't know what they're talking about.[74]

This final extract captures much of how doctors appear to have been perceived around the middle of the twentieth century. They were thought to vary. Some were thought to be admirable. But many were thought to be self-interested, reactionary, and incompetent.

When writing about politicians and doctors, the range of panellists we sampled – who drew on cultural resources circulating in wider society to construct and express their understandings and judgements – did not sound particularly deferent in 1945. Instead, they sounded rather critical in two senses: careful to distinguish between different kinds of politician and doctor and quite willing to criticise politicians and doctors for their perceived failings (their selfishness, dishonesty, arrogance, ignorance). How does this compare with writing on scientists from the same dataset? The similarities are clear. Panellists may not have commonly distinguished between good and bad scientists, but they did commonly identify good and bad qualities of scientists. Put differently, a range of panellists repeated a certain way of describing scientists as admirable 'but' (that pivot again). Take this teacher from Watford: 'I think most of us feel that they are clever and brainy, but that most have one-track minds and are only clever in their special studies.'[75] Or this civil servant from Purley:

I have great admiration for scientists . . . But they often lack a wide background of knowledge and experience – due perhaps to too early and too complete specialisation. Now research is usually a team affair and one man is concentrated on a very small point for a very long time. It is a temptation to develop a one-track mind.[76]

Scientists were described as clever and brainy but with one-track minds. For one panellist, they were 'a mixed lot'.[77] Another responded to the question as follows: 'Scientists I talk of with a certain respect, although I also feel their outlook is often narrow.'[78]

Some MO panellists at this time were members of a new cadre of the scientifically engaged who emerged from the military regime of the Second World War (Savage 2010). Therefore, it is hardly surprising that some panellists described scientists in less mixed and more positive

[74] Panellist 2199, male, 40, factory manager, Lancing.
[75] Panellist 1048, female, 48, teacher, Watford.
[76] Panellist 1066, female, 38, civil servant, Purley.
[77] Panellist 1534, female, 47, farmer, Campbeltown.
[78] Panellist 3545, female, 28, clerk, Glasgow.

terms – such as this clerk from Edinburgh: 'I think that the future of society depends so much on the work of scientists and scientific planning and that they are very important.'[79] But we sampled a range of panellists to include young and old, men and women, from various occupational groups, and various regions of the UK. And some of these panellists described scientists in much less positive terms – which is just as unsurprising in its own way, given the immediate context of the Second World War. A clerk from Letchworth's response to the question was brief and to the point: 'Should not invent explosives.'[80] A nurse from Bristol responded to the question as follows: 'A conversation about scientists would find me deploring the fact that so many of their discoveries have been used for evil ends.'[81] For this teacher from Bingley, scientists 'prostitute their brains to make weapons of war more and more deadly'.[82] And for many panellists, scientists were described as 'inhuman',[83] 'not human enough',[84] or 'slightly inhuman'.[85]

These panellists often sound critical regarding scientists – as they did regarding politicians and doctors – in two senses: they distinguish between the 'good' and 'bad' qualities of scientists, and they condemn scientists for their perceived faults (using shared categories like the 'one-track mind' or the 'inhuman' scientist). Before summarising the picture for 1945, let us finally turn to writing about lawyers. Here, the cultural resources used were overwhelmingly negative in character. Panellists repeated a storyline that lawyers are dishonest. Our clerk from Edinburgh wrote of his own position: 'I feel that many of them are legal twisters. I don't trust them to any extent.'[86] A factory manager from Leek wrote of what he perceived to be the general position: 'Lawyers are regarded as thieves and liars.'[87] One respondent who did not take this position was an accountant from Sheffield who still felt the need to defend lawyers against 'the popular belief they are all fobbers'.[88]

Another storyline repeated by a range of panellists was that lawyers work to relieve clients of their money, often by dishonest means. In this line, lawyers are 'legalised highway robbers' who 'always get their fees'.[89]

---

[79] Panellist 1682, male, 25, clerk, Edinburgh.
[80] Panellist 1190, male, 73, clerk, Letchworth.
[81] Panellist 2466, female, 58, nurse, Bristol.
[82] Panellist 3120, female, 79, teacher, Bingley.
[83] Panellist 3230, male, 64, technical author, Coventry.
[84] Panellist 3034, female, 46, research laboratory assistant, Wembley.
[85] Panellist 1534, female, 47, farmer, Campbeltown.
[86] Panellist 1682, male, 25, clerk, Edinburgh.
[87] Panellist 2800, male, 40, factory manager, Leek.
[88] Panellist 2539, male, 44, accountant, Sheffield.
[89] Panellist 1095, male, 69, railway draughtsman, Wilmslow.

They are in the business of 'feathering their own nests' by 'making lawsuits draw out as long as possible'.[90] Most commonly, they are 'sharks'[91] or 'cold-blooded consumers of human flesh'.[92] Take this brief response from a teacher in Bingley: 'Sharks, pure and simple.'[93] Or consider this longer response from a clerk in Glasgow: 'Lawyers I regard as sharks who overcharge the unwary and who make their money out of unnecessarily complicated documents which they themselves produce to give a chance of money-making to other lawyers in the future.'[94]

Lawyers were almost universally condemned by the MO panellists, drawing on shared storylines (lawyers are dishonest) and categories (the shark). They were described using more straightforwardly negative terms than were politicians, doctors, and scientists. But these latter three groups were still often described using negative terms or at least mixed terms (for groups considered by panellists to be mixtures of 'good' and 'bad'). The overall picture of 1945, provided by volunteer writing for MO, is certainly not one of generalised deference – generalised to a range of objects representing authority or social standing (politicians, doctors, scientists, lawyers) but also generalised to a range of subjects (from the twenty-eight-year-old businessman in Torquay to the forty-seven-year-old farmer in Campbeltown to the fifty-eight-year-old nurse from Bristol to the seventy-nine-year-old teacher from Bingley).

To readers familiar with Almond and Verba's (1963) depiction of Britain in the late 1950s, this picture constructed from MO data may seem a little strange. Almond and Verba famously compared the more 'participant' civic culture of America to the more 'deferential' civic culture of the UK. But when recalling Almond and Verba's comparison, we should also recall their full depiction of Britain at this time, which was not of a straightforwardly deferential society but of a 'mixed' political culture – combining parochial, subject, and participant elements (consensus and diversity, moderation and change, traditionalism and rationalism). We should also set Almond and Verba's interpretation of their survey results from 1959 against other assessments of post-war British society. If we do this, we find that our picture of 1945 actually works to complement other existing accounts.

One such account is Richard Hoggart's (1957) study of the British working class between the First World War and the mid-1950s. Towards the beginning of this period, for Hoggart, such citizens were deferent in

---

[90] Panellist 1534, female, 47, farmer, Campbeltown.
[91] Panellist 2475, female, 60, lecturer, Norwich.
[92] Panellist 3359, male, 42, engineer, place of residence not known.
[93] Panellist 3120, female, 79, teacher, Bingley.
[94] Panellist 3545, male, 24, clerk, Glasgow.

some respects – cheerfully tolerant and fatalistic regarding life's hard-
ships – but not others. They distinguished between 'us' and 'them', where
'them' included the bosses and public officials who were not to be trusted
and who were to be debunked at every opportunity. Then, during the
course of this period, such citizens became less deferent as they became
more literate and mass publications used this improved literacy to encourage and persuade working people to favour 'the opinion' of 'the common
man' over the 'full understanding' of 'the intellectual'.

Another such account is found in the publications of Steven Fielding.
They use responses to polling by the British Institute of Public Opinion
(BIPO), alongside material collected by MO, to demonstrate
a widespread ignorance, indifference, apathy, and disengagement but
also alienation and cynicism in British society around the general election
of 1945 (Fielding 1992). They also use content analysis of 'political' films
released between 1944 and 1964 to demonstrate that mixture of deference and criticism first identified by Hoggart (Fielding 2008). These films
depicted figures of authority and social standing – politicians, civil servants, teachers, police officers, magistrates – who advanced themselves at
the expense of 'the little people', alongside examples of citizens who were
powerless in the face of such corruption.

Finally, in this context, it is worth mentioning Selina Todd's (2014)
history of the British working class. Todd notes that in 1945 the vast
majority of people in Britain were positioned as workers by capitalist relations of production. But they were not so much striving for respectability,
knowing their place, and making that place clean and tidy (as has been
suggested or implied by narratives of deference and its decline). Instead,
they were striving for autonomy from want and anxiety, for some of the
good things in life, for just a better life – by joining a picket line but equally
buying a pools coupon. Furthermore, these people had become conscious
of their class during the Second World War. They had mixed with each
other on the factory floor. They had come to realise their power in the
context of full employment. They had come to imagine the possibilities of
a better life by watching the Hollywood films now shown at cinemas.

Our picture constructed from volunteer writing for MO – which depicts
no generalised deference towards figures of authority and high social
status in 1945 – fits closely these accounts of distrust regarding
a corrupt 'them', a longstanding tradition of debunking such authority
figures, and a gathering will to power on the part of ordinary British
citizens. But how does this writing for MO in 1945 compare with writing
in response to a similar question asked of MO panellists in 2014?

Regarding politicians, panellists repeated the storylines familiar from
Chapter 4 – politicians are self-interested, not straight-talking, out of

touch, and all the same – using the strong terms familiar from earlier sections of the present chapter. For example, they described politicians less as talkers, gasbags, and orators, who play to the gallery, with the gift-of-the-gab (see Table 4.1), and more as liars and cheats. 'Typical characteristics of politicians include: 1. Lying', wrote a civil servant from Bath.[95] Here is the full set of characteristics from a concise writer in Johnstone: 'Liars, cheats, obstructive, obtuse, overpaid, fat cats in suits, shiny buffed-up faces (David Cameron).'[96] Then we have this university administrator from Newcastle: 'I do tend to associate politicians at the national level with lying, cheating, and feathering their friends' nests.'[97]

Politicians were described as liars and cheats. They were also described as 'bland, career-driven, manipulating, truth-benders, ego-maniacs, untrustworthy, corrupt, and full of double-standards'.[98] They were even described as 'a separate breed' for being 'cunning, arrogant, overly self-confident ... untrustworthy and unreliable, mean, selfish, and out for their own ends'.[99] This particular panellist, a broadcaster from Scotland, went on to write of politicians: 'If I shook their hand, I would need to count the number of fingers on my hand in case I had been robbed.'

Writing about politicians in 2014, panellists also mobilised the subject position of the citizen with strong negative feelings about politicians and politics. They were angry, like this factory worker from Lowestoft: '[I]t makes me angry that they claim for expenses. What do they spend their wages on!'[100] They were disgusted, like this student from Leeds: '[A]s a group they disgust me and I'd trust them about as far as I could throw them. Especially those from the three main parties.'[101] Then some panellists described their loathing for politicians and politics. A retired civil servant from East Boldon answered the question almost as if he was being asked specifically about his loathing of politicians: 'The thing I loathe the most about politicians in modern Western democracies is their dishonesty and slipperiness, and their abuse of language.'[102] Then we have a response from a locksmith in Northallerton that provides an insightful comment on many of the other responses in the archive: 'Politicians serve the very useful function of being people we can loathe.'[103]

---

[95] Panellist E5014, male, age not known, civil servant, Bath.
[96] Panellist J4793, female, 33, writer, Johnstone.
[97] Panellist B4290, female, 44, university administrator, Newcastle.
[98] Panellist M5198, male, 43, tree inspector, Harpenden.
[99] Panellist H1470, female, 60, broadcaster, Scotland.
[100] Panellist C2579, female, 69, factory worker, Lowestoft.
[101] Panellist S5202, male, 25, student, Leeds.
[102] Panellist M3190, male, 55, retired civil servant, East Boldon.
[103] Panellist R3546, female, 50, locksmith, Northallerton.

We have argued that citizens were not particularly deferent in 1945. In this respect, there was no golden age of political support in the UK immediately after the Second World War. But now it can be seen – or heard in the last three paragraphs – that something nevertheless changed between 1945 and 2014. Citizens may have become a little less deferent and more critical regarding politicians. But more than this, we hear something akin to rage in the voices of panellists – which are the voices of citizens more generally, insofar as panellists draw on widely available cultural resources in their writing (the storyline that politicians cheat and lie or the subject position of the angry, disgusted citizen). So the question is begged: Were responses to other figures of authority and high social status equally strong, emotional, and negative in 2014?

The brief answer to this question is 'no'. In fact, responses to doctors, scientists, and lawyers in 2014 were generally more positive than was the case in 1945. Let us begin with doctors. In 1945, the most prominent storyline was that doctors vary. Some are kind and attentive. Others are incompetent and self-interested. As a group, represented by the BMA, they constitute a reactionary force in society. So how did panellists write about doctors in 2014? They described doctors as caring. Listen to this restaurant worker from the East Midlands: 'I am very healthy, so have had little contact with them, but have found them honest, kind, and willing to listen.'[104] Or listen to this student from Walsall: 'I always view such people with a great deal of respect, because the caring nature of their job.'[105] Panellists also described doctors as professional. A local government officer from Sale wrote: 'Knowledgeable, trustworthy, professional, truthful. I would say that I would trust what the doctors said to me and would treat them with respect and respect for their opinions.'[106] Then we have this teacher from Stone: 'I associate doctors with the word "professional". Highly educated, dedicating their lives to the ailments of others. Fully deserving of the salary which accompanies the role they do.'[107]

The last line of this quotation – which refers to how doctors fully deserve their salaries – reminds us that MO asked this question at a particular historical moment (which contrasts to the immediate historical context of the 1945 directive, discussed previously). In early 2014, the NHS received plenty of news media coverage, largely focused on the UK's aging population and the so-called 'patient surge', rising costs and the so-called 'funding gap', and the pay of NHS staff (the subject of a dispute between Health Secretary Jeremy Hunt and the unions).

[104] Panellist H266, female, 91, restaurant worker, East Midlands.
[105] Panellist W5345, male, 18, student, Walsall.
[106] Panellist T4409, female, 35, local government officer, Sale.
[107] Panellist B5152, female, 22, teacher, Stone.

In this context, a prominent storyline repeated by a range of panellists in 2014 was that doctors are overworked and underpaid – and so are to be defended against their critics in the coalition government. This was the case – unsurprisingly, perhaps – for public sector workers like this local government officer from Cromer: 'Hard-working, caring, losing the fight to look after people under mounds of paperwork. I have great respect for doctors and think they work ridiculous hours ... for very little reward.'[108] But it was also the case for a range of other panellists: from a literary events coordinator in London ('overworked, caring')[109] to a retired banker in Brentwood ('overworked, many underpaid, generally reliable')[110] to this housewife from Newcastle: 'I regard doctors as knowledgeable and intelligent. I do believe the majority of doctors are well-meaning and interested in their chosen field ... I am a proud supporter of the NHS and hope it can be safeguarded.'[111]

It does not sound like citizens were raging against doctors in the same way they were raging against politicians in 2014. And the same can be said of scientists. In 1945, the prominent storyline was that scientists have 'good' and 'bad' qualities, and the bad include an association with modern weapons of war (which provided the prototypical figure of the 'inhuman' scientist with the 'one-track mind'). What cultural resources did panellists use to write about scientists in 2014? The long-running storyline that scientists are not quite human or at least a little strange was repeated occasionally. They are 'not so good at human relationships'.[112] They are 'a decidedly odd bunch'.[113] They 'find human relationships difficult'.[114] But the most prominent storyline, repeated by a range of panellists, was that scientists are professional, hard-working, and trustworthy and make an important contribution to society.

Consider the following two extracts:

Mad, exciting, cutting-edge, at the forefront of the world – leading health and environmental advances in things such as stem cell research, a cure for cancer, prosthetics, using 3D printing in operations! Hidden away from public view, white coats, detailed and laborious work. A methodological approach. Out of these professions, I have the most respect for scientists. They get to the lab, they do a job, they work intensely in strictly controlled environments, and they are shaping our real future.[115]

[108] Panellist C3691, female, 49, local government officer, Cromer.
[109] Panellist W5214, male, 28, literary events coordinator, London.
[110] Panellist R3422, male, 66, retired banker, Brentwood.
[111] Panellist R5429, female, 39, housewife, Newcastle.
[112] Panellist I1610, female, 70, retired nursery nurse, Ducklington.
[113] Panellist K5246, male, 45, railway signalling designer, Crewe.
[114] Panellist S2083, male, 83, retired shopkeeper, Lewes.
[115] Panellist J4793, female, 33, writer, Johnstone.

I consider them to be dedicated and studious. I also know that a good scientist never stops learning and searching for answers. I consider them to be important because of their contribution to society as a whole, because of new innovations, or finding solutions to long-lasting problems or cures for illness. Without scientists, society will stagnate and become useless.[116]

These extracts capture much of the most prominent storyline about scientists used by panellists in 2014. Scientists are dedicated and studious; involved in detailed, intense, laborious work; making advances and new innovations; contributing to society and shaping the future. In the words of other panellists, they are 'professional, knowledgeable, logical, methodical'.[117] They are known for their 'professionalism' and 'the contribution they make to society'.[118] By their 'dedication and knowledge', they are 'benefitting mankind'.[119]

Like the picture of doctors emerging from responses to the spring 2014 directive and unlike the picture of politicians, this picture of scientists is clearly favourable – and more favourable than the corresponding picture from 1945. To complete the comparison, let us consider lawyers. In 1945, the cultural resources used by panellists to write about lawyers were overwhelmingly negative in character (the storyline that lawyers are dishonest or the category of 'the shark'). In 2014, one set of cultural resources was equally negative in character. Lawyers may not have been described as 'sharks', but they were described as 'shysters',[120] 'vultures',[121] and 'blood-sucking parasites who would bleed you dry financially if given a chance to represent you in a court case'.[122]

However, taken as a whole, the descriptions of lawyers in the 2014 material were less overwhelmingly negative and more mixed than those in the 1945 material. A second storyline – less prominent but still repeated by a range of panellists in 2014 – was that lawyers are professional and knowledgeable. A pharmacist from Solihull wrote: 'I think of lawyers as knowledgeable and clever professionals who do their best for whoever their clients are, whether prosecuting or defending.'[123] A housewife from St Gennys wrote simply: 'Trustworthy, highly educated.'[124] And this local government officer from Sale described lawyers as '[p]rofessional,

[116] Panellist R5429, female, 39, housewife, Newcastle.
[117] Panellist T4409, female, 35, local government officer, Sale.
[118] Panellist E5014, male, 48, civil servant, Bath.
[119] Panellist P3209, male, 74, artist, Welton.
[120] Panellist R3422, male, 66, retired banker, Brentwood.
[121] Panellist W5214, male, 28, literary events coordinator, London.
[122] Panellist H1470, female, 60, broadcaster, Scotland.
[123] Panellist V3773, female, 52, pharmacist, Solihull.
[124] Panellist W3163, female, 56, housewife, St Gennys.

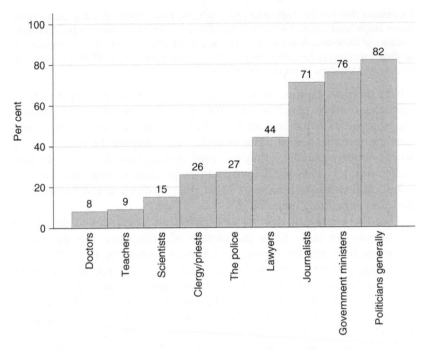

Figure 5.5 Do not trust to tell the truth, Ipsos MORI, 2016.

knowledgeable, confident, and truthful'.[125] She continued in direct response to the question: 'I would say that I would respect the solicitor's opinion and take their advice.'

The cultural resources used by panellists in their writing for MO suggest a less negative view of lawyers in 2014 than 1945. This was the case for scientists and doctors too. The rage against politicians we see in 2014 was not generalised to other figures of authority and high social status, just as we saw no generalised deference towards such figures in 1945.

This account of political exceptionalism in 2014 is consistent with available survey evidence. Since 1983, Ipsos MORI has regularly fielded a question asking people about their perceptions of the trustworthiness of various groups of professionals: 'Now I will read you a list of different types of people. For each would you tell me if you generally trust them to tell the truth, or not?' While levels of trust in the different groups fluctuate slightly from year to year, there is a good degree of structure in

---

[125] Panellist T4409, female, 35, local government officer, Sale.

the public's relative evaluations of trustworthiness. The figures for the survey fielded in 2016 are shown in Figure 5.5, which reports the percentage of respondents saying they generally do not trust particular groups to tell the truth. Here, we see the lowest levels of distrust for doctors, teachers, and scientists and the highest levels for journalists, government ministers, and 'politicians generally' (with clergy, lawyers, and police falling somewhere in between). These responses differ little from the original responses collected in 1983 – and in many years in between – by seeing politicians at the top of the league in terms of the least trusted groups in society.

Conclusions

In this chapter, we have used the writing of a carefully sampled range of MO panellists to establish the cultural resources circulating in society at two different historical moments: the mid-twentieth century (the so-called 'golden age' for British democracy) and the early twentieth century (the so-called 'age of anti-politics'). These cultural resources are summarised in Table 5.1, the contents of which are supplementary or additional to those of Table 4.1.

We have made an argument of two parts. First, we have completed our account of the rise of anti-politics in the UK. Negative sentiment held by citizens towards the institutions of formal politics has long been present, but over the past half century or so, it has increased in social scope (Chapter 3), political scope (Chapter 4), and intensity (the *strength* of this negative sentiment). In the period following the Second World War, many citizens approached formal politics with concerns about the self-interested motivations and lack of straight-talking of politicians but also with a reticence to judge politicians and governments. A prominent storyline

Table 5.1 *Additional cultural resources, 1945–1955 and 2001–2015*

	1945–1955	2001–2015
Storylines	Politicians and governments vary and are difficult to judge	Politicians are a joke, an embarrassment, to be ridiculed, not to be taken seriously
Categories	The difficult question	The gaffe
Subject positions	The citizen who takes little interest, knows little, and so cannot judge	The citizen who feels strongly about politicians, parties, elections, governments – angry, disgusted, depressed, full of loathing

of the time was that politicians and governments vary and are difficult to judge. A prominent subject position of the time was the citizen who takes little interest in politics, knows little about it, and so cannot judge politicians and governments. In the period following the turn of the twenty-first century, many citizens approached formal politics with concerns that politicians are self-interested, not straight-talking, out of touch, and all the same. They also now expressed these concerns in the strongest possible terms. A prominent storyline of this later period was that politicians are a joke, an embarrassment, to be ridiculed, and not to be taken seriously. A prominent subject position of the time was the citizen who feels strongly about politicians, parties, elections, and governments; who feels contempt, anger, disgust, depression, and loathing when faced by formal politics.

Second, we have begun to address the question of what explains this rise of anti-politics. Specifically, we have considered evidence for demand-side accounts focused on broad socio-cultural change, modernisation, the decline of deference, and the rise of critical citizens. What have we found? Citizens generally did not sound particularly deferent towards politicians in the mid-twentieth century. Actually, they sounded rather critical in various ways. They made negative judgements of politicians. Or they were reluctant to judge politicians and governments without more information. Or they discriminated between different kinds of politician. Furthermore, citizens generally did not sound particularly critical towards politicians in the early twenty-first century. They made negative judgements of politicians. But they also lacked seriousness in their engagement with politics. They were frequently embarrassed by politicians. In their ridicule of politicians, they were often led by elites – other politicians, journalists, comedians.

The conclusion reached is that many citizens felt discontented by formal politics in the early twenty-first century, but to an extent – with a strength – that is not easily explained by modernisation. Why should economic security or improved educational attainment lead to such contempt, anger, disgust, depression, and loathing? Furthermore, this rage of citizens was narrowly focused – on politicians, parties, governments (as opposed to doctors, scientists, lawyers) – in a way that, again, is not easily explained by broad socio-cultural change. This political exceptionalism is also not easily explained by some generalised shift in styles of communication (say, from a more hesitant and careful style to a more confident, self-aware, emotionally literate style).

6 Beyond Depoliticisation: The Persistent Force of Stealth Democratic Folk Theories

A Supply-Side Problem?

In this chapter, we continue our discussion of what explains the rise of anti-politics in the United Kingdom (UK) by considering evidence for existing accounts focused on broad political-economic change, which are sometimes called 'supply-side' accounts (e.g. Hay 2007, Norris 2011). In particular, we consider a set of influential theories focused on depoliticisation and post-democracy (see Crouch 2004, Hay 2007, Mair 2013, Mouffe 2005, Rancière 1999, Žižek 1999, Wilson and Swyngedouw 2014).

The authors, texts, and theories in this set vary by argument and position, but, taken together, they provide a potential explanation for the rise of citizens' negativity towards the activities and institutions of formal politics. It is claimed that politicians in the late twentieth century, in countries like the UK, generally came to believe three things. First, the end of the Cold War heralded the end of an era of ideological conflict and adversarial politics. Second, politicians were no longer best placed to govern societies – in the view of public choice theory and neoliberalism, where politicians, parties, and governments appear as both self-interested and inefficient (Hay 2007). Third, a new era had arrived, characterised by globalisation – by powerful global firms (Crouch 2004), new global problems (e.g. climate change), and global governmental actors appropriately scaled/networked to this globalising world (Held et al. 1999).

It is then claimed that politicians generally responded to these beliefs with a particular set of actions. They depoliticised issues and functions, relocating responsibility for them from the governmental sphere of elected politicians to the public sphere of agencies, boards, and commissions of bureaucrats and technocrats (Colin Hay's 'depoliticisation 1' – see Hay 2007). Or they relocated responsibility from the public sphere to the private sphere by way of privatisation (Hay's 'depoliticisation 2'). In addition, they replaced government with governance, characterised by policy networks, participation limited to approved stakeholders, and negotiations found opaque by most citizens (Offe 2006). Also, they refocused away from input legitimacy, based on citizen participation, towards a procedural legitimacy based on checks and balances, transparency, legality, and stakeholder access (Mair 2013).

Finally, it is claimed that such actions produced the particular condition in which we now find ourselves. There is consensus on what governments can and should do. Contestation, antagonism, and agonistic disagreement have disappeared – have been excluded or contained by narratives of necessity (Hay's 'depoliticisation 3'). Elected national governments have lost power. They have lost sovereignty, autonomy, and self-determination (Held et al. 1999). They have lost the ability to secure output legitimacy (Scharpf 2000). Citizens, unsurprisingly, have withdrawn from national political institutions, either by failing to participate in parties and elections or by joining insurrectional movements (Wilson and Swyngedouw 2014). This condition has been given various labels – behind which, of course, lie subtle differences of emphasis and argument – from 'post-democracy' (Crouch 2004, Rancière 1999) to 'post-politics' (Žižek 1999) to 'the post-political' (Mouffe 2005).

Given such theories of depoliticisation, what should we expect for each of the periods under consideration in this book? We should expect a mid-twentieth century 'golden age' of sovereign, active, effective government; political debate and choice; and citizens both satisfied and mobilised by such a positive supply of politics. Then we should expect an early twenty-first century 'age of anti-politics' characterised by small and ineffective government, opaque and distant governance, political consensus, and citizens disaffected by such a poor supply of politics.

In the rest of this chapter, we test these expectations against evidence from existing studies of British political history and our two datasets: volunteer writing for Mass Observation (MO) and responses to various public opinion surveys. We do find something of a golden age in the period immediately following the Second World War, characterised as it was by relatively active and effective government and political debate and choice (at least in the early years). And we do find a more recent period of relatively ineffective government, distant governance, and consensus or lack of electoral choice. But, contrary to expectations, we don't find much evidence that citizens in the mid-twentieth century felt positively towards the activities and institutions of formal politics because of the supply of politics at the time. And we find mixed evidence regarding the relationship between citizens' judgements of politics and the supply of politics in the early twenty-first century. Ultimately, we conclude that citizens' judgements of the supply of politics – and especially the extent to which parties are 'responsible' or responsive to citizens needs and preferences –

are mediated by their folk theories of democracy. And we argue that something akin to a 'stealth' understanding of democracy (Hibbing and Theiss-Morse 2002) has been a significant force in British politics for many decades. This folk theory encourages citizens to be disaffected with elite polarisation at least as much as elite consensus and to prefer coalitions of competent and independent leaders, working in the perceived 'national interest', at least as much as political debate and party competition.

In demonstrating these findings, we begin with the period 2001–2015, which overlaps with the period on which accounts of depoliticisation and post-democracy are most directly focused (usually the 1980s to the present day).

2001–2015: A Lack of Political Debate and Choice, But ...

Was the early twenty-first century a period of small and ineffective government, opaque and distant governance, and consensus or lack of political choice for citizens? Before we turn to the datasets used elsewhere in the book, let us consider some relevant historical events and associated commentary and historiography. If we do that, we learn that care should be taken when periodising history in such a way. The UK experienced numerous instances of government ineffectiveness – or perceived government ineffectiveness – in the decades prior to the late twentieth century. One such instance was the political-economic performance described in Michael Shanks' *The Stagnant Society*, published in 1961. The UK also experienced numerous moments of political consensus during the post-war period. One of these was described favourably by Daniel Bell in *The End of Ideology* – published in 1960, focused on 1950s America, but with an argument of broader relevance. That same moment was depicted less favourably in Herbert Marcuse's *One-Dimensional Man*, published in 1964 and focused on growing consensus but also a growing emphasis on questions of technique, productivity, and efficiency – questions of 'means' – over questions of politics and morality, or questions of 'ends' (described by Marcuse as 'depoliticisation'). We have already seen in Chapter 1 that a slightly later moment was also portrayed unfavourably by Trevor Smith (1972) – 1960s Britain, characterised by consensus, managerialism, and pluralism.

To repeat, care should be taken when periodising history in this way. Nevertheless, what can be said of the period since the late 1970s? Considering historical events and associated commentary and historiography, this period does look to have been characterised – *especially* characterised, *on balance* – by (perceived) government ineffectiveness, political consensus, and the rise of governance. Government ineffectiveness was a key theme for political commentators from the mid-1970s onwards. Anthony King (1975) wrote of an 'overloaded' national government. Geoffrey Mulgan (1994) wrote of an 'exhausted' national government. And if government seemed increasingly ineffective by the late twentieth century, then political consensus appeared to be increasingly pervasive too. The Cold War ended in 1991 and was quickly followed by pronouncements like Francis Fukuyama's (1992) *The End of History and the Last Man*. Tony Blair became leader of the Labour Party in 1994 and sought to move the party (further) onto the 'centre-ground' (as 'New Labour'). Intellectual justification for this was provided by Anthony Giddens' (1998) *The Third Way*. By the early 2000s, this way – self-styled as centrist, non-ideological, pragmatic – had also become the way of the Conservative Party, at least according to David Cameron, its leader from 2005 (Pierce 2005). Finally, during the same period, many perceived a shift from government to a distant and opaque governance. The UK had joined the European Economic Community in 1973. During the 1980s, Margaret Thatcher's Conservative government had privatised numerous parts of the British state. During the late 1990s and early 2000s, Blair's Labour government had practised a 'politics of depoliticisation' (Burnham 2001), including the reassignment of tasks (e.g. to the Bank of England, made independent in 1997), the external validation of policy (e.g. by the National Audit Office), and the acceptance of binding rules (e.g. from the European Union or EU).

To summarise the argument so far, there were certainly examples of government ineffectiveness and political consensus in the decades prior to the 1980s, but a brief consideration of historical events and associated analysis provides plenty of support for narratives of change – from the 1980s onwards – towards *especially* small and ineffective government, opaque and distance governance, and consensus or lack of political choice. Such narratives would include detailed studies of British political history like David Marquand's (2004) *Decline of the Public*. They would also include works of global synthesis like Eric Hobsbawm's (1994) *Age of Extremes*. Here, the UK is one of many national states 'eroded' since the early 1970s – 'eroded from above' by globalisation and 'eroded from below' by neo-liberal politicians. The UK is one of many national states facing increasingly complex problems and dependent increasingly on expert opinion. Hobsbawm describes this reorientation of politicians away from the public and towards elites – 'the political class' – as 'depoliticisation'.

We are now in a position to pose the next question in our sequence: If 'the age of anti-politics' was distinguishable by extraordinary depoliticisation – and even if that remains arguable in some respects and from certain historical perspectives – how, then, did citizens perceive the supply of politics during this period? Did they find it lacking? Did they wish for stronger national government, more political debate, greater party competition and electoral choice? We can begin to answer these questions by considering the cultural resources used by MO panellists to write about formal politics during the period. There was a storyline that government remains important, but only really for certain localities dependent on public services and certain people dependent on government benefits. There was a storyline that government faces a number of difficult problems at the moment – including terrorism and immigration – for which there are no obvious or easy solutions. And there was a storyline that national governments are now constrained in their ability to act – by the super-power of the USA or the rules and regulations of the EU or the mediation of large and dominant news organisations (owned by powerful individuals like Rupert Murdoch) or the assumptions of the post-2008 fiscal crisis (that public debt is too high, the deficit must be reduced, and this makes public spending generally unaffordable).

Taken together, these storylines indicate a view of national government as relatively limited. But these were not the most prominent, frequently repeated, fully developed storylines in the MO material. We now consider these most prominent storylines – of relevance to our theme of depoliticisation and post-democracy – in some detail. The first was a line that, since the 1990s, there has been a lack of difference between the platforms of the main parties, a lack of alternatives available to voters, a lack of electoral choice. There has been a lack of debate and position-taking by politicians regarding the issues of concern to many people. There has been a lack of representation for many people in the UK's party system. We covered some of this in Chapter 4 where politicians appeared as 'all the same' for not only their similar educational backgrounds, practices in pursuit of electoral success, and suspect motivations but also their similar beliefs and policies. There is more to cover here to develop the point in full.

One category in this storyline was 'New Labour'. It was used in the 2001 election diaries, when the term was relatively fresh. For example, a student from the North East wrote: 'We may as well live in a one-party state . . . There is nothing left of centre that I'd like to see and, by winning the public service debate, New Labour have the right of centre ground sewn up.'[1] She continued:

---

[1] Panellist B2917, female, 23, student, North East.

I voted New Labour but have come to realise that the New in Labour stands for disappointment. But even though this is the case, a Conservative option is no better ... what that does mean for someone like me is that if I don't like any option, I refuse to play a part. I find it difficult to respect a government with such a large majority that doesn't want to make radical changes as it is scared of what middle England would do. I'm not what New Labour sees as middle England so New Labour or indeed any of the political parties are not for me.

This panellist found New Labour to be 'right of centre'. She found no options on the 'left of centre', where she positioned herself. She perceived all the main parties to be focused on the swing voters and marginal constituencies of 'middle England'. Not identifying as middle England herself, she was minded to withdraw participation – 'to refuse to play a part' – regarding the coming election.

By the spring 2014 directive, the term 'New Labour' was no longer being used much by panellists – perhaps unsurprisingly, since it had been dropped by the party itself (when Ed Miliband became leader in 2010). But Labour's perceived rightwards move remained an essential part of the storyline. A retired typesetter from the South East wrote: 'When the next election arrives, I am going to find it very difficult to decide a party to support, for though I have always voted Labour, I feel now we have one Conservative and two Liberal parties.'[2] If the Labour Party had become a 'Liberal party' for this panellist, for another panellist – a housewife from London – it had become 'the Conservative Party in sheep's clothes'.[3] A care worker from Leeds went further still: 'I'm not going to vote for [Ed Miliband] because his policies seem to be trying to be more right wing than the Tories.'[4]

A second part of this storyline was that citizens were being offered nothing different, no viable alternative, little meaningful choice – not just by Labour but by all the main parties. In the 2001 election diaries, a Navy Lieutenant from Helensburgh reported how 'the Conservative Party didn't seem to have anything radically different to say ... so the Labour Party just got back in by default'.[5] A child carer from London made a similar assessment of the Conservative Party: 'I think the key issues in the election were education, health, asylum seekers, and the Euro, and I certainly did not feel the Conservative Party presented a viable alternative in relation to any of these.'[6] A decorator from Derby saw little difference between the attitudes of Labour and the

---

[2] Panellist H1806, male, 88, retired typesetter, South East.
[3] Panellist M3055, female, 39, housewife, London.
[4] Panellist M4780, female, 30, care worker, Leeds.
[5] Panellist H2480, male, 38, Navy lieutenant, Helensburgh.
[6] Panellist H2870, female, 38, child carer, London.

Conservatives but also between those two parties and the UK's third party of the time, the Liberal Democrats: 'We have no true choice. We see clearly there is so little difference in the attitudes of the three main parties, it has become immaterial who gets the prize – except to the politicians themselves.'[7]

These categories were repeated by numerous panellists in 2001 but also in responses to later directives. Consider the following two responses from spring 2010. 'I felt like there isn't much difference between the policies of the three main political parties.'[8] 'One of the Tory slogans is "Time for a change". I think this is fatuous rubbish. One should not vote just for the reason that it's "Buggins' turn". There must be a strong alternative policy, but I have not yet seen evidence of this'.[9] Then consider the following three responses from spring 2014: 'As time goes by, the differences between all the parties becomes more and more slight. They are all a bit of left and a bit of right';[10] '[Labour] have consistently failed to provide an alternative set of policies the public might be persuaded to vote for';[11] 'The reason turnout is low is that people can't see much difference between the parties these days, and so they don't have strong enough feelings'.[12] From a variety of panellists, across the entire period, we get a familiar set of complaints: there is no longer much difference between the policies of the main parties; and there is no real alternative offered by the opposition (whether the Conservative Party in the early 2000s or the Labour Party more recently).

A third part of this line was a set of claims about how the main parties lack clear values or principles and avoid certain issues or debates of concern to citizens. In his 2015 election diary, a retired film editor from Scotland wrote:

Repetition has been the order of the day, and yet many of the most significant issues have been neglected. Where were the environment? Climate change ... ? Trident? Europe? Even immigration (beyond puerile sloganising) – nowhere. As ever, real policy issues were either largely ignored or reduced to bullet-points. The word 'debate' has been abused by the media and politicians in favour of repeated sound-bites and outright lies shouted above the sound-bites of other 'debaters'.[13]

---

[7] Panellist R1418, male, 79, decorator, Derby.
[8] Panellist D3958, female, 28, secretary, Wallsend.
[9] Panellist P3209, male, 71, artist, Yorkshire.
[10] Panellist B5342, female, 28, unemployed, Salisbury.
[11] Panellist C3167, male, 42, warehouse worker, Stoke.
[12] Panellist C3691, female, 49, local government officer, Cromer.
[13] Panellist H1541, male, 70, retired film editor, Scotland.

We return to soundbites and mediated debates in Chapter 8. Here, our focus is on repetition by the main parties of slogans and 'bullet-points' while together they neglect or ignore 'the most significant issues'.

Many such claims became populated by a new character in 2014 and 2015: the United Kingdom Independence Party (UKIP). While not one of the UK's main parties, it came to represent for some panellists a set of things perceived to be lacking in those main parties. In spring 2014, a teacher from Kingston-upon-Thames wrote of the main parties: 'Despite what they say, none of them have addressed the points which UKIP have tapped into, namely that the UK is losing sovereignty to the EU.'[14] Then a housewife from St Gennys wrote of UKIP:

This party is giving people the opportunity to speak out against the Conservative and Labour parties. Without them, many issues would never be discussed as the main parties don't want to talk about them. This lot have forced issues such as immigration and the EU out into the daylight and made the other parties acknowledge that people have serious concerns.[15]

In spring 2015, a retired decorator from Derby wrote:

The more unlikely it is that I will ever again see Conservatives or Labour returning to strong moral principles, the less I wonder at the apathy of those who decide it is not worth the effort to go out and use their vote. I do believe, however, that more non-voters are coming to see some relief in the rise of UKIP.[16]

UKIP was positioned as the party addressing the points and issues about which 'people have serious concerns' – the EU and immigration. Through discussion of UKIP, the main parties were positioned as lacking a willingness to talk about what matters to people and as lacking 'strong moral principles' regarding such matters.

We now turn to the final part of this storyline: the subject position of the unrepresented voter. If the Labour Party has moved to the right, there is little difference between the main parties, the opposition offers no real alternative, and the main parties communicate few clear values and avoid debate regarding many of the salient issues of the day, then – notwithstanding the rise of UKIP – many citizens feel unrepresented in the UK's party system. A range of panellists described themselves, other people, or certain views as being unrepresented or not represented by the main parties. In 2001, for example, a student from Leeds remarked of the low turnout in that year's general election: 'I think a lot of non-voters are making a specific political point about their alienation from the

---

[14] Panellist P2915, male, 55, teacher, Kingston-upon-Thames.
[15] Panellist W3163, female, 56, housewife, St Gennys.
[16] Panellist R1418, male, 93, retired decorator, Derby.

democratic process and the fact that they don't feel represented by any of the political parties.'[17] In response to the next directive from MO on formal politics, fielded in spring 2010, a retired youth and community officer from Redbourn wrote:

Labour no longer represents many of my political views. In significant areas of policy – I am utterly opposed to them. Going to war in Iraq was wrong. Utterly wrong. Allowing the banks to operate by their own rules ... I could go on ... So – for the past 13 years (of the Labour government) – I have not had a natural 'political home' ... Labour was not a natural choice for me (I didn't leave them – they left me!).[18]

'I didn't leave them – they left me!' This exclamation succinctly captures the supply-side explanation for anti-politics outlined at the top of this chapter. It especially captures the claim that citizens perceive a consensus among the main parties, a lack of representation for certain views, and so have become disaffected with formal politics.

This category of 'political representation' was used in response to multiple directives. We finish with two examples from spring 2014. 'Surely there would be an increase in voting if ... there was a wider representation of what people want', wrote a podiatrist from Dunblane.[19] 'Labour really have lost touch with their roots as a party that represents working people – they're not left wing at all any more', wrote a care worker from Leeds.[20] And also two examples from spring 2015. This customer sales assistant from Midsomer Norton: '[N]o party truly represents the working people anymore.'[21] And this museum consultant from North Shields, reflecting on the general election of 2015: 'I am fed up with it ... I don't feel that I have any options available to me that represent my views.'[22] The claim is that certain groups or interests are no longer represented sufficiently by the main parties – not least because of Labour's move to the right (or to 'middle England') – and this explains citizens' disaffection and withdrawal.

Let us now summarise this first storyline. It was a line that Labour had moved to the right, the main parties now all occupied what they perceived to be the centre-ground, and voters were now offered little by way of meaningful alternatives and electoral choice. It was a line made up of categories like New Labour, the avoided issue, the unrepresented position/citizen, and – looming on the horizon – the populists of UKIP.

[17] Panellist J2893, female, 24, student, Leeds.
[18] Panellist C3603, male, 66, retired youth and community officer, Redbourn.
[19] Panellist E5296, female, 33, podiatrist, Dunblane.
[20] Panellist M4780, female, 30, care worker, Leeds.
[21] Panellist R556, female, 22, customer sales assistant, Midsomer Norton.
[22] Panellist C4131, female, 33, museum consultant, North Shields.

We can assume that such a line and set of categories were circulating widely in the UK during this period – were widely available to citizens as cultural resources from which to construct and express their understandings and judgements of politics – because they were repeated by numerous panellists, embedded in a range of networks and in response to multiple directives.

Now, if this was the only prominent storyline in the MO material from 2001 to 2015, and we had no means of historical comparison with material from the mid-twentieth century, we might conclude at this stage that evidence from MO supports those supply-side explanations for the rise of anti-politics. Citizens perceived a limited, small, ineffective national government and a lack of serious political debate and party competition. Citizens perceived a situation of depoliticisation and elite consensus and were disaffected by such a supply of politics. But there was a second prominent storyline in the MO material from the early twenty-first century. Before moving to conclusions, therefore, we now consider that second storyline as well as results from relevant public opinion surveys and also – in the next section – comparable material from the 1940s and 1950s.

The second prominent storyline in the MO material from 'the age of anti-politics' was quite different from the first. It was that political debate is not really necessary. It creates divisions that otherwise would not exist. Party political arguments are little more than petty squabbles. Or they are the battles of extremists. In this context, might not a coalition of moderates push the extremists to the margins and govern in the interests of all?

We start with a set of categories commonly used to describe political debate and argument. These first appear in the 2001 election diaries. Early in the campaign, a quality engineer from Bracknell was 'fed-up with the posturing of politicians'.[23] For a telephonist from Yarmouth:

Whether it's foot and mouth, the health service, education, whatever, there are too many arguments among the parties ... In all the debates, these arguments drone on and on interminably ... It's boring to read about all the parties squabbling with each other, and anyway, how will this solve any of the problems?[24]

Then we have this lorry driver from Southwick: 'The biggest annoyance with any election is the petty bickering between the parties.'[25] Political debate and argument were described as posturing, squabbling, and petty bickering and also 'back-biting', 'playground arguing', 'name-calling', 'point-scoring', and 'mud-slinging'. These categories were common to

[23] Panellist B1426, male, 65, quality engineer, Bracknell.
[24] Panellist N2058, female, 57, telephonist, Yarmouth.
[25] Panellist W2910, male, 34, lorry driver, Southwick.

election diaries from other years too. For example, in 2015, a retired aircraft engineer from West Dorset wrote: 'A very quiet few weeks election-wise in this part of the country, despite the usual mud-slinging between politicians that nobody around here seems to take much notice of; it certainly doesn't help their cause.'[26]

Now, it should be acknowledged that sometimes these categories were used not to dismiss political argument entirely but rather to distinguish between 'genuine' political debate – between different parties holding different positions – and manufactured political argument between parties all positioned on the centre-ground. Here, we have a link back to the storyline discussed previously. 'Slagging off' is what politicians do when they have no alternative ideas to offer.[27] 'Yah-boo posturing' is what politicians do when their policies are similar and thus difficult to argue about properly.[28]

Having said that, sometimes these categories were used, it would seem, precisely to dismiss political argument entirely. This brings us to a second part of the storyline: the category of 'the nation' or 'country' or (local) 'area', assumed to have one coherent set of needs and interests, at risk of artificial division by party politics. Some panellists wrote of 'the nation', like this technician from Bagstone:

At the time of Hume/Heath – 'one-nation' period, [the Conservative Party] worked for the nation's good. They may have done the wrong thing, but they usually did it for the right reasons. During the Thatcher period, they were nasty, vindictive, self-destructive ... and divisive.[29]

Some panellists wrote of the 'country', like this student from Gateshead:

I understand that the competition between the Labour Party and the Conservative Party is possibly the most famous British political rivalry, however their approaches disappointed me ... It seemed like they each cared more about beating each other than about what was best for this country.[30]

Then some panellists wrote of the local 'area', like this music teacher from Hebden Bridge: 'I decided I did not want the Labour Party to be returned, nor did I want the Conservatives. I voted for the Liberal Democrat as he was a local man and knew our area and needs.'[31]

Who would serve the nation, the country, or the local area best? For such panellists, it was not partisan politicians. It could be independent

---

[26] Panellist R1719, male, 71, retired aircraft engineer, West Dorset.
[27] Panellist W2910, male, 34, lorry driver, Southwick (spring/summer 2001).
[28] Panellist P3209, male, 71, artist, Yorkshire (spring 2010).
[29] Panellist S5292, male, 63, technician, Bagstone (spring 2014).
[30] Panellist R5583, female, 18, student, Gateshead (spring 2015).
[31] Panellist M1381, female, 69, music teacher, Hebden Bridge (spring/summer 2001).

politicians. Thus, when an independent candidate was elected in the general election of 2001, a nurse from Scotland wrote: 'I am very glad that an independent Member of Parliament was elected – oh for many more like him!'[32] Or it could be 'the wisest and cleverest people' from any party or none. Listen to this sales assistant from Shipley:

I suggest that instead of political parties, we choose some of the wisest and cleverest people throughout the land to run the country ... Both main parties spend too much time ridiculing each other ... When we were deciding who to vote for, both my husband and I thought that in our case we should vote for the man, regardless of party.[33]

These last two quotations come from the 2001 election diaries. By 2010, there was a new context that provided two more categories for this storyline. During the campaign for the general election of 2010, the polls were so close that a hung parliament was a real possibility. Media coverage of the campaign focused on this possibility and what the various parties would do in the event of a hung parliament (Kavanagh and Cowley 2010). That event came to pass, and the main parties entered coalition negotiations. The result was a coalition between the Conservative Party and the Liberal Democrats that survived until the general election of 2015.

One category provided by this context was 'coalition government'. During the 2010 campaign, a retired youth and community officer from Redbourn wrote: 'If only there was a space on my voting slip to put a cross for – "none of the above – prefer coalition".'[34] After the election and the outcome of coalition negotiations, a retired executive from London wrote: 'I really do wish them well. If there is anything this country needs right now, it's a long period of steady, stable government, with no bickering, name-calling, point-scoring etc.'[35] By the spring 2014 directive, a retired counsellor from the Fylde Coast was looking forward to the next general election: 'I would like to see a Lib-Lab coalition.'[36] In her 2015 election diary, a retired nursery nurse from Ducklington reflected on that next general election campaign: '[T]he three parties should have got together to work on tackling the financial problems.'[37]

If 'coalition government' was one category provided by the context of the general elections of 2010 and 2015, then a second category was 'extreme' politicians or policies, the likes of whom could presumably be

[32] Panellist T2150, male, 58, nurse, Scotland (spring/summer 2001).
[33] Panellist W571, female, 66, sales assistant, Shipley (spring/summer 2001).
[34] Panellist C3603, male, 66, retired youth and community officer, Redbourn.
[35] Panellist D1602, male, 67, retired executive, London.
[36] Panellist G226, female, 73, retired counsellor, Fylde Coast.
[37] Panellist I1610, female, 71, retired nursery nurse, Ducklington.

excluded from government where a coalition was formed in the national interest. From the 2010 election diaries, consider this from a cinema projectionist based in Hilton: '[I]f no one party has all the power and is forced to make deals and compromises, it's unlikely they will be able to bring in any extreme policies, which must be a good thing.'[38] Or this from a retired banker writing from Southwick:

I have always advocated that a coalition of all three parties would be best for the country, provided they could work together. This would prevent the extremes of their ideas being implemented. However, in practice they tend to bicker and try to score points off one another, instead of working for the good of the country.[39]

Here, we have displayed the various parts of our second prominent story-line: the positioning of party-political argument as bickering and point-scoring, the assumption of one united country with one coherent set of needs, the advocacy of coalition government, and the extreme ideas that could be excluded by such coalition-building.

Let us finish with some voices from 2014 and 2015. An air traffic services assistant from Southampton wrote: 'Why do people always want one extreme or the other? What you want is quiet, stable, sensible government that you almost don't notice is there, just quietly keeping the economy on track.'[40] Then we have this retired civil servant from Bolton: '[C]oalition government hasn't worked out at all badly, with the more extreme politicians of both parties effectively side-lined.'[41] Or take this marketing manager from Basingstoke: 'I think that the Coalition Government has been a good thing for the UK. One party has tempered the other.'[42] Or this orchestra director, looking forward to the general election of 2015: 'We will end up with a coalition that will make sensible decisions, that will water down the more extreme policies of whoever ends up involved.'[43] Coalition government was positioned as quiet, stable, sensible government that tempers, side-lines, or waters down the extreme policies of extremist partisans.

We are now in a position to summarise and reflect on these findings from the 2001–2015 period. A range of panellists, responding to multiple directives, commonly drew on two sets of cultural resources to write about the supply of politics in the early twenty-first century. One was a storyline that little difference now exists between the main parties. They

---

[38] Panellist D4101, male, 49, cinema projectionist, Hilton.
[39] Panellist S3035, male, 63, retired banker, Southwick.
[40] Panellist D4736, male, 47, air traffic services assistant, Southampton.
[41] Panellist M3190, male, 55, retired civil servant, East Boldon.
[42] Panellist P5340, male, 37, marketing manager, Basingstoke.
[43] Panellist G4373, male, 49, director of chamber orchestra, South West.

don't exhibit strong values or principles. They don't take clear positions on the issues of concern to citizens. They don't debate these issues. Voters are left with few alternatives and little electoral choice. Citizens are left without adequate representation in Parliament. A second storyline, however, was that little debate is needed between parties. Such debate is just petty squabbling, bickering, posturing, point-scoring, mud-slinging. The nation or the country or the local area has one set of needs. These are best served by independent leaders or coalition government. Such government does not create divisions where none existed – which is what party politics does – but rather side-lines the extremists (the unnecessarily partisan).

How do these findings compare with evidence from public opinion surveys? Regarding the first storyline, we have a question fielded in 1963 by the first British Election Study (BES) – and, in a similar form, at every general election since. Between 1963 and 1974, a period dominated by the Conservative and Labour parties, the question asked: 'Considering everything the parties stand for, would you say that there is a great deal of difference between them, some difference, or not much difference?' With the rise of the Liberals in the 1970s, a new question wording was introduced (1979 to 2015): 'Considering everything the Conservative and Labour parties stand for, would you say that there is a great deal of difference between them, some difference, or not much difference?' The percentage of respondents expressing the view that there is 'not much difference' between the parties is plotted in Figure 6.1. There are three things to note. First, perceptions of elite consensus do appear to have become more common since the late 1980s. Second, despite this trend, such perceptions were not as common in the early twenty-first century as they were in the 1960s. Third, in both periods, split by a period of perceived elite polarisation during the 1980s, perceptions of political consensus were common but by no means dominant (being expressed by roughly a quarter to a third of respondents). These points confirm what has already been argued on the basis of the MO material. Care should be taken when periodising history in the way done, often implicitly, by theorists of depoliticisation and post-democracy. A storyline of elite consensus circulated widely in the early twenty-first century but was by no means dominant and constituted just one of two prominent storylines about party politics at this time.

The prominence of both storylines is further confirmed by BES data collected since 2001. These survey questions asked people if they agreed or disagreed that parties 'don't tell people about the really important problems facing the country', 'don't offer voters real choices in elections because their policies are pretty much all the same', 'spend too much time

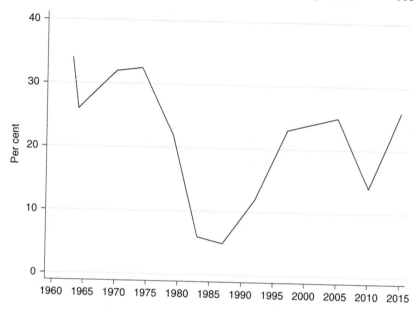

Figure 6.1 Not much difference between the parties, BES, 1963–2015.

bickering with each other', 'do more to divide the country than to unite it', and 'are more concerned with fighting each other than with furthering the public interest'. In Figure 6.2, we plot the percentage of people indicating that they either agree or disagree with the first four of these statements (combining the responses for 'agree' and 'agree strongly' and for 'disagree' and 'disagree strongly'). Across the first two of these questions, plotted in the top panels of Figure 6.2, substantially more citizens agreed than disagreed with statements tapping perceptions of a lack of political choice and that parties are not straight with voters about the problems facing the country (see also Figure 4.5 for similar evidence collected by the British Social Attitudes survey). At the same time, a majority of citizens concurred with statements tapping perceptions of party politics as divisive, as shown in the lower panels of the figure. This is also the case for the last question listed previously – about whether parties and politicians are more concerned with fighting each other than furthering the public interest – which was only asked in 2015 and the response to which is shown in Figure 6.3.

What are we to make of these two contrasting storylines, prominent in volunteer writing for MO and confirmed in their prevalence by survey research? The first storyline reminds us of the supply-side explanations for the rise of anti-politics introduced at the top of this chapter. Indeed, it

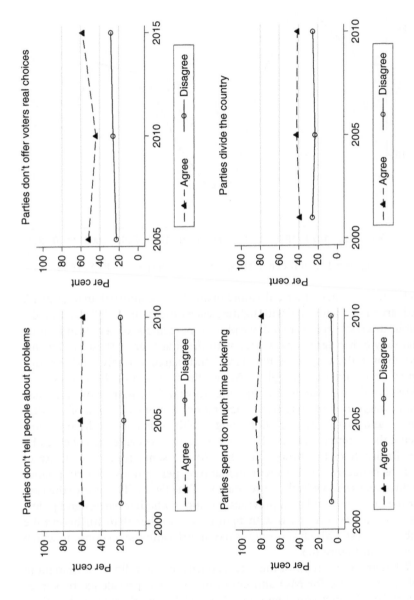

Figure 6.2 Public opinion about political parties, BES, 2001–2015.

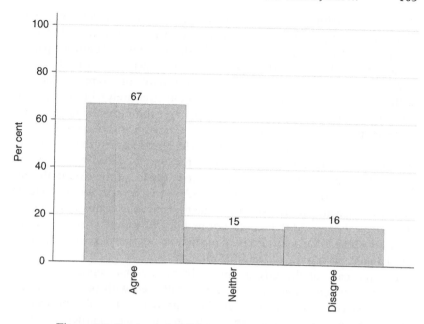

Figure 6.3 Parties and politicians in the UK are more concerned with fighting each other than with furthering the public interest, BES, 2015.

provides evidence to support those explanations. There was a view taken by many citizens that *politics had left them, so they were leaving politics.* National government had become small and ineffective, governance had become distant and opaque, but, most importantly, politics had become characterised by consensus and a lack of electoral choice.

However, the second storyline – and the two storylines taken together – remind us of another literature. There has been a long-running debate in political science about 'responsible parties'. This probably began in 1950 when the American Political Science Association's (APSA) Committee on Political Parties argued that, for parties to be responsible to their electorates, they need to be cohesive and have distinctive programmes offering a clear alternative to competing parties (APSA Committee on Political Parties 1950). Otherwise, voters at elections don't know quite what they are voting for (or against) and cannot hold parties responsible for their proposals and actions. This apparently was the situation in 1940s America. There was not enough party responsibility because the parties operated only as loose associations of state and local organisations, with little national machinery, cohesion, or programme. There was a fear among APSA members that extremist parties would take advantage of this situation with clear programmes at either end of the left-right spectrum, producing an undesirable cleavage in American society (ibid.).

Since 1950, debate has focused on the distance needed between parties for a responsible party system: too close and citizens may leave the main parties for extremist parties with more distinctive programmes (or may withdraw from engagement with formal politics entirely); but too distant and citizens may view the main parties as extremists themselves and become disaffected with perceived unnecessary polarisation among political elites. For example, David King (1997) has argued that American citizens remained consistent in their preferences for centrist policies and political compromise during the last three decades of the twentieth century, but the two main parties in the USA moved away from the political centre and became more extreme in their positions over the same period. The result was a void that could not be filled by a third party, given the hostility of the US electoral system to small or new parties, so it was filled by citizens' frustration, alienation, and cynicism.

For the case of the UK in the early twenty-first century, we have presented evidence that citizens were disaffected with politics because of a perceived consensus between the main parties but also because of perceived unnecessary polarisation between those same parties. What are we to conclude from this? On the one hand, it may still be that anti-politics is explained by the supply of politics, if in more complex and paradoxical ways than is often appreciated. On the other hand, it may be that contemporary anti-politics in the UK is not fully and best explained by theories of depoliticisation and post-democracy. Before we develop these conclusions, however, let us now consider the evidence for our comparison period: 1945–1955. Was this a period of sovereign, active, effective government, political debate and choice, and citizens satisfied and mobilised by such a supply of politics – as theories of depoliticisation and post-democracy would lead us to expect?

1945–1955: A Wealth of Political Debate and Choice, But . . .

Following the structure of the previous section, we begin by considering some relevant historical events and associated commentary and historiography. In doing so, we find many reasons for thinking of the immediate post-war period as one of (apparent) strong and effective national government. David Kynaston (2007: 22) describes 1940 as 'arguably the British state's finest hour'. It mobilised for war, introduced rationing in a way that was generally perceived as equitable, and created numerous ministries. 'The 1945 moment', for Kynaston (p437), found 'the state fresh from its finest hour and now offering the opportunity to transform society'. In 1946, the National Health Service (NHS) was established. That same year, the Bank of England, the coal mines, and civil aviation were nationalised. We also find reasons for thinking of this period as one of political debate and struggle. The Second World War had been, for many, a fight against fascism. By the end of the 1940s, the Cold War was becoming, for many, a fight against communism.

Like in the previous section, however, we also find plenty of reasons to be cautious about periodising history in this way. Despite victory in the Second World War, in the late 1940s many British citizens still remembered the Great Depression (1930–1931) and how ineffective government could be in the face of unemployment (Kynaston 2007). The mid-twentieth century was also a moment of internationalisation and the sharing of power by nation-states with inter-governmental organisations (from the International Monetary Fund to the United Nations to the North Atlantic Treaty Organisation). Finally, if this period was characterised by ideological war at the European or global scale, then it was also characterised by much political consensus and compromise at the national scale.

For G R Searle (1995), the early 1940s were characterised by antipathy towards partisanship in British politics. The war-time commandeering of property, food rationing, and conscription of labour was thought to require total unity. This antipathy was led by Churchill himself, who was never really a party figure and saw himself more as 'father of his people' (ibid.). Indeed, when Churchill did introduce a partisan note to his campaigning for the general election of 1945, this partisanship was viewed by many as being out of keeping with the shared suffering and sacrifices of war and also the respected war-time coalition government (McCallum and Readman 1947). With Labour having won that election, the Conservative Party adopted its Industrial Charter (1947), committing them to full employment and the welfare state. In the general election of 1950, the manifestos of Labour and the Conservatives differed in emphasis but not substance (Nicholas 1951). Finally, in 1954, *The Economist* coined the term 'Butskellism' to capture the similarity in policies between Richard (Rab) Butler (Chancellor for the incumbent Conservative Government) and Hugh Gaitskell (Chancellor for the previous Labour Government). The term captured what historians would later refer to as the post-war 'consensus' or 'settlement' (e.g. Addison 1975) – driven by memories of economic hardship during the 1930s and collectivist achievement during the Second World War and focused on full employment, Keynesianism, the mixed economy, and the welfare state (ibid.).

Considering such historical events and associated commentary and historiography, the mid-twentieth century does look to have been a period of strong national government and ideological conflict. But it also looks to have been a period of new governmental actors at the international scale and significant political consensus at the national scale. The picture, it would seem, was more mixed than is often implied by theories of change from a post-war period characterised by politicisation and democracy to a later period characterised by depoliticisation and post-democracy. That being said, perhaps the more important question – as we saw in the previous section – concerns *how citizens themselves perceived things at the time*. Did they perceive a sovereign, active, effective government? Did they perceive sufficient political debate and electoral choice? Were they satisfied and mobilised by such a supply of politics?

We start, again, by identifying the cultural resources used by MO panellists to write about formal politics during the period. There was a storyline that national government is important, and is becoming more important, because of nationalisation. There was a similar storyline that local government is important because, increasingly, it provides local services that 'touch the lives' of citizens (housing, roads, schools, antenatal clinics, maternity homes, libraries, water, electricity). There was also a contrasting storyline that government is constrained by post-war conditions – including the need for rationing and controls, whichever party is in government.

But let us focus on the two most prominent sets of cultural resources found in the MO material from the mid-twentieth century – the two storylines and associated categories most frequently repeated and fully elaborated by a range of panellists in response to multiple directives. The first was a storyline that Labour and the Conservatives, the two main parties, represent different sections of the population, different political ideologies, and different programmes for government. What were these different sections of the population? They were the different social classes produced by the industrial capitalism of the period. We see this in the 1945 election diaries, where a librarian from Evesham described Labour as 'a working class movement' and wrote: 'In my particular department, the tone is predominantly Labour, with a sprinkling of Tory diehards who are Tory because they hate socialism.'[44] A domestic nurse distinguished between 'the Conservatives – the majority of whom are "haves" [and] object sharply to nationalisation', and 'the Labour "have-nots"' who 'advocate' for nationalisation.[45] Similar language was used by

---

[44] Panellist 3119, female, 21, librarian, Evesham.
[45] Panellist 3402, female, 40, domestic nurse, Leicestershire.

this office worker from Blackpool: 'I believe the Tories are mainly interested in looking after the upper classes – the Socialists are mainly interested in looking after the workers, especially the "have-nots".'[46] She continued: 'I think the Labour Party will do a lot for this country, given the chance, especially for the man in the street.'

The Labour Party was associated with the working class, the workers, the 'have-nots', the man in the street. It was associated with socialism and nationalisation. By contrast, the Conservative Party was associated with the upper classes, the 'haves', and opposition to socialism and nationalisation. We see this again in responses to the June 1947 directive. When asked about the Conservative Party, a clerk from Letchworth wrote: 'I suggest the capitalists and their policies which seem to be against working people having control.'[47] When asked about the Labour Party? 'I agree with nationalisation of public services to prevent private profit and exploitation.' A lieutenant from Dartford took a less favourable view of Labour, but did so using familiar categories: 'Socialism ... I have been fighting against National Socialism for seven years; the red light is already glowing dully in this country; it's a matter of time and degree ... Workers are the new and more dangerous parasite.'[48] Then we have this youth leader from Porthmadog, who in his response took all the main parties altogether: 'I imagine that our three main parties now represent on a broad basis the three main classes of our people – the Conservatives for the landed and industrial class, the Liberals for the middle class and small trader,[49] and Labour for the average working man.'[50]

For many panellists, political competition between the Labour Party and the Conservative Party reflected and captured societal competition between capitalists or the landed and industrial class on the one hand and, on the other, working people or workers or the average working man, now advocating for socialism and nationalisation. These categories were commonly used again in responses to the August 1949 directive. For this office worker from Orpington, the Labour Party represented '[r]eckless spending, too much nationalisation, hatred of everyone not their own class ... the over-heavy burden of taxation'.[51] For this housewife from Birmingham, '[the city] suffered so badly through capitalists owning our

---

[46] Panellist 3640, female, 31, office worker, Blackpool.
[47] Panellist 1190, male, 75, clerk, Letchworth.
[48] Panellist 3635, male, 26, lieutenant, Dartford.
[49] The Liberal Party was Britain's third party during this period, but they never won more than twelve seats at a general election, and were often treated as only a minor party – for example, during allocation of party election broadcasts on BBC radio (Nicholas 1951).
[50] Panellist 4146, male, 32, youth leader, Porthmadog.
[51] Panellist 1015, female, 74, office worker, Orpington.

industries'.[52] She continued: 'I shall vote Labour.' Such categories were also commonly used in responses to the November 1950 directive. Panellists were asked to 'give an account' of their 'political outlook and sympathies'.[53] A steel worker from Kilbirnie wrote: 'Labour Party as my father was a socialist, I was raised to recognise that anything the working man got would have to come out of the pocket of the rich.'[54] A shoehand from Maresfield wrote: 'I have always been socialist in outlook and I have never considered changing. Why am I socialist? Because in the first place I belonged to the working class.'[55] Finally, listen to these two panellists, a warehouseman/commercial traveller followed by a commercial artist:

I have always felt that I have had a raw deal at the hands of the moneyed classes and, by extension, at the hands of the members of the Conservative Party. On the other hand, I have always been socially minded, desiring a better deal for the under-dog, and have seen in the Labour Party the better of the two instruments to carry this policy into effect.[56]

I was apprenticed to Process Engineering at the age of 15 and joined the trade union, of which I have been a member for over 30 years. My contacts with trade unionists gave me the impression that there was a constant cold war between the Employers and their Employees. This gave me a left bias which is so strong that I cannot imagine myself voting Conservative under any circumstances.[57]

The Conservatives were viewed as representing the capitalists, the rich, the moneyed classes, the employers. Labour was viewed as representing the working class, the working man, the under-dog, the employees (and also socialism and nationalisation; or, for some, burdensome taxation and excessive government spending).

If the two main parties represented different sections of capitalist-industrial society, they also represented different political ideologies and programmes for government. We now demonstrate more fully these latter parts of the storyline. Panellists often justified their support for the Labour Party in terms of their own socialism. For example, in June 1947, a teacher from Great Missenden wrote: 'As a socialist, I am in general agreement with the policy of the Labour Party.'[58] Or in November 1950, a railway draughtsman from Paignton wrote: 'I am LABOUR. I have been a Socialist since my teens and never been anything else.'[59] Indeed, the Labour Party was associated so closely with socialism during this period that often it was

[52] Panellist 2254, female, 48, housewife, Birmingham.   [53] Directive SxMOA1/3/130.
[54] Panellist 1393, male, 41, steel worker, Kilbirnie.
[55] Panellist 2713, male, 40, shoehand, Maresfield.
[56] Panellist 2921, male, 28, warehouseman and commercial traveller, Leicester.
[57] Panellist 4042, male, 47, commercial artist, place of residence not known.
[58] Panellist 1056, female, 65, teacher, Great Missenden.
[59] Panellist 1095, male, 74, railway draughtsman, Paignton.

referred to simply as 'socialist' or 'the socialists'. For example, in August 1949, a teacher from Boscastle reported: 'I voted Socialist.'[60] Looking forward to the next general election, an officer worker from London wrote: 'I shall vote Socialist.'[61] Or listen to this from a Conservative Party supporter located in Birmingham: 'I am very anxious to see the Socialists out of office.'[62]

Distinctive policies and values were also associated with the two main parties. The Labour Party was associated with nationalisation. When asked about the main parties in June 1947, a domestic worker from Dartmouth wrote of the Labour Party: 'I agree with Labour Party policy – nationalisation of transport etc.'[63] A nurse from Steyning wrote of the Labour Party: 'I believe in the nationalisation of the mines and the Bank of England.'[64] Also of the Labour Party, a buyer from Matlock declared: 'I am a supporter of the Labour Party and approve of their belief in nationalisation of basic industries and public utility services.'[65] Throughout the period, supporters of the Conservative Party contrasted nationalisation to free enterprise or freedom in general. In November 1945, for example, a housewife from London wrote: 'I am becoming violently anti-socialist and feel that we're all in danger of losing our liberties and becoming almost totalitarian ... It is said that equality and freedom cannot exist side by side. Then give me freedom everyday.'[66] Or in June 1947, a farmer from Chelmsford wrote:

I cannot agree with the Labour Party's policy to nationalise all key industries. When the government takes control, everything is slowed up, the wheels of the machine become clogged with red tape. As Government stands the expense, all costs are wasteful, extravagant, out of all proportion to what can be done under private enterprise.[67]

A further example is this from a Conservative-voting sales executive in November 1950: 'Socialism puts a premium on efficiency and enterprise, and superimposes the dead weight of bureaucracy on an unwilling electorate.'[68]

This storyline, then – that Labour and the Conservatives represent different sections of the population, political ideologies, and programmes for government – was made up of numerous categories: the various social

---

[60] Panellist 2859, female, 52, teacher, Boscastle.
[61] Panellist 3640, female, 35, officer worker, London.
[62] Panellist 1216, male, 42, buyer, Birmingham.
[63] Panellist 1642, female, 42, domestic worker, Dartmouth.
[64] Panellist 1980, female, 67, nurse, Steyning.
[65] Panellist 4236, female, 59, buyer, Matlock.
[66] Panellist 2916, female, 54, housewife, London.
[67] Panellist 3653, male, 66, farmer, Chelmsford.
[68] Panellist 4870, male, 37, sales executive, place of residence not known.

classes, socialism, capitalism, nationalisation, free enterprise. These categories were repeated in writing from across the period by a range of panellists. Their prominence suggests a common view of politics at the time – that national government is important and the main parties offer citizens a genuine choice (of who should govern, in the interests of whom, and with what programme for government). This view is expected by theories of depoliticisation and post-democracy, which imagine a post-war period of strong government, political debate, and electoral choice. As such, the material presented so far in this section is broadly supportive of such theories.

However, there was a second, equally prominent storyline in the MO material from 1945 to 1955. This was a line – also repeated frequently and often developed at length – that democracy is important and citizens have a duty to participate (see Moss et al. 2016), but party politics is problematic in various ways. It limits the freedoms of individual politicians. In doing so, it discourages people of merit from standing for election. It also denies the existence of one common good. In this context, party politics equates to unnecessary talk. Action is needed and is best taken – for the good of the country as a whole – by national government, or coalition government, made up of independent candidates, or at least statesmen (as opposed to partymen). Some of this line will sound familiar to readers of the previous section. Before we discuss the two periods together, let us first demonstrate this alternative line from the mid-twentieth century.

In May 1949, MO asked panellists the following question: 'What is your attitude to the principle of obedience to "party line"?'[69] Responses included some arguments that parties and party discipline are needed because citizens generally vote for party representatives (not individuals), and governments need votes in Parliament in order to get anything done. But responses also included many expressions of significant discontent with party politics. Party discipline was perceived to require that politicians go against their conscience. This was judged to be wrong – by this medical inspector from Northallerton, for example: 'I don't believe that anyone should vote against their conscience and I think the whip system in Parliament is very wrong. I would never enter Parliament except as an independent on this account.'[70] It was judged to be wrong because going against one's conscience is dishonest, as expressed by this housewife from Sheffield: 'A man who is against his conscience is dishonest. That is for me the flaw in party politics and the

---

[69] Directive SxMOA1/3/121.
[70] Panellist 3426, female, 50, school medical inspector, Northallerton.

chief reason why I could never join a political party.'[71] It was judged to be wrong also because to ask someone to go against their conscience is to limit their freedom and so to go against the freedom associated with democracy. A housewife from Sevenoaks responded to MO: 'This is a difficult question to answer because I so strongly disapprove of "party". To have to be obedient to a party programme against one's own conscience leaves one without our toasted democratic freedom.'[72] Now listen to these two panellists, a youth leader followed by a sales organiser:

In all cases where the principle of 'partyline' comes against conscience, I would much rather have a man ... express his own truthful opinion than to force him to abandon his scruples for the sake of party unity ... No party is infallible, and unless that party gives scope to individual conscience and opinion, we may as well scrap democracy and have a dictatorship.[73]

I think political doctrines should be for education and guidance of members, not a yard-stick or straight-jacket for their conduct ... No group of people, I almost state emphatically no two persons, agree in equal degree on any subject or group of subjects. I consider that such insistence on obedience is a forerunner to 'nationalism' and eventually of Communism and other forms of police state dictatorship.[74]

These panellists were discontented with party politics – and specifically party discipline – because it required that politicians and party members go against their conscience, be dishonest, and submit to constraints associated more with dictatorship than democracy.

Panellists were also discontented because such requirements and constraints discouraged people of merit from standing for election and so favoured lesser individuals – with implications for the quality of government received by citizens. This was the concern of one clerk from Glasgow, writing in 1949 and looking forward to the general election of 1950: 'I shall probably vote for the man I consider the best candidate, irrespective of party. I feel strongly that the present Parliament is made up of non-entities and yes-men ... [S]o many candidates slide into Parliament simply on the party label.'[75] It was also the concern of one hospital worker from Penzance, when asked about municipal elections in November 1945: 'I deprecate the importation of party politics into local affairs; merit should be the sole test.'[76]

---

[71] Panellist 1669, female, 47, housewife, Sheffield.
[72] Panellist 2892, female, 56, housewife, Sevenoaks.
[73] Panellist 4146, male, 34, youth leader, Porthmadog.
[74] Panellist 4512, male, 52, sales organiser, place of residence not known.
[75] Panellist 3545, female, 32, clerk, Glasgow.
[76] Panellist 2703, male, 60, hospital worker, Penzance.

Indeed, responses to the November 1945 directive suggest a particular discontent with party competition and discipline in local politics. A lecturer from Norwich wrote on behalf of herself and her husband: 'We both think municipal elections are important. I regret the fact that they are political. I think local government should not begin on such narrow party lines.'[77] A domestic nurse from Leicester wrote: 'I think municipal elections are important but completely ruined in principle by the political party idea which has got into them. Local govt should be non-party.'[78] Some panellists even used the term 'party' like a negative adjective to express their discontent with local politics. This from a researcher in Wembley: 'I do realise that [municipal elections] should be more important to me, but I am so little interested in politics and local m. elections do tend to become more and more "party".'[79] And this from a housewife in Bradford:

The Bradford City Council is run purely and simply on party political lines – with 'whips' and all the rest of the indecent party methods . . . 'Party' politics rule every move. There is no working together whatsoever. Every question which is raised is thrashed out in the most venomous, vindictive, 'party' manner.[80]

Whether national or local in scale, politics and government were described by many panellists as being dominated by parties, which in turn were described as promoting 'rigid' or 'narrow' party lines, 'nonentities' and 'yes-men' over 'best candidates' of 'merit', and party competition over 'working together'.

Why might panellists have thought 'working together' possible (and party politics unnecessary)? This brings us to a second part of this line that democracy is important but is undermined by party politics. It brings us to the category of 'the common good' or 'the country as a whole'. This family of categories was used by panellists when writing about local politics in November 1945. The housewife from Bradford, quoted previously, wrote: 'The municipalities are in the absolute power of the cliques – spending their energies and the citizens' money in fighting each other rather than in working together for the common weal.'[81] Asked if he considered his local council 'to be a good or bad one',[82] a commercial traveller from Leamington Spa replied: 'I consider this council to be a bad one as it is not a balanced one. Too many with stakes in boosting the place in a manner which might well not be to the benefit of

---

[77] Panellist 2475, female, 60, lecturer, Norwich.
[78] Panellist 3402, female, 40, domestic nurse, Leicester.
[79] Panellist 3034, female, 46, researcher, Wembley.
[80] Panellist 2903, female, 49, housewife, Bradford.   [81] Ibid.
[82] Directive SxMOA1/3/88.

the townspeople at large dominate too many of the committees.'[83] Such categories were also used by panellists when writing about national politics. In July 1947, a farmer from Chelmsford wrote of the Labour Government: 'The government seem to be too class conscious, instead of running the business of the country for the benefit of the country as a whole.'[84] In July 1950, a commercial traveller from Leicester wrote of Stafford Cripps (Labour Member of Parliament and Chancellor of the Exchequer): '[A] conscientious, able politician who sometimes allows political philosophy and expediency to usurp the place of the common economic good.'[85] Also, in November 1950, the manager of a textile mill in Loughborough wrote of Labour and the Conservatives: '[B]oth ... parties seem to represent sections of the community and not the interests of the country as a whole.'[86]

Many panellists imagined one 'common economic good' or 'common weal' and expected politicians to serve 'the townspeople at large' or 'the country as a whole'. Having done so, they viewed party competition and political argument as just unnecessary talk – a game created by politicians looking to make themselves appear useful. In February 1945, a housewife from Ogmore-by-Sea described politics as 'a dirty game and largely talk anyway'.[87] The May 1945 election diaries are full of complaints about party political argument described as 'accusations and counter accusations'[88] or 'justifying and defending themselves' or 'slanging individuals'[89] or 'an unnecessary war of class against class' or 'squabbles about proceedings or past grievances' or 'animosity ... whipped up'[90] or 'lying propaganda'[91] or 'constant dissention' or 'finding fault'.[92] If one category was repeated more than any other, it was 'mud-slinging'. A housewife from South East England wrote: 'I hate party mud-slinging.'[93] An electrical engineer from Ringwood wrote: 'I am sure this mud-slinging is not liked and gives people a bad view of politics.'[94] A member of the armed forces reported from Manchester on how 'many are tired of the mud-slinging and argument'.[95] A civil engineer

[83] Panellist 3438, male, 37, commercial traveller, Leamington Spa.
[84] Panellist 3653, male, 66, farmer, Chelmsford.
[85] Panellist 2921, male, 27, commercial traveller, Leicester.
[86] Panellist 2576, male, 40, manager of textile mill, Loughborough.
[87] Panellist 3137, female, 34, housewife, Ogmore-by-Sea.
[88] Panellist 1056, female, 63, teacher, Wycombe.
[89] Panellist 2684, male, 37, goods packing manager, Belmont.
[90] Panellist 3402, female, 40, domestic nurse, Leicestershire.
[91] Panellist 1644, female, 59, housewife, Coventry.
[92] Panellist 3432, female, 66, domestic worker, Ware.
[93] Panellist 3388, female, 54, housewife, South East.
[94] Panellist 1165, male, 39, electrical engineer, Ringwood.
[95] Panellist 2385, male, 30, armed forces, Manchester.

from the East of England recorded his surprise at the 'absence of mud-slinging' in his local constituency.[96]

The storyline was that if one common good exists, then party politics is unnecessary. Such a view helps to explain popular reaction to the general election of 1945. It was held after victory in Europe but before victory over Japan. For many, it should have been delayed. Listen to this from the May 1945 election diary of a domestic nurse in Leicestershire: '[T]he coalition should have continued until the end of the Japanese war. International affairs are in a state too precarious to allow for us lowering our prestige and lessening our ability by petty squabbles at home.'[97] And this from the election diary of a commercial traveller based in Leamington Spa: 'I have nothing but condemnation for those who pressed for this election. There is no point in indulging ourselves in this exercise in democratic exhibitionism when the war is but half won.'[98] These panellists were concerned about losing focus on the war. But in expressing their concern, they also communicated their view of political argument ('petty squabbles') and party competition (indulgent 'democratic exhibitionism').

Such a view also helps to explain popular reaction to the party election broadcasts of Winston Churchill during the 1945 campaign. In the first of these, Churchill claimed that a socialist system could not be established without a Gestapo. Listeners were generally not impressed (McCallum and Readman 1947). We see this in the May 1945 election diaries. Churchill's broadcasts were judged to be not in keeping with recent events (i.e. the successful war-time coalition): 'Emotionally, they aroused resentment, that he should attack, personally, colleagues who had given good service. Intellectually, they aroused disbelief and, indeed, derision.'[99] They were judged to signal a descent from justified war-time leadership to unjustified peace-time party politics: '[Churchill was] a brilliant war leader and orator who should have had the sense to retire at the end of the war. He is cheapening his reputation by engaging in petty party squabbles.'[100] Churchill's broadcasts were received not as arguments in a necessary political debate but as vote-mongering, abuse, ranting, and, of course, mud-slinging. A housewife from Monmouth wrote: 'I was not at all impressed by Churchill's election speeches ... There seemed to be so much mud-slinging.'[101] A weaver from Huddersfield

---

[96] Panellist 2794, male, 24, civil engineer, East of England.
[97] Panellist 3402, female, 40, domestic nurse, Leicestershire.
[98] Panellist 3484, male, 37, commercial traveller, Leamington Spa.
[99] Panellist 1075, female, 56, film strip producer, London.
[100] Panellist 3960, male, 29, farm labourer, place of residence not known.
[101] Panellist 3419, female, 32, housewife, Monmouth.

reported how 'the Churchill broadcast disgusted most people. A man weaver: "Well, he's gone down in my estimation". A housewife: "No programme. Nothing but abuse". Me: guttersnipe. No trace of statesmanship. Nothing but a ranting party man.'[102] Or consider this from a Ripon-based university tutor:

There is no doubt that Churchill has done himself a great deal of harm and that public opinion is badly shocked by his sudden descent, as most people think, from the inspired national leader to the tricky politician, trying to make party capital by every vote-mongering device.[103]

With all this 'petty party squabbling' and attempted 'party capital' making, Churchill the 'partyman' and 'tricky politician' compared poorly with Clement Attlee, his more statesmanlike opponent. The manager of a textile mill in Leicester, for example, described one of Attlee's broadcasts as 'a gentlemanly speech, not much throwing'.[104] A goods packing manager from Belmont wrote of Attlee: 'I like … his lack of abuse of the Conservatives.'[105]

If such panellists desired something different to the narrow party line and the mud-slinging partyman, what was that something different? The final categories in this storyline were 'the national government', 'the coalition', 'the independent candidate', 'the best man' (or occasionally woman), and 'the statesman'.

In May 1945, when Churchill resigned as Prime Minister to fight the general election of that year, there had been an electoral truce between the main parties since 1939 and a coalition government for the preceding five years. Furthermore, this coalition government had been a national government with power genuinely shared between the Conservatives, Labour, and various non-party administrators, technocrats, and civil servants (Searle 1995). 'National government' and 'coalition government' were prominent figures in this storyline. In the election diaries of May 1945, a technical assistant from Winchester reported a conversation with 'Mrs M': 'She was definite in her opinion that it would always be better to have a national government rather than party politics.'[106] A teacher for Orpington reported public opinion in her constituency: 'National govt is hoped for by many. Frequently, one is asked "why need there be parties?"'[107] Then we have this

---

[102] Panellist 3648, female, age not known, weaver, Huddersfield.
[103] Panellist 2156, female, 56, university tutor, Ripon.
[104] Panellist 2576, male, 35, manager of textile mill, Leicester.
[105] Panellist 2684, male, 37, goods packing manager, Belmont.
[106] Panellist 1346, female, 29, technical assistant, Winchester.
[107] Panellist 3121, female, 62, teacher, Orpington.

housewife from Reading, describing her own position: 'I am normally non-party and prefer an independent, or one will stand for a coalition. I hate party mud-slinging.'[108]

'National government' and 'coalition government' were commonly used by panellists throughout the period. In August 1949, pondering the challenge of on-going recovery after the war, a clerk from Manchester expressed the need for 'a concerted national effort involving a revival of that remembered adjective – the Dunkirk Spirit. In the hope that this is possible, I shall endeavour to vote for a National Govt at the next election'.[109] In November 1950, reflecting on 'the development of [her] feelings about politics and of [her] political outlook and sympathies',[110] a civil servant from Morecambe wrote: 'I went to a course of lectures on current affairs ... This made me feel that there was so much right and so much wrong in each of the parties that there wasn't much to choose between them ... I was rather fed-up with politics anyhow and wished we could be governed by a perpetual coalition.'[111]

Who were the individual governors most appropriate to such 'national' or 'coalition' governments? They were 'Independents'. Reflecting on the party system in May 1945, a journalist from Dundee wrote: 'I am glad that the other three parties exist to moderate the worst excesses and deficiencies of the two great parties, but would be gladder still if there were more Independent members.'[112] Reflecting on what makes a 'good or bad' local council,[113] a housewife from Coventry wrote: '24 Independents sitting round a table have only the business to be loyal to.'[114] The preferred leaders in this storyline were also the 'best men' or 'best brains' of all parties. In May 1945, the manager of a textile mill in the East Midlands wrote in his election diary: 'I don't like party politics. We had the best men for the job regardless of party in the war. Why can't we have the same during peace?'[115] The November 1945 directive focused on municipal elections and local councils.[116] An office worker from Orpington wrote: 'I deplore greatly that politics should enter municipal elections; it should be the best man or woman for the post – it's all wrong.'[117] We also have this from a vicar in Boston: 'I decline in local affairs to vote on party lines. I know the men standing and I vote for those

---

[108] Panellist 3388, female, 54, housewife, Reading.
[109] Panellist 3878, male, 35, production manager, London.
[110] Directive SxMOA1/3/130.
[111] Panellist 2675, female, 59, civil servant, Morecambe.
[112] Panellist 3655, male, age not known, journalist, Dundee.
[113] Directive SxMOA1/3/88.   [114] Panellist 1644, female, 59, housewife, Coventry.
[115] Panellist 2576, male, 35, manager of textile mill, East Midlands.
[116] Directive SxMOA1/3/88.   [117] Panellist 1015, female, 70, office worker, Orpington.

I think will be the best.'[118] For many panellists, the same applied to national politics. Listen to this from a teacher in Coventry, writing in May 1949: '[W]e should be able to put the best men in high places, irrespective of party, to carry out majority wishes.'[119] Or this from a clerk in Glasgow, writing in August of that year: 'I shall probably vote for the man I consider the best candidate, irrespective of party.'[120] Or this from a civil servant in Blackpool, writing in November 1950: 'I should prefer government by the best of all parties, not a "Tory" government or a "Labour" government – the times demand it, the best brains we have working for the country, not a party.'[121] Or, finally, this from a housewife in Gateshead, responding to the same directive: 'If only we could have a govt of the best men from all parties!!!'[122]

The storyline was that national or coalition government worked well during the war. Party mud-slinging is not needed. What is needed, instead, is independent candidates or the best individuals from all parties, focused on the business before them and working together in the interests of the country as a whole. What is needed – instead of mud-slinging politicians – is 'statesmen'. This is the final category for us to demonstrate here. In February 1945, a member of the army wrote of politicians: '[They] almost have to be dishonest, squeezing themselves into some party formula, and not really caring about their constituents, but merely seeking self-advancement. When a politician becomes a statesman with a broad vision ... then one respects him.'[123] In May 1945, a weaver from Huddersfield wrote this after listening to one of Churchill's party election broadcasts: 'I think he would like to be remembered as a great statesman more than anything, but he is too much of a politician ever to have been or become a great statesman. A statesman must put the real needs of his country first.'[124] Finally, in July 1950, when asked about a list of named individuals,[125] a farm labourer responded: 'They are all statesmen, as distinct from politicians.'[126] Statesmen were the ideal alternative to politicians. While politicians were narrowly focused on the needs of themselves and their party, statesmen were broadly focused on the needs of their constituents and the country as a whole.

[118] Panellist 3187, male, 45, vicar, Boston.
[119] Panellist 1644, female, 62, teacher, Coventry.
[120] Panellist 3545, female, 32, clerk, Glasgow.
[121] Panellist 3640, female, 36, civil servant, Blackpool.
[122] Panellist 1016, female, 63, housewife, Gateshead.
[123] Panellist 1213, male, 28, army, place of residence not known.
[124] Panellist 3648, female, age not known, weaver, Huddersfield.
[125] Directive SxMOA1/3/127.
[126] Panellist 3960, male, 27, farm labourer, place of residence not known.

Stealth Democratic Folk Theories

In this chapter, we have considered supply-side explanations for the rise of anti-politics in the UK. In particular, we have considered influential theories of depoliticisation and post-democracy. Such theories led us to expect certain characteristics from our two periods. We expected a mid-twentieth century 'golden age' of sovereign, active, effective government; political debate and choice; and citizens satisfied and mobilised by such a supply of politics. Then we expected an early twenty-first century 'age of anti-politics' characterised by small and ineffective government; opaque and distant governance; political consensus; and citizens disaffected by such a supply of politics.

What did we find in existing studies of British political history, existing surveys of British public opinion, and volunteer writing for MO? We found that care should be taken when periodising history in such a way. Neither period was as distinct or one-dimensional as theories of historical change would often lead us to believe. Second, focusing on the most important question for our purposes – concerning *what citizens perceived* regarding the supply of politics in each period as opposed to what characterised the supply of politics according to some objective standard – we found a degree of empirical support for theories of depoliticisation and post-democracy. One prominent storyline in the mid-twentieth century – that each of the two main parties represented different sections of the population, political ideologies, and programmes for government – suggests that many citizens perceived a good supply of political debate and choice during the period. One prominent storyline in the early twenty-first century – that formal politics exhibited a lack of difference between the main parties, a lack of political debate about the most salient issues, a lack of electoral choice for voters, and a lack of representation for certain popular views – suggests that many citizens perceived a poor supply of politics during that later period.

Third, however, we found something else: evidence of a long-term force in British political culture – a widespread discontentment with party competition and political debate and a preference for coalitions of independent leaders focused on 'the common good' – that appears to have been overlooked by theories of depoliticisation and post-democracy. (It should be said that such a force has not been overlooked by historians of British politics. For example, G R Searle (1995) notes that British political life has not always been dominated by the competitive struggle between parties. Alongside party feeling, there has often existed significant antipathy towards partisanship. There have been persistent attempts to break with 'party strife' and restrictive party programmes. This 'coalitionist tradition' in British politics includes some of the country's most celebrated politicians, from Austen Chamberlain to David Lloyd George to Winston Churchill.)

Evidence for this long-term force comes especially from two alternative storylines found prominently in the MO material. In the mid-twentieth century, the line was that one 'common good' exists, party politics is therefore unnecessary, and what is needed instead is national or coalition government made up of independents and statesmen. In the early twenty-first century, the similar line was that political debate is not needed and, instead, coalition government could serve 'the nation' (and, in doing so, side-line the extreme partisans).

Taken together, these storylines lead us to question the power of depoliticisation and post-democracy as explanatory theories for the rise of anti-politics in the UK. They also lead us to other literatures in political science. One, as we saw earlier in the chapter, is the debate on responsible parties – which reminds us that citizens can become disaffected by elite polarisation at least as much as elite consensus. A second literature, introduced in the opening pages of this book, is that focused on 'stealth democracy'. Hibbing and Theiss-Morse (2002) use 'stealth democracy' to describe Americans' attitudes to governmental procedures and processes around the turn of the twenty-first century. In surveys and focus groups, they found a citizenry adverse to political conflict, not least because many citizens believe that most Americans have the same goals – 'the silent majority' – and so believe that political debate is unnecessary and driven by special interests. What follows from such assumptions is a belief that government should just be technical in character. It should be management by 'empathetic non self-interested decision-makers' or ENSIDs. Democratic procedures should exist but should not be visible on a routine basis (as with, say, deliberative democracy) – hence 'stealth democracy'.

Others have debated the extent to which stealth democratic preferences are prevalent in the UK at the beginning of the twenty-first century (e.g. Webb 2013, Stoker and Hay 2017). One lesson worth taking from this debate is that survey responses to questions of democratic preferences depend, to a significant extent, on the kinds of questions asked. For example, if researchers ask questions designed to confirm stealth theories, they tend to achieve such confirmation; but if they ask questions designed to confirm alternative 'sunshine' theories, they also tend to achieve such confirmation (see Neblo et al. 2010). One way around this empirical problem is to consider what citizens say about their democratic process preferences when given the opportunity to speak or write freely about formal politics without being guided by tightly worded survey instruments.

Much of this chapter has been devoted to such an exercise. In both periods, we found a prominent storyline reminiscent of Hibbing and Theiss-Morse's stealth democracy. The relationship between these storylines and stealth democracy is presented in Table 6.1. The first thing to note is that, for each period, what we identified as a prominent storyline in the preceding sections is actually – or better thought of as – a *folk theory* of democracy. It is a model of the world (Kahneman 2011) that is only loosely made up of non-technical abstractions (Kempton 1986, Lakoff 2002) but provides cognitive cues or shortcuts for understanding and judgement (Keesing 1987). It is commonly held by citizens and so presumably acquired from a combination of everyday experience, social interaction, and expert knowledge. It is made up of shared categories, subject positions, and storylines. So a prominent folk theory of democracy in mid-twentieth century Britain was made up of the following lines: one 'common good' exists; therefore party politics is unnecessary; therefore government should be national or coalition government. And a prominent folk theory of democracy in early twenty-first century Britain was made up of the similar lines: the country or local area has one set of needs; so political debate is unnecessary; so government is best done by coalitions of moderates.

The second thing to note in Table 6.1 is the main difference between these folk theories and the American stealth model. The assumption of one 'common good' is similar. The judgement that political debate is unnecessary is also similar. But the image of the ideal government is notably different. While Americans around the turn of the twenty-first century expressed a preference for government by businesspeople and non-elected experts, many citizens of the UK, in both periods, expressed a preference for government still by elected leaders – whether completely independent of party or just moderate partisans.

Something akin to stealth democracy has been one prominent folk theory in the UK for many decades. Given the available data, we cannot say quite how prevalent such a popular understanding has been at different historical moments. But we can say that supply-side explanations for the rise of anti-politics – focused on depoliticisation and post-democracy – have neglected this long-term force in British politics. They have missed that citizens' judgements of the supply of politics are mediated by their folk theories of democracy. They have missed that many citizens do not hold the same belief systems or ideologies as elite political actors (Converse 1964) – where elite political actors, defined by their high levels of political information, education, and involvement, would include political theorists themselves. These supply-side explanations beg the following question: If many citizens during the second half of the twentieth

Table 6.1 *Stealth democratic folk theories*

	Hibbing and Theiss-Morse (2002) on stealth democracy in late twentieth-century America	A folk theory of democracy prominent in mid-twentieth-century Britain	A folk theory of democracy prominent in early twenty-first-century Britain
Assumptions regarding citizens' needs and desires	Citizens have the same basic goals – 'the common good' or 'the silent majority'	There is one common good or common weal. Government should serve the townspeople at large or the country as a whole	There is one national good. Government should serve the country or the local area (as a whole)
Judgements of politics, political debate, party competition etc.	Political debate, deal-making, concession-making, compromise etc. is unnecessary and driven by special interests	Party politics is unnecessary talk. It is a game of mud-slinging and petty squabbling. Furthermore, narrow and rigid party lines favour party yes-men over individuals of merit. They even limit individual freedom and so are undemocratic	Political debate is not necessary. It is petty squabbling and bickering. It is posturing and point-scoring. Or it is what a minority of extremists do
Images of the ideal democratic system and government	Government should just be technical in character – management – and done by non-self-interested decision-makers (ENSIDs – businesspeople, non-elected experts)	Democracy is better than dictatorship, but government should be national or coalition government, made up of independents, or the best men from all the parties – statesmen working together for common good	Government is best done by a coalition of moderates, working together in a quiet, steady, sensible manner that tempers or side-lines the extremists

century assumed a *popular* consensus in the UK, why should so many citizens have become disaffected when *elite* consensus (re)emerged around the turn of the twenty-first century?

The rise of anti-politics is no doubt a complex phenomenon to be explained by multiple factors. But in this chapter and the previous one, we have used evidence from the UK to cast doubt on two of the most influential explanations in the literature. These sets of demand- and supply-side factors may well have played some role in the rise of anti-politics in the UK. But there is a need to consider other explanations too. In the next two chapters, we follow the MO material – inductively – towards two such additional explanations: changing images of the good politician (Chapter 7) and changing modes of political interaction (Chapter 8). Then, in Chapter 9, we revisit and develop our argument concerning folk theories, stealth democracy, and historical change.

7   Changing Images of the Good Politician

From the Good Citizen to the Good Politician

In the previous two chapters, we have cast doubt on two of the most influential explanations for the rise of anti-politics in the United Kingdom (UK): the replacement of deferential citizens by critical citizens (Chapter 5) and depoliticisation (Chapter 6). We now consider what else changed between the middle of the twentieth century and the turn of the twenty-first century that might help to explain the rise of negative sentiment among citizens towards the activities and institutions of formal politics. In this chapter, we consider the changing image of 'the good politician' held by citizens, against which politicians might be judged.

Recently, there has been much discussion of 'the good citizen' (e.g. Dalton 2009). The idea here is that norms of good citizenship have changed over time. Good citizens, it is thought, used to feel respect for political authority and a duty to participate by way of voting, paying taxes, and belonging to political parties. Today, good citizens are thought to demand and celebrate social rights and participate by way of volunteering, protesting, and buying products for political reasons. We argued in Chapters 1 and 5 that citizenship norms may not have changed quite so much as some commentators have claimed. We argue in this chapter that, while citizenship norms may not have changed in the way often supposed, norms for politicians – images of the good politician held by citizens – have changed in ways that help to explain the rise of anti-politics.

We argue in this chapter for a focus on the good politician. This focus should not be on the elite image of the good politician (e.g. Machiavelli 2003), though there is a growing literature on this elite image using political theory to defend politicians against contemporary anti-politics (see Corbett 2014). Rather, this focus should be on the popular image of the good politician, not least because popular understandings of political ethics have been shown to differ from, and especially to be more expansive than, elite understandings (Allen and Birch 2015b). Our focus on the good politician is also a focus on how the popular image of the good politician has changed over time. This contrasts with much of the existing literature, which focuses not only on the elite image of the good politician but also on the timeless tensions in that elite image. We have found this existing literature helpful and return to it later in the chapter. Let us briefly introduce two examples from the literature here.

For Kane and Patapan (2012), democratic leadership is forever characterised by tensions and contradictions. The central tension is that politicians, and especially those holding high office, have to be leaders in a system that celebrates popular sovereignty (i.e. rule by all the people, or equality). There are other tensions too. One attempt to address this central tension is representation. But representation produces its own contradictions. There are numerous forms of representation, from identity representation (when leaders represent their people by resembling them as closely as possible) to agent representation (when leaders represent their people by following their instructions and defending their interests) to trustee representation (when leaders represent their people by embodying their best qualities and using their own judgement on behalf of their people). Politicians cannot achieve all three forms of representation at the same time. A further tension identified by Kane and Patapan is that between accountability and transparency on the one hand and persuasion or the winning of consent on the other (which they label 'systemic hypocrisy'). Politicians must be honest and truthful to achieve accountability and transparency. But to win consent from a coalition of groups in society, they must say at least slightly different things to these different groups. And to persuade citizens and win support for a position, politicians must use rhetoric (which citizens often receive as dangerous propaganda or else just empty words).

A second example is Stephen Medvic's (2013) study of the perennial traps faced by politicians in democracies. Politicians are caught in 'the leader-follower trap' when citizens demand leadership, so long as it takes the country in what they perceive to be the right direction. Otherwise, they want politicians to listen and follow the will of the citizenry (as perceived by those citizens). Politicians are caught in 'the principled-pragmatic trap' when citizens demand that politicians hold to their principles, so long as those principles are shared by those citizens. Otherwise, they want politicians to compromise and solve problems; to reject ideology for pragmatism. Finally, politicians are caught in 'the ordinary-and-exceptional trap' when citizens want politicians to be just like them and so to understand how the world looks from their perspective but also to be far above average in the qualities they possess – commitment, competence, integrity – and the standards to which they are held.

In the rest of this chapter, we consider the popular image of the good politician and how it has changed over time. We argue that citizens in the mid-twentieth century generally wanted politicians to be sincere, hardworking, able, human, moderate, and strong. This image was characterised by tensions but was just about possible for politicians to perform – if not by individual politicians then at least by politicians as a group, with different politicians representing the different virtues. By the early twenty-first century, citizens generally still wanted politicians to be trustworthy, able, moderate, and strong. But they also wanted politicians to be 'normal' in a variety of ways and situations. Politicians should behave, look, and sound normal. They should be normal – or behave appropriately and look and sound appropriate – on the 'world stage', for the national political context, for the age of the digital image, and in everyday life. They also wanted politicians to be 'in touch' with 'reality' as experienced by 'ordinary people'. In short, we argue that citizens increasingly expect politicians not only *for* the people – honest, hard-working, strong – but also *of* the people. Towards the end of the chapter, we discuss three plausible origins of these new expectations: the professionalisation of politics, the ideology of intimacy (Sennett 1977), and democratic egalitarianism (Hoggart 1957).

The Good Politician in the Mid-Twentieth Century

In July 1950, Mass Observation (MO) asked its panel of volunteer writers the following question: 'How do you feel about: a) Attlee; b) Churchill; c) Bevin; d) Cripps; e) Bevan?'[1] Labour had won a small majority in the general election of February 1950. Clement Attlee remained Prime Minister. Ernest Bevin remained his Foreign Secretary, Stafford Cripps his Chancellor, and Aneurin Bevan his Minister for Health. At this time, Winston Churchill was Leader of the Opposition (the Conservative Party). In responding to this question, panellists told MO what they felt or thought about these particular politicians. In the responses, however, we can also read something else. We can read the responses for the shared criteria panellists used to judge these politicians. This is what we do in the rest of this section. We are not so much interested in how panellists graded Attlee or Churchill or Bevin (as good or bad politicians). We are interested in the general 'marking criteria' used by panellists to reach particular grades. These criteria can be reconstructed from the cultural resources repeated across multiple responses from a range of panellists, as we now demonstrate.

[1] Directive SxMOA1/3/127.

The named politicians were judged for their 'integrity', 'moral courage', 'plain-speaking', and refusal to 'play to the gallery'. They were generally praised for being 'sincere'. A Methodist minister from Uppingham wrote of Attlee: 'I like the man for his sincerity.'[2] An assistant registrar from London wrote this of Cripps: 'Ruthlessly, efficiently, sincerely doing his job as well as it can be done.'[3] Bevan was described by a shopbuyer from Matlock as 'sincere and brave in his convictions'.[4] Another shared category here was 'honesty'. A publisher's assistant from Paignton wrote: 'Bevin strikes me as a genuine man, honestly trying to do his best.'[5] A housewife from Pontfadog also described Bevin as honest: '[H]e puts Britain first always and is, I am sure, an honest man.'[6] Then we have this tax inspector from Northampton on Cripps: 'Rather an enigma – certainly ascetic and one hopes as honest as one thought.'[7] A third shared category was 'principles' or the 'principled' politician. Here is a commercial traveller from Leicester on Attlee: 'Seems to be a high-principled man, one who relies on honesty rather than oratory, and who likes to get on quietly and efficiently with the job in hand.'[8] Here is an administrator from Horsham on Cripps: 'I admire his steadfast principles.'[9]

Most of the named politicians were praised for possessing this family of virtues: sincerity, honesty, being principled, being genuine. Then occasionally they were criticised for lacking these virtues. Listen to this secretary from London on Attlee: 'My opinion of his integrity has gone down. He can't run with the hare and hunt with the hounds, but he's trying to.'[10] Or this farmer from Thetford on Churchill: 'An excellent statesman. Less sincere than [Attlee].'[11] Or this timber merchant from Leeds on Cripps: 'I dislike people who tell lies in the house and conduct themselves in a cathedral afterwards. A hypocrite and a nasty bit of know-all altogether.'[12] The MO panellists mostly praised the named politicians for their integrity and truth-telling. But even when they criticised these politicians, we still see traces of the marking criteria used by panellists. The good politician should pick a position and stick to it (they should not 'run with the hare and hunt with the hounds'). Their conduct should be

[2] Panellist 2817, male, 26, Methodist minister, Uppingham.
[3] Panellist 2484, male, 27, assistant registrar, London.
[4] Panellist 4236, female, 62, shopbuyer, Matlock.
[5] Panellist 2852, male, 51, publisher's assistant, Paignton.
[6] Panellist 3371, female, 56, housewife, Pontfadog.
[7] Panellist 1432, female, 34, tax inspector, Northampton.
[8] Panellist 2921, male, 27, commercial traveller, Leicester.
[9] Panellist 3463, female, 69, administrator, Horsham.
[10] Panellist 1635, female, 35, secretary, London.
[11] Panellist 3808, male, 50, farmer, Thetford.
[12] Panellist 2771, male, 51, timber merchant, Leeds.

consistent across situations and also between talk and action (they should not 'tell lies in the house and conduct themselves in a cathedral afterwards').

A second family of virtues, against which panellists judged the listed politicians, centred on 'hard work'. Now almost seventy years old, with deteriorating health, Bevin was especially assessed in these terms. A chartered accountant from Edinburgh wrote of Bevin: 'I think he has tried hard to improve international relations in the world, but feel that he is not sufficiently fit to cope with the strain of a Foreign Secretary's job.'[13] Our administrator from Horsham concurred: '[Bevin] I consider too unwell to give the attention, judgement, and hard work necessary for a Foreign Secretary.'[14] Our shopbuyer from Matlock was a little more positive: 'I think his greatness is waning, but he has accomplished much through his hard work.'[15]

Bevin was seen as hard-working, trying hard, doing 'his level best'.[16] He was the prototypical hard-working politician, not least because of his waning capacity for precisely such hard work. But other politicians were also judged against these criteria, which appear to have been general criteria for assessing politicians at the time. So a teacher from Ripon wrote: 'Attlee is doing his best for the country.'[17] A housewife from Bishop Auckland wrote of Cripps: 'Excellent character and admirable worker.'[18] Also of Cripps, a cardboard-box maker from London wrote: 'As Chancellor of the Exchequer, he is doing his level best to make our position nationally sound in the sphere of economics.'[19] The good politician, whether Bevin or someone else, works hard and does their best for the country.

Since doing one's best is rarely enough on its own, however, the good politician was also 'competent',[20] with a 'first-rate brain'.[21] And if Bevin was the prototypical hard-working politician, then Cripps was the prototypical competent politician. He was 'able'. A shoehand from Maresfield described him as '[v]ery able and efficient'.[22] An electrical engineer from Witley described him as '[v]ery sound and able'.[23] A letter-press printer

[13] Panellist 1682, male, 30, chartered accountant, Edinburgh.
[14] Panellist 3463, female, 69, administrator, Horsham.
[15] Panellist 4236, female, 62, shopbuyer, Matlock.
[16] Panellist 2921, male, 27, commercial traveller, Leicester.
[17] Panellist 2984, female, 42, teacher, Ripon.
[18] Panellist 1974, female, 49, housewife, Bishop Auckland.
[19] Panellist 2209, female, 80, cardboard-box maker, London.
[20] Panellist 4000, male, 26, physicist, Salford.
[21] Panellist 2457, female, 51, civil servant, Newcastle.
[22] Panellist 2713, male, 39, shoehand, Maresfield.
[23] Panellist 4043, male, 33, electrical engineer, Witley.

from Nailsworth wrote: 'Stafford Cripps is my political hero. He has got ability and courage, and he works harder than most of us.'[24] Another shared category here was brilliance. An army officer from Oswestry described Cripps as '[a] brilliant man, in fact a genius'.[25] Our publisher's assistant from Paignton wrote: 'I consider Cripps brilliant, trustworthy, but inclined to be self-conscious.'[26] Wisdom was another category shared by numerous panellists. 'Inclined to be less optimistic about him, yet wise on the whole', wrote a teacher from Ripon.[27] 'I think he is a combination of saintliness and worldly wisdom', wrote our shopbuyer from Matlock.[28]

Cripps was judged to be clever. An estate agent from Newport wrote: 'I have great respect for Cripps. If anyone can manage our finances, he can ... I believe him to be clever.'[29] An administrator from Horsham described Cripps as 'a genuine, honest man, a true socialist, and a clever man, and a Christian'.[30] This category was used to characterise other politicians too. On Churchill, a journalist from Glasgow wrote: 'Exceedingly clever, a great politician, a fighter, great spirit.'[31] On Bevan, an office worker from Sunbury-on-Thames wrote: 'Quite clever, but I have never liked him.'[32]

We should also note how other politicians were assessed for their 'ability'. Attlee was assessed by this insurance broker from Cheadle Hulme: 'Grown considerably in stature since he became Prime Minister. He is an able man.'[33] Churchill was assessed by our shoehand from Maresfield: 'Able, best judgement uninfluenced by political bias.'[34] Bevan was assessed by this civil servant from Newcastle: 'With Cripps ... one of the ... best brains in the Labour Party.'[35]

So the good politician of the mid-twentieth century was able, in addition to being sincere and hard-working. But they were also expected to be 'human', by which was meant genial, warm, sympathetic. Again, we see this most clearly in the case of Cripps. Praised for his ability and efficiency, Cripps was also criticised for his lack of humanity. Our chartered accountant from Edinburgh wrote: 'A clever man who I admire for his consistency since he has been chancellor. I feel, however, that he lacks the

[24] Panellist 3857, male, 35, letter-press printer, Nailsworth.
[25] Panellist 3627, male, 32, army officer, Oswestry.
[26] Panellist 3852, male, 51, publisher's assistant, Paignton.
[27] Panellist 2984, female, 42, teacher, Ripon.
[28] Panellist 4236, female, 62, shopbuyer, Matlock.
[29] Panellist 1688, male, 39, estate agent, Newport.
[30] Panellist 3463, female, 69, administrator, Horsham.
[31] Panellist 4654, male, 70, journalist, Glasgow.
[32] Panellist 3116, female, 50, office worker, Sunbury-on-Thames.
[33] Panellist 2776, male, 52, insurance broker, Cheadle Hulme.
[34] Panellist 2713, male, 39, shoehand, Maresfield.
[35] Panellist 2457, female, 51, civil servant, Newcastle.

common human touch which might make him more popular. Tends rather to ignore the human factor in his calculations.'[36] Similarly, an ambulance driver from London wrote: 'A wonderful chancellor. A bit inhuman perhaps, but the best man for the job.'[37] The problem here was Cripps's 'high-minded' approach and his austerity policies, which seemed to reflect his 'austere', 'puritanical', 'ascetic' character. A teacher from Manchester wrote of Cripps: 'Scholarly, clever, incorruptible, but rather too high-minded and austere to appeal to ordinary people.'[38] Or take this railway draughtsman from Paignton: 'What a pity not more genial! So "austere"!'[39] Or this bank clerk from London: 'Cripps I have every confidence in. He isn't afraid of unpleasant facts and doesn't hesitate to act on them. A rather unnecessary puritanical type at times, but that's a minor fault compared with his virtues.'[40] Then we have our housewife from Pontfadog: 'I can't help admire him because he goes on with a thing if he believes in it – but he is an ascetic and intellectual socialist and that probably over-colours his ideas and actions and makes it a bit hard on the ordinary [man].'[41] Finally, we have this nursery superintendent on Cripps: 'Clever – but somehow something is lacking – he seems cold and unsympathetic. He may be admired – but never liked.'[42]

What was Cripps missing that other politicians might have? He was missing the 'amusing personality' of Churchill or the 'warm personality' of Bevan.[43] But just as the good politician should be capable, clever, and brilliant but not so intellectual, high-minded, and calculating as to make them inhuman, the good politician should also be genial, warm, and sympathetic but not so human as to make them 'emotional' and 'unreasonable'. If Cripps was the prototypical able politician, then Attlee was the prototypical level-headed politician. This was another family of virtues against which politicians were judged in the mid-twentieth century. The good politician was level-headed. Listen to this estate agent from Newport on Attlee: 'I believe he is an able man and a good day-to-day party leader, but a very uninspiring statesman, at any rate in public. However, he is level-headed and I do not wish to see him replaced just now.'[44] Then we have our teacher from Manchester on Attlee:

---

[36] Panellist 1682, male, 30, chartered accountant, Edinburgh.
[37] Panellist 1420, female, 39, ambulance driver, London.
[38] Panellist 2975, female, 40, teacher, Manchester.
[39] Panellist 1095, male, 74, railway draughtsman, Paignton.
[40] Panellist 3366, female, 31, bank clerk, London.
[41] Panellist 3371, female, 56, housewife, Pontfadog.
[42] Panellist 4744, female, 65, superintendent of nursery, place of residence not known.
[43] Panellist 2975, female, 40, teacher, Manchester; Panellist 1420, female, 39, ambulance driver, London.
[44] Panellist 1688, male, 39, estate agent, Newport.

'Intelligent, competent, and sincere. Adequate for his position. A relief to have someone so quiet and level-headed.'[45] The good politician, then, was also quiet. Listen to this upholsterer on Attlee: 'I believe him to be rather purposeful and an efficient minister, though quiet in manner with a total (and admirable) lack of showmanship.'[46] Or this tax inspector from Belfast: 'I like Attlee's moderation and quiet determination, and admire his skill behind the scenes in managing such a difficult team.'[47] The good politician, then, was also moderate. A seventy-one-year-old woman for whom we have no occupation or place of residence wrote: 'I think Attlee is sincere and a good man who does his best under most difficult circumstances. I don't think he is a great man, and I think it was his moderateness and lack of fanaticism which made him the best man to keep his queer group together.'[48]

Attlee was also praised for his 'coolness of method';[49] for being 'steady',[50] 'unobtrusive',[51] and 'modest';[52] for being a 'gentleman' who 'does not seek publicity' and does his job 'without the usual ballyhoo'.[53] Meanwhile, other politicians were criticised for lacking Attlee's moderation and quiet style. Churchill was criticised for his vanity and showmanship. Our retired railway draughtsman from Paignton wrote of Churchill: 'What a mixture of grandeur and vanity!'[54] Our shopbuyer from Matlock wrote of Churchill: 'I don't like him. I admit his great courage, but I feel that he is so vain.'[55] Then we have this upholsterer on both politicians: 'I dislike Churchill more than any other politician, chiefly because of his love of showmanship (it is Attlee's lack of this sort of thing that makes me admire him).'[56]

Churchill may have lacked Attlee's quiet, unobtrusive, modest style, but it was Bevan who was most criticised for lacking Attlee's moderation. If the good politician was level-headed, steady, cool, and a gentleman, they were not 'emotional',[57] 'unreliable',[58] 'boisterous',[59] and 'vulgar'.[60]

---

[45] Panellist 2975, female, 40, teacher, Manchester.
[46] Panellist 4601, male, 53, upholsterer, place of residence not known.
[47] Panellist 1066, female, 44, tax inspector, Belfast.
[48] Panellist 4191, female, 71, occupation not known, place of residence not known.
[49] Panellist 3627, male, 32, army officer, Oswestry.
[50] Panellist 3808, male, 50, farmer, Thetford.
[51] Panellist 1095, male, 74, retired railway draughtsman, Paignton.
[52] Panellist 3857, male, 35, letter-press printer, Nailsworth.
[53] Panellist 2457, female, 51, civil servant, Newcastle; Panellist 3886, male, 30, chemist, Falkirk; Panellist 4446, male, 53, food inspector, Chester.
[54] Panellist 1095, male, 74, retired railway draughtsman, Paignton.
[55] Panellist 4236, female, 62, shopbuyer, Matlock.
[56] Panellist 4601, male, 53, upholsterer, place of residence not known.
[57] Panellist 2975, female, 40, teacher, Manchester.
[58] Panellist 1974, female, 49, housewife, Bishop Auckland.
[59] Panellist 4556, female, 31, school meals assistant, place of residence not known.
[60] Panellist 3463, female, 69, administrator, Horsham.

Bevan, the former coal miner and union activist, was described as all of these things and more. His partisan feeling was too strong. This was the case for our housewife from Pontfadog: 'He seems to let his class-hatred dominate his mind to the exclusion of all excuse.'[61] Perhaps unsurprisingly, it was the case for a retired farmer from Latchington who described Bevan as '[a] stirrer-up of class-hatred'.[62] It was also the case for this chemist from Falkirk: 'I dislike Bevan ... chiefly because he seems to be motivated largely by class-hatred.'[63] Bevan allowed his bitterness and resentment to get the better of him. Our tax inspector from Belfast wrote this of Bevan: 'I feel his political judgement (and politically all his opinions) are warped by a hard childhood. He shows a bitterness and resentment that can do neither him nor anyone else good.'[64] Our letter-press printer from Nailsworth wrote this: 'I feel he is not adult enough to control his very understandable bitterness against the Tories.'[65] Then listen to this from our teacher in Manchester on Bevan:

Interesting and attractive personality, but seems to lack the patience, diplomacy, and toleration needed by a man in high political office. A keen, ardent, and class-conscious worker, rather too much hampered by strong emotion and personal bitterness to make objective decisions.[66]

Bevan's judgement was thought to be warped. He was thought to be out of control. He was thought to lack patience, diplomacy, toleration; to be overly emotional, personal, and subjective. The good politician, by contrast, would be unbiased, self-controlled, patient, diplomatic, tolerant, reasonable, objective. They would have the 'manners' and 'customary courtesies of civilisation' lacked by Bevan.[67] They would be 'sober' and not 'doctrinaire', 'rabble-rousing', a 'demagogue' like Bevan.[68] They would be 'tactful' and not 'injudicious', too 'forthright', pressing 'too hard' like Bevan.[69] They would not have Bevan's 'ungoverned temper' lamented by one clergyman from Harrogate.[70]

This brings us to a final group of virtues by which politicians appear to have been judged at this time. If Attlee was praised for his moderation and

[61] Panellist 3371, female, 56, housewife, Pontfadog.
[62] Panellist 3653, male, 69, retired farmer, Latchington.
[63] Panellist 3886, male, 30, chemist, Falkirk.
[64] Panellist 1066, female, 44, tax inspector, Belfast.
[65] Panellist 3857, male, 35, letter-press printer, Nailsworth.
[66] Panellist 2975, female, 40, teacher, Manchester.
[67] Panellist 4440, male, 48, police inspector, place of residence not known.
[68] Panellist 2921, male, 27, commercial traveller, Leicester; Panellist 1688, male, 39, estate agent, Newport.
[69] Panellist 4000, male, 26, physicist, Salford; Panellist 3366, female, 31, bank clerk, London; Panellist 4446, male, 53, food inspector, Chester.
[70] Panellist 3204, male, 74, clergyman, Harrogate.

quiet, well-mannered style of politics, he was also criticised for lacking the brilliant, inspiring personality of a strong leader. One category commonly used by a range of panellists when writing about Attlee was 'personality'. A sales manager from Ilford described Attlee as '[c]apable but without personality'.[71] More positively, our ambulance driver from London wrote of Attlee: 'He seems more of a personality than I had thought.'[72] Another shared category of relevance here was inspiration. What Attlee lacked was an inspirational personality. This was the case for a physicist from Salford: 'Competent chairman. No personality. Can't inspire.'[73] It was the case for our nursery superintendent: 'I think he is sincere but very uninspiring ... a boring speaker.'[74] Attlee was judged by some panellists to be boring, 'dull', and in no way 'spectacular' (in a way that excites and inspires citizens).[75] Another shared category here was weakness/strength. For this journalist from Glasgow, Attlee was '[a] very decent man ... but not enough of spirit and fight in him to be Premier. Weak in choosing his ministers'.[76] Our administrator from Horsham wrote of Attlee: 'I suppose he is a good conscientious worker, but I feel his personality is not sufficiently strong or evident to carry full confidence.'[77] Then we have this from our shopbuyer in Matlock: 'I trust Attlee's integrity and I feel his is a much stronger character than I used to think it was. I wish he was a little more emotional and less gentle.'[78] The good politician had a strong, inspirational personality. This is what made them a leader. Indeed, leadership was a final category to be demonstrated here. A railway clerk from Watford wrote of Attlee: 'I feel [he] is a genuine, high-principled socialist from pure conviction. He lacks personality so useful to a leader and man in public position.'[79] A police inspector described Attlee as '[a] great man lacking in personality and the power to lead'.[80] Or take this from a young wood finisher: 'Attlee is completely colourless and is completely lacking in the quality of leadership which we shall be needing in the dark times ahead.'[81]

Was there such a colourful personality and leader among this group of politicians? Of course there was: Churchill, the prototypical strong and

[71] Panellist 3858, male, 42, sales manager, Ilford.
[72] Panellist 1420, female, 39, ambulance driver, London.
[73] Panellist 4000, male, 26, physicist, Salford.
[74] Panellist 4744, female, 65, superintendent of nursery, place of residence not known.
[75] Panellist 1974, female, 49, housewife, Bishop Auckland; Panellist 2852, male, 51, publisher's assistant, Paignton.
[76] Panellist 4654, male, 70, journalist, Glasgow.
[77] Panellist 3463, female, 69, administrator, Horsham.
[78] Panellist 4236, female, 62, shopbuyer, Matlock.
[79] Panellist 3481, female, 56, railway clerk, Watford.
[80] Panellist 4440, male, 48, police inspector, place of residence not known.
[81] Panellist 4535, male, 29, wood finisher, place of residence not known.

Table 7.1 *The good politician of the mid-twentieth century*

Virtue family	Shared categories	Prototypical politician
Sincerity	Sincerity	
	Honesty	
	Principles	
Hard work	Hard work	Bevin
	Trying one's best	
Ability	Ability	Cripps
	Brilliance	
	Wisdom	
	Cleverness	
Humanity	Humanity	
	Personality	
Moderation	Moderation	Attlee
	Level-headedness	
	Quietness	
Leadership	Leadership	Churchill
	Personality	
	Inspiration	
	Strength	

inspirational leader. Churchill may have been criticised for his vanity and showmanship, but he was praised for being a 'warrior', a 'fighter', with 'guts' and 'vision'.[82] He was praised for being 'brilliant' and 'inspiring'.[83] In particular, he was repeatedly described as 'outstanding' in personality and character. Listen to this tax inspector from Northampton on Churchill: 'The most outstanding character in this country today and maybe the world.'[84] Or this administrator from Horsham: 'An excellent leader in time of war, an outstanding personality delighting in being in the limelight, a clever speaker, genuine in what he says.'[85] And finally, this estate agent from Newport: 'Churchill is of course a genius, a remarkable and outstanding personality. Discretion and patience he has little, but great courage and audacity'.[86]

We are now in a position to characterise the good politician of the mid-twentieth century. This good politician was sincere, hard-working, able, human, moderate, and strong (Table 7.1). These families of

---

[82] Panellist 1066, female, 44, tax inspector, Belfast; Panellist 2484, male, 27, assistant registrar, London; Panellist 3116, female, 50, office worker, Sunbury-on-Thames.
[83] Panellist 3366, female, 31, bank clerk, London.
[84] Panellist 1432, female, 34, tax inspector, Northampton.
[85] Panellist 3463, female, 69, administrator, Horsham.
[86] Panellist 1688, male, 39, estate agent, Newport.

virtues and associated categories were shared and repeated by a range of panellists. In this section, we have only considered responses to one directive from one particular year (July 1950). But what we have found matches what we found in other chapters drawing on responses to other directives. For example, in Chapter 4 we saw politicians criticised across the period for being talkers, twisters, gasbags; for being dishonest; for practising oratory; for having the gift of the gab and playing to the gallery. In other words, we saw politicians criticised for not fitting the image of the sincere, honest, principled (good) politician. Then in Chapter 6, we saw politicians criticised across the period for being party yes-men engaged in mud-slinging and petty squabbling and also praised for honestly following their conscience, for being individuals of merit, for standing as independents or joining coalitions, for acting as statesmen on behalf of the common good. In other words, we saw politicians judged against the image of the sincere, able, moderate (good) politician.

These findings also fit with elements of the existing historiography. Jon Lawrence (2006, 2009) studied electioneering in Britain during this period. He argues that electioneering changed between the 1920s and 1950s. It became less assertive, exuberant, passionate, volatile, explosive, unruly, disrespectful, irreverent. It became more rational, serious, orderly, sober, calm, restrained. There were a number of explanations for this transformation. Legal changes to the conduct of elections saw political meetings moved from expensive private halls to cheaper school halls thought more appropriate to a quieter form of political argument. Second, the enfranchisement of women cast the macho rough-and-tumble of the old-style politics in a new and less flattering light. Third, the breakdown of the belief in natural hierarchies that happened during the First World War disassociated disorder from harmless popular exuberance and instead associated it with potentially dangerous dysfunctional class relations. Finally, Britain sought to distinguish itself during this period from revolutionary continental Europe – perceived to be passionate but also barbaric, brutal, and fascist or communist. In this context, the good politician was human and moderate in addition to being sincere, hard-working, able, and strong.

The image of the good politician was also characterised by tensions at this time. They were meant to be able (intellectual, scholarly, calculating, efficient) yet human (genial, warm, likeable). They were meant to be human (sympathetic, emotional) yet moderate (civilised, self-controlled, self-governed, level-headed, cool, sober, steady, reliable, objective). They were meant to be moderate (tolerant, diplomatic, not too forthright, not too doctrinaire) yet sincere (principled, steadfast, with convictions, with integrity). And they were meant to be moderate (quiet, modest) yet inspirational (brilliant, spectacular, audacious, strong, with fight, with spirit).

We have three additional reflections on this image of the good politician and these tensions. First, as we argue throughout the book, the immediate post-war period was no democratic 'golden age'. The image of the good politician was difficult to achieve then, as probably it has always been. Second, these tensions do not quite map onto those timeless tensions of democratic leadership identified by others and reviewed in the introduction to this chapter (except perhaps for moderation versus sincerity, which overlaps with Medvic's principled-pragmatic trap). Still, we can imagine these tensions existing beyond the context of mid-twentieth-century Britain. As such, we have identified here some additional potentially timeless tensions of democratic leadership. Finally, and most importantly, these tensions do not appear to have caused much of a problem for political support at the time. Panellists mostly wrote about the virtues possessed by certain politicians as opposed to the virtues *lacked* – or *vices* possessed – by those politicians. The different virtues were represented by different politicians (see Table 7.1). Bevin represented hard work. Cripps: ability. Attlee: moderation. Churchill: leadership. There was no prototypical sincere or human politician, but all the named politicians except Churchill were generally viewed as sincere, honest, and principled, and all but Attlee and Cripps were generally seen as genial, warm, and sympathetic. Our point here is that citizens during this period may have placed contradictory demands on politicians, as perhaps they have always done, but they could see their expectations being met by politicians as a group. They could see their image of the good politician being performed, if not individually by one particular, heroic politician, then collectively by the most prominent politicians of the day.

The Good Politician in the Early Twenty-First Century

In spring 2014, we partnered with MO to ask its panel a similar question to that asked in July 1950: 'How do you feel about: a) David Cameron; b) Ed Miliband; c) Nick Clegg; d) William Hague; and e) George Osborne?'[87] There had been a Conservative-led Coalition Government since the general election of 2010. Cameron was Prime Minister. Clegg (Leader of the Liberal Democrats) was his Deputy, Hague his Foreign Secretary, and Osborne his Chancellor. Miliband was Leader of the Opposition (the Labour Party). What did panellists write about these

---

[87] Directive SxMOA2/1/99/1.

prominent politicians of the early twenty-first century? What cultural resources did they draw upon? What marking criteria for grading politicians are suggested by these cultural resources? What image of the good politician is suggested by these marking criteria? And did this image of the good politician differ from that found in the mid-twentieth century?

All the named politicians were judged in terms of 'trust' and related categories. On Cameron, we have this data architect from Wigan: 'He's a bit like the geography teacher that sits on your desk trying to be friendly, but you know he has a bottle of Purell ready for when he goes back to his office.[88] I don't know – I basically agree with a lot of what he says, but I don't quite trust him.'[89] On Miliband, we have this writer from Johnstone: 'I don't feel any affinity towards him and wouldn't trust him to get the job done. He's wiry and gangly, and doesn't exude honesty or truth'.[90] On Hague, a retired shopkeeper was brief: 'Don't trust him.'[91] On Osborne, a local government officer from Sale wrote: 'Seems to command quite a presence when he is interviewed, but I wouldn't trust what he says.'[92]

The listed politicians were assessed on whether they could be trusted – to get the job done, to be honest, to tell the truth. Within this family of virtues, Hague was occasionally praised for being 'direct' and 'to the point'. A music teacher from Newark wrote of Hague: 'Direct, unfussy, on the ball.'[93] A railway signal designer from Crewe wrote: 'I have grown to like William Hague. He comes across as being focused and to the point.'[94] Miliband was also occasionally praised, but more for being 'genuine'. 'I like Ed Miliband. He's genuine!', wrote a youth worker from Llanelli.[95] 'I like Ed Miliband. He seems to be a good, genuine man, but where is the fire?', wrote a cleaner from Devon.[96]

Miliband was criticised for lacking 'fire', which we return to later, but also for lacking a 'position' or 'convictions'. Listen to this retired civil servant from East Boldon:

To me, Ed is more the 'policy wonk' ... Ed Miliband is still struggling to 'make his soul' politically: sure, he knows roughly where he stands on the political spectrum, but gives the impression that he's yet to 'harden' and become a finished product with a definite brand, ready to be marketed to the public. In fact, I'd say he gives

---

[88] Purell is a popular hand sanitiser in the UK.
[89] Panellist G5421, male, 35, data architect, Wigan.
[90] Panellist J4793, female, 33, writer, Johnstone.
[91] Panellist W853, female, 78, retired shopkeeper, Birkenhead.
[92] Panellist T4409, female, 35, local government officer, Sale.
[93] Panellist P2034, male, 36, music teacher, Newark.
[94] Panellist K5246, male, 45, railway signalling designer, Crewe.
[95] Panellist F1560, female, 93, youth worker, Llanelli.
[96] Panellist S496, female, 87, cleaner, Devon.

the impression that he'll never completely settle into any position – that his thinking will continue to evolve over time and could well move sharply away from wherever it is at the moment.[97]

This quality of Miliband's was to be approved of and admired 'on a purely personal level' but was 'not the quality most people look for in a political leader'. A broadcaster from Scotland was less generous in her assessment of Miliband's lack of 'soul': 'A lacklustre, incompetent "yes"-man with no personal or political presence whatsoever. He has as much appeal as a "conviction" politician as a wet dishcloth. He is a ghost, a shadow, a nothing, an invisible person and politician.'[98]

If Hague was direct and Miliband was genuine – but lacking a 'hard', 'definite', 'settled' position – then Cameron was 'smooth' and 'slippery': difficult to get hold of and pin down. 'He's smooth, too smooth', wrote a retired counsellor from the Fylde Coast.[99] A retired shopkeeper from Birkenhead just wrote this of Cameron: 'A smooth operator.'[100] Another retired shopkeeper, this time from Lewes, wrote slightly more but in the same vein: 'David Cameron projected himself as a sincere family man, but comes across as a smooth performer with a privileged background.'[101] Finally, on Cameron, listen again to our writer from Johnstone: 'He always appears to have squeaky clean and buffed-up skin when appearing on television, and to have a youngish face, but in terms of his politics, he's been very slippery and reneged on promises and plans.'[102] Cameron was not sincere. He was smooth and slippery. We return to his looks and privileged background later.

This family of virtues included trustworthiness, honesty, truthfulness, directness, genuineness, sincerity, and conviction. The corresponding vices included smoothness and slipperiness. They also included deviousness. Most of the named politicians were suspected of cunning and deception. A podiatrist from Dunblane wrote of Miliband: 'He seems nice enough, but then they always do when they want in!'[103] She suspected Miliband of just acting nice in order to win her vote. Cameron was also suspected of acting by our broadcaster from Scotland: 'He uses the media to give himself a high profile, in order to be "seen" by those who seem to matter ... He thinks he is so clever with his strategies, but some of the public are not that stupid and can see

---

[97] Panellist M3190, male, 55, retired civil servant, East Boldon.
[98] Panellist H1470, female, 60, broadcaster, Scotland.
[99] Panellist G226, female, 73, retired counsellor, Fylde Coast.
[100] Panellist W853, female, 78, retired shopkeeper, Birkenhead.
[101] Panellist S2083, male, 83, retired shopkeeper, Lewes.
[102] Panellist J4793, female, 33, writer, Johnstone.
[103] Panellist E5296, female, 33, podiatrist, Dunblane.

198   Changing Images of the Good Politician

through his little act.'[104] A literary events coordinator from London discussed Cameron and Osborne together:

David Cameron and George Osborne are two of a kind – public school educated men, career politicians, with a flawed, divisive ideology, but the ability to appear reasonable and caring in the public eye. They are from the [former Prime Minister] 'Tony Blair' school of politics – bland but hiding an ulterior motive below that.[105]

Indeed, it was Osborne who was most commonly depicted as operating with ulterior motives – as 'devious'. He was 'Clever, devious, unattractive' (youth worker, Llanelli).[106] 'Out of all of them, he looks the most devious!', wrote a podiatrist from Dunblane.[107] Then we have this tree inspector from Harpenden: 'George Osborne, like Cameron, I find to be a slimy character who is very good at twisting the truth.'[108]

All the named politicians, with perhaps the exception of Hague, were commonly criticised for lacking this family of virtues. But the prototypical untrustworthy politician – most associated with lacking these virtues or possessing their corresponding vices – was Clegg. We saw in Chapter 4 how Clegg, during the general election campaign of 2010, formally pledged 'to vote against any increase in [university tuition] fees in the next parliament', before joining the Conservative Party in Coalition Government and abstaining when a vote was taken that almost tripled the annual fee cap. In spring 2014, panellists had plenty to say about Clegg's broken promises. A retired sales consultant from Rochester found them noteworthy but not fatal: 'Nick seems ok. I don't dislike him, but he's reneged on certain pre-election 2010 promises such as the tuition college fees.'[109] The same cannot be said for this artist from Welton:

He will always be remembered for his broken promise on students' fees. Such a high profile betrayal is irredeemable. As a person, I am sure he is perfectly decent and honest, but he leaves me with a feeling of being the classic tragedy of a political career. To gain a front bench seat, he has betrayed many in the electorate.[110]

By breaking this pledge, Clegg was judged to have betrayed his voters. We see the same judgement in this response from a housewife in Newcastle:

[104] Panellist H1470, female, 60, broadcaster, Scotland.
[105] Panellist W5214, male, 28, literary events coordinator, London.
[106] Panellist F1560, female, 93, youth worker, Llanelli.
[107] Panellist E5296, female, 33, podiatrist, Dunblane.
[108] Panellist M5198, male, 43, tree inspector, Harpenden.
[109] Panellist L1002, female, 67, retired sales consultant, Rochester.
[110] Panellist P3209, male, 74, artist, Welton.

I would never trust Nick Clegg, even if he was the last man standing. How can you have your own face plastered around on billboards purporting to support the freezing of student fees, then within six months introduce higher tuition fees?? How can you betray your students so blatantly? ... I also believe he sold his soul when forming a coalition. Again, how could you form a coalition with the Conservative Party, whose policies were so far removed from your own?[111]

Clegg pledged one thing before doing another. In doing so, he betrayed those relying on him. Why did he do this? Why did he 'change policies', 'backtrack', 'compromise' (in a way that 'let down' those who supported him)?[112] Many suspected it was because he was 'a moral vacuum, desperate for power';[113] that he would 'sleep with anyone to get power (in the political sense)';[114] that he had 'sold out', 'sold his soul', 'jumped at the illusion of power at the expense of dancing to the Conservative's tune'.[115]

The good politician, then, was trustworthy. They were sincere and genuine, honest and direct. They were not smooth or slippery. They did not break promises and sell their souls for power. This was one family of virtues comprising the image of the good politician in the early twenty-first century. It was reminiscent of the sincere, honest, principled (good) politician of the mid-twentieth century. A second family of virtues, evident in MO writing from spring 2014, was reminiscent of the able, wise, clever (good) politician of the mid-twentieth century.

Hague was praised for being wise and clever. Our housewife from Newcastle wrote of Hague: 'I think his profile has been raised and improved with his foreign ministerial duties, which have seen him mature and become more diplomatic and wiser.'[116] For a technician from Bagstone, Hague was '[c]lever, educated'.[117] Then we have this civil servant from Nottingham: 'He seems to me to be a safe pair of hands, trustworthy and reliable, a professional.'[118] And this planning officer from Sheffield: 'I think [Hague] is perhaps a more effective politician now than he ever was.'[119]

Osborne was also praised for his ability, competence, and efficiency. Listen to this teacher from Belfast: 'Doing an excellent job and has shown

---

[111] Panellist 5429, female, 39, housewife, Newcastle.
[112] Panellist E5296, female, 33, podiatrist, Dunblane; Panellist W5345, male, 18, student, Walsall; Panellist H1806, male, 88, retired typesetter, South East.
[113] Panellist M3190, male, 55, retired civil servant, East Boldon.
[114] Panellist H3784, male, 41, postroom officer, Sutton.
[115] Panellist D5428, male, 40, nurse, Belfast; Panellist 5429, female, 39, housewife, Newcastle; Panellist E5014, male, 48, civil servant, Bath.
[116] Panellist R5429, female, 39, housewife, Newcastle.
[117] Panellist S5292, male, 63, senior technician, Bagstone.
[118] Panellist F3409, female, 63, civil servant, Nottingham.
[119] Panellist S3711, male, 38, planning officer, Sheffield.

great improvement in his ability to speak effectively in the [House of Commons].'[120] Or this civil servant from Nottingham: 'Another one branded as a "toff", but actually quite competent.'[121] Or this artist from Welton: '[Osborne] has proved to be very efficient as Chancellor.'[122] The good politician was clever, educated, wise. They were able, effective, competent, efficient. We return to the 'professional politician' and the 'toff' later.

If Hague and Osborne were judged to have ability, though not so frequently that one might reasonably label one or both of them as proto-typical able politicians, the other named politicians were generally criti-cised for lacking ability. Of Cameron, a retired sales consultant from Rochester wrote: 'He is OK, quite benign, but not as well-educated as one would expect from someone who has been to Eton.'[123] Our civil servant (retired) from East Boldon took a similar view of Cameron: 'He appears to have little sense of history and hasn't opened a book since he left Oxford, and probably thinks that culture is something to do with probiotic yoghurt.'[124] He added: '[B]ut that's what you'd expect from a modern politician.' As for Miliband, the repeated line was that, as Leader of the Labour Party, he was being asked to operate beyond his abilities. Listen to this from a retired clergyman in Newcastle: 'I wonder if [Miliband] is an example of someone who has risen to a position beyond his abilities.'[125] And this from a warehouse worker in Stoke-on-Trent: 'Oh dear. He reminds me of nothing so much as a sixth-form debating captain promoted beyond his abilities.'[126] The same line was applied to Clegg: 'He talks the talk', wrote our panellist from Johnstone, 'but it seems to be a lot of hot air. I think he means well, but could be out of his depth.'[127]

Our primary concern here is not with judgements of Clegg or Miliband or any of these politicians as individual politicians – though of course some readers may find such particular judgements interesting. It is with how politicians in general were judged – by what implicit marking criteria or 'grade descriptors' or popular image of the good politician. So far, we have identified two virtue families against which politicians appear to have been assessed in the early twenty-first century. The good politician was trustworthy (honest, genuine) and capable (competent, educated).

---

[120] Panellist R4526, male, 53, teacher, Belfast.
[121] Panellist F3409, female, 63, civil servant, Nottingham.
[122] Panellist P3209, male, 74, artist, Welton.
[123] Panellist L1002, female, 67, retired sales consultant, Rochester.
[124] Panellist M3190, male, 55, retired civil servant, East Boldon.
[125] Panellist B2710, male, 84, retired clergyman, Newcastle.
[126] Panellist C3167, male, 42, warehouse worker, Stoke-on-Trent.
[127] Panellist J4793, female, 33, writer, Johnstone.

We now turn to a third family of virtues that again reminds us of the good politician from the mid-twentieth century: this time, the moderate, level-headed, quiet politician.

Cameron was praised for being level-headed and offering stability. A senior marketing manager from Basingstoke wrote: 'I think David Cameron is a credible PM. He seems level-headed and not inclined to knee-jerk reactions. I think that stability is important.'[128] But he was also criticised for bickering and squabbling in the House of Commons – for example, by this retired typesetter from the South East: 'At Parliamentary Question Time, he acts like a schoolboy brawling over a conker result.'[129] This panellist criticised Miliband for much the same thing: '[T]he way he follows the traditional slanging match at Question Time disappoints me.' He also found Hague's political style too aggressive: 'My memory of him in the Thatcher years is the time when, as a long-haired student, he confronted a Labour MP in a most aggressive manner. At the time, his voice was similar to the rasping one he has today and I took an instant dislike to him.'

So the good politician should be level-headed. They should not react, be aggressive, slang, or brawl. But they should also be strong. Hague was praised by some writers for being strong. 'I feel like he's strong and dependable', wrote an unemployed panellist from Salisbury.[130] A teaching assistant from Bythorn wrote of Hague: 'Strong and opinio-nated. I always think he talks a lot of sense. Not a good leader, irritating to listen to, but I usually agree with him. Fair! Clever too.'[131] Hague was strong, dependable, opinionated. He was also decisive: '[Hague] has really grown in stature ... he is decisive and [has] most leadership skills in/on the world stage' (retired sales consultant, Rochester).[132]

The other politicians, by contrast, were generally criticised for being weak. Of Cameron, our teaching assistant from Bythorn wrote: 'I think he's a decent enough man, but probably a bit "weak" at times.'[133] Of Miliband, a postroom officer from Sutton wrote: 'Weak, annoying voice, not up to the job.'[134] Or take this tree inspector from Harpenden on Clegg: 'Nick Clegg is also a weak personality on the political stage and was never likely to hold much sway after back-tracking over tuition fees.'[135] These politicians were judged to have weak personalities and to lack the

[128] Panellist P5340, male, 37, senior marketing manager, Basingstoke.
[129] Panellist H1806, male, 88, retired typesetter, South East.
[130] Panellist B5342, female, 28, unemployed, Salisbury.
[131] Panellist D4400, female, 43, teaching assistant, Bythorn.
[132] Panellist L1002, female, 67, retired sales consultant, Rochester.
[133] Panellist D4400, female, 43, teaching assistant, Bythorn.
[134] Panellist H3784, male, 41, postroom officer, Sutton.
[135] Panellist M5198, male, 43, tree inspector, Harpenden.

strong personalities of the good politician. So Cameron was '[a] rather pitiful figure who isn't really strong enough to withstand the pitfalls of government' (youth worker, Llanelli).[136] On Miliband, a local government officer from Sale wrote: 'He seems fairly normal, but I am not sure that I can see him leading the country as he doesn't seem to have a strong enough personality.'[137] The same applied to Clegg: 'Nick Clegg seems to be the puppet of David Cameron. Again, I don't think he could be Prime Minister as he doesn't seem to have a strong enough personality and seems very submissive.' Clegg was described as 'weak',[138] 'wet',[139] 'spineless',[140] a 'yes man' with 'no backbone',[141] lacking in 'strength'.[142] Miliband was described as 'weak',[143] 'wet',[144] 'feeble', and easily 'intimidated'.[145] Cameron was described as lacking 'ruthlessness' and a 'strong personality'.[146]

The good politician, by contrast, was trustworthy, capable, level-headed, and strong. In possessing these virtues, to the degree expected by citizens, the good politician was, presumably, an extraordinary character. But this brings us to another family of virtues expected of the good politician in the early twenty-first century. Politicians were also judged against an image of what is 'ordinary' or 'normal'. And they were criticised for being 'odd' or 'strange'. They were criticised for being 'a bit . . . odd', in the case of Miliband;[147] or 'a bit of a creep', in the case of Hague (with his 'strange voice' – his 'distinctive voice . . . that works against him');[148] or 'creepy' and 'reptilian in his demeanour', in the case of Osborne.[149]

The good politician was expected to perform their normality by achieving the appropriate look, voice, and conduct for a variety of situations. If we stay with Osborne, he was associated at this time with austerity policies and public spending cuts. He was 'the austerity Chancellor'

---

[136] Panellist F1560, female, 93, youth worker, Llanelli.
[137] Panellist T4409, female, 35, local government officer, Sale.
[138] Panellist D4400, female, 43, teaching assistant, Bythorn.
[139] Panellist C4102, male, 50, graphic designer, Norfolk.
[140] Panellist W729, female, 56, supply teacher, Dundee.
[141] Panellist H1470, female, 60, broadcaster, Scotland.
[142] Panellist P2034, male, 36, music teacher, Newark.
[143] Panellist S5292, male, 63, technician, Bagstone.
[144] Panellist E5014, male, 48, civil servant, Bath.
[145] Panellist A2212, female, 57, writer, Watford.
[146] Panellist M3190, male, 55, retired civil servant, East Boldon; Panellist T4409, female, 35, local government officer, Sale.
[147] Panellist S5202, male, 25, student, Leeds.
[148] Panellist A2212, female, 57, writer, Watford; Panellist B5342, female, 28, unemployed, Salisbury; Panellist G226, female, 73, retired counsellor, Fylde Coast.
[149] Panellist M3005, female, 39, housewife, London; Panellist K5246, male, 45, railway signalling designer, Crewe.

(Cowley and Kavanagh 2016). And he was criticised for lacking the appropriate comportment for such a difficult national context. On behalf of herself and her husband, a cleaner from Devon wrote of Osborne: 'We cannot stand his face. He looks so smug. He has a face that looks like he is laughing at us all. I expect he is.'[150] Then a writer from Watford wrote: 'He is a dreadful person, constantly smirking while pursuing evil policies that harm the poor. He always looks so smug and there is the suggestion of the psychopath about him, on account of his inappropriate affect'.[151]

Another context in which the good politician was expected to seem normal – *in place* – was 'the world stage'. Cameron was praised for behaving appropriately and achieving the appropriate look for this context. Listen to this unemployed panellist from Salisbury: 'I like that he's Eton-educated and that he comes from such a well-off family – it's great to have the best of society in charge. He comes across well on the world stage. I like the way he dresses and conducts himself.'[152] Panellists generally worried about the other politicians in this context. For example, a civil servant from Bath wrote this of Hague: '[E]very time he used to appear in public, he had a habit of making a fool of himself – wearing a silly hat or sharing a hotel room with his young male colleague! ... I am worried that William represents the UK abroad.'[153]

A third context for the good politician to master was the age of the digital image – easily produced, circulated, manipulated. Clegg was praised for being 'presentable' and 'photogenic': 'Despite his lack of conviction, he is much more likeable and presentable than Miliband. He is photogenic and appealing, with a strong wife and nice kids. His personal image is his best feature' (unemployed, Salisbury).[154] But most of our named politicians were graded poorly for presentation. If we take Miliband as an example, a retired sales consultant from Rochester wrote: 'He is ok, but not inspirational, not inspiring. He mumbles. He is very adenoidic. And when he ate a bacon bap – during the recent Newark by-election, well, it was enough to put you off your food!'[155] Then we have this from a care worker in Leeds: 'It's a shame he's not very photogenic.'[156] And this from a planning officer in Sheffield: '[U]nfortunately, we are in such an image-driven age that he is let down a little here in the public's perception.'[157]

---

[150] Panellist S496, female, 87, cleaner, Devon.
[151] Panellist A2212, female, 57, writer, Watford.
[152] Panellist B5342, female, 28, unemployed, Salisbury.
[153] Panellist E5014, male, 48, civil servant, Bath.
[154] Panellist B5342, female, 28, unemployed, Salisbury.
[155] Panellist L1002, female, 67, retired sales consultant, Rochester.
[156] Panellist M4780, female, 30, care worker, Leeds.
[157] Panellist S3711, male, 38, planning officer, Sheffield.

Finally, the good politician needed to appear normal – *at ease* – in the context of everyday life. Consider the following two extracts – the first from a retired civil servant in East Boldon and the second from a marketing manager in Basingstoke:

There's a further problem that I can't gloss over and that's Ed Miliband's social gaucherie. Gaucherie outside of a very limited range of places and social situations, I mean. He's presumably at ease in a few milieu, such as university lecture rooms, conferences, and think tank seminars, and politico-literary lunches, but put him in a supermarket, a church hall, a busy high street, or a pub and he looks like a polite, mild-mannered Martian bemusedly trying to orient himself in an unfamiliar world. He's *so* metropolitan, *so* North London, that to people from, say, Huddersfield or Bristol, he's almost a foreigner. And that in turn raises the question of anti-Semitism.[158]

George Osborne always seems very awkward in the media, but the fact that he is Chancellor of the Exchequer in spite of this makes me think he must be incredibly intelligent ... He does come across as odd and uncomfortable and I cannot imagine being relaxed in his company.[159]

The good politician was expected to appear as if they belonged not only on the world stage but also in a provincial supermarket or pub. They were expected to appear at ease themselves but also to put others at ease – to appear as relaxing company for citizens. The same marketing manager from Basingstoke wrote this of Hague: 'I like William Hague and think he would be someone it would be easy to talk to.'

The good politician, then, was trustworthy, capable, level-headed, strong, and normal in a variety of ways (look, voice, behaviour) and situations (from the national political context to the world stage to the age of the digital image to everyday life). Finally, and connected to this last family of virtues, the good politician of the early twenty-first century was 'in touch' with the 'real lives' of 'regular', 'common', 'ordinary' people. None of the listed politicians were found by panellists to meet this final standard. Cameron and Osborne were judged to be especially 'out of touch'. One frequently repeated category here was the 'toff'. Some panellists used the term to describe Cameron and Osborne. For example, a retired counsellor from Fylde Coast wrote of Osborne: 'Looks like a schoolboy, but has matured somewhat. In some ways, I think he's done a good job with our finances. But to me, he's still another High Tory "toff".'[160] Other panellists felt the need to defend Cameron and Osborne against such descriptions. For example, our retired civil servant from East

---

[158] Panellist M3190, male, 55, retired civil servant, East Boldon.
[159] Panellist P5340, male, 37, marketing manager, Basingstoke.
[160] Panellist G226, female, 73, retired counsellor, Fylde Coast.

Boldon wrote: 'I'm sick of people banging on about the fact that Cameron went to Eton. I don't care where a man went to school. And as for being a "toff" – his father was a stockbroker, I believe. Hardly the Duke of Westminster.'[161]

Related categories here were the 'posh', 'rich', 'privileged' politician. Cameron was described as an 'arrogant posh boy. Sticks up for the middle/upper classes' (postroom officer, Sutton).[162] A retired nursery nurse from Ducklington wrote of Cameron: 'He is a very privileged man who went to Eton etc. so that must colour his attitudes.'[163] Also of Cameron, a supply teacher from Dundee simply wrote: 'Too posh for me.'[164] Then we have Osborne. Listen to this civil servant from Bath: 'I particularly dislike his arrogant attitude towards the electorate who earn so much less than the multimillionaire posh boy.'[165] Then listen to this housewife from Newcastle, also on Osborne: 'He doesn't have any character appeal to the general public. Again, the upper class posh boy image doesn't really appeal to the common voter who is struggling to cope on his lower salary.'[166]

This was the primary concern for many panellists. If Cameron and Osborne were posh, rich, privileged – toffs – then how could they understand the struggles of 'the common voter'? Of Cameron, a music teacher from Newark asked: 'Works hard and well, but does he really know the plight of so many people?'[167] Similarly, a care worker from Leeds wrote: 'I think he's a pompous, prejudiced rich boy who knows nothing about the problems of normal people.'[168] The same applied to Osborne. Our care worker from Leeds again: 'I absolutely detest him. He is rich and doesn't know how hard it is to live on a low income. He's also really smug and ugly looking.' Our music teacher from Newark again: 'Direct, sure of himself, but like D Cameron, does he really understand the plight of so many people?' Or listen to this cleaner from Devon: 'People like George Osborne have never lived on a very low income and have no idea what they are talking about . . . The problem with George is he has no idea how people manage to live on low incomes.'[169]

Cameron had been educated at Eton and Oxford. His grandfather was Sir William Mount of Wasing Place, a Lieutenant Colonel and Second Baronet. Osborne had been educated at St Pauls and a close friend of

---

[161] Panellist M3190, male, 55, retired civil servant, East Boldon.
[162] Panellist H3784, male, 41, postroom officer, Sutton.
[163] Panellist I1610, female, 70, retired nursery nurse, Ducklington.
[164] Panellist W729, female, 56, supply teacher, Dundee.
[165] Panellist E5014, male, 48, civil servant, Bath.
[166] Panellist R5429, female, 39, housewife, Newcastle.
[167] Panellist P2034, male, 36, music teacher, Newark.
[168] Panellist M4780, female, 30, care worker, Leeds.
[169] Panellist S496, female, 87, cleaner, Devon.

Cameron at Oxford. They were perhaps obvious targets for criticism along these lines. They were the prototypical 'out of touch' politicians. But it should be noted how the other named politicians were judged harshly in this regard too. A retired banker from Brentwood gave a general response to MO's question: 'Five names you quote are all rich men, all men not women, who are only interested in themselves and their cronies. Osborne is the worst and exemplifies the lack of knowledge of the world.'[170] A local government officer from Cromer focused on Miliband: 'Where are the true socialists from ordinary backgrounds and schools who are really in touch with people?'[171] Our retired nursery nurse from Ducklington noted of Clegg: 'Also comes from a privileged background.'[172] Then there was Hague: 'Typical Tory politician – upper middle class and privileged upbringing' (local government officer, Sale).[173]

Our point here is not whether Hague or anyone else actually had the upbringing or background ascribed to them by panellists. It is that politicians were assessed on how 'normal', 'ordinary', 'real' they were – and, in most cases, were found wanting. They were found wanting because they were upper middle class, privileged, rich. But they were also found wanting because they were 'career politicians' or 'professional politicians'. A housewife from St Gennys took all the named politicians together: 'David Cameron, Ed Miliband, Nick Clegg, William Hague, and George Osborne are all career politicians. They have never had a regular job in commerce or industry and have no comprehension of how we mere mortals live'.[174] Another housewife from Newcastle focused on Cameron (elected to Parliament after spells as a political researcher and special advisor): '[H]e is a professional politician and as a result I cannot create an association with him or his wife. Maybe if Mr Cameron had a "story" to tell, some struggle, some affinity, then I would feel differently, but he remains detached.'[175] A retired nursery nurse from Ducklington focused on Miliband (son of human rights campaigner Marion Kozak and Marxist academic Ralph Miliband): 'Ed Miliband comes from a "political family" and has been brought up in that "bubble".'[176] Finally, we have our unemployed panellist from Salisbury on Hague (former President of the Oxford University Conservative Association and also the Oxford Union): '[A]s I know he has

---

[170] Panellist R3422, male, 66, retired banker, Brentwood.
[171] Panellist C3691, female, 49, local government officer, Cromer.
[172] Panellist I1610, female, 70, retired nursery nurse, Ducklington.
[173] Panellist T4409, female, 35, local government officer, Sale.
[174] Panellist W3163, female, 56, housewife, St Gennys.
[175] Panellist R5429, female, 39, housewife, Newcastle.
[176] Panellist I1610, female, 70, retired nursery nurse, Ducklington.

Table 7.2 *The good politician of the early twenty-first century*

Virtue family	Shared categories	Prototypical politician
Trustworthiness	Trustworthiness Honesty Genuineness Convictions Soul	None, but Clegg was the prototypical untrustworthy politician
Ability	Ability Education	None really, but perhaps Hague and Osborne at a push
Moderation	Level-headedness Stability	None really
Strength	Strength Strength of personality	None really, but perhaps Hague at a push
Normality	Normality Look/face/dress Voice Easiness	None really, but perhaps Cameron and Clegg at a push
In touch with reality	In touch with reality Normality Ordinariness	None, but Cameron and Osborne were the prototypical out of touch politicians

been in politics from a very young age, I feel he is out of touch with reality.'[177]

We are now in a position to characterise the good politician of the early twenty-first century. This good politician was trustworthy, able, moderate, strong, normal – in a variety of ways and situations – and in touch with reality as experienced by most people (Table 7.2). These families of virtues and associated categories were shared and repeated by a range of panellists. In this section, we have only considered responses to one directive from one particular year (spring 2014). But what we have found matches what we found in other chapters using other evidence. In Chapter 3, we saw how survey questions across the period focused on the trustworthiness of politicians (whether they tell the truth, keep promises, give straight answers, use official figures correctly) and their (dis)connection to voters (whether they lose touch with people and whether they only care about people with money). So the good politician, here, was trustworthy and in touch with reality. Then in Chapter 4, we saw how responses to MO directives from across the period repeated the story-lines (and associated categories) that politicians are not straight-talking (the broken promise, the spin doctor, the stage-managed encounter, the

[177] Panellist B5342, female, 28, unemployed, Salisbury.

avoided topic or question) and out of touch/all the same (the rich boy, the posh boy, the toff, the career politician). Again, the good politician here was trustworthy and in touch with reality. Then, in Chapter 5, we saw how responses to multiple directives repeated the storyline that politicians are a joke – an embarrassment, to be ridiculed for making gaffes, not to be taken seriously. The good politician, here, was capable and normal (especially normal-looking and -sounding on the world stage and in front of the camera or microphone). Finally, in Chapter 6, we saw how responses to directives from across the period focused on whether politicians and parties differ from one another, offer voters alternatives and choice, engage in debate, take positions regarding the issues of concern to people, and represent people. Alternatively, they focused on whether politicians and parties create unnecessary debate, create divisions that otherwise would not exist, engage in petty bickering, and adopt extreme positions. Here, the good politician was trustworthy and strong (with convictions and soul) but also moderate (not extreme).

Regarding Table 7.2, and comparing it with Table 7.1, we find some historical continuity. Like the good politician of the mid-twentieth century, the good politician of the early twenty-first century was sincere (trustworthy), able, moderate, and strong. But we also find some historical change. The expectation that politicians be 'human' appears to have developed from a relatively minor and undemanding expectation that politicians be genial, warm, and sympathetic to a relatively major and more demanding expectation that politicians be 'normal' in a variety of ways and situations and especially 'in touch' with the 'real' lives of 'ordinary' people.

Also like the good politician of the mid-twentieth century, we find the good politician of this later period to be characterised by tensions and contradictions. Indeed, some of these tensions appear to have continued from the immediate post-war period. The good politician was imagined to be trustworthy (genuine, with convictions) yet moderate (willing to compromise and form coalitions in the interests of the country as a whole). They were imagined to be moderate yet strong (with a strong enough personality to lead others). Some of these tensions, however, appear to be new. The good politician was imagined to be trustworthy yet normal (good-looking and -sounding in a variety of situations). They were imagined to be capable (extraordinarily educated) yet in touch with reality (with experience of life as an ordinary citizen). They were imagined to be normal – in place, at ease – in a range of situations from the world stage to the provincial high street.

These latter tensions were 'new' in one sense, since they were not prominent in mid-twentieth-century Britain, but not in another sense, since we can imagine them existing in other contexts (beyond the UK in the early twenty-first century). Indeed, they map onto some of the time-less tensions and traps identified by others and introduced at the top of this chapter. In particular, the tension between trustworthiness and mod-eration is reminiscent of Medvic's principled-pragmatic trap. The tension between being trustworthy and being good-looking and -sounding in a variety of situations is reminiscent of Kane and Patapan's systemic hypocrisy. And the tension between being extraordinary (trustworthy, capable, strong) and ordinary (normal, in touch) is reminiscent of numer-ous formulations in political theory. These include Medvic's ordinary-and-exceptional trap. They include Kane and Patapan's central tension of democratic leadership (i.e. the challenge of leadership in a system celebrating equality). They also include Kane and Patapan's distinction between trustee representation (where citizens want leaders to represent the very best of them and be exceptionally capable) and mirror represen-tation (where citizens want leaders to mirror them and be normal).

We have learned much from this existing literature on democratic leadership. We have also made some original contributions in this chap-ter. We have demonstrated how the popular image of the good politician changed between the middle of the last century and the start of the present century. Certain criteria for judging politicians came to the fore and became salient for citizens. Certain tensions, which may well be timeless in theory, became more important. Many citizens came to expect politicians not only *for* the people (sincere, hard-working, able, moderate, strong) but also *of* the people (normal, in touch).

The Good Politician in the Early Twenty-First Century: Survey Data

To further test these findings, we conducted a national survey asking respondents how important they thought particular criteria were for jud-ging politicians.[178] Specifically, the survey asked: '[H]ow important, if at all, would you say the things I am going to read out are to make a good politician?', with respondents choosing from a four-point scale ('very important', 'fairly important', 'not very important', and 'not at all impor-tant' – with 'don't knows' also permitted). The criteria used in the survey were informed by the MO research (i.e. the virtue families and shared categories summarised in Tables 7.1 and 7.2).

In Figure 7.1, we plot the percentage of respondents saying the virtue or trait is 'very important' (indicated by the lower, dark grey–shaded bar)

---

[178] The survey of a nationally representative sample of 2055 adults from across the UK was conducted online by Populus between 9 and 10 August 2017.

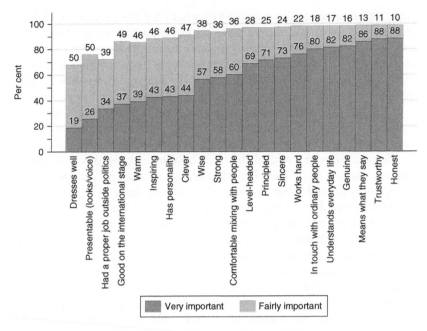

Figure 7.1 Traits making a good politician, 2017.

and 'fairly important' (indicated by the upper, light grey–shaded bar), with criteria ordered from left to right on the x-axis from the lowest to the highest ranking in terms of being 'very important'. Strikingly, criteria associated with trustworthiness – politicians being trustworthy, honest, genuine, and meaning what they say – are prominent, taking the top four places when only 'very important' responses are considered (with sincerity and being principled ranked only slightly lower). The next most prominent virtue family is that of being in touch with reality, with 'understands everyday life' and 'in touch with ordinary people' ranked as the fifth and six most important traits. Moderation ('is level-headed'), strength ('is strong', 'has personality', 'is inspiring'), and ability ('is wise', 'is clever') are each placed towards the middle in terms of importance, whereas 'normality' ('dresses well', 'is presentable in terms of their looks and voice', 'is comfortable mixing with most people in most situations', 'is warm') tends to figure lower down the ranked list. This latter finding may be due to social desirability bias in the behaviour of survey respondents aware that they should not be influenced by superficial factors such as the appearance of politicians – though note how the lowest ranked category of all, dressing well, is still considered important by almost 70 per cent of respondents.

These findings are consistent with our argument that citizens appear to want many things – some of which are not easily combined – from their politicians. For the majority of our traits, more than 80 per cent of respondents considered them very or fairly important, presenting politicians with a difficult task of being viewed favourably across such a wide range of criteria. Even just for those items considered 'very important' by citizens, politicians must be honest, trustworthy, genuine, in touch with ordinary people, hard-working, sincere, principled, and level-headed. In the early twenty-first century, politicians face the challenge of matching up to these expectations – while knowing that other elites such as journalists may focus on the presentational side of politics.

It is also possible to consider how perceptions of what makes for a good politician vary by social group. To do this, we estimated an ordinal logistic regression of the association of particular demographic predictors (gender, age, social class, and education) with the perceived importance of each of the traits, with values of the dependent variable ranging from 'not at all important' to 'very important' on the four-point scale described previously. The ordinal logistic regression provides us with a coefficient for each of the predictors, where a coefficient of 0.75 can be interpreted as meaning that a one unit increase in the predictor – in our case, whether a survey respondent is in a particular group – leads to a 0.75 increase in the *log-odds* of a given trait (e.g. honesty, warmth) being important to the survey respondent, if all the other variables in the model are held constant. In Figure 7.2, the coefficient is indicated by a diamond, while the whiskers indicate the standard errors of the coefficients to show where the effects are statistically significant (where the error bars do not intersect the zero line), at the 95 per cent confidence level. What is most crucial when reading the figure is which side of the zero line the coefficient lies on (i.e. whether the association is positive or negative) and whether the whiskers intersect it (i.e. whether that association is statistically significant). The results reveal a number of interesting patterns.

First, there are clear gender differences for most criteria: women are more likely than men to believe that such qualities are important for making the good politician. The most pronounced effects are for being warm, strong, comfortable mixing with people, understanding everyday life, and having personality. There are some generational differences too, with older respondents (aged fifty-five and over) tending to consider it more important that politicians mean what they say and be sincere, principled, strong, in touch with ordinary people, level-headed, honest, and hard-working. Interestingly, there are few differences by social class. The exceptions are that working-class voters (C2DE) consider being principled to be less important and being warm to be more important.

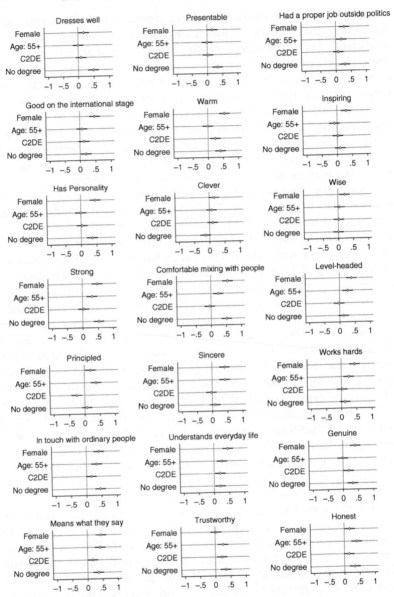

Figure 7.2 Demographic predictors of perceived importance of traits making a good politician.

The effects of education are consistent with these effects of social class: people with lower levels of education (i.e. no degree) tend to favour the virtue families of trustworthiness, 'normality', and being 'in touch with reality' (specifically, they are more likely to consider it important for politicians to be strong, warm, trustworthy, honest, and genuine, to mean what they say, to be in touch with ordinary people, to be comfortable mixing with most people, to dress well, to have personality, and to be presentable).

There is much that could be explored further here. But we have now established the two main points worth taking from these survey data for the purposes of our main argument. First, despite some variation by trait and social group, most UK citizens in the twenty-first century consider most of the listed criteria to be important. The image of the good politician is thus multi-faceted and difficult to perform. Second, if the traits are ranked by perceived importance, not only are the two relatively new virtue families established from the MO data widely perceived to be important ('normality' and 'in touch with reality'), but also being in touch with reality is perceived to be second in importance only to 'trustworthiness'.

The Political Class, the Ideology of Intimacy, and Democratic Egalitarianism

Considering these survey data alongside the historical comparative analysis made possible by the MO material analysed earlier in the chapter, we are left with some claims and questions for discussion. One claim is that criteria by which politicians are judged appear to have become more demanding over time. The associated question is this: Where did these more demanding criteria come from? Put differently, why did these more demanding criteria, and the tensions they create, move to the foreground around the turn of the twenty-first century? A second claim is that politicians appear to have performed poorly against these more demanding criteria in the early twenty-first century. They were praised less and criticised more than in the mid-twentieth century. Vices were mentioned more often than virtues. In contrast to the earlier period, when most of the virtue families were represented by a prototypical politician (Table 7.1), some of the virtue families most important for citizens in the later period – trustworthiness or being in touch with reality – were not represented by any prototypical politician (Table 7.2). The associated question here is this: Why did politicians appear to perform so poorly against these admittedly demanding criteria in the early twenty-first century?

Let us begin with the question of where these more demanding criteria came from (that politicians be 'normal' and 'in touch' with 'real life') and the associated question of why these tensions came to the fore around the turn of the twenty-first century (between the trustworthy politician and the politician with appropriate performances for multiple situations, between the extraordinarily capable politician and the politician in touch with life as it is ordinarily experienced, and between the politician at home on the world stage but also in the provincial supermarket). One possible explanation is that, over time, politicians themselves have become less normal and more out of touch; have become more different from and less connected to citizens. If this was the case, the virtues of politicians being normal and in touch may not have seemed relevant to citizens in the mid-twentieth century but may have been pushed front and centre by a change in the profile of politicians during the second half of the twentieth century. So what does the evidence tell us about politicians during this period?

There is a large literature on the changing social background and associated political style of politicians in the UK and similar democracies (e.g. Best and Cotta 2000, Borchert and Zeiss 2003, Cotta and Best 2007, Guttsman 1963, Mellors 1978, Norris 1997a, Norris and Lovenduski 1995, Riddell 1993, Rush 1969). Most of these studies suggest that, since 1945, the background and style of politicians have been shaped by numerous processes. The state has been expanded and modernised. Occupations have been professionalised. Financial rewards for politicians – pensions, allowances, salaries – have been introduced and improved. Career opportunities for politicians have been expanded (to positions on parliamentary select committees, in quangos, as lobbyists or consultants for interest groups, in the institutions of the European Union, in the devolved administrations of Scotland, Wales, and Northern Ireland). One outcome of all this has been the decline of amateur politicians, aristocratic politicians, and working-class politicians (most of whom spent only a few years in Parliament, worked part time, had other occupations, and returned to those occupations after a few years – Jun 2003). A related outcome has been the rise of 'professional politicians' and 'career politicians' – where, in Max Weber's (1984) terms, the former live *off* politics (making their money from politics) and the latter live *for* politics (making their careers in politics). Within this group of university-educated, middle-class politicians, there has also been a decline in those coming from 'brokerage occupations' like teachers and lawyers, where these occupations provide time and/or skills and/or networks for aspiring politicians, and an increase in those coming from 'instrumental occupations' like party workers, assistants to MPs, think tank researchers, and office holders in quangos (Cairney 2007). Overall, there has been convergence in the social background and associated style of politicians despite a small rise in the proportions of women and ethnic-minority politicians (Criddle 2016). There has emerged a 'political class' comprised of politicians but also political consultants, advisers, researchers, and lobbyists that is relatively homogeneous and well connected internally but relatively detached from citizens in wider society.

This literature suggests that politicians may well have become more abnormal and out of touch over the second half of the twentieth century. It suggests that citizens' recent concerns about the normality of politicians and the extent to which they understand real life may well be a response to the changing social profile and associated style of politicians. However, this argument should not be taken too far. There may not have been many professional politicians and career politicians in mid-twentieth-century Britain. There may not have been a political class at this time – not least because politicians back then were more divided by social class (Jun 2003). Nevertheless, many well-known politicians in that period were hardly normal or ordinary (in the way meant by MO panellists quoted in the preceding section). For every Ernest Bevin (who entered Parliament with little formal education, having worked as a labourer, a lorry driver, and a union official) or Aneurin Bevan (who left school at thirteen and followed his father down the local coal mine), there was at least one Churchill (educated at Harrow and Sandhurst and whose father was the Seventh Duke of Marlborough and Chancellor of the Exchequer). If we consider the other Labour politicians named in MO's July 1950 directive, Attlee was educated at Oxford, while Cripps was educated at Winchester and University College London before becoming one of the highest-paid barristers in all of England (Rubinstein 2003). Yet panellists hardly, if ever, questioned the ability of Cripps or Attlee or Churchill to understand their lives. They hardly, if ever, referred to the social background of these politicians – or, indeed, any politicians (when asked about politicians as a group in February 1945 or local councillors in November 1945 or MPs in May 1949 or their own MP in August 1949). It would seem that citizens in the early twenty-first century judged politicians to be abnormal and out of touch not only because politicians have changed – have become professional politicians, career politicians, and members of a political class – but also because citizens valued normality and being in touch with reality more highly than in the mid-twentieth century.

This last point leads to another question: Where did these heightened expectations on the part of citizens come from? This is a difficult question to answer empirically, given the available data. Instead, we have two theories, both of which make sense, we think, as explanations for this change in citizens' expectations. The first comes from Richard Sennett's (1977) *The Fall of Public Man*. He studied London and Paris in the 1750s when the bourgeoisie began to flourish, the 1840s when the effects of industrial capitalism became manifest, and the 1890s (a third 'posthole' in his comparative-static analysis). In both cities, in archived material and publications from across this period of almost 150 years, he observed changes to public behaviour, speech, dress, and belief. He observed how industrial capitalism had traumatised people and led them to withdraw from the public life of their Enlightenment cities. Capitalism had provided mass-produced clothing that mystified public life and made strangers difficult to read. At the same time, secularism had encouraged people to approach others not by their assigned place in nature but by their immediate sensation and feeling, their relation to personal needs and experience, their value in the formation of personality and self.

What does this have to do with images of the good politician in twentieth-century Britain? Sennett argues that capitalism and secularism worked slowly to produce, eventually, by the 1960s and 1970s, an ideology of intimacy in societies like the UK. People turned inwards, away from public life and exchanges with strangers in the cosmopolitan city. They expected warmth, trust, and the open expression of feeling from all experiences ('the tyranny of intimacy'). In our specific field of politics, they became focused less on actions and programmes, such as the drafting and execution of legislation, and more on personality and character, such as the motives and feelings of politicians. For Sennett, during the second half of the twentieth century, citizens became self-absorbed and narcissistic. They became unable to understand what belongs to the domain of the self and self-gratification and what belongs outside that domain. They came to find politics that is not intimate to be impersonal, inauthentic, and alienating. The result, for Sennett, was a narrowing of the content of political discourse.

This is one potential explanation for the changing image of the good politician. It is a theory predicting the increased focus we have seen on how politicians look, sound, and behave; the appropriateness of this comportment and conduct to a variety of both traditionally public and private situations; and the personal experiences of politicians. A second potential explanation comes from Richard Hoggart's (1957) *The Uses of Literacy*. Hoggart's geographical, historical, and social focus was narrower than Sennett's: on working-class culture in Britain from the end of the First World War to the mid-1950s. Over this period, he noted that 'working people' had become better off with better living conditions, health, consumer goods, and, crucially, educational opportunities. He asked how improved literacy, in particular, was being used – by working people themselves but also those keen to persuade working people through appeals and encouragements in mass publications. Drawing on his own experience, supplemented by literary analysis of popular magazines and periodicals, he made a series of claims.

First, in the early twentieth century, there was an 'us' and 'them' working-class culture in Britain. 'Us' described working people, celebrated for their independence, self-reliance, thrift, cleanliness, friendliness, co-operation, and neighbourliness. 'Them' described other people – the bosses and public officials – denigrated for being at once both powerful and unhelpful. Thinking back to Chapter 5, it is worth emphasising how this working-class culture, for Hoggart, was not a deferential culture. Working people were celebrated. They did not generally view themselves as inferior. Bosses and public officials were denigrated. They were not generally viewed by working people as superior.

Second, around the middle of the twentieth century, mass publications emerged that built on these existing attitudes and extended them in various ways. In particular, they built on the old ideas of independence and self-reliance and extended them so far as flattery of 'the common man' and worship of 'the little man as hero'. Again, it is worth emphasising that, for Hoggart, improved literacy did not automatically produce more critical citizens. His focus was on how improved literacy among working people was *used by elites* (working through mass publications). What were the products of this cultural work? They were less the first signs of a more critical citizenry – educated, skilled, questioning, active – and more the first signs of decidedly uncritical 'high-brow hunting', 'inverted snobbery', and 'levelling down'. For Hoggart, looking forward to the second half of the twentieth century, this fledgling 'democratic egalitarianism' threatened to undermine political democracy. It threatened to divert attention away from the important qualities of democratic leaders – their intellect, courage, and discipline – and towards other qualities like 'the common touch' and blind faith in 'the rightness of majority opinion'. It threatened, we might say, to supplement expectations that politicians be sincere, capable, and strong with expectations that politicians be 'normal' and 'ordinary'.

Conclusion

In this chapter, in order to explain the rise of anti-politics described in Chapters 3 to 5, we have argued for a focus on 'the good politician', in addition to 'the good citizen'; also on the *popular* image of the good politician, in addition to the elite image; and also on the *changing* image of the good politician, in addition to the timeless tensions of democratic leadership. Drawing on volunteer writing for MO, we have demonstrated how the good politician of the mid-twentieth century was imagined to be sincere, hard-working, able, human, moderate, and strong. This image was characterised by tensions and contradictions. But it was just about possible for politicians to perform – if not as individuals then at least as a group (with different politicians representing the different families of virtue). By contrast, the good politician of the twenty-first century was imagined to be trustworthy, able, moderate, and strong but also 'normal' – with a look, voice, and behaviour appropriate to a variety of situations – and 'in touch' with 'real life' as experienced by 'ordinary' people. The long standing but relatively minor expectation that politicians be 'human' – genial, warm, sympathetic – had developed into something more prominent and demanding. Citizens now expected politicians not only *for* the people but also *of* the people. And they did not see politicians achieving this more demanding image of the good politician – either as individuals or as a group.

These new expectations, we have argued, might be explained by at least three processes. Politics became professionalised over the second half of the twentieth century, such that many politicians and other political professionals gradually formed a relatively homogeneous class, seemingly detached from the rest of society. Over the same period, the ideology of intimacy spread through societies like the UK, encouraging citizens to expect intimacy – warmth, trust, open expression, personality, character, authenticity – in their engagements with formal politics. Then, over the same period, democratic egalitarianism spread through societies like the UK, encouraging citizens to expect 'the common touch' – majority opinion, the low brow, the simple – in their engagements with formal politics.

Finally, we have noted that twenty-first-century politicians appear to perform poorly against the image of the good politician held by twenty-first-century citizens. This might be just because that image is especially demanding of politicians. It might also be that politicians have become a homogeneous class. There are not so many different politicians to represent the different families of virtue in the twenty-first century (as there were in the mid-twentieth century, when no single politician represented the good politician of that period but each virtue family had its own prototype among the most prominent politicians of the day). In the next chapter, we propose a third explanation for why politicians appear to have performed increasingly poorly against the popular image of the good politician. This image would be difficult for politicians to achieve under any circumstances, but it is especially difficult to achieve since the mediatisation of politics and the professionalisation of political campaigning. What explains the rise of anti-politics in the UK and similar democracies is not only the changing image of the good politician, against which citizens judge politicians, but also the changing contexts in which politicians and citizens encounter each other, which shape the performances of politicians, on which the judgements of citizens are based.

8 Changing Modes of Political Interaction

Introduction

Citizens' judgements of politics are shaped by their understandings or folk theories, but also their encounters and interactions. Understandings, particularly images of 'the good politician', were the focus of Chapter 7. That chapter made two main claims. Politicians in the early twenty-first century were judged by citizens against particularly demanding criteria. Furthermore, such politicians were judged by citizens generally to perform poorly against these criteria. In this chapter, we now consider the role of political interaction in these judgements and in the rise of anti-political sentiment over the second half of the twentieth century.

By political interaction, we mean something beyond the supply and demand factors discussed in Chapters 5 and 6. In part, we mean what some researchers have called 'intermediary factors' (e.g. Norris 2011). There have been changes in the media sector. It has been deregulated. New outlets have been established, and programming has expanded. Overall, the sector has become more competitive. In this context, news reporting of politics has changed. It has become more negative – because stories of partisan conflict or institutional failure are thought to attract consumers and so to attract advertisers (Baumgartner and Bonafont 2015, Kepplinger 2000, Robinson 1976, Soroka and McAdams 2015). News reporting of politics has become dominated by strategic news frames, in which politicians are positioned as self-interested and unconcerned with the public good (Cappella and Hall Jamieson 1997). For Mark Thompson (2016), former Director General of the British Broadcasting Corporation (BBC) and, at the time of writing, President of The New York Times Company, such news reporting has become dominated by the following items. *Short stories* focus on soundbites and edit out all conditional clauses and qualifications. *Forensic journalism* involves hero-journalists exposing villain-politicians by way of adversarial interviews. *Opinion* has replaced the more expensive analytical journalism of specialist correspondents and is used to differentiate media organisations in the increasingly crowded marketplace. *Instant reaction* is freely available from social media but contributes to the noisy feedback loop known by media professionals as 'howlround'.

There have also been changes in political campaigning. The context here was expansion of the franchise, embourgeoisement, partisan dealignment, declining party membership, and rising voter volatility. Political campaigning has become professionalised and populated by 'the new campaign professionals' (Kavanagh 1995): advertising agents, pollsters, public relations advisors, speechwriters, spin doctors, researchers. It has become more negative – because 'knocking copy' is thought by these professionals to be more effective than positive advertising (Crewe and Harrop 1989, Rosenbaum 1997). It has become nationalised, with the 'premodern doorstep campaign' of leafleting, canvassing, public meetings, and direct communication between local politicians, constituency volunteers, and voters (Norris 1997b) replaced by the 'modern national campaign' of press conferences, rallies, opinion polls, and so on. Then political campaigning has become targeted on floating voters in marginal constituencies via direct mail ('the postmodern campaign' – ibid.).

Of course, these two sets of changes – in political campaigning and the media sector – are related, and this relationship is captured by the concepts of 'political communication' (see Blumler and Kavanagh 1999) and 'the mediatisation of politics' (see Mazzoleni and Schulz 1999, Strömbäck 2008). With the expansion of the franchise, politics became more dependent on media coverage. Initially, in the 'era of mass propaganda' (Wring 1995), politics controlled such media coverage through regulation. But over time, as media became more abundant, politics lost control (Black 2005, Kandiah 1995, Wring 1995). Politics had to adapt to media logic (mediatisation): simplification, visualisation, personalisation, intimacy, drama, conflict. During the second half of the twentieth century, politics especially adapted to television (Blumler and Kavanagh 1999, Kavanagh 1995) – by, for example, repeating short statements appropriate to television soundbites or providing 'good pictures' in the form of leader walkabouts and other photo opportunities. Today, political communication is best characterised as a struggle between politicians trying to set the agenda and manage the stage and disdainful journalists focused on meta-campaign stories and the unmasking of politicians (Kavanagh 1995).

What have been the effects of all these developments? Journalists and the new campaign professionals have come between citizens and politicians (Neustadt 1997). Citizens have come to hear less from politicians themselves, and politicians have come to meet fewer citizens in person (Kavanagh 1995). But how these developments have been received by citizens themselves is the subject of much debate. 'Popular culturalists' see media and political abundance as grounds for optimism, while 'critical traditionalists' see fragmentation and spectacle as grounds for pessimism (Blumler and Kavanagh 1999). There is a large literature on media effects and political support. Simple models of propaganda and stimulus-response have gradually been replaced by more complex models accounting for how citizens choose and use media content and make multiple readings of what are polysemic texts (Franklin 2004, Norris 1997b, Philo 1990). Broadly focused claims about media, citizens, and political support in general have gradually been replaced by specific claims about particular media ('old media' or 'new media', newspapers or television, television news or television entertainment), citizen groups (more or less educated citizens, partisans and non-partisans, younger and older generations), and dimensions of political support (interest, knowledge, trust, efficacy, participation). This field of study has produced numerous findings, but its focus has been rather narrow – on relationships between tightly defined indicators that are relatively easy to measure. It has also faced numerous methodological difficulties – for example, the difficulty of disentangling media effects from other effects and of establishing long-term effects from relatively short-term studies (Franklin 2004).

In this chapter, we take a different approach by focusing on political interaction. In doing so, as discussed in the Introduction, we are influenced by American pragmatism, cognitive science, deliberative democratic theory, the argumentative turn in policy analysis, and especially Erving Goffman (1961) on social encounters and Nigel Thrift (1983) and Anthony Giddens (1984) on contextual theories of social action. For Goffman, encounters are social arrangements or activity systems (e.g. meetings, games, dances), which provide local resources (e.g. rules, etiquette, roles), to be realised by participants in the making of events. Goffman distinguishes between face-to-face and multi-situated interaction. In face-to-face encounters, participants tend to get caught up and carried away by their activities. They convey their intentions verbally and non-verbally, which enhances the security of others. Solidarity, relatedness, psychic closeness, and mutual respect often follow. By contrast, multi-situated activities create looser worlds for participants, allowing for periods of disinterest and demanding only of light investment.

Goffman's writing on social interaction influenced Thrift and Giddens. For Thrift, time and space are central to the construction of social action. Human activity is not only compositionally determined – in families or schools, for example – but also contextually determined by the immediate spatial and temporal setting. These settings might be thought of as locales: containers of opportunities and constraints on action; contextual fields made up of geology, hydrology, climate, organised production, social divisions, forms of state, forms of sociability, forms of knowledge. Locale is also a key concept for Giddens. Space is a medium through which social relations are produced. It provides settings or contexts or situations – locales – for interaction. These locales are both enabling, providing resources like knowledge on which action can be based, and constraining, providing a limited milieu of rules and institutions in which knowledge can be interpreted and used. So people act within locales, drawing on knowledge and working within institutional rules. Of course, they also interpret, reproduce, and change that knowledge and those rules (structuration).

Since the early 1980s, contextual theories of social action have been developed in various ways. For example, there has been a greater focus on the spatial extensivity of contexts (Thrift 1996). Given new information and communication technologies, containers of opportunities and con- straints – that still might be called locales or at least translocales – are often stretched across space. Despite these developments, or perhaps because of them, the central insight of such theories remains highly relevant. Contexts are productive and constitutive. They provide resources and affordances. They provide orientations to action (ibid.). We might also say: they provide orientations to *inter*action.

If these are the social theories influencing our approach in this chapter, then a few recent empirical studies also influence our approach. One is Jon Lawrence's (2009) study of political interaction through electioneer- ing. For Lawrence, the nomination hustings of eighteenth- and nine- teenth-century Britain positioned candidates in physical proximity to an often irreverent, disrespectful public. They were physical ordeals that 'tested the mettle' of politicians. For citizens, they were fun and enter- taining. In the name of accountability, politicians had to humble them- selves before their heckling, mocking, derisive constituents. They had to display 'the common touch' and 'be a good sport'. During the twentieth century, this 'spirit of the hustings' was gradually replaced by party organisation, mobilisation of core supporters, and selective campaigning. Television became more important, and local face-to-face campaigning was replaced by national mediated campaigning. Political interaction was reduced to managed and choreographed photo opportunities, press con- ferences, and rallies.

A second study of interest here is Maarten Hajer's (2009) on the performance of political authority in conditions of governance. Like Lawrence, and influenced by Goffman among others, Hajer focuses on the micro-sociology of political communication. He studies how political authority is achieved through discourse and dramaturgy. Classical modern governance, he argues, performed its authority through rules, conventions, and in situ performances (provided especially by the parliamentary setting). Network governance, by contrast, must perform its authority by staging deliberation. The problem here is that deliberation is difficult to stage. Meeting rooms and draft agreements, for example, do not provide journalists with 'good stories' and 'good pictures'.

A final example is Andrew Dobson's (2014) study of democratic listening. For Dobson, democracy rests on responsive communication, and yet good listening has been ignored in political conversation (at least compared to good speaking). Representatives and constituents must listen to each other. Deliberation involves listening to all points of view. Importantly, for our purposes, Dobson argues that good listening requires planning, organisation, rules, and skills. It requires institutionalisation. It requires well-structured political encounters, such as the truth and reconciliation committee in Dobson's study. One argument of Dobson's is that neither party politics nor twenty-first-century media encourage good listening.

Our approach in this chapter builds on these studies and theories. We begin with contexts of political encounter: the settings in which citizens encounter politics and especially politicians. Then we consider how such contexts – by providing resources, knowledge, rules, orientations – afford certain modes of political interaction (speaking, listening, questioning, challenging, testing). Finally, we consider how such modes of political interaction afford certain performances by politicians and judgements by citizens – including performances and judgements regarding those virtues of the good politician identified in Chapter 7.

We are able to do all of this because the general election diaries of Mass Observation (MO) panellists contain plenty of material on contexts of political encounter, modes of political interaction, performances by politicians, and judgements by citizens. Indeed, we can see in the diaries clear illustrations of how these different items are related and how these relationships have changed over time. What we don't see in the diaries, of course, is political interaction outside general election campaigns. This is a limitation of the research. We don't see this weakness as fatal, however, for two reasons. First, ever since Sydney Blumenthal's (1982) *The Permanent Campaign*, it has been widely acknowledged that prominent modes of political interaction during election campaigns have become prominent modes during other periods too – and, indeed, have become a mode of governing between elections. Second, few other modes of political interaction exist beyond those associated with election campaigning. The most frequently used example in the UK is probably constituency surgeries, where Members of Parliament (MPs) meet face-to-face with individual constituents who need help or wish to raise a grievance. But Emma Crewe's (2015) anthropology of MPs at work sheds important light on such constituency surgeries. While they afford the telling of personal stories on the part of constituents and the performing of empathy and practical assistance by politicians (or at least their case workers), it is estimated that less than 1 per cent of citizens participate in constituency surgeries, experience such interaction, and witness such performances.

In the rest of this chapter, we compare political interaction around the general election of 1945 – the only set of election diaries we have for the mid-twentieth century – with political interaction around three general elections of the early twenty-first century (2001, 2010, and 2015 – when MO asked its panellists to keep election diaries).[1] We argue that contexts of political encounter have changed. As a result, modes of political interaction have changed. As a result, performances of virtue – the virtues identified in Chapter 7 – were less prominent in the early twenty-first century than half a century earlier. And judgements of politicians and politics were more negative. Overall, our explanation for the rise of anti-politics is given a second part by this chapter. Not only has the image of the good politician become more demanding, such that it would be difficult to perform in any circumstances (Chapter 7). Also, the image of the good politician is difficult to perform – and receive – especially in the particular circumstances of media deregulation, abundance, and competition and also professionalised and mediatised political campaigning.

The General Election of 1945

One view of 1945 is that it was a particularly unusual general election. It was the first to be held for a decade, after a period of political co-operation 'unequalled in the history of this country' (McCallum and Readman 1947: 1). The Second World War had not quite finished, the register was out of date, and turnout figures are generally thought to be unreliable and incomparable (Denver et al. 2012). Labour won its first overall majority: 'one of the greatest reversals in our political history' (McCallum and Readman 1947: 246). The war had apparently moved citizens to the left because of the suffering and sacrifice they shared – or should have shared – and the government controls that were perceived to have worked (Pugh

[1] MO also asked panellists to keep election diaries in 1987. For analysis of those diaries, see Clarke et al. 2017.

1982). But there is another view of the 1945 general election (Fielding et al. 1995). Labour won a landslide of seats but not votes. They did so for some of the 'usual' reasons. Voters were disappointed by the incumbents, who they associated with depression, appeasement, war, and foot-dragging over implementation of the Beveridge Report. Labour campaigned in response to the practical concerns held by voters regarding wages and housing.

If there are multiple views of the 1945 general election, there is one thing on which most commentators agree: 1945 was 'the radio election' (Kandiah 1995, Rosenbaum 1997). The BBC had been established in 1922. The first official party political broadcasts had appeared on BBC radio in 1929. Citizens had become used to listening to radio news during the war. By the campaign of 1945, nightly political broadcasts – usually involving a speech by a politician of up to thirty minutes in length – were listened to by 45 per cent of the population (McCallum and Readman 1947).

What did citizens make of these broadcasts and the other means by which they encountered politicians, parties, and politics during the campaign? In May 1945, MO asked panellists to 'report at intervals on the election campaign'.[2] The diaries they returned describe a range of political encounters and interactions. Most of the panellists received election addresses and leaflets through their letterboxes. Many were visited at home by canvassers. National and local newspapers make regular appearances in the diaries, as do window cards, posters, and loud-speaker vans. But the two most prominent means by which panellists encountered politicians in 1945 – about which panellists wrote most frequently and at greatest length – were speeches on the radio and local political meetings.

Panellists wrote of listening to and hearing politicians on the radio: 'I turned on to listen to Mr E Brown last evening';[3] 'listened in to all the wireless talks up to now';[4] 'I've just heard Churchill's second broadcast';[5] 'heard Eden last night'.[6] They wrote of attending political meetings outside pubs; at the local works; on greens, squares, and market-places; and in schools, Co-op halls, town halls, gardens, village rooms, and ambulance halls (Figure 8.1). Alternatively, they wrote of failing to attend such

---

[2] Directive SxMOA1/3/86.
[3] Panellist 1980, female, 69, nurse, Steyning. ('Mr E Brown' was Ernest Brown, Leader of the National Liberal Party.)
[4] Panellist 2576, male, 35, manager of textile mill, Leicester.
[5] Panellist 1346, female, 29, technical assistant, Winchester.
[6] Panellist 3207, male, 39, occupation not known, Prestwick. ('Eden' was Anthony Eden, most recent Secretary of State for Foreign Affairs and Leader of the House of Commons.)

Figure 8.1 Clement Attlee campaigning in his Limehouse constituency, 1945 (© Getty Images).

meetings in a way that suggests attendance was something approaching a norm of the period: 'I really should be attending more meetings';[7] 'the girl conductor on the bus was bewailing the fact that she had not been able to get to any election meetings owing to late duties.'[8]

What did these contexts afford by way of political interaction? They allowed for the testing of politicians, for politicians to demonstrate virtues

[7] Ibid.   [8] Panellist 1048, female, 47, teacher, Watford.

(and vices), and for citizens to know, judge, and distinguish politicians. Long radio speeches were a test for politicians. Consider the following two diary entries – the first from an electrical engineer in Ringwood, the second from a weaver in Huddersfield:

My wife felt that half an hour is too long, or anyway, very few speeches were good enough to last that length of time. This was shown by Sir W Beveridge's speech. In many ways it was good and I was biased in that long before hearing it I expected it to be good, but it was too long. It seems difficult to make a well-knit speech ranging over a variety of topics and perhaps there should have been more concentration on one thing.[9]

Not much heard about Tom Johnson. His delivery was rather hard on the ear, although his matter was good ... Sinclair is speaking on the liberal policy as I write. His delivery is vile and irritating with too much emphasis, mostly in the wrong places. Nothing but platitudes and nothing to offer. Ernest Brown was another washout. Nothing to say and neither personal charm nor sincerity ... Sinclair still speaking. Small men cannot get over on the air. Neither can insincere men. The voice cannot be disguised in a long talk and character comes out.[10]

These nightly radio broadcasts (Figure 8.2) asked politicians to speak for half an hour without interruption. They exposed politicians on two fronts. 'Delivery' had to be easy on the ear – neither monotonous nor irritating. 'Matter' had to describe a well-knit argument and not just platitudes. Over the course of these speeches, politicians could demonstrate their character (or lack of character).

Political meetings were still more of a test. These meetings were participatory for citizens who laughed, applauded, and donated money but also moaned, booed, jeered, heckled, shouted, and howled. Reports of rowdy meetings appear in many of the diaries:

The meeting was literally up-roarious. No slight, innuendo, misrepresentation, or sneering remark was allowed to go unchallenged ... Another speaker, announced as an industrialist, was heckled about profits and cartels ... Any reference to Churchill being indispensable was greeted with moans of dissent ... The Tory candidate came in and there were some boos for him ... My hands were sore with clapping and my face was still with laughter.[11]

Last evening, I attended a meeting at the town hall ... There were quite lively questions asked. At one time it got hot and one young man started to attack another and had to be called to order by the chairman ... One local man kept the

[9] Panellist 1165, male, 39, electrical engineer, Ringwood. ('Sir W Beveridge' was William Beveridge, MP for Berwick-upon-Tweed and author of the 1942 Social Insurance and Allied Services report.)
[10] Panellist 3648, female, age not known, weaver, Huddersfield. (Tom Johnson was the most recent Secretary of State for Scotland. 'Sinclair' was Archibald Sinclair, Leader of the Liberal Party.)
[11] Panellist 1048, female, 47, teacher, Watford.

Figure 8.2 William Beveridge recording a speech for use in the 1945 campaign (© Getty Images).

candidate arguing about the question: was Mulberry produced by government or private enterprise? He said private enterprise. (I heard today that probably he had had a drop and that made him talkative).[12]

Went to Moore's meeting tonight ... I arrived at the hall near the end of Moore's speech. The local miners in a solid block at the back of the hall were giving him

[12] Panellist 1980, female, 69, nurse, Steyning. ('Mulberry' refers to the Mulberry harbours – floating harbours made to support the Allied invasion of Normandy.)

a hard time. They were rude and occasionally funny ... Moore made as much as he could of the Attlee/Laski business but at every reference to it there were loud howls of 'Beaverbrook'.[13]

Politicians were challenged at these meetings. Citizens would ask questions, express their views, fight among themselves – their confidence boosted by alcohol in some cases. From the perspective of the previous century, these meetings may have seemed less rowdy and more sober (Lawrence 2009). But from the perspective of the following century, as we shall see, they appear to be relatively participatory and challenging contexts for political interaction.

Politicians were challenged in such contexts but were also able to pass the test and demonstrate virtues. One prototypical category of the time was 'the good speaker': a type of politician who thrived on the long radio speech and the rowdy political meeting. Politicians were good speakers when they communicated policy in a pleasant voice: 'I heard Lord Woolton speak on the radio and thought it the best speech on the Conservative side as he did not abuse anyone but said why he had joined Churchill's Government and what the future policy would be. He is an excellent speaker with a very pleasant voice.'[14] They were good speakers when they refrained from abuse and mud-slinging, communicated reason and authenticity, and answered questions:

Liberal meeting, town hall, Hunstanton. Began with excellent speech by a young women who had social work in the East End of London. Then speech by candidate Penrose. Both very authentic – Beveridge and a rising party and very reasonable. Absence of mud-slinging ... Good question intelligibly answered and admission of difficulty. Penrose a good debating speaker.[15]

By contrast, there were bad speakers who babbled, seemed to have no policies, and failed to answer questions. Consider this report of a Conservative meeting:

[13] Panellist 3207, male, 39, occupation not known, Prestwick. ('Moore' was probably Thomas Moore, MP for Ayr Burghs. 'The Attlee/Laski affair' refers to Harold Laski, Chairman of the British Labour Party and Professor at London School of Economics, whose writing on class conflict and the possibility of violent revolution was attacked by Churchill for being anti-democratic, leading Attlee to distance himself from Laski. 'Beaverbrook' was Lord Beaverbrook (Max Aitken), the most recent Lord Privy Seal and owner of multiple partisan newspapers including *The Daily Express*.)

[14] Panellist 3426, female, 46, school medical inspector, Northallerton. ('Lord Woolton' was Frederick Marquis, 1st Earl of Woolton and the most recent Lord President of the Council.)

[15] Panellist 2794, male, 24, civil engineer, West Bridgford. ('Penrose' was probably Alexander Penrose, Liberal candidate for King's Lynn.)

Chairman tried to close without questions. They had had enough experience of
heckling with the RAF as reported by The News Chronicle, but we did not.
Barrage of questions from soldiers followed. McCullough could not answer
them but avoided them quite clearly. Had to admit he has no policy at all ...
McCullough a poor speaker.[16]

Or consider this report of another town-hall meeting:

At 5.30pm I went in to the Town Hall and found Sir Bedford Dorman in the chair
and just starting to speak. He made a babbling speech which I in the gallery found
difficulty in hearing ... By this time, the Labour and Commonwealth people
poured in and began to heckle. The poor speaker was getting more and more
hot and bothered when the candidate arrived amid mixed clapping and booing.
I had been told that Sir Thomas Dugdale was not a good speaker but really he did
not do at all badly and was easily heard.[17]

This panellist, a school medical inspector from Northallerton, was able to
distinguish between good and bad speakers and to be impressed by good
speakers (even when not primed to be so).

This is the final point to make about political interaction during the
1945 campaign: long radio speeches and rowdy political meetings
allowed citizens to know, judge, and distinguish politicians. They allowed
the virtues of some politicians to be heard. 'I did listen to the end of
Stafford Cripps and thought him very good. What a pleasant voice he has
and he speaks with sincerity and conviction.'[18] 'Samuel was very able and
made a good case for liberalism.'[19] 'Went to the liberal meeting in the
evening ... Candidate didn't turn up until 9.15 ... However, he gave
a straightforward, unpretentious speech – he was an unpretentious sort of
man.'[20] Some politicians could be judged on the basis of these political
encounters as sincere, able, unpretentious; in possession of a pleasant
voice, conviction, and a good case. They could also be distinguished from
lesser politicians. For a nurse from Steyning: 'I heard last night the best
speech over the radio that I have heard in this contest. Noel-Baker.'[21] For
a clerk from London: 'Samuel impressed well as the best speech yet and
I heard two people say they would vote Liberal as a consequence.'[22] Also

---

[16] Ibid. ('McCullough' was probably Donald McCullough, Conservative candidate for
     King's Lynn.)
[17] Panellist 3426, female, 46, school medical inspector, Northallerton. (Thomas Dugdale
     was MP for Richmond.)
[18] Panellist 1980, female, 69, nurse, Steyning.
[19] Panellist 3310, female, 33, teacher, Edinburgh. ('Samuel' was Herbert Samuel, Leader
     of the Liberal Party in the House of Lords.)
[20] Panellist 3351, male, 26, clerk, Beverley.
[21] Panellist 1980, female, 69, nurse, Steyning. ('Noel-Baker' was Philip Noel-Baker, MP
     for Derby.)
[22] Panellist 1325, male, 37, clerk, London.

from London (Barnet), we have this civil servant: 'As regards personality, I feel that Dr Taylor is by far the best of the three candidates. At the only political meeting I attended he impressed me very much by his obvious sincerity and high standard of values.'[23]

It was possible in 1945 to describe politicians in comparative and superlative terms. There were good and bad speakers, better and worse speeches, and best candidates. We can see in the diaries of MO panellists that such judgements – often positive – were possible at least in part because of logical connections between contexts of encounter, modes of interaction, and performances. Citizens encountered politicians most prominently through speeches on the radio and local political meetings. These settings afforded speaking on the part of politicians and listening, hearing, reacting, and challenging on the part of citizens. This political interaction tested the material and delivery of politicians. It oriented them to performances of virtue – of sincerity, ability, character – by which citizens could judge and distinguish them. How would any of this change by the end of the century?

The General Elections of the Early Twenty-First Century

Between 1945 and 2001, much changed in political communication. Some of these changes can be seen in data collected by the British Election Study (BES). While the wording varied slightly between general elections, survey questions asked respondents if they had attended a political or candidate meeting during the campaign (from 1964 to 1992), whether they had been canvassed by a political party (1964 to 2015), whether they had watched or heard a party election broadcast (1979 to 2015), and, after they were introduced in 2010, whether they had watched or heard any of the leader debates (2010 to 2015).[24] Figure 8.3 plots the percentage of people claiming to have done each of these things. In doing so, it reveals a number of interesting patterns. First, the political meetings that were prominent in the MO election diaries of 1945 saw a decline in participation from the 1960s to the 1990s – so much so that BES researchers ceased asking about political meetings after 1992. Levels of canvassing also saw a long-term decline, though the 1980s saw an increase compared to the 1964 election and levels of canvassing increased in 2015 compared to 2010. The proportion of people hearing

---

[23] Panellist 2675, female, 53, civil servant, Barnet. ('Dr Taylor' was Stephen Taylor, Labour candidate for Barnet.)

[24] The most important variation in wording to note here is that respondents were asked in 1964 if they had 'attended' a political meeting, whereas in other years they were asked if they had 'heard a candidate' at a political meeting.

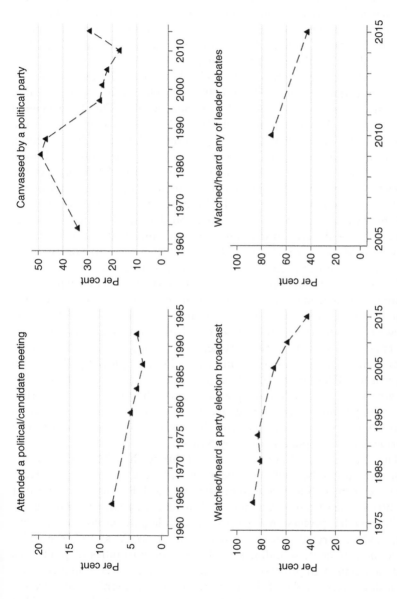

Figure 8.3 Participation in general election campaigns, BES, 1964–2015.

or watching a party election broadcast also declined substantially over the period, falling by more than half from above 80 per cent in 1964 to around 40 per cent in 2015. By 2010, many citizens were watching or listening to the new leaders' debates, although the proportion declined substantially in 2015 – perhaps as the novelty wore off or the format changed. We discuss these leaders' debates in detail later, drawing on the MO election diaries of the early twenty-first century.

Beyond what can be seen in the BES data, many changes in political communication between 1945 and 2001 are well described in the existing literature (e.g. Kandiah 1995, Rosenbaum 1997). The 1955 general election was labelled 'the first television election' by journalists at the time – with reason, in that viewing figures at least matched listening figures during the campaign. Initially, from 1951, television just showed party political broadcasts. But the Television Act of 1954 made provisions for commercial television, and the new actors this brought pushed at existing rules and conventions. The Conservative Party Conference was covered by television in 1954. The 'fourteen-day rule' – banning coverage of issues to be debated in Parliament within a fortnight – was allowed to lapse in 1956. Two years later, the Granada Network was the first to cover an election campaign (the Rochdale by-election of 1958).

Politicians responded to this increased television coverage with media training. At Central Office, the Conservatives established a broadcasting school (1950) and mock television studio (1952). Labour did the same a few years later (1958). After a period when control seemed to be lost – the era of 'ordeal by television' (Rosenbaum 1997) – politicians wrestled back control of political communication. They employed pollsters and advertisers. They used press conferences to set agendas. Their rallies became ticketed and free of questions from the floor, at first to stop journalists from foregrounding hecklers in their reports but later in response to security concerns (after the murder in 1979 of Conservative Northern Ireland spokesman Airey Neave).

This 'packaging' of politics increased during the 1980s and became obsessive during the 1990s (Franklin 2004). By the end of the century, as we have seen, political communication in the UK – as in many other countries – had become characterised by: deregulated, abundant, competitive media; professionalised, mediatised, largely negative campaigning; and a struggle between disdainful journalists and the spin, stage-management, soundbites, and photo opportunities of politicians and their campaign professionals. At the start of the twenty-first century, what did citizens make of this political communication? What were the most prominent contexts in which they encountered politicians? What performances of politicians did they witness? With what judgements did they respond? And how did all this differ from political interaction in the mid-twentieth century?

We have three sets of election diaries for the early twenty-first century – from the general elections of 2001, 2010, and 2015.[25] These elections all differed from each other in certain respects, as all elections do. The 2001 election was delayed because of the foot-and-mouth epidemic of that year. When eventually it happened, Labour won a widely predicted majority on a historically low turnout of 59 per cent. The 2010 election came soon after the global financial crisis and the parliamentary expenses scandal. The campaign was dominated by the UK's first ever televised leaders' debates (Kavanagh and Cowley 2010). The election was closely fought and resulted in a hung Parliament and, eventually, the UK's first peace-time coalition government in more than seventy years. As for the 2015 election, it came soon after the Scottish independence referendum. The campaign was dominated by speculation on what would happen in the event of another hung Parliament and a strong performance by the Scottish National Party or SNP (Cowley and Kavanagh 2016). Ultimately, the Conservatives won a majority, against the predictions of most pollsters (on which see Sturgis et al. 2016).

These elections all differed from each other in certain respects, then, but they were also similar to each other in certain respects, and, crucially, in how they differed from the general election of 1945. First, campaigning in all three elections was highly professionalised – and all the campaigns were found to be boring by journalists, who sought to liven them up by capturing and making the most of moments when politicians briefly lost control (Butler and Kavanagh 2002, Cowley and Kavanagh 2016). Second, all three campaigns were played out primarily on television – in televised news reports, interviews, and debates – despite the gradual rise of messaging by direct mail and social media, which was narrowly targeted by parties at floating voters in key marginal constituencies (Kavanagh and Cowley 2010, Cowley and Kavanagh 2016). Indeed, the general election of 2015 may well have been the last 'television election' before the predicted 'internet' and 'social media' elections of the coming period. We discuss this coming period in the Preface and Conclusion of this book, but it had not arrived by 2015 – in the sense that most people still encountered politicians through broadcast media coverage and especially on television. We found evidence of this in the MO general election diaries. Other researchers have drawn on other evidence to make a similar point (e.g. Cowley and Kavanagh 2016). Finally, all three elections were heavily polled, with opinion poll results

[25] Directives SxMOA2/1/62/2 (spring 2001), SxMOA2/1/63/3 (summer 2001), SxMOA2/1/88/3 (spring 2010), and SxMOA2/1/102 (spring 2015).

influencing the agendas of politicians and journalists during the campaign itself (ibid.).

Given these similarities, we now discuss all three general elections together. Panellists encountered the campaigns by old means – canvassing, posters, leaflets, newspapers, party election broadcasts, radio news – some of which panellists found notable for being less prominent compared to previous years and decades. They also encountered the campaigns by various 'new' means: television news; political comedy shows (on radio, television, and the Internet); and social media (mostly used for sharing jokes and links to reporting and analysis by journalists working for 'old' media organisations). But the most prominent contexts of political encounter in the early twenty-first century, about which panellists wrote most frequently and at most length, were broadcast media coverage of the campaign and especially television coverage of 'debates' (between politicians, journalists, and other politicians) and reporting of opinion polls and expert analysis. We return to opinion polls and expert analysis later. Before that, we consider televised debates and related media events.

Debates, Photo Opportunities, Soundbites – and Evasive, Gaffe-Prone, Childish Politicians

In 2001, panellists watched interviews between journalists and politicians or panel discussions between politicians (chaired by journalists) and called these 'debates'. 'I look forward to Sunday's debates on the tele', wrote a radio programme monitor from Ipswich.[26] She continued: 'I enjoy them both: BBC1 "On the Record" and ITV "Jonathan Dimbleby".' Alternatively, panellists wrote of not watching such debates when usually they would have done. 'I have not followed this run-up to the election as closely as I usually do', wrote a cleaner from Ely.[27] 'I have not watched any debates.'

'The debates' came to mean something different in 2010. For this election, televised debates between the leaders of the main parties were introduced for the first time in the UK (Figure 8.4). For Kavanagh and Cowley (2010), these debates dominated the campaign, effectively becoming the national campaign, sucking the life from other aspects – the leaders' tours, the manifestos, the press conferences, the party election broadcasts – because they took so much preparation time for the parties and because so much media space was given over to each one. There were three such

---

[26] Panellist C1939, female, 66, radio programme monitor, Ipswich.
[27] Panellist F1634, female, 58, cleaner, Ely.

Figure 8.4 One of the televised leaders' debates, 2010 (© PA Images).

debates. The first and third were watched by 10 million and 8 million viewers respectively (ibid.). The second was watched by 4 million, which was still a very large audience for a subscription channel (Sky News). MO diarists wrote of having 'watched' these 'debates': 'I've been watching the debates';[28] 'I watched the debates with a group of about 10 friends';[29] 'There was a third and final TV debate last night on BBC1. My husband watched it, but I couldn't really be bothered.'[30]

They also wrote of having watched – or sometimes not watched – debates in 2015, when again the format changed. Prime Minister David Cameron only agreed to participate in one debate with seven leaders from the seven largest parties plus a special edition of *Question Time*, where the leaders of the three main parties appeared, but only one after the other. A third show was called *The Challengers' Debate* and included leaders of the opposition parties but not the two parties in coalition government (the Conservatives and Liberal Democrats). Again, the diarists wrote: 'I watched most of the Leaders' debates';[31] 'have watched the debates on TV';[32] or, alternatively, 'I missed the keynote coverage such as the leader debates.'[33]

[28] Panellist B3631, female, 38, librarian, West Midlands.
[29] Panellist B4419, male, 24, student, Brighton.
[30] Panellist D4400, female, 39, display assistant, Bythorn.
[31] Panellist B5342, female, 29, blogger, Wiltshire.
[32] Panellist T3155, male, 67, retired vehicle mechanic, Woodville.
[33] Panellist N5545, male, 22, occupation not known, North West.

If televised debates of various formats constituted the 'keynote coverage' of these election campaigns, what kind of political interaction did they afford? They allowed politicians to speak, but usually fairly briefly, either because this was demanded by the format and previously agreed strict rules of engagement or because politicians would be interrupted by journalists or other politicians after only a short period of time. These debates allowed citizens to listen, if only briefly, or more commonly to watch (as we have seen). But reacting, challenging, and testing was now done mostly by journalists or other politicians as opposed to citizens. Sometimes, this arrangement appeared to satisfy citizens. In *The Challengers' Debate* of 2015, many panellists responded well to Leanne Wood, Leader of Plaid Cymru, when she challenged Nigel Farage, Leader of the UK Independence Party (UKIP). 'I thought that UKIP only wanted to demonise non-British or other races', wrote an office worker from Hill Mountain, for example.[34] She continued: 'I was glad when the Plaid Cymru leader put him in his place.' But at other times, this arrangement appeared to disappoint citizens. In 2001, for example, a lecturer from Bolton wrote: 'I avoided party political broadcasts but watched some Newsnight debates ... It seems that problems were swept under the carpet.'[35]

This latter quotation is more illustrative of how diarists generally received these debates: as providing opportunities for evasion by politicians. The most prominent storyline – repeated by a range of panellists, writing during all three campaigns – was that debates of this kind were 'stage-managed'. In 2001, our radio programme monitor from Ipswich wrote: 'Today we had Tony Blair with Jonathan Dimbleby ... The debate went well, but felt it was a bit stage-managed e.g. a lady in the audience put the question "why was the French Health Service better than ours". The question was quickly pushed aside and not answered.'[36] Later, in the same diary, she wrote:

There is more stage-management these days. I remember the candidates calling on everyone. Not today. You wouldn't know there was an election pending here ... I think in some ways life is easier for the candidates today, not having to knock on doors and hold meetings in shopping malls etc. They honestly don't know what people feel. At these debates on TV, which are stage-managed, they seem to have groups of like-minded people around them.

This panellist found the debates of 2001 – the televised interviews between journalists and (panels of) politicians – to be stage-managed.

---

[34] Panellist R2862, female, 42, office worker, Hill Mountain.
[35] Panellist R2862, female, 42, lecturer, Bolton.
[36] Panellist C1939, female, 66, radio programme monitor, Ipswich.

Politicians were insulated from citizens, allowed to evade questions, and surrounded by their own peers, aides, and supporters (putting them 'out of touch', we might say, with 'what people feel').

In 2010, panellists generally took a similar view of the televised leaders' debates. They commented on how they were managed by party strategists and over-rehearsed:

I watched the leaders' debate on ITV tonight … The audience members could only put their pre-selected questions; they could not respond to the answers … I don't warm to Cameron … and his consciousness over what Tory strategists must see as the pressure points of their appeal occasionally showed (he had met 'a forty year old black man' in Plymouth who had been in the Royal Navy for three years, he said at one point).[37]

So far, we have had two much-hyped television debates … neither of which I have watched. The clips which I have been forced to watch through their inclusion in news programmes have confirmed my opinion that these would be over-rehearsed both in content and TV technique, and I was better off watching something else.[38]

The first quotation comes from an unemployed man writing from Birmingham. He notes that audience participation was tightly circumscribed, something we return to shortly. He views Cameron's performance in a strategic frame (as viewers have been encouraged to do by media news frames since at least the 1990s – Cappella and Hall Jamieson 1997). The second quotation comes from a retired HGV driver in Basildon. It captures how televised debates were prominent in the early twenty-first century not only because many citizens watched them but also because citizens who didn't watch them often saw parts of them anyway and heard comment on them too, on other television programmes (or radio programmes or in newspapers or on the Internet). This panellist found the 'clips' he saw to be 'over-rehearsed both in content and TV technique'.

A regular complaint in the 2010 diaries was that studio audiences for these debates were too constrained in their behaviour – that political interaction was too constrained – by the rules agreed between political parties and media organisations. A counsellor from the Fylde Coast noted of one debate that Gordon Brown 'harped on the same points over and over again. Well, they all did really, and of course with an alleged 70 plus rules about the debate, the audience had to stay silent'.[39] A display assistant from Bythorn described the scene of another debate: 'All three of them standing in front of a live audience (who had been told not to boo,

---

[37] Panellist B3227, male, 43, unemployed, Birmingham.
[38] Panellist R470, male, 76, retired HGV driver, Basildon.
[39] Panellist G226, female, 69, counsellor, Fylde Coast.

cheer, or clap, and they didn't much either, much to my dismay).'[40] Such constrained political interaction was found to be 'sterile' and 'unreal' – for example, by our counsellor from the Fylde Coast. Of the first debate, she wrote: '[T]he way it was presented was all very strategy with no real response allowed from the audience, as the latter were not allowed to continue the debate. It seems a bit sterile.'[41] Of the second debate, she wrote: 'With the audience not being able to answer back, it seemed a bit unreal.'

The format of debates in 2015 was different again, but the storyline shared by many panellists was familiar. The debates were too stage-managed, with too many constraints on political interaction, allowing politicians to say little beyond carefully prepared soundbites, providing citizens with little on which to judge and distinguish politicians. Listen to this from a warehouse worker in Stoke-on-Trent:

> The debates between the party leaders, or rather the squabbling about who was going to take part, where they were going to stand, and whether or not the prime minister was even going to take part, occupied an inordinate amount of space in the media. When they finally happened, the debates were damp squibs, telling us little we didn't already know about the leaders of the three main parties.[42]

And listen to this from a student in Cheshire: 'I watched the leaders' debates but I didn't find them very useful. There were too many people speaking and it felt like they were mostly delivering short, pre-prepared speeches. It was too planned.'[43] Like the interviews and panel discussions of 2001 and the first televised leaders' debates of 2010, these debates of 2015 were received by viewers as planned, structured to give politicians only short periods to fill with pre-prepared content, and unhelpful in providing a basis on which to judge politicians and parties.

It is also worth noting here that other ways by which citizens encountered politicians during these campaigns – beyond debates on television (and, less prominently, radio) – were also widely perceived to be stage-managed. Our warehouse worker from Stoke-on-Trent wrote of the 2015 campaign: 'David Cameron . . . looked ever more stiff as he trundled from one staged appearance to the next.'[44] A market researcher from Wigan wrote of the same campaign:

> The recent election was on the whole a rather disappointing affair. From the very start, it all seemed a little bit low-key and stage-managed. It lacked real passion,

---

[40] Panellist D4400, female, 39, display assistant, Bythorn.
[41] Panellist G226, female, 69, counsellor, Fylde Coast.
[42] Panellist C3167, male, 43, warehouse worker, Stoke-on-Trent.
[43] Panellist C4271, female, 26, PhD student, Cheshire.
[44] Panellist C3167, male, 43, warehouse worker, Stoke-on-Trent.

with all the party leaders playing safe, never being directly challenged. They appeared to arrive at pre-arranged venues to a hand-picked loyal band of supporters where questions were carefully kept on-message. There was never any chance of direct questioning. It was as if the campaign managers could not trust the politicians to get it right. Is it any wonder people get bored and cynical over politics.[45]

The problem for these two panellists was that politicians appeared only at stage-managed events. At such events, they were insulated from citizens (except for 'a hand-picked loyal band of supporters') and their questions (except for questions 'carefully kept on-message'). Politicians, controlled by their campaign managers, appeared 'stiff'. Citizens, kept at a distance, appeared justified in their boredom and cynicism.

One type of stage-managed event about which panellists had plenty to say in their diaries was the photo opportunity. Panellists used the category itself: 'For a long time, it seemed like 2015 was an election of tranquillisers. There was lots of talk and photo opportunities, but none of it seemed to capture the public imagination.'[46] Or they noted the 'posing on TV' and 'posed photographs' in the newspapers.[47] Or they described particular photographs they had seen:

On 15th April, the cover of *The Daily Mail* featured a picture of David and Samantha Cameron, strolling along, hand-in-hand, in casual clothes – snapped as though all unknowing. He was wearing a leather jacket and dark blue jeans, both of which looked so new that if he bent down in them, they would probably creak. Obviously, we were meant to think, He's an ordinary guy after all – married, youngish, informal – somebody I can identify with (despite his Eton education) and will therefore vote for.[48]

Here, our unemployed panellist from Birmingham provides a strategic reading of the photograph. He assumes that it was carefully stage-managed, with carefully chosen costumes, to communicate a particular message. Reading this panellist's diary in full, one is left with an impression of someone disappointed and alienated by such political interaction.

A final aspect of stage-managed events, whether TV debates or photo opportunities, commented on by a range of panellists in diaries from across the period, was the soundbite. Again, some panellists used the category itself. 'I keep seeing clips of "Call me Dave"', wrote our retired HGV driver from Basildon, referring to a line used by David Cameron and reported during the 2010 campaign.[49] He continued: 'When I see the

[45] Panellist P4287, male, 58, market researcher, Wigan.
[46] Panellist C3167, male, 43, warehouse worker, Stoke-on-Trent.
[47] Panellist G3655, male, 71, retired company director, North East (spring 2010).
[48] Panellist B3227, male, 43, unemployed, Birmingham (spring 2010).
[49] Panellist R470, male, 76, retired HGV driver, Basildon.

clips, I wonder if he said anything other than the soundbites all channels seem to pick up on.' Other panellists complained of 'the same slogans and phrases being overused'.[50] For this particular diarist, a teacher from Newcastle-under-Lyme writing in 2015, it was Ed Miliband 'determined to be "clear with you" at every possible opportunity', and Cameron's '"long term economic plan"'. Finally, consider this report on the 2015 campaign from a software company manager based in Devon:

I started off excited about the possibility of removing the Tories. But this had given way to a feeling of 'What the hell, let's just get the thing over with' before we were half way through the 6 weeks of campaigning. Lies, damned lies and manifestos, and totally sick-making TV appearances and soundbites: Cameron and Osborne with hardhats and sleeves rolled up, as if they know what it's like to work for a living. Miliband doing his best not to look like he's just landed and is all confused because they don't have TV on his planet. Visiting schools, visiting hospitals, making promises that can't possibly be kept. TV interviewers who are willing to be rude but unable to challenge the underlying assumptions of their interviewees. I've had enough now.[51]

Soundbites, photo opportunities, and television appearances are discussed together by this panellist. They don't fool her. She listens to soundbites and interviews but hears only 'lies', 'promises that can't possibly be kept', and the same old 'underlying assumptions'. She looks at photos and watches television but sees only 'sick-making' politicians pretending to work and be normal (or just not from another planet!).

This brings us to the performances of politicians and judgements of citizens afforded by such contexts of encounter (media coverage of debates, photo opportunities, and soundbites) and modes of interaction (posing and speaking, if only briefly, by politicians; watching and, to a lesser extent, listening and reading by citizens; and questioning of politicians, but mostly by journalists and other politicians on behalf of citizens). Three kinds of performance by politicians were noted frequently in the MO diaries. First, there were the avoidance of topics and evasion of questions. Politicians were able to do this when protected from citizens in stage-managed settings. So in 2001, a quality engineer from Bracknell wrote: 'One issue that all parties pussyfooted around was illegal immigration/asylum.'[52] And an occupational therapist from Wales wrote: 'I turn off the radio if Ann Widdicombe comes on, or Hague, or any of them actually. They do not listen to the question asked and they do not answer the question either.'[53] Or in 2015, a retired typesetter from

[50] Panellist L5604, male, 34, teacher, Newcastle-under-Lyme.
[51] Panellist M4859, female, 37, manager of software company, Devon.
[52] Panellist B1426, male, 65, quality engineer, Bracknell.
[53] Panellist J2891, female, 36, occupational therapist, Wales.

Woking wrote: 'The most important subject I wanted to hear about was defence, which was hardly discussed.'[54] Campaigning by way of stage-managed media events, politicians could evade the questions of interviewers and avoid the topics on which they felt weak – topics that were sometimes highly salient for citizens and so were perceived as ignored or neglected.

A second kind of performance by politicians, found notable by a range of diarists, was the gaffe. When campaigns are so controlled, the conditions are set for a brief loss of control. And when controlled campaigns are perceived to be so boring by journalists and citizens, the conditions are set for these brief losses of control to become major news items. In 2001, the most prominent gaffe in the MO diaries, though panellists did not commonly used the term 'gaffe' until 2010, was 'Prescott's punch'. Deputy Prime Minister John Prescott was campaigning in Rhyl when Craig Evans, a local farm worker, threw an egg at him, and Prescott responded with a punch in the direction of Evans. Panellists referred to this as 'Prescott's punch'. 'The big news item today is John Prescott's punch at a man who threw an egg at him', wrote our radio programme monitor from Ipswich.[55] 'I cleverly left the country on May 13th for 6 weeks in America', wrote a planning officer from the North West.[56] She continued: 'Whilst in America, I read very few papers and saw little news … The only thing I heard about was Prescott's punch.' The incident was 'big news' that circulated widely in the UK and beyond. For 'apathetic' and 'wary' citizens, it 'livened up' an otherwise dull, overly stage-managed campaign. A researcher from Walsall wrote: 'The general feel was apathy; none of the parties seems to have new or exciting ideas. For most people, the most exciting moment in the campaign was the moment when John Prescott threw a punch in response to having an egg thrown at him.'[57] Or listen to this from a museum assistant in Isleham: 'I am already extremely wary of anything to do with the Election – I do not find any of them worthy of a vote … At least the Deputy Prime Minister's punch has livened up the whole proceedings.'[58] Before sending off their diaries to MO, some panellists looked back on the campaign and found the Prescott punch foremost in their memories: 'My overriding memory of the run-up to the election was of John Prescott punching a member of the public';[59] 'Two things

[54] Panellist H1806, male, 89, retired typesetter, Woking.
[55] Panellist C1939, female, 66, radio programme monitor, Ipswich.
[56] Panellist D2739, female, 22, planning officer, North West.
[57] Panellist M2933, female, 27, researcher, Walsall.
[58] Panellist W2107, female, 60, museum assistant, Isleham.
[59] Panellist J2893, female, 24, student, Leeds.

Figure 8.5 Gordon Brown meets Gillian Duffy in Rochdale, 2010 (© PA Images).

remain in my memory of the election campaign: 1) John Prescott's straight left to the jaw of his assailant ...'[60]

By 2010, such incidents of lost control were commonly referred to as 'gaffes', and the most prominent example in the 2010 diaries was Gordon Brown's mistake when campaigning in Rochdale (Figure 8.5). A retired Executive from London takes up the story:

> On a visit to Rochdale today, [Brown] had a long conversation with a 65 year old woman Labour supporter that covered immigration, education and other subjects too. He wished her and her family well at the end ... and got into his car without realising his microphone was still switched on, allowing BBC, ITV and Sky people to hear what he was saying ... and what he was saying was a tirade about the woman being a bigot and he should not have been allowed to meet her etc. ... This evening, I was browsing through the online version of a newspaper in Barcelona and the story was already there, so presumably it has gone all around the world.[61]

This extract provides a description of the event, as perceived by this panellist. It also remind us how gaffes – 'Gordon's gaffe',[62] his

---

[60] Panellist R1389, male, 87, licensed victualler, Brighton. (The second thing remaining in this panellist's memory was an image of William Hague, Leader of the Conservative Party, campaigning against the Euro by 'waving a pound coin in the air, triumphantly, as if he'd just won the lottery or scored the winning goal in a cup final'.)

[61] Panellist D1602, male, 67, retired executive, London.

[62] Panellist G226, female, 69, counsellor, Fylde Coast.

'tremendous gaffe'[63] – become widely circulated news items, not least because they 'keep the circus interesting, rather than boring bleatings about promises and manifestos'.[64]

Gaffes were a prominent feature of the 2015 campaign too. Diarists wrote, for example, of Ed Miliband tripping over the *Question Time* set at the end of one debate. But let us move on to a final kind of performance afforded by the context of professionalised campaigning and televised 'debates'. Positioned opposite one another or opposite a combative journalist, given only a brief time to speak, and primed with negative messages from campaign professionals, politicians were seen by citizens to squabble and bicker. In 2001, panellists complained of 'petty bickering',[65] 'playground arguing',[66] 'each side slagging off the other',[67] and 'too much criticising of the other side'.[68] They saw this across the campaign, including in party election broadcasts found to be 'awful – promises and threats'.[69] This restaurant worker from Northern Ireland went on to ask rhetorically: 'Why are they so negative?' But panellists especially saw squabbling and bickering in what one aircraft engineer from the South West called 'the nightly TV slanging matches' (i.e. the televised interviews and panel discussions involving politicians, journalists, and other politicians).[70]

Diarists complained of such things across the period. If we jump forward to 2015, they wrote phrases like 'off they rant at each other',[71] 'plenty of mud flying around from each to the other',[72] and 'parties just bicker and trade insults'.[73] They wrote about 'leaders of parties slagging off other parties',[74] the 'knocking' of 'the other parties',[75] and 'the blame culture and the culture of fear'.[76] Importantly, they wrote about such things particularly in direct response to having watched or listened to debates (and coverage of debates by news programmes). Listen to this PhD student from North West England: 'I think the TV debates summed up my thoughts about the election and the parties. There was a lot of unhelpful bickering and point-scoring, which I think politics has descended to. I would like more positive campaigning and less throwing

[63] Panellist R4526, male, 49, teacher, Belfast.
[64] Panellist G4296, male, 33, radio broadcast assistant, Cardiff.
[65] Panellist W2910, male, 34, lorry driver, Southwick.   [66] Ibid.
[67] Panellist B1426, male, 65, quality engineer, Bracknell.
[68] Panellist C1191, female, 46, carer, Limavady.
[69] Panellist H266, female, 77, restaurant worker, Northern Ireland.
[70] Panellist R1719, male, 57, aircraft engineer, South West.
[71] Panellist R1719, male, 71, retired aircraft engineer, West Dorset   [72] Ibid.
[73] Panellist K3146, female, 37, publishing manager, Saltaire.
[74] Panellist C3603, male, 71, retired youth and community officer, Sheffield.
[75] Panellist T1961, female, 67, retired nursery nurse, East Sussex.
[76] Panellist W4376, female, 45, designer and creator of scrapbooks, Bishop Auckland.

mud at other parties.'[77] Or, for those who prefer a differently positioned diarist, take this retired decorator from Derby:

> I turned on Radio 4 this morning in an effort to make what I could out of two hours of political 'debate' on Women's Hour and in which seven women party representatives talked away. And how they talked! A lot of contrary rubbish (we did this and you failed to do that). I stuck it for half an hour and had I been one of the undecided when tuning in, I would have been more of a non-voter when switching off.[78]

We may detect the presence of sexist tropes in this extract ('how [the women] talked!'). But we can also detect a relationship between contexts of encounter, modes of interaction, and performances by politicians. The diarist encountered politicians on the radio. These politicians were positioned alongside six other politicians and given brief opportunities to speak. The listener had no means of questioning or challenging the politicians. That responsibility, if it existed, lay with a journalist chairing the discussion and the six other politicians. What kind of performance resulted from this arrangement? The diarist heard a series of claims, counter-claims, and accusations: 'a lot of contrary rubbish'. They heard what another diarist called, reflecting on the previous evening's *Newsnight*, 'the usual slanging match' – with 'each side quoting facts and figures that are favourable to themselves, whilst they take the time out to rubbish each other'.[79] This retired aircraft engineer from Dorset continued: 'As usual, we have no idea who is telling the truth, so at the end of yesterday we were none the wiser.'

This last quotation brings us to the judgements of citizens. What judgements of politicians and politics did citizens make on the basis of these interactions and performances? In the diaries, we find that panellists could still just about distinguish between good and bad performers. Nick Clegg, Leader of the Liberal Democrats, was commonly thought to have performed well in the first televised leaders' debate of 2010. Nicola Sturgeon, Leader of the SNP, was commonly thought to have performed well in *The Challengers' Debate* of 2015. But the judgements we find most frequently in the diaries, and most forcefully stated, are familiar from earlier chapters of this book. First, because they stage-manage events, avoid topics, and evade questions, politicians were judged to be not straight-talking (as we saw in Chapter 4). For example, after one televised panel discussion in 2001, a secretary from South East England wrote of how the participants 'slimed their way through the various

---

[77] Panellist H5557, female, 25, PhD student, North West.
[78] Panellist R1418, male, 93, retired decorator, Derby.
[79] Panellist R1719, male, 71, retired aircraft engineer, West Dorset.

questions'.[80] If politicians were slimy or slippery, they were also fraudulent. The same panellist wrote:

Tony Blair ridiculously launched the election at a girls' school ... when they started singing hymns, he looked into the middle distance, all trembling chin and watery-eyed. He's such a fraud! On Sunday, David Frost had a go at him, and again, you look into his face and you can see he just looks as if he doesn't believe what he's saying.

Photo opportunities and stage-managed debates encouraged the judgement of politicians as not trustworthy, honest, or genuine (virtues expected of politicians by citizens in the twenty-first century – see Chapter 7).

Second, because they make gaffes, politicians were judged to be a joke (as we saw in Chapter 5). For example, a display assistant from Bythorn wrote in 2010:

Gordon Brown did a pretty daft thing and made a 'gaffe', as the news reporters keep calling it. On Wednesday, he interviewed an elderly lady who was a lifetime Labour voter. He was nice to her face, then forgot he had his microphone on and was recorded saying bad things about her afterwards, like mainly she 'was a bigot'. I think he's a right pillock.[81]

Here, we see the judgement of Brown as 'a right pillock' (a fool) following directly from the witnessing of his gaffe – his brief loss of control, performed in the context of a professionalised campaign and newly forensic journalism (focused on exposing the assumed hypocrisy of politicians and their campaigns).

A final judgement afforded by such interactions and performances was that squabbling and mud-throwing politicians are like badly behaved children. Here, again, we have our display assistant from Bythorn in 2010: 'I'm getting bored of it already. They just seem like a bunch of kids who love to bicker and quarrel. They are not very good at listening to anyone else either. They talk over each other a lot.'[82] As another example, take this retired typesetter from Woking, writing in 2015: 'The party leaders' debates were just as I expected, as I feel politicians act like school children and I did not enjoy them at all.'[83]

Opinion Polls, Expert Analysis, and Alienated Citizens

We have argued that, by the end of the twentieth century, citizens encountered formal politics most prominently through media coverage

---

[80] Panellist J2891, female, 36, secretary, South East.
[81] Panellist D4400, female, 39, display assistant, Bythorn.   [82] Ibid.
[83] Panellist H1806, male, 89, retired typesetter, Woking.

of debates, photo opportunities, and soundbites. But there was a second context of political encounter also given prominence in the MO diaries: media reporting of opinion polls and expert analysis regarding politicians, parties, elections, the political system, and even anti-politics itself.

In 2001, panellists mentioned 'experts' and especially 'polls' frequently in their diaries. They wrote: 'Labour seem to be in the lead at the present time in the polls';[84] or 'The opinion polls have the Conservatives trailing badly with Labour ahead with some 55% of the poll';[85] or 'It says in the papers that Labour are still 15 points ahead of the Conservative Party.'[86] A cleaner from Ely wrote at some length:

I have to admit that in the last two months before it was called, I thought that maybe the Labour majority would be down . . . But if we are to believe all the polls and the experts, I am wrong because they are saying that not only will Tony Blair win but he will have an even bigger majority. I do not know if this will be the case but I heard a newspaper person say on Channel 4 last night that the reason for this is that on the whole the people of this country feel safe and are content with this government.[87]

Later in her diary, she continued:

According to the experts who know about these things, even if the Labour vote was down, William Hague could not win because the Labour majority at the present time is so huge. Edward Heath was interviewed last night. He is not standing this time because of his age. But he said that Labour would win.

In her diary, this panellist reported at least as much of what 'the polls and the experts' said as what the politicians said. The polls told her that Labour would secure 'an even bigger majority'. The experts – a newspaper columnist and a former politician in this case, both interviewed for their analysis on television news – told her that Labour 'would win' (and why).

More generally, what did panellists take from this reporting of opinion polls and expert analysis? They came to assume the general election of 2001 was a 'foregone conclusion' – regardless of their own judgements of politicians and parties. This was a category used in most of the diaries. 'The result was a foregone conclusion', wrote a shop manager from South West England.[88] 'In 2001 it was just a foregone conclusion', wrote a researcher from Walsall.[89] 'It was a foregone conclusion that Labour

[84] Panellist N403, female, 63, cleaner, Galleywood.
[85] Panellist J2819, female, 36, secretary, South East.
[86] Panellist C2204, male, 49, labourer, Nottingham.
[87] Panellist F1634, female, 58, cleaner, Ely.
[88] Panellist H260, female, 71, shop manager, South West.
[89] Panellist M2933, female, 27, researcher, Walsall.

would get in again', wrote a third respondent – an engine inspector from Derby.[90] This category was often used alongside discussion of opinion polls. For example, an aircraft engineer from the South West wrote towards the end of their diary: 'I've always been wary of so-called foregone conclusions, but in this case it certainly was a rout. The opinion polls were right.'[91] Or listen to this from our decorator in Derby:

As for the pre-election lies and misrepresentations mouthed by the three main parties, to be daily thrust down our throats by the media, and if we are further to take into account the opinion polls, then we are heading for the biggest yawn-producing event of the new century on June 7th. That Labour are still far ahead to be overtaken by the Conservatives, no matter the promises and bribes made to voters, makes all a foregone conclusion and hardly worth going to the polls.[92]

The opinion polls predicted a 'foregone conclusion'. An election that is a foregone conclusion is neither exciting nor worthy of participation by citizens (who are denied political efficacy by such a discourse). We see the same connection between predictions of a foregone conclusion and citizen withdrawal – through lack of interest – in the following entry by a housewife from East Sussex: 'I think, like so many others, this year's election didn't seem to interest me as much as former elections. It seemed to be very much a foregone conclusion.'[93]

Political scientists have long understood that indicators like voter interest and turnout are partly influenced by the characteristics of particular election races, including the degree to which they are closely fought. But what has been less well understood is the way that discussion of opinion polls by politicians, journalists, and other commentators can give citizens a set of cultural resources – a vocabulary and set of justifications – from which to construct anti-political sentiment, practices, and subject positions. In 2001, this appears to have happened. Diarists picked up on expert discussion of Labour's lead in the polls and associated discussion of whether voters would participate in such a foregone conclusion. For example, a quality engineer from Bracknell wrote: 'Both sides are worried about voter apathy. Labour because the polls put them so far ahead, the Tories because they are being given no chance.'[94] Panellists then used the terms of this discussion – 'apathy', 'disillusionment', 'cynicism' – to write about citizens in general: 'I think the whole country seems to be taken over by apathy';[95] 'I think people . . . are very

---

[90] Panellist R1468, female, 77, engine inspector, Derby.
[91] Panellist R1719, male, 57, aircraft engineer, South West.
[92] Panellist R1418, male, 79, decorator, Derby.
[93] Panellist T1961, female, 52, housewife, East Sussex.
[94] Panellist B1426, male, 65, quality engineer, Bracknell.
[95] Panellist F1373, female, 69, former shop assistant, Wales.

disillusioned with politics';[96] 'most people I know are now quite cynical on all political questions.'[97] Finally, some panellists recognised themselves in this group of apathetic or anti-political citizens. Listen to this journalist from Durham: 'More and more people are saying they can't, in all honesty, vote for anyone ... That is awful. Cynicism and disillusion must be overcome or we'll get government by default. The trouble is that I feel the same way.'[98] Or, if a journalist seems like too much of a usual suspect for this point, take instead our decorator from Derby: 'If I show less than enthusiasm for the approaching day of the General Election ... then it must be that my attitude is a general reflection of the apathy that abounds.'[99]

Around the general election of 2001, a prominent means by which citizens encountered formal politics was media reporting of opinion polls and expert analysis. Many took from such reporting a characterisation of the election as a 'foregone conclusion' – and, insofar as a foregone conclusion happens regardless of citizens' forthcoming judgements, presumably a reduced sense of political efficacy too. Many also took from such reporting a set of cultural resources for constructing and justifying negative sentiment regarding formal politics. Did media reporting of opinion polls and expert analysis play a similar role during the campaigns of 2010 and 2015?

In 2010, diarists again frequently mentioned 'the polls': 'The polls are showing a surge of support for Nick Clegg';[100] '[Cameron's] lead in the latest opinion poll ... is down to just two points';[101] 'The polls suggested when we were going to vote that it was likely we'd end up with a hung parliament.'[102] During this campaign, panellists especially mentioned opinion polls and expert analysis when discussing the televised leaders' debates: 'The opinion polls this morning have put Nick Clegg as the most successful performer of the night';[103] 'The news said it was David Cameron that won tonight in the polls they have done already';[104] 'It's the morning after the night before and radio, tv and the press are full of comment, analysis and almost word by word dissection of the first of the prime ministerial debates on ITV last night.'[105] This retired executive

---

[96] Panellist J2893, female, 24, student, Leeds.
[97] Panellist R450, male, 75, retired builder, London.
[98] Panellist W633, female, 58, journalist, Durham.
[99] Panellist R1418, male, 79, decorator, Derby.
[100] Panellist B3227, male, 43, unemployed, Birmingham.
[101] Panellist D1602, male, 67, retired executive, London.
[102] Panellist G4296, male, 33, radio broadcast assistant, Cardiff.
[103] Panellist B3227, male, 43, unemployed, Birmingham.
[104] Panellist D4400, female, 39, display assistant, Bythorn.
[105] Panellist D1602, male, 67, retired executive, London.

from London went on to write: 'The second of the three debates is next Thursday – I definitely won't watch it (partly because I don't think I can get Sky) but I'll doubtless hear all about it on Friday's radio.' In 2010, citizens encountered politicians by watching the debates themselves, but also – or alternatively – by hearing about the debates afterwards (from journalists, other politicians, and other experts). We see this demonstrated again in the diary of our Fylde-Coast counsellor: 'My friend . . . said on the phone last week that there's so much analysis and discussion on TV and radio that although she didn't watch either of the two TV debates, she feels as if she has!'[106]

What judgements by citizens were afforded by such indirect, double-mediated interaction with politicians – involving the challenging of politicians by journalists and other politicians but also the judging of politicians' performances by journalists, other politicians, and other expert analysts? In the diaries, we see panellists deferring in their judgement to others. Whereas in the 1945 diaries, panellists would frequently describe a politician's performance before offering a judgement on the performance, the politician, and often their party too, in 2010, as opposed to the position of judge, panellists would frequently write from the position of a relatively distant, passive, late-coming spectator (of a show incorporating its own judges). The voice in which panellists wrote about politicians and their performances in 2010 was notable in this regard. They used formulations like 'it's emerged': 'They have polled people watching the 3 leaders as they talk, and it's emerged that Nick Clegg is a clear winner on tonight's battle.'[107] Or they used formulations like 'has been thought to be' – 'The three main leaders of the parties have already had two debates, with a third coming up shortly. Nick Clegg, the leader of the Liberals, has been thought to be the favourite up to now.'[108] Or they used formulations like 'he seems': 'Clegg is a force to be reckoned with at the moment. He seems to have come off much better than the others from the first live debate.'[109]

So the role played by media reporting of opinion polls and expert analysis was a little different in 2001 and 2010 but significant in both years. The same can be said for 2015. Again, panellists frequently mentioned opinion polls in their diaries: 'The opinion polls . . . have changed very little';[110] 'Ed Miliband has had a (tiny) boost, according to the polls';[111] 'polls consistently suggest that the SNP will effectively wipe

[106] Panellist G226, female, 69, counsellor, Fylde Coast.
[107] Panellist D4400, female, 39, display assistant, Bythorn.
[108] Panellist J1890, female, 78, retired, Hull.
[109] Panellist F4125, female, 45, clerical assistant, Northern Ireland.
[110] Panellist C3603, male, 71, retired youth and community officer, Sheffield.
[111] Panellist C4131, female, 33, museum consultant, North Shields.

out the majority of Labour (and possibly Lib Dem) seats.'[112] This time, in contrast to what we saw in 2001, the polls were predicting a closely fought contest: 'The papers say the polls are a dead heat between Tories and Labour';[113] 'opinion polls still suggest no party will have overall control';[114] 'Final opinion polls still showing level pegging for Labour and Conservatives.'[115] What effect did these polls have on media discussion? If discussion of a foregone conclusion in 2001 led to further discussion about potential voter apathy and disillusionment, did discussion of a 'dead heat' in 2010 lead to further discussion about potential voter engagement and satisfaction? Other scholars have noted how the opinion polls in 2015 actually directed media commentary away from the issues and towards the possibility of a hung Parliament and speculation on processes in that event (Cowley and Kavanagh 2016). This 'coalitionology' (ibid.) did not go down well with MO diarists – especially because the eventual result in 2015 was a Conservative majority and not the widely predicted hung Parliament. A retired film editor from Scotland spoke for many panellists when he wrote of feeling 'led astray' and 'exhausted' by media reporting of opinion polls and expert analysis in 2015:

The election has been a long haul for everyone; far too long in the run-up; far too excitable and far too much at the mercy of the media and pollsters, who in various ways led us astray at the end. Having exhausted us with the prospect of a seriously hung parliament, we were then whacked on the head with a surprise result in the middle of the night.[116]

Conclusion

In this chapter, we have further developed our account of what explains the rise of anti-politics. Our starting point was that citizens make judgements about politics on the basis of prior understandings or folk theories or images (especially images of the good politician – see Chapter 7) but also political interaction between citizens, politics, and especially politicians. We have argued that, over the second half of the twentieth century, a number of changes took place, including further expansion of the franchise; embourgeoisement and partisan dealignment; media deregulation, abundance, and competition; and the professionalisation and mediatisation of political campaigning. These developments resulted in one set of contexts in which citizens encountered politicians becoming less

---

[112] Panellist H1541, male, 70, retired film editor, Scotland.
[113] Panellist S2207, female, 63, teaching assistant, Brighton.
[114] Panellist F5629, male, 55, retail assistant, Upholland.
[115] Panellist C3603, male, 71, retired youth and community officer, Sheffield.
[116] Panellist H1541, male, 70, retired film editor, Scotland.

Table 8.1 *Political interaction compared*

	1945	2001–2015
Contexts of political encounter	Long speeches on the radio Rowdy local political meetings	Media coverage of stage-managed debates and photo opportunities Media reporting of opinion polls and expert analysis
Modes of political interaction	Speaking at length by politicians Attending, listening, participating, questioning, challenging, testing, reacting by citizens	Posing and speaking (briefly) by politicians Watching and to a lesser extent listening and reading by citizens Questioning, challenging, testing, reacting, and judging mostly by journalists and other politicians (double-mediation)
Performances by politicians	Delivery and material Virtues and vices	Stage-management, evasion, soundbites, gaffes, bickering
Judgements by citizens	Distinctions between better and worse speeches, good and bad speakers, better and worse candidates	Politicians are not straight-talking Politicians are a joke Politicians are like badly behaved children Or citizens make no judgements of politicians but instead defer in their judgement to others (opinion polls and expert analysis)

prominent (long speeches on the radio and rowdy local political meetings) and another becoming more prominent (media coverage of stage-
managed debates and photo opportunities and media reporting of opinion polls and expert analysis). We see this in the MO election diaries.
We also see how these different contexts afforded different modes of
political interaction, performances by politicians, and judgements by
citizens.

Table 8.1 provides a summary of our main findings. In the mid-
twentieth century, contexts of political encounter allowed and encouraged politicians to speak at length. They allowed and encouraged citizens
to listen to politicians and, in the case of meetings, to question and
challenge politicians. Politicians were oriented by these modes of interaction towards performances of virtue and vice, including of good/bad
material, delivery, and character. Citizens were oriented, in turn, towards
calibrated judgements that distinguished between better and worse
speeches, speakers, and candidates. By contrast, early twenty-first-
century contexts of encounter allowed and encouraged politicians to

speak only briefly. They allowed and encouraged citizens to watch politicians and, to a lesser extent, to listen and read (at least *about* politicians). Questioning and challenging of politicians was now done mostly by journalists or other politicians on behalf of citizens. In a process of double-mediation, reacting to and judging politicians was now also done mostly by journalists, other politicians, and other expert analysts. Politicians were oriented by these modes of interaction towards performances of stage-management, evasion, soundbites, gaffes, and bickering. Citizens were oriented, in turn, towards judgements of politicians as not straight-talking, a joke, and badly behaved children. Alternatively, citizens deferred their judgements of politicians to expert analysts and their opinion polls, almost as if elections and formal politics more broadly had little to do with citizens' own judgements (except to make citizens feel ineffective, exhausted, and increasingly disaffected).

Our overall argument is that anti-politics is explained by numerous factors. Among these, for the case of the UK at least, the decline of deference may not be so important as some people have argued (Chapter 5), and the same can be said for depoliticisation and movement to a post-political condition (Chapter 6). Moreover, changing images of the good politician appear to be important (Chapter 7), as do changing modes of political interaction (this chapter). The twenty-first-century image of the good politician – as *for* the people but also *of* the people – is particularly demanding. It would be difficult to perform successfully in any circumstances. It is especially difficult to perform in circumstances characterised by media deregulation, abundance, and competition and also professionalised and mediatised political campaigning.

9 Changing Folk Theories: From Stealth Democracy to Stealth Populism

We have used evidence from survey research and Mass Observation (MO) to challenge the claims of others and present some claims of our own regarding the rise of anti-politics. Let us now suggest a series of propositions that capture and expand important parts of our argument. The aim is to explore our broader understanding of how citizens think about politics and how changes to those patterns of thought help to explain the shifting forms of anti-politics in contemporary democracies. More specifically, this chapter serves three purposes. First, we situate folk theories, as they are used in this book, more firmly in cognitive science and related fields. Second, we develop more fully the concept of stealth populism covered only briefly in previous chapters. Third, we prepare the way for a concluding chapter focused on reform options and well grounded in both empirical evidence and theoretical debates.

Our starting point is widely shared: in most contemporary democracies, citizens generally do not pay a great amount of attention to the hubbub of formal politics (Marcus et al. 2000, Zaller 1992) and are minimally informed about mainstream politics and policy issues (Delli Carpini and Keeter 1996). This view does not deny that citizens can and do talk about politics or that they have political ideas and interests (Gamson 1992). But it does leave open the issue: How then do they make judgements about formal politics? Insights from the cognitive sciences have proved influential in framing answers to this question. Many political scientists agree that citizens use cognitive cues to steer them to their political choices (for a good selection, see Lupia et al. 2000). It is at this point that the consensus breaks down. There is a broadly optimistic line of argument suggesting that citizens can use heuristics – mental shortcuts requiring little effort or information to be brought into play – to make political judgements that are good enough and a reliable guide to what they might choose if they had more information or put more cognitive effort into making the judgement (Popkin 1991, Sniderman et al. 1993). There is a strong counter-view, however, suggesting that citizens are not able to choose their heuristics but rather adopt them more automatically and intuitively, without a great deal of concern (Kuklinski and Quirk 2000). Their judgements in this 'fast thinking' mode (Kahneman 2011) are likely to be partial and prone to bias. A second front in this conflict emerges when it comes to cumulative judgements by citizens. The optimistic line is that individual errors cancel one another out and that public opinion moves roughly in line with real-world events. The counter-argument is that if individual judgements are prone to the same biases and the same limited information sources, then there are few grounds for assuming wisdom in the crowd. To some extent, the variance between these arguments is about a difference in starting point. The optimistic line of argument is premised on emphasising the idea that citizens are not clueless, while the alternative focuses on the bounded quality of judgement (Kuklinski and Quirk 2000).

Most work drawing on this debate about political judgements refers to the bounded nature of the rationality used by citizens in placing their vote in an election or making a policy choice. We focus on diffuse support for the political system rather than support for particular candidates or policies, but our assumption would be that the same cognitive rules apply to these political judgements as well. From the perspective of seeking to understand shifting patterns of anti-politics, the insights from the cognitive sciences suggest that the way that citizens reason about politics is not an approximation to the rational actor favoured by some democratic and constitutional thought but an altogether messier and flawed process. Citizens reason, yes, but not always consciously, logically, unemotionally, or in direct tune with their interests. We need to take into account 'real reason – what the cognitive sciences have discovered about how we really think' (Lakoff 2009: 220).

Building on that insight, our argument can be broken down into four propositions. First, humans reason about the political system mostly in fast thinking mode and employ narratives and stories developed in that mode to explain how politics works. Second, it is possible to identify 'folk theories' about politics, which are distinct from beliefs or ideologies and perform the functions of helping citizens to understand politics, to explain their position to others, and to make political choices. Third, between the middle of the twentieth century and the beginning of the twenty-first century, the folk theory of stealth democracy used by a critical mass of British citizens mutated into the folk theory of stealth populism. One set of expectations – that politicians should be sincere, hard-working, able, and moderate and that many politicians are such *politicians for the people* – was replaced by another: that politicians be *for* the people but also *of* the people ('normal' and 'in touch') and that many politicians are *not* such 'good' politicians. Fourth, this development frames the contemporary expression of anti-politics and the dilemmas associated with achieving political competence and engagement in democratic societies at the beginning of the twenty-first century – given the inherent limits to our cognitive capacities. The underlying argument of our book is that citizens have become more negative about their political system in response to both conscious reflection and less conscious cognitive changes in how they understand politics and shifting patterns of engagement with politics. Giving citizens more facts about politics or explaining the way the political system works – classic political education – is unlikely to change their outlook; an issue explored when examining the construction of reform measures in the Conclusion. To challenge anti-politics, we need to change people's narratives about and experiences of politics.

Reasoning about Politics

How do citizens reason about politics? Colin Hay (2007: 162) argues that we still know very little 'about the cognitive process in and through which they come to attribute motivations to the behaviour [they] witness, or how [they] come to develop and revise the assumptions about human nature [they] project on to others'. Yet reason they do, not as omniscient calculators but with bounded rationality. Starting with the pioneering contribution of Herbert Simon (1985) – who emphasised the idea that human cognition is limited – and with the considerable input of the cognitive sciences, we can agree that citizens reason, in the sense they have reasons for doing what they do, but those processes of reason are framed by the bounds of their cognitive capacity and the environment in which they are located (Lupia et al. 2000).

Without denying the scope for further research and developments in understanding, it can be argued that we have a range of firm insights to aid our capacity to explain the limits to human cognition. One helpful starting point is dual process theory that rests on a distinction between two types of cognition: System 1 and System 2. The terms 'System 1' and 'System 2' were first coined by Stanovich and West (2000), but the ideas and experimental work on which they draw have a longer history. Table 9.1 presents a representation of some of the properties of each system of reasoning that are open to individuals to use. Following Daniel Kahneman (2011), we refer to these two systems as fast and slow thinking modes. The differences between System 1 and System 2 reasoning reflect relative rather than absolute divisions (Stanovich and Toplak 2012), and not all features outlined in Table 9.1 have to be observed for a certain type of thinking to be identified as present. Overall, the fast thinking of System 1 operates quickly and automatically, generates

Table 9.1 *Properties of fast and slow thinking (adapted from Stanovich and Toplak 2012)*

System 1 (fast thinking)	System 2 (slow thinking)
Intuitive More influenced by emotions and feelings	Analytic Less influenced by emotions and feelings
More automatic Relatively undemanding of cognitive capacity Relatively fast Parallel Innately present but also acquired by exposure and personal experience	More controlled Capacity demanding Relatively slow Sequential Learnt more by formal tuition and culture input

impressions and inclinations, and infers and invents causes and intentions. Type 2 thinking, by contrast, requires a lot more effort. It involves concentration and is experienced more directly as conscious reflection and as a choosing between cognitive alternatives.

Thinking in System 1 mode is the dominant form of human reasoning. There are many kinds of this type of thinking, and they come from different sources and paths. Some are innate to the human condition, the product of evolution and reflective of the need for humans to respond quickly and effectively to a complex range of ever-changing messages about their environment, as in the flight response when a surprise threat arises. System 1 thinking is an invaluable tool in a complex world where information is limited or difficult to process. Its role is to enable people to make sense of their world. 'The main function of System 1 is to maintain and update a model of your personal world, which represents what is normal in it ... it determines your interpretation of the present as well as your expectations of the future' (Kahneman 2011: 71). Yet as Kahneman (2011: 85) comments: 'The measure of success for System 1 is the coherence of the story it manages to create. The amount and quality of the data on which the story is based are largely irrelevant.' System 1, in short, is quick to judgement, and its guess may be good enough, but it is prone to systematic errors.

Critical voices have been raised against dual process theories. Some query whether there are two coherent types of reasoning and argue that there is a single process going on (Osman 2004). Others question whether there are only two forms of reasoning and speculate about there being more (Moshman 2000). The critique that has gained most traction is one aimed at definitional issues and the boldness of the distinction between the two forms of reasoning (Evans 2012) and the less explored weaknesses of Type 2 reasoning. These challenges, however, are not sufficient to prevent students of politics benefiting from using the distinction between fast and slow thinking. To understand anti-politics means understanding the narratives developed by System 1 fast thinking.

It means also exploring the environments that help to shape the development and deployment of those narratives. In particular, it may be that cognitive limitations could be overcome by the role of institutions that can frame and shape the decisions of citizens. Lupia and McCubbins (2000: 47) argue that 'political institutions make it easier for citizens to learn *what they need to know* by affecting citizens' beliefs about who can and cannot be trusted'. Their suggestion is that citizens need relatively modest amounts of knowledge to make reasoned choices and that institutional devices can provide a substitute for more detailed information about politicians' character – by telling citizens that the politicians they have an interest in, for example, will face punishment for lying or will have to verify their claims. In short, creating institutional devices that give the chance of providing a credible commitment could help the citizen take a shortcut in their decision-making. Another line of argument is that affective or emotional experiences may focus people's attention on an issue or provide them with the appropriate cues to make a decision and therefore could be a functional asset to them in low information contexts with modest cognitive effort (Marcus et al. 2000, Rahn 2000).

The possibility of the environment shaping understanding is a valuable insight, but from the perspective of our interest in anti-politics, the lessons to be drawn from the evidence presented earlier in this book are that both the institutional and affective environments have turned against allowing citizens to judge better about who to trust or not to trust. In general, it would seem that institutions or emotions do not necessarily have to have a positive effect in terms of enabling citizens to act more effectively in making political choices. The effects could be negative, and that is what our evidence suggests they have been. The professionalisation of politics means that politicians are now less diverse as a group, so they are less able collectively to represent the different virtues expected of them. The contexts of encounter between politicians and citizens have changed so that modes of interaction afforded by media events and professionalised campaigning make it more difficult for politicians to perform virtues and for citizens to calibrate judgements. Over time, many citizens have become angered, sickened, and depressed by formal politics. In short, the institutional devices that might have promoted more trust in politics – by, for example, allowing politicians to perform acts of public speaking or campaign interaction that gave them credibility – have been downplayed, and those that create suspicion and doubt have been substituted. Add in a more challenging and negative emotional environment, then both cognitive and environmental factors appear to be working together to intensify anti-politics.

Narratives about Politics: The Role of Folk Theories

Citizens understand politics using narratives and the relatively unconscious process of fast thinking. As George Lakoff (2009: 34) argues: '[W]e cannot understand other people without such cultural narratives . . . We understand public figures by fitting them into such narrative complexes. That goes for politicians as well as celebrities.' These cognitive maps also become cultural products when they are shared and circulated informally. One way of capturing the idea of cultural narratives is through the concept of folk theories (Holland and Quinn 1987, Lakoff 2002). People routinely develop their own theories to explain the physical, technological, and social phenomena they encounter. The concept of folk theories seeks to capture that process. As Willett Kempton (1986: 75) explains:

Human beings strive to connect related phenomena and make sense of the world. In so doing, they create what I would call folk theory. The word 'folk' signifies both that these theories are shared by a social group, and that they are acquired from everyday experience or social interaction. To call it 'theory' is to assert that it uses abstractions, which apply to many analogous situations, enable predictions, and guide behaviour.

Folk theories are common-sense or taken-for-granted ways of understanding. Folk theories 'serve pragmatic purposes; they explain the tangible, the experiential . . . they hold sway in a realm in which exceptions prove rules and contradictions live happily together' (Keesing 1987: 374). As Quinn and Holland (1987: 3) suggest: '[A] large proportion of what we know and believe derive from these shared models that specify what is in the world and the how it works.'

Folk theories offer non-technical explanations of how things work that can be very different to the institutionalised, professionally legitimated conceptions held by experts and system designers. People understand the way thermostats work in a way different to engineers (Kempton 1986), or they can explain how Facebook posts appear at greater or lesser frequency on their screen but not in the same way as those who design the filtering algorithms that drive that process (Eslami et al. 2016). Similarly, citizens may understand politics but not in the same way as its practitioners or political scientists.

Folk theories are different from political beliefs or coherent ideologies. They are constructed more loosely and not as fixed. Folk theories are not as systematic or coherent as more technical or specialised forms of knowledge or discourse. Rather, they 'comprise sets of short-cuts, idealisations, and simplifying paradigms that work well enough yet need not fit together without contradictions into global systems of coherent knowledge' (Keesing 1987: 380). Folk theories are the ways people try to make sense of what is happening. They are revised in the light of experience and reinforced by social exchanges. Folk models are often loosely constructed and act as both representations of how things are supposed to work and a more pragmatic guide about what to do. The models can take a variety of forms and are by no means easy to discern, since they are not always vocalised or rendered explicit.

Moreover, an individual's allegiance to a model may shift depending on the setting or context. In this sense, folk theories are not iron cages that determine thought patterns, but they may nonetheless prove important in guiding the reasoning used by people. One of the most important lessons from studying folk theories is that 'not all citizens have coherent ideologies' and it is 'normal for people to operate with multiple models in various domains' (Lakoff 2002: 14–5). However, people do not generally act randomly; rather, they tend to apply different models in different settings, orienting themselves to specific social and political practices in predictable but often context-specific ways.

Folk theories are what we need to orient ourselves to the situations in which we find ourselves – in order to act and to make sense of our world. In particular, they provide 'what one needs to know in order to *say* culturally acceptable things about the world' (Quinn and Holland 1987: 4). Folk theories are models in people's minds, but they are more than that in that they steer social acts (Malle 2000).

Lakoff (2002: 9–11) argues that such folk worldviews are composed of ways of categorising that are both commonplace and normal to the human mind. Typically, people can identify a category (e.g. a good politician); a typical case (a person doing something that matches the requirement of a good politician); an ideal case (a model politician); an anti-ideal or dystopic prototype (a politician who lies or is not authentic); a social stereotype to support snap judgements (politicians just have to open their mouths and lies fall out); a salient exemplar (someone who shows that it is possible to be a good politician); and an essential prototype (a set of properties or a model whose features, according to the folk theory, would be observed to enable us to know we were looking in practice at a good politician). As this suggests, folk theories tend to be developed through the application of categories and prototypes. As Lakoff (2002: 11) notes, 'none of this should be strange or unfamiliar.

All of these are normal products of the human mind, and they are used in everyday discourse. There is nothing surprising about their use in politics, but we need to be aware of how they are used.'

From Stealth Democracy to Stealth Populism

When discussing politics with others – or, indeed, explaining their position to interviewers – citizens use the forms of reasoning implied by folk theories. We argue that part of the explanation for changing patterns of anti-politics is a mutation of the stealth-democratic folk model used by many citizens to understand politics. In Chapter 6, we saw that stealth democracy was a prominent folk theory in post-war Britain. Many citizens believed democracy to be important. They felt a duty to vote. But they viewed party politics as just unnecessary mud-slinging and yearned for independent candidates, statesmen, coalitions, and national governments (working on behalf of a perceived singular local or national interest). In Chapter 7, we saw how some content of this folk model became changed over the second half of the twentieth century. In the years following the Second World War, many citizens expected politicians of competence and independence. By the early twenty-first century, many citizens expected politicians *for* the people (trustworthy, able, moderate, strong) but also *of* the people (normal and in touch with everyday life). Furthermore, in Chapter 8, we saw how contexts of political encounter in the immediate post-war period encouraged judgements of politicians as *representatives for the people*. In the later period, such contexts encouraged more negative judgements. In short, a critical mass of citizens used to expect government by representatives for the people and could imagine politicians – or enough politicians – as these competent and independent leaders. Citizens heard politicians give long radio speeches. They saw them handle rowdy political meetings. Over time, however, a critical mass of citizens have come to expect representatives *both for and of* the people. Furthermore, these citizens cannot imagine their politicians – or enough of their politicians – in this way. Citizens see the photo opportunities of politicians, hear their soundbites, note their gaffes. A stealth understanding of politics has transformed into a stealth populist understanding, by which many citizens imagine 'the people' – who largely agree and so just need action from competent, independent representatives – but also an incompetent and out-of-touch political elite (who act, the story goes, against the interests of the people).

Let us explore these folk models in a little more detail and see how they relate to the more formal technical models that might be used by politicians or political scientists. The stealth democracy model has been identified as present in the understanding of citizens in a range of studies and

Table 9.2 *Comparing stealth democracy and elitist democracy*

	Folk model: Stealth democracy	Formal model: Elitist democracy
Typical case	Established post–Second World War democracies in North America and Western Europe	Established post–Second World War democracies in North America and Western Europe
Ideal case	A political system that delivers what citizens want	A political system that does not ask too much of citizens
Anti-ideal	A political system where there is all talk and no action, and unnecessary conflict	A political system that places too much influence on the voice of the public
A social stereotype to support model	Memory of a politician taking the right decisive action	Trusted and legitimate political elite
An exemplar or prototype	An effective politician	A deferential citizen

countries (Evans and Stoker 2016, Hibbing and Theiss-Morse 2002, Stoker and Hay 2017). We are not alone in identifying it as a folk model of democracy held by citizens. In the United Kingdom (UK), we argue that its heyday was in the second half of the twentieth century. During the early part of that period, its closest family resemblance in formal theory was the elitist democracy model (Held 2006, Walker 1966). The starting point for both models is an image of post-war western democracy, but at that point the two models diverge (Table 9.2).

The elitist model of democracy developed as a critique of the classical model that looked to provide more active citizen engagement. The critique was based on a view of citizen participation as both unrealistic (citizens have neither the time nor the inclination to participate extensively in politics) and undesirable (a fear of the role of demagogic leadership, mass psychology, group coercion, and mob rule). Democracy required citizens to select and endorse their leaders but stay out of the detail of policy-making and show trust and deference to those elected to carry out measures in the public interest.

The stealth model shares some of the same ground but heads off in a different direction. It too thinks that citizens should not be expected to do too much or put too much effort into direct engagement, but this is not because citizens cannot be trusted or lack capacity. Rather, it is that citizens have busy lives with better things to do than political engagement. Moreover, since most sensible people agree on what is the right thing to do, then citizens should be able to expect political leaders to get on and take the action necessary without detailed oversight or input from

Table 9.3 *Comparing stealth democracy and stealth populism*

	Stealth democracy	Stealth populism
Typical case	Established post–Second World War democracies in North America and Western Europe	Twenty-first century democracies, old and new, that have a highly professionalised and media-dominated politics
Ideal case	A political system that delivers what citizens want	A political system that is failing to deliver what citizens want
Anti-ideal	A political system where there is all talk and no action, and unnecessary conflict	An anti-system or anti-establishment politician
A social stereotype to support the model	Memory of a politician taking the right decisive action	Politicians that are 'bland but hiding an ulterior motive below that'.[1]
An exemplar or prototype	An effective politician	A smooth-talking politician who is all spin and no substance

citizens. The fear in this model is of politicians that put party conflict or personal interests ahead of doing the right thing. But the hope is that there are enough good politicians around to make for effective government. Stealth democracy sees citizens combine fear of politicians creating division and selling out on their promises with some faith that the political system can still deliver enough – without requiring a more sustained level of political participation from themselves. Citizens reason that they do not want to pay much attention to politics, but they do want it to work for them in the background, quietly and efficiently dealing with those issues which need to be managed collectively. The stealth democracy view is that politics should work smoothly and competently for citizens – rather than requiring a great deal of effort from them – and it stands a good chance of doing so if the right kind of politician is in charge.

We argue that, by the early twenty-first century, this stealth under-standing of politics had transformed into a stealth-populist understand-ing. Now, many citizens imagined 'the people' who share a common interest but also an incompetent and out-of-touch political elite who act, if at all, against that interest. The stealth perspective has mutated as a folk theory from a grudging hope that the political system might deliver to a populist expression of angst, railing against the failing of democratic politics. The differences between the stealth democracy folk narrative and its populist replacement are presented in Table 9.3.

---

[1] Panellist W5214, male, 28, literary events coordinator, London (spring 2014).

The stealth populist folk theory offers a distinctively more negative view of the political system than the far from rosy depiction provided within the stealth democracy narrative. It has become more prominent among citizens in the early twenty-first century. The judgement of many citizens has shifted from one view of a political system that might deliver to another view of a system that cannot deliver. Politicians should be close to the people, empathetic, and engaged but also effective and determined to keep their promises. Stealth populism wants politicians who deliver, but in addition to the requirements of the stealth democracy narrative, politicians should be *of the people*. These qualities are conspicuous by their absence in twenty-first-century British politics. Politicians are seen as non-entities, bland, sneaky, liars who apparently break promises as regularly as they breathe. The political system has become a focus for angst and disappointment. The journey captured in the chapters of this book has been from scepticism to cynicism, from stealth democracy to stealth populism.

Where Next for Democratic Politics?

Cognitive studies tell us that 'not only are citizens minimally informed . . . but [they] are also prone to bias and error in using the limited experience they receive' (Kuklinski and Quirk 2000: 182). Many citizens find the machinations of the formal political system to be disappointing and alienating. Although citizens remain interested in political ideas and choice, many feel that formal politics, as it is currently offered to them, is not going to deliver on their concerns. Cognitive limitations join negative narratives and failing institutions to provide the perfect storm that is driving anti-politics.

This chapter has argued that significant cognitive limitations are faced by citizens in approaching the political system. They engage with politics largely in a fast thinking mode that allows conscious reflection to be dominated by unconscious and largely negative framing. Overall, the fast thinking of System 1 operates quickly and automatically and generates impressions and inclinations and further infers and invents causes and intentions. Yet it is possible to offer, with only a little effort, a partial list of the multiple biases in judgement that tend to creep in under System 1 reasoning. System 1 is biased to confirm existing explanations, neglects ambiguity and suppresses doubt, focuses on existing evidence rather than new evidence, uses potentially misleading prototypes to make judgements, will try to answer an easier question rather than a harder one, overweighs low-probability actions in coming to a judgement, is more sensitive to change than stable states, can exaggerate risk based on high-intensity or -profile events, is more concerned about loss aversion, and frames decisions narrowly. 'System 1 is highly adept in one form of thinking – it automatically and effortlessly identifies causal connections between events, sometimes even when the connection is spurious' (Kahneman 2011: 110).

The folk theories or narratives that citizens tell themselves about politics are far from positive. Indeed, more generally it could be argued that fast thinking about politics is prone to presenting and supporting negative understandings (Stoker et al. 2016). A significant proportion of citizens has gradually moved from a grudging acceptance of the stealth-democratic idea that politics might deliver, to the more angst-ridden certainty of stealth populism and the belief that politics cannot and will not deliver. The most prominent folk story of politics at the beginning of the twenty-first century describes an activity dominated by bland, self-interested, and out-of-touch politicians. The cognitive approach to politics is framed by fast thinking, and the narratives that have been created are strongly negative.

It could be that institutional or other interventions might challenge some of these cognitive biases or negative narratives, but the professio-nalised character of politics, its slick marketing and sloganising, and its determined effort to stay on message has meant that many citizens have lost what little capacity they had to distinguish between good and bad politicians and parties. People are more than capable of using information and making decisions under favourable conditions. People can usually engage in complex tasks like making friends and parenting and, given training, can easily undertake more complex tasks – from engineering to running businesses. There are major obstacles, though, placed in their way when it comes to judging politics (Kuklinski and Quirk 2000). First, the business of politics is complex and involves a multi-faceted mix of deciding about evidence, values, the positions of others, power dynamics, and acceptable outcomes. Second, political debate rarely has as its goal to provide reliable information; its focus is more on persuasion. Third, there are few opportunities given to citizens for thinking carefully about politics. Finally, there is rarely any useful feedback provided in a way that might help time-poor citizens to make decisions.

The dilemma for the future of democracy is clear. Anti-politics frames the debate, and we cannot wish away the factors lying behind it. The cognitive dynamics that steer our understanding of politics will remain in place. The narratives about politics that show it as practised by politi-cians who are failing cannot easily be overthrown. The institutional prac-tices of politics that are reinforcing negativity on the part of citizens have a logic of their own in the context of a professionalised, media-driven, and marketing approach to the delivery of politics. To argue that we need better political education overlooks the dynamics of fast thinking. To call for more citizen engagement and deliberative-democratic innovations runs counter to a widely held stealth view that politics should deliver without requiring too much input from the public. To ask politics to change its ways without a capacity for credible commitment to do that from all competitors is perhaps to ask too much. Our research has helped us to frame the problem of anti-politics. In the Conclusion, we see if we can address that problem, but in a way that is consistent with our research findings.

Conclusion

There is a need to provide an overview of the argument so far, and this task occupies the first section of this chapter. Our book contributes at four levels. First, there is an element of conceptual clarification regarding how to understand the term 'anti-politics' and relate it to other more established concepts. Second, overcoming several methodological challenges, we bring into play empirical data from Mass Observation (MO) and a wide range of surveys and polls. Third, as we draw on datasets enabling us to take a longer historical view, we can show that although there never was a golden age when citizens were enchanted by formal politics, the scope and intensity of anti-politics have grown over the decades. Finally, having taken this long view, we can sift through various explanations of trends in anti-politics and show that some explanations are more plausible than others. Our original contribution is an account of how anti-politics has grown because citizens' criteria for judging politics have become more demanding, and this development is compounded by the more restricted environment in which politicians and citizens now interact.

But our ambition in this concluding chapter goes beyond a restatement of our main arguments. It is to engage with the tricky issue of what if anything could be done about the problem of anti-politics. We think our analysis suggests that some of the common reform prescriptions might have only modest chances of addressing the problem. There has been much focus in contemporary democracies on citizenship education aimed at young people, constitutional reform, and new practices of participation and deliberation. We can concede that each of these reform strategies might be of value in itself, but none of them can really get to grips with anti-politics – if our analysis and understanding of anti-politics are correct. Negativity about politics is not exclusively an issue among younger citizens. Some constitutional reforms are too tokenistic to make a difference, and others do more to change the relationships between politicians and other elite decision-makers than shift ingrained negative patterns of interaction between citizens and politicians. Citizen participation and deliberation initiatives tend to be attractive options for only some citizens and appear to have little impact on restoring trust in the political system. Our view is that the challenge of reinstating a better balance in the dynamic between politicians and citizens requires us to accept those features of the relationship that cannot be changed and identify some that can. We make suggestions for reform measures that could address the complex dimensions of anti-politics that our study has revealed but recognise further research and the trialling of options are needed.

The Argument So Far

Anti-Politics: An Attitudinal Definition

We defined anti-politics as citizens' negative sentiment towards the activities and institutions of formal politics. Our focus, then, is on what other scholars have referred to as political alienation or withdrawal of political support or political disaffection. Anti-politics in our study is largely captured by shifts in the attitudes of citizens towards politicians, politics, and the political system. Our argument touches on two other ways of defining anti-politics. The first sees it as an opportunity that has been exploited, as reflected in the rise of populism. Anti-elite politicians rail against the corrupt politics of the establishment and present themselves as champions of the people. The second sees anti-politics as a strategy used by those very elites to keep issues off the political agenda and control the democratic process, offering citizens only an anaemic and controlled form of political engagement.

We see merit in these other depictions of anti-politics but suggest that the danger of these approaches is that they contain ready made within them an answer to the questions that we argue can be explored empirically: Has anti-politics grown, and what are its causes? Both the alternative definitions assume that anti-politics has grown and offer competing explanations of its emergence – one focused on the failings of the political system to deliver and the other on the usurpation of democratic processes by political elites. We argue, rather, for a more empirically grounded approach and, of course, for taking the long view of anti-politics. What we do share with many other studies is a sense that anti-politics matters. A certain degree of scepticism about politics is healthy in any democracy, but not when it is associated with non-participation, non-compliance with legitimate laws, or support for aggressive forms of populism that undermine the mutual respect and tolerance essential to the practice of democracy. Anti-politics can make government more difficult, and it may lead to the neglect of so-called 'wicked' or difficult-to-resolve issues and long-term challenges as politicians fear they lack the legitimacy to engage with citizens over these issues. Nor do we assume that negativity towards formal politics is being cancelled out by citizens' positive sentiment towards informal politics (the democratisation thesis). Our evidence suggests that many citizens are not clamouring for more opportunities to participate. They have an interest in politics – and indeed do self-organise collectively – but we cannot assume that this engagement is a replacement for connecting to formal democratic processes.

Meeting the Challenge of Taking the Long View

We took a longer view of anti-politics than has been taken by most researchers to date, covering both the so-called current 'age of anti-politics' and the so-called post-war 'golden age'. This longer view was possible for the case of the United Kingdom (UK) because of two data-sets: collected survey and opinion poll data (which date back further for the UK than for most other countries) and volunteer writing from MO (a unique dataset). These datasets each had their own strengths and weaknesses. Used together, they allowed us to generate new insights (most often from the MO data) and confirm those findings (most often using the survey data).

Regarding the MO material, we undertook our own systematic analysis of the 'raw' data rather than using the summaries produced by MO's own researchers (which is what most existing studies have done). This involved sampling thirteen 'directives' or occasions when MO asked its panellists to write about formal politics across the two periods. Then we sampled sixty panellists per directive to construct datasets broadly representative of the UK population (by gender, age, region, and occupational category) and broadly comparable between the two periods. Then we read this material for the cultural resources used by panellists to write about formal politics – categories, storylines, and folk theories – focusing especially on those resources shared by a broad range of panellists (and so presumably circulating in wider society at the time, to be used by citizens in the construction of understandings, expectations, and judgements regarding formal politics).

The analysis of survey data also required some innovation as tracking long-term trajectories of political disaffection in a way that overcomes data limitations poses a substantial methodological challenge. Survey questions relevant to the problem of anti-politics are relatively scarce prior to the 1970s, and for various reasons, different questions and variations of questions are more prominent in some time periods than others.

We overcame this obstacle in two ways. First, we used trend data from repeated survey measures and supplemented this with comparison of responses to survey questions asked at different points in time. Second, we used Stimson's dyad-ratios algorithm to construct an over-time index of political discontent that combines data from multiple poll series.

The Expansion of an Anti-Politics Mood

Moving from methods to results, we established that no golden age of political engagement existed in the UK. A substantial proportion of citizens even in the 1940s were dissatisfied with government, thought politicians to be 'out for themselves', thought politicians to be 'not straight-talking', expected contradictory things of politicians, or at least found politicians difficult to judge. Nevertheless, and contrary to claims of trendless fluctuation or Britain's unchanging anaemic political culture, we established that anti-politics increased in the UK over the second half of the twentieth century in three respects: social scope, political scope, and intensity.

More citizens from across all social groups now judge politicians and politics to be flawed. If anything, older citizens are slightly more negative than younger ones. But the main point is that disillusionment with politics is not confined to one social group. Furthermore, anti-politics has increased in political scope. Citizens hold more grievances with formal politics. As the twenty-first century gets into its stride, they judge politicians to be self-serving and not straight-talking but also out of touch, all the same, and a joke. One of the features of the evidence from MO panellists was the increased intensity or strength by which the criticisms of politics found expression. In the period immediately after the Second World War, respondents wrote about politicians in relatively measured terms. This finding cannot be dismissed as simply a reflection of a general culture of deference at the time. In the same responses, they wrote about doctors as 'selfish' and 'ignorant', scientists as 'inhuman' with 'one-track minds', and lawyers as dishonest, thieving 'sharks'. By the early twenty-first century, stronger negative terms for these other professionals were not really apparent in the writing of MO panellists, but such strong terms were now prominently used for politicians. Citizens described their 'loathing' for politicians who made them 'angry', 'disgusted', and 'depressed'.

Explaining Anti-Politics

We cast doubt on some existing influential theories explaining the rise of anti-politics. We noted earlier some doubts about the decline of deference, given that deference was rarely found in the MO responses of the

1940s. The flip side of the decline of deference thesis is a set of theories about the rise of critical or assertive citizens who are secure, educated, and keen to take the initiative in making societal decisions. But our citizens in the more recent period sounded angry, sickened, and depressed – rather than critical – and these feelings were targeted specifically at politicians (as opposed to all figures of authority). It would be fair to say that, in the round, British citizens are not moving along post-material tramlines towards a new, assertive culture of critical citizenship. Rather, evidence points to an entrenched anti-politics mood; a sense of feeling terminally let down by the political system and frustrated by the antics of politicians.

We noted that anti-politics is also explained by some as the product of a watering down of political choice. According to some theories of depoliticisation and post-democracy, a neo-liberal consensus gripped formal politics from the late 1970s onwards, and the more controlled and limited form of politics on offer pushed citizens into a minimalist role. Together, these factors had the effect of turning many away from political engagement. We found some MO panellists writing about contemporary politics dismayed by the lack of choice offered by the main parties. However, it should not be assumed that citizens were content with party politics in previous eras, as some post-democracy theorists imply. Indeed, in the mid-twentieth century, many citizens struggled to see the need for party politics at all. They judged politicians to be compromised by party discipline (to be professional politicians and 'partymen'). They viewed party politics as just unnecessary mud-slinging and axe-grinding. They longed for independent statesmen, coalitions, and the national governments of recent war-time. We argue that citizens were not positively engaged with formal politics in the 1940s and 1950s simply because politicians and parties were clearly distinguishable along ideological lines, so we must look elsewhere – beyond accounts of depoliticisation and post-democracy – to explain fully the rise of anti-politics.

Beyond offering critiques of established theories, we offered a new explanation of anti-politics based on two ideas. First, we showed that popular images of the good politician have changed. The new image is rooted in the professionalisation of politics, the ideology of intimacy, and democratic egalitarianism. Second, we argued that this new image is more difficult for politicians to perform. It is more demanding, since it asks politicians to be not only *for* the people – to be honest, capable, moderate, and strong – but also *of* the people – to be 'normal' and 'in touch' with 'real' life and 'ordinary' people. In addition, the professionalisation of politics means that politicians are now less diverse as a group, so they are less able collectively to represent the different virtues expected of them. Furthermore, the contexts of encounter between politicians and citizens have changed. The modes of interaction afforded by media events and professionalised campaigning make it more difficult for politicians to perform virtues and for citizens to calibrate judgements.

Responding to the Evidence: Reform Options

Citizens at the start of the twenty-first century appear to want a multi-faceted relationship with their elected representatives but are offered a series of one-dimensional experiences that disappoint and frustrate and so provide the driving force behind negative attitudes towards formal politics. In thinking about how to respond, it is important to follow through on the thread of evidence presented in our book. Beyond that, there seems little point in arguing for reforms that would require a political process that asked more from human cognition than could reasonably be expected and more from a political system than could reasonably be delivered. Most citizens are highly likely to continue to pay attention to politics to a limited degree and will use a combination of fast or intuitive thinking and, to a lesser extent, slow, reflective thinking to deliver their judgement on politics. Most political systems will – in the context of global forces, entrenched inequalities, and imperfect implementation practices – continue to generate a certain degree of disappointment. Indeed, as one of our group of authors has argued (Stoker 2006/2017), political systems are characterised by designed-in disappointment. As a centralised form of decision-making, politics is inherently controlling. It may protect freedoms, but it does so by imposing collective choice over individual choice. To take part in politics is time-consuming and challenging – given the scale and quality of communication that is required and the challenge of using voice but also listening to others. Finally, the outcomes of the political process are seldom clear-cut and often messy compromises.

For long periods, there appears to be nothing noble about politics at all. Politics, after all, is a battle for influence and the exercise of power. That this activity involves politicians in hustle, intrigue, lies, and deceit provides little surprise to most citizens who have long understood that politics is prone to such a dynamic. Politics has the quality of being both the decent pursuit of the common good and a rather unedifying process that involves humans behaving badly. So, any reforms offered will have to embrace this split personality of politics and work with the grain of an inherently imperfect system. In the discussion that follows, we review some widely advocated and implemented reform measures and indicate why our evidence suggests that success might be limited. We then move on to consider some non-standard responses that might be worthy of further consideration and trialling.

The Limits to Citizenship Education

Citizenship education aimed at schoolchildren and young adults has been a preferred reform option in the past two decades. From September 2002, schools in England were legally required to deliver citizenship education for all eleven- to sixteen-year-olds. A commitment to citizenship education is a common feature of many contemporary democracies (Peterson et al. 2016). Jon Tonge and colleagues (Tonge et al. 2012: 599) argue that, in England, at least:

> Citizenship education *has* made a significant impact upon political understanding and engagement. Using our key tests of understanding of local and national issues and likelihood of voting, receipt of citizenship education *is* consistently an important positive factor, regardless of age, social class, ethnicity and gender. Our study demonstrates that young people who have received citizenship classes are more likely to engage in civic activism, contributing to a healthier polity.

The core argument to emerge from their evidence is that it is worth persevering with citizenship education. Indeed, if anything, the challenge is to make it more engaging and impactful. Similar patchy but positive assessments emerge from other studies. Lawless and Fox (2015) suggest politically themed video games, an app identifying local political offices and how to run for them, an extended volunteer programme for getting involved in politics, and making knowledge of current events part of college admissions requirements – all as ways of extending the impact of citizenship schemes.

Our argument is not with the value per se of citizenship education, but rather we agree with and extend the argument of Stephen Macedo and colleagues (2005: 6) that schools' citizenship efforts need to be put in a broader framework: 'Schools did not create our current civic engagement crisis single-handedly, and they cannot solve it on their own.' The evidence presented in this book shows that it is not only younger citizens who lack faith in politics; if anything, many have a naïve level of hope about its capacity to repair and improve itself, compared to older citizens who are likely to feel that experience has taught them only negative lessons about politics. Moreover, our evidence suggests that political discontent is not made simply by failures of citizenship. It is made by failures of interaction between citizens and politicians. For these reasons, we hold that citizenship education may have benefits but that it is unreasonable to expect it to be able to tackle the issue of anti-politics, at least on its own.

Constitutional Reforms May Not Be the Answer

Faced by popular discontent, a common response on the part of political elites is to propose a range of constitutional reforms. In the UK, we have seen a large number of reforms (Bogdanor 2009, McLean 2010) aimed at enshrining human rights, greater devolution, reform to the House of Lords and the way that Parliament operates, shifts in the calling of and voting procedures for elections, and the use of referendums. Constitutional change has also played a part in the reform programmes of many countries, including many emerging democracies (Lijphart 1996, 2004, Reynolds 2011, Farrell 2014). In the case of the UK, at least, our evidence suggests that the reforms have not had an immediate impact on quelling levels of political discontent.

But beyond that basic empirical observation, there are two underlying reasons why constitutional reform may not be the main answer to anti-politics. First, many reforms are limited in impact because their focus is on moving power around within the political elite. As Vernon Bogdanor (2009: 298) argues, British reforms have largely involved a redistribution of power 'from one part of the elite to another'. Reforms have moved influence around among those professionally involved in politics and law but have not done much to move power to citizens from these elites. Even when it comes to referendums and changes to the electoral system, it is elites that have set the terms and timing of new practices. This point leads on to a second general concern. In a significant review of some of the reforms of political systems in recent decades, Bowler and Donnovan (2013) make it abundantly clear that reforms are often undermined in implementation or indeed fatally flawed from launch. Above all, Bowler and Donovan show that a significant constraint on political reform is the interests of the current political elite, in that they tend to choose reform options that will benefit their party or give their interests an advantage. Although the pressure of public opinion – and sometimes even the value choices of elites – can play a part in making decisions, their evidence is that political and constitutional reforms from around the world are often selected by political elites with partisan advantage in mind (as opposed to the impact of reforms on diffuse political support).

Constitutional reform can be of value, of course, for a range of reasons, but our analysis of the causes of anti-politics suggests that it is unlikely to get to the heart of the anti-politics problem. Our evidence tells us that the problem lies in how citizens judge politics and interact with politicians, and constitutional reforms may not have the capacity to address those issues (and, indeed, perhaps are unlikely to be designed to achieve that end).

More Participation and Deliberation: Answering the Wrong Question

Many writers promote the idea of citizen participation and deliberative mini-publics as a way of addressing the issue of anti-politics, and there are multiple examples of the practice of this idea (Fung and Wright 2003, Smith 2009, Geissel and Newton 2012). Vincent Jacquet (2017: 1) notes that such democratic innovations are seen as 'a key ingredient to curing the democratic malaise of contemporary political regimes because they provide an appropriate means to achieve inclusiveness and well-considered judgment'. The evidence from studies of these schemes shows that so-called 'ordinary' members of the public can, 'given the right circumstances, discuss with respect the views of others, change their minds in the light of evidence and argument, and reach judicious conclusions that take into account the public interest' (Newton 2012: 155). There is also little doubt that, in most instances, the participants in mini-publics take a great deal out of their engagement – both in the short run and in the long run and often in terms of an increased sense of personal political efficacy (Smith 2009). What is not clear is whether the schemes directly improve the legitimacy of decision-making by elites and there-fore, by implication, address the issue of anti-politics. One difficulty is that although participants feel positively about their engagement, the bulk of citizens are not involved and may have little awareness of the initiative, or, if they do, have received an interpretation of it through the normal dynamics of politics and media. There is evidence that involvement in making a decision is likely to make one feel better about that decision, but it is not clear that such judgements are then stretched to views of the political system as a whole (Hibbing and Theiss-Morse 2002). Claudia Chwalisz (2017) provides a positive assessment of experience in Australia and Canada, largely on evidence from government sponsors and partici-pants of the schemes, but a direct study of participants in a British mini-assembly revealed only a weak effect on ameliorating political alienation among participants (Spada et al. 2017). The verdict on the impact of mini-publics in terms of tackling anti-politics must remain open. Crucially, success is most likely, as Chwalisz argues, where the decision-making of the mini-public is very much integrated into the policy-making processes of elected representatives. That opportunity to see elected representatives in a different light – and in a more reflective and sustained mode of operating – would fit with the pointers from our research about how to change the dynamic of anti-politics.

The broader issue facing mini-publics and other forms of democratic innovation is just how scalable the initiatives are. In part, the concern is that setting them up both is time-consuming and involves considerable expense, and so it would appear difficult for them to be anything other than isolated experiences for just a modest number of citizens. But beyond these issues, there is the finding identified in our research and that of others that advocates of engagement are prone to over-estimate the extent and intensity of political engagement that most people desire. Jacquet (2017:1) provides evidence to show that reluctance to engage is not simply a product of how well designed the intervention is but rooted in how 'individuals conceive their own roles, abilities and capacities in the public sphere, as well as in the perceived output of such democratic innovations'. Drawing on extensive interviews with non-participants, a range of reasons emerge that are consistent with the complex understanding of political citizenship shown by our research (p15):

Some prefer to concentrate on the private sphere and do not feel competent to express political judgments in these arenas. The deliberative feature of mini-publics prevents participation because certain people dislike speaking out in public and are afraid of others' judgments. Non-participants with the political alienation logic dislike politics and consider that every form of engagement will be manipulated by political elites. Finally, some selected citizens decline the invitation because there is no guarantee of actual external political output on the political system.

Hibbing and Theiss-Morse (2002: 183), in their initial study of stealth democracy, noted that 'people's dislike of politics runs deep and is unlikely to be eliminated if only they would get involved with other people in political procedures'. Indeed, these authors go on to suggest that more participation or even greater transparency might have negative effects by encouraging more anti-politics. In the former case, citizens will be forced to confront directly that others disagree with them and getting a collective choice is a messy process; and in the latter case, more openness reveals more about the way that politics really works than most people want to know. Since our work reveals stealth-democratic understandings held by citizens as a persistent force in British political culture, we agree with Hibbing and Theiss-Morse that the key to challenging anti-politics may rest not with more participation but rather a better engagement with representative politics by citizens. It is to that challenge that we turn in the final section of this Conclusion.

A Call for a New Programme of Trials: Creating Sites for Interaction

The analysis we have offered suggests that for many citizens, their negativity towards politics has increased in scope and intensity in part because they are more demanding in what they want from political leaders and in part because they only get to judge performances by those leaders through the lens of stage-managed media events. The journey for citizenship has been less from allegiance to assertiveness, as is commonly claimed (Dalton and Welzel 2014), and more from reticence to a combination of flippancy and vehement antagonism regarding formal politics. Many citizens now ridicule politicians while at the same time feeling angry, disgusted, and depressed by politics. Many citizens now demand intimacy and egalitarianism from representative democracy (in a way that is quite new in the case of the UK). Politicians, in this light, need to offer more than just ability and hard work. They need to seem 'normal' and 'in touch' to the great variety of citizens in twenty-first-century society. Furthermore, they need to do this in the context of a citizen group that on the whole is interested in, has opinions about, but is relatively inattentive to politics. The task of reaching out has been made harder still by the way that politics has turned in on itself. The journey for politics has been from a practice driven by voluntary activity feeding into a mixed cadre of political representatives to an operation dominated by top-down organisation and slick marketing resting on a cadre of highly professionalised representatives. Long-term societal changes combined with changes in what is viewed as good and effective political practice have created a tougher environment for representative politics to be seen as palatable and engaging.

We think there is little hope of persuading citizens to see politics through a different lens. This lens, with its filters for intimacy and egalitarianism, emerged from decades if not centuries of cultural change (that was in many ways for the better). Nor do we imagine that citizens can be convinced to spend a lot more time engaging with politics. So, the first part of the driving forces behind anti-politics is made up of givens that cannot be imagined or wished away. What is left is the second part of the driving forces behind anti-politics, and here we can hope for some change. The actors who adopted professionalised, mediatised, largely negative communication practices could be persuaded to think about adjusting them in the light of our findings regarding the intensity of anti-politics that surrounds their current practice.

The first thing to say here is that we should not expect too much from these politicians, political parties, journalists, and media organisations. Their current behaviour is largely a result of the competitive pressures they face, and we are not advocating for a less competitive political system or a more regulated media sector. But having said that, we find hope in signs that such competitive pressures might now be changing. Professionalised parties and political campaigning appear to be facing difficulties in winning the support of voters disaffected by such offers and modes of political communication. Adversarial journalism appears to be facing difficulties in winning the support of audiences disaffected by the soundbites, bickering, and evasion afforded by such contexts of political encounter. We also find hope in alternative models provided by the past century but also the past year or two. There are lessons to be learned from political communication of the mid-twentieth century, when radio broadcasts or political meetings gave politicians time to explain themselves, to expose themselves, and sometimes to undermine themselves and provided citizens with opportunities to listen, react, question, and make calibrated judgements and distinctions on the basis of what they heard. There are also lessons to be learned from innovations of the past couple of years.

Many politicians are now using social media to communicate more directly with citizens, bypassing the double-mediation of journalists, other politicians, and other political professionals. Some of these politicians have enjoyed considerable success in recent elections. There is a fast-moving literature on the Internet, social media, and political communication. At the time of writing, the picture remains mixed at best. Some researchers have found associations between higher Internet use and stronger democratic preferences (e.g. Stoycheff and Nisbet 2014), but others have found little relationship between Internet use and political interest, trust, and efficacy (Richey and Zhu 2015) or have argued that online worlds – characterised by anonymity and flexibility – encourage uncivil debate that decreases political trust and efficacy (Åström and Karlsson 2013). What is certain is that new technologies offer a multiplicity of opportunities to actors in this field. To give just one example, what Matthew Wood and colleagues (2016) term 'everyday celebrity politicians' are currently experimenting with social media and especially the way it affords performances of more human, feminine, authentic politicians – as a means not only to win votes but also to re-engage disaffected citizens.

Let us finish this Conclusion by suggesting three areas for trials by reformers keen to provide new institutional contexts for politicians and citizens to meet and come to know each other better. Relatively few initiatives have invested in bringing citizens and elected representatives directly together. One ambitious model is provided by the Irish Constitutional Convention of 2013, an assembly composed of both citizens and politicians (Farrell 2014). Other examples can be found in the final stages of some participatory budgeting exercises (Smith 2009). An experimental intervention that brought elected representatives and citizens together through a web-based exchange has demonstrated positive impacts on a range of citizens regardless of educational or social characteristics (Neblo et al. 2010). In that work, a range of positive impacts on citizens' political engagement were identified, but it was not clear from the research design if it was contact with an elected representative or the opportunity to deliberate that was doing the work. The challenge of these initiatives is that they rely quite heavily on drawing a small fraction of citizens into a relatively intensive form of engagement, yet there is an argument that there might be multiplier effects with participants using their social networks to diffuse discussion and debate through a wider public (Lazer et al. 2015). It might be possible to build on these types of initiatives by adopting a practice from the mini-publics and citizen-juries discussed earlier in the chapter and regularly asking for randomly selected citizens to join with politicians on select committees in the UK Parliament and its corresponding institutions in Scotland, Wales, and Northern Ireland. The practice could also be extended to overview and scrutiny committees that operate in much of local government. Elected representatives would need to change their practices to support these schemes and become facilitators of public engagement and deliberation rather than straightforward decision-makers. Funding and other support would need to be provided to citizen participants.

A second set of initiatives might build on the work of several elected representatives who not only construct an individual casework connection with constituents but also engage in collective conversations, reporting back and asking for ideas about the policy choices they need to make. Independents in Australian politics have pioneered some of these types of consultation practices (Hendriks forthcoming), identifying those issues over which they can offer a clear advanced stance for electors to make a judgement on but leaving open for discussion their position on a range of other issues. They have also actively encouraged volunteer engagement with their office on a non-partisan basis (Bettles 2016). If this form of politics was to grow in the context of a politics still dominated by parties, then manifestos would need to become slimmed-down commitments on a number of key issues to which all party members were bound, leaving room for constituency engagement on other issues. Policies hidden in the detail of manifestos often give a false sense of legitimacy to party decision-making and are used to close down conversations rather than open them up. The idea proposed here is about limiting rather than extending those issues over which party discipline and control could be exercised, giving elected representatives greater scope to express their independence and character – in tune with the preferences of many citizens at the start of the twenty-first century.

More mainstream institutional practices might also lend themselves to a process by which citizens could judge politicians in a multi-dimensional way. More devolved decision-making and more localism could, if they connected power and control to local elected representatives closer to communities, provide the basis for a different form of politics. It is not automatically the case, but the early experiences of those mayoral offices where real power has been located – London or Greater Manchester, for example – provide hopeful signs. Benjamin Barber (2013) argues in *If Mayors Ruled the World* that regardless of city size or political affiliation, local elected executives exhibit a non-partisan and pragmatic style of governance that is lacking in national and international halls of power. Early work on the English experience made a similar argument (Greasley and Stoker 2008). Many citizens like a politics of action and getting things done, which is part of the 'stealth' folk theory of how democracy should work. At its best, the mayoral model can deliver that politics – although any local governance system would need strong and appropriate checks and balances, with opportunities for citizen engagement designed in.

The ideas presented in this last section of the book are about designing a politics more in tune with what most citizens appear to want from politics. They seem to want politicians who are both exceptionally virtuous and in touch with ordinary life and who act on behalf of the people without asking too much of citizens in terms of attention and participation. It is a difficult task to balance these requirements and to balance them against the difficult role politics must always play in reconciling conflicting interests and values. Therefore, we support both the further trialling of these ideas and the generation of further ideas to be tested. Our book calls into question currently favoured reform strategies by showing how they fail to address our core findings about what is driving anti-politics. We need a new debate that starts from where we are and how we got here. This book, we hope, has made a valuable contribution to that challenge by providing a novel and long-term perspective on the rise of anti-politics.

Appendix

Table A1 Survey questions relating to anti-politics

Question	2016	2015	2014	2013	2012	2011	2010	2009	2008	2007	2006	2005	2004	2003	2002	2001	2000	1999	1998	1997	1996	1995	1994	1993	1992	1991	1990	1989	1988	1987	1986	1985	1984	1983	1982	1981	1980	1979	1978	1977	1976	1975	1974	1973	1972	1971	1970	1969	1968	...	1966	...	1964	1963	...	1959	...	1946	1945	1944
Do you think that British politicians are out merely for themselves, for their party, or to do their best for their country?			×																																										×															×
Government approval.	×	×	×	×	×	×	×	×	×	×	×	×	×	×	×	×	×	×	×	×	×	×	×	×	×	×	×	×	×	×	×	×	×	×	×	×	×	×	×	×	×	×	×	×	×	×	×	×	×		×		×	×		×		×		
Prime ministerial approval.	×	×	×	×	×	×	×	×	×	×	×	×	×	×	×	×	×	×	×	×	×	×	×	×	×	×	×	×	×	×	×	×	×	×	×	×	×	×	×	×	×	×	×	×	×	×	×	×	×		×		×	×		×		×		
Speaking generally, what are the things about this country that you are most proud of?																																																								×				
On the whole, do the activities of the national government tend to improve conditions in this country, or would we be better off without them?																																																								×				
In your opinion, do people like yourself have enough say in … the way the government runs the country?																																												×					×											
Some people think that government is too much centralised in London. Others are quite content with things as they are. What do you think?																																															×													
Which of these statements best describes your opinion on the present system of governing Britain?		×				×	×	×	×	×	×	×	×	×					×	×		×				×																		×																
You see the card gives you some words to choose from which might describe your feelings about different things. Could you tell me the one which best describes how you feel about: Politicians in Britain today?																																											×																	
Compared with other European countries, do you feel that Britain is relatively well governed, relatively badly governed, or is it about average?																																											×																	
How much do you trust a British government of either party to place the needs of this country and the people above the interests of their own political party?																	×		×	×			×			×				×	×												×																	
Some people think that changing our whole political system is the only way to solve Britain's problems. Some think the system should be changed to give ordinary people much more say in what goes on. But others think the system should be changed so that the country's political leaders have much more power and authority to get on with the job without interference. Which … comes closest to your view?																																						×																						

Table A1 (cont.)

Question	2016	2015	2014	2013	2012	2011	2010	2009	2008	2007	2006	2005	2004	2003	2002	2001	2000	1999	1998	1997	1996	1995	1994	1993	1992	1991	1990	1989	1988	1987	1986	1985	1984	1983
Now I will read out a list of different types of people. For each, would you tell me whether you generally trust them to tell the truth or not? Government ministers.		X	X			X		X	X	X	X	X	X	X	X	X	X	X		X				X										X
Now I will read out a list of different types of people. For each, would you tell me whether you generally trust them to tell the truth or not? Politicians generally.		X	X			X		X	X	X	X	X	X	X	X	X	X	X		X				X										X
Most MPs will tell lies if they feel the truth will hurt them politically.								X					X										X				X					X		
Most MPs have a high personal moral code.													X										X									X		
Most MPs care more about special interests than they care about people like you.								X																			X					X		
Most MPs make a lot of money by using public office improperly.								X					X										X				X					X		
How much do you agree or disagree that … generally speaking those we elect as MPs lose touch with people pretty quickly?						X	X	X				X		X	X	X	X		X		X		X			X				X	X			
How much do you agree or disagree that… parties are only interested in people's votes, not in their opinions?						X	X	X				X		X	X	X	X		X		X		X			X				X	X			
How much do you agree or disagree that … People like me have no say in what the government does?																X														X	X			
How much do you trust British governments of any party to place the needs of the nation above the interests of their own political party?										X																				X	X			
How much do you trust politicians of any party in Britain to tell the truth when they are in a tight corner?						X	X	X				X		X	X	X	X		X		X		X											
In general, whose interests do you think MPs put first? Their own, their party's, their constituents', the country's, other, don't know.				X							X										X													
For each of the following institutions, please tell me if you tend to trust it or tend not to trust it. The British government.		X	X	X	X	X	X	X	X	X	X	X		X	X	X	X	X																
For each of the following institutions, please tell me if you tend to trust it or tend not to trust it. The British parliament.		X	X	X	X	X	X	X	X	X	X	X	X		X	X	X																	
How much do you agree or disagree that … it doesn't really matter which party is in power, in the end things go on much the same?			X		X	X	X	X	X	X	X	X		X	X	X																		

Question legend:

- **Q1.** How much do you trust the following to tell the truth? A great deal, a fair amount, not much, not at all. Leading Labour politicians / Leading Conservative politicians / Leading Liberal Democrat politicians / My local MP.
- **Q2.** Please tell me on a score of 0–10 how much you personally trust each of the institutions I read out. 0 means you do not trust an institution at all, and 10 means you have complete trust. Politicians.
- **Q3.** Please tell me on a score of 0–10 how much you personally trust each of the institutions I read out. 0 means you do not trust an institution at all, and 10 means you have complete trust. The national parliament.
- **Q4.** Are you satisfied or dissatisfied with the way MPs in general are doing their job?
- **Q5.** How satisfied or dissatisfied are you with the way that Parliament works?
- **Q6.** Overall, how would you rate the standards of conduct of public office holders in the United Kingdom?
- **Q7.** Please tell me how many MPs you think do each of the following. Would you say all of them, most of them, about half, a few or none? They use their power for their own personal gain.
- **Q8.** Most politicians are in politics only for what they can get out of it personally.
- **Q9.** I am going to read out some different types of people. Please tell me which you would generally trust to tell the truth and which you wouldn't. MPs in general.
- **Q10.** I am going to read out some different types of people. Please tell me which you would generally trust to tell the truth and which you wouldn't. Your local MP.
- **Q11.** How much do you trust British politicians generally?
- **Q12.** How much do you trust the Parliament at Westminster?
- **Q13.** On balance, do you agree or disagree with the following statement? I trust the government to tell the truth.
- **Q14.** On balance, do you agree or disagree with the following statement? I trust the government to act in the best interests of the country.

Year	Q1	Q2	Q3	Q4	Q5	Q6	Q7	Q8	Q9	Q10	Q11	Q12	Q13	Q14
2016														
2015	X	X	X	X	X	X					X			
2014	X	X				X			X					
2013	X	X	X			X	X		X					
2012	X	X	X		X		X	X	X	X				
2011	X	X	X			X	X							
2010	X	X					X				X	X		
2009	X	X		X	X		X			X	X	X		
2008	X					X			X					
2007	X	X	X										X	X
2006	X	X	X	X	X	X	X		X	X			X	X
2005		X	X			X					X	X		
2004						X	X	X	X	X	X	X		
2003	X	X	X	X	X									
2002														
2001														
2000														
1999														
1998														
1997														
1996														
1995														
1994														
1993														
1992														
1991														
1990														
1989														
1988														
1987														
1986														
1985														
1984														
1983														
1982														
1981														
1980														
1979														
1978														
1977														
1976														
1975														
1974														
1973														
1972														
1971														
1970														
1969														
1968														
...														
1966														
...														
1964														
1963														
...														
1959														
...														
1946														
1945														
1944														

Table A1 (*cont.*)

Question	2016	2015	2014	2013	2012	2011	2010	2009	2008	2007	2006	2005	2004	2003	2002	2001	2000	1999	1998	1997	1996	1995	1994	1993	1992	1991	1990	1989	1988	1987	1986	1985	1984	1983	1982	1981	1980	1979	1978	1977	1976	1975	1974	1973	1972	1971	1970	1969	1968	...	1966	...	1964	1963	...	1959	...	1946	1945	1944
In (OUR COUNTRY), do you think that the giving and taking of bribes, and the abuse of positions of power for personal gain, are widespread among any of the following? Politicians at national level.						X		X																																																				
How much trust do you have in Members of Parliament in general?	X	X	X																																																									
How much do you agree or disagree with the following statements? Politicians only care about people with money.	X	X	X																																																									
How much do you agree or disagree with the following statements? It doesn't really matter which party is in power.	X	X	X																																																									

Table A2 *Survey questions and response options*

Gallup

'At the present time, is the government doing its job well or badly?' / 'Do you approve or disapprove of the Government's record to date?' (Well; Badly; Don't know / Approve; Disapprove; Don't know)

'Are you satisfied or dissatisfied with ... as prime minister?' (Satisfied; Dissatisfied; Don't know)

'Do you think that British politicians are out merely for themselves, for their party, or to do their best for their country?' (Themselves; Their party; Their country; Don't know)

'Please tell me whether you agree or disagree with the following statements. Most MPs make a lot of money by using public office improperly' (Agree; Disagree; Don't know)

'In your opinion, do people like yourself have enough say in ... the way the government runs the country?' (Yes; No; Don't know)

'Please tell me whether you agree or disagree with the following statements. Most MPs have a high personal moral code' (Agree; Disagree; Don't know)

'Please tell me whether you agree or disagree with the following statements. Most MPs care more about special interests than they care about people like you' (Agree; Disagree; Don't know)

'Please tell me whether you agree or disagree with the following statements. Most MPs will tell lies if they feel the truth will hurt them politically' (Agree; Disagree; Don't know)

Ipsos MORI

'Are you satisfied or dissatisfied with the way ... the Government is running the country?' (Satisfied; Dissatisfied; Don't know)

'Now I will read out a list of different types of people. For each, would you tell me whether you generally trust them to tell the truth or not? Politicians generally' (Trust to tell truth; Do not trust to tell truth)

'Now I will read out a list of different types of people. For each, would you tell me whether you generally trust them to tell the truth or not? Government ministers' (Trust to tell truth; Do not trust to tell truth)

'Please tell me whether you agree or disagree with the following statements. Most MPs make a lot of money by using public office improperly' (Agree; Disagree; Don't know)

'Please tell me how many MPs you think do each of the following. Would you say all of them, most of them, about half, a few or none? They use their power for their own personal gain' (All; Most; About half; A few; None; Don't know)

'I am going to read out some different types of people. Please tell me which you would generally trust to tell the truth and which you wouldn't. MPs in general' (Trust to tell truth; Do not trust to tell truth)

'I am going to read out some different types of people. Please tell me which you would generally trust to tell the truth and which you wouldn't. Your local MP' (Trust to tell truth; Do not trust to tell truth)

'Please tell me whether you agree or disagree with the following statements. Most MPs have a high personal moral code' (Agree; Disagree; Don't know)

'In general, whose interests do you think MPs put first?' (Their own; Their party's; Their constituents'; The country's; Other; Don't know)

Table A2 (*cont.*)

'On balance, do you agree or disagree with the following statement? I trust the government to tell the truth' (Strongly agree; Agree; Neither agree nor disagree; Tend to disagree; Strongly disagree; Don't know)

'On balance, do you agree or disagree with the following statement? I trust the government to act in the best interests of the country' (Strongly agree; Agree; Neither agree nor disagree; Tend to disagree; Strongly disagree; Don't know)

'Which of these statements best describes your opinion on the present system of governing Britain?' (Works extremely well and could not be improved; Could be improved in small ways but mainly works well; Could be improved quite a lot; Needs a great deal of improvement; Don't know)

Almond and Verba (1963)

'Suppose a law were being considered by [appropriate national legislature specified for each nation] that you considered to be unjust or harmful. What do you think you could do? If you made an effort to change this law, how likely is it that you would succeed? If such a case arose, how likely is it you would actually try to do something about it?' (Open-ended)

'Speaking generally, what are the things about this country that you are most proud of?' (Open-ended)

'Thinking about the national government, about how much effect do you think its activities, the laws passed and so on, have on your day-to-day life? Do they have a great effect, some effect, or none? On the whole, do the activities of the national government tend to improve conditions in this country, or would we be better off without them?' (Great effect; Some effect; Better off without them)

Political Action Committee

'Generally speaking, those we elect as MPs to Westminster lose touch with the people pretty quickly' (Strongly agree; Agree; Disagree; Strongly disagree; Don't know)

'How much do you trust a British government of either party to place the needs of this country and the people above the interests of their own political party?' (Just about always; Most of the time; Almost never)

Eurobarometer

'In (OUR COUNTRY), do you think that the giving and taking of bribes, and the abuse of positions of power for personal gain, are widespread among any of the following?' (Politicians at national level; None; Don't know)

'I would like to ask you a question about how much trust you have in certain institutions. For each of the following institutions, please tell me if you tend to trust it or tend not to trust it. The British parliament' (Tend to trust it; Tend not to trust it; Don't know)

'I would like to ask you a question about how much trust you have in certain institutions. For each of the following institutions, please tell me if you tend to trust it or tend not to trust it. The British government' (Tend to trust it; Tend not to trust it; Don't know)

Committee for Standards in Public Life

'Overall, how would you rate the standards of conduct of public office holders in the United Kingdom?' (Very high; Quite high; Neither high nor low; Quite low; Very low; Don't know)

Table A2 (*cont.*)

European Social Survey

'Please tell me on a score of 0–10 how much you personally trust each of the institutions I read out. 0 means you do not trust an institution at all, and 10 means you have complete trust. The national parliament'

'Please tell me on a score of 0–10 how much you personally trust each of the institutions I read out. 0 means you do not trust an institution at all, and 10 means you have complete trust. Politicians'

British Social Attitudes Survey

'Do you agree or disagree that ... most of the time we can trust people in government to do what is right' (Agree strongly; Agree; Neither agree nor disagree; Disagree; Disagree strongly; Can't choose)

'How much do you agree or disagree that ... parties are only interested in people's votes, not in their opinions' (Agree strongly; Agree; Neither agree nor disagree; Disagree; Disagree strongly; Don't know)

'How much do you agree or disagree that ... generally speaking those we elect as MPs lose touch with people pretty quickly' (Agree strongly; Agree; Neither agree nor disagree; Disagree; Disagree strongly; Don't know)

'How much do you trust British governments of any party to place the needs of the nation above the interests of their own political party?' (Just about always; Most of the time; Only some of the time; Almost never; Don't know)

'How much do you trust politicians of any party in Britain to tell the truth when they are in a tight corner?' (Just about always; Most of the time; Only some of the time; Almost never; Don't know)

'How much do you agree or disagree that ... it doesn't really matter which party is in power, in the end things go on much the same' (Agree strongly; Agree; Neither agree nor disagree; Disagree; Disagree strongly; Don't know)

'How much do you agree or disagree that ... most politicians are in politics only for what they can get out of it personally' (Agree; Neither agree nor disagree; Disagree)

YouGov

'Do you approve or disapprove of the Government's record to date?' (Approve; Disapprove; Don't know)

'Please tell me whether you agree or disagree with the following statements. Most MPs will tell lies if they feel the truth will hurt them politically' (Tend to agree; Tend to disagree; Do not have an opinion)

'Please tell me whether you agree or disagree with the following statements. Most MPs make a lot of money by using public office improperly' (Tend to agree; Tend to disagree; Do not have an opinion)

'Please tell me whether you agree or disagree with the following statements. Most MPs have a high personal moral code' (Tend to agree; Tend to disagree; Do not have an opinion)

'Do you think that British politicians are out merely for themselves, for their party, or to do their best for their country?' (Themselves; Their party; Their country; Don't know)

Hansard Society

'Which of these statements best describes your opinion on the present system of governing Britain?' (Works extremely well and could not be improved; Could be improved in small ways but mainly works well; Could be improved quite a lot; Needs a great deal of improvement; Don't know)

Table A2 (*cont.*)

'How satisfied or dissatisfied are you with the way that Parliament works?' (Very satisfied; Fairly satisfied; Neither satisfied nor dissatisfied; Fairly dissatisfied; Very dissatisfied)
'Are you satisfied or dissatisfied with the way MPs in general are doing their job?' (Very satisfied; Fairly satisfied; Neither satisfied nor dissatisfied; Fairly dissatisfied; Very dissatisfied)

British Election Study

'Which of these statements best describes your opinion on the present system of governing Britain?' (Works extremely well and could not be improved; Could be improved in small ways but mainly works well; Could be improved quite a lot; Needs a great deal of improvement; Don't know)
'How much do you agree or disagree that ... people like me have no say in what the government does?' (Agree strongly; Agree; Neutral; Disagree; Disagree strongly; Don't know)
'How much do you agree or disagree with the following statements? It doesn't really matter which party is in power, in the end things go on much the same' (Agree strongly; Agree; Neither; Disagree; Disagree strongly; Don't know)
'How much do you trust British governments of any party to place the needs of the nation above the interests of their own political party?' (Just about always; Most of the time; Only some of the time; Almost never; Don't know)
'Now, thinking about British political institutions like Parliament, please use the 0 to 10 scale to indicate how much trust you have for each of the following, where 0 means no trust and 10 means a great deal of trust. And how much do you trust the Parliament at Westminster?'
'Now, thinking about British political institutions like Parliament, please use the 0 to 10 scale to indicate how much trust you have for each of the following, where 0 means no trust and 10 means a great deal of trust. How much do you trust British politicians generally?'
'How much trust do you have in Members of Parliament in general?' (1 to 7 scale, where 1 means no trust and 7 means a great deal of trust)
'How much do you agree or disagree with the following statements? Politicians only care about people with money' (Strongly Agree; Agree; Neither agree nor disagree; Strongly disagree; Disagree; Don't know)

References

Abrams M and Marsh A J (1981) *Political Action: An Eight Nation Study, 1973–1976* (data collection, UK Data Service, SN: 1389, http://dx.doi.org/10.5255/UKDA-SN-1389-1).

Addison P (1975) *The Road to 1945: British Politics and the Second World War* (London, Jonathan Cape).

Allen N and Birch S (2015a) 'Process preferences and British public opinion: Citizens' judgements about government in an era of anti-politics', *Political Studies* 63(2): 390–411.

(2015b) *Ethics and Integrity in British Politics: How Citizens Judge Their Politicians Conduct and Why It Matters* (Cambridge, Cambridge University Press).

Allen P and Cairney P (2017) 'What do we mean when we talk about the "political class"?', *Political Studies Review* 15(1): 18–27.

Almond G A and Verba S (1963) *The Civic Culture: Political Attitudes and Democracy Five Nations* (Boston, MA, Little, Brown and Company).

Amin A and Thrift N (2013) *Arts of the Political: New Openings for the Left* (Durham, NC, Duke University Press).

Amnå E and Ekman J (2013) 'Standby citizens: Diverse faces of political passivity', *European Political Science Review* 6(2): 261–281.

Anderson B (1983) *Imagined Communities* (London, Verso).

APSA Committee on Political Parties (1950) 'Toward a more responsible two-party system: A report of the Committee on Political Parties', *American Political Science Association* 44(3): Part 2, Supplement.

Åström J and Karlsson M (2013) 'Blogging in the shadow of parties: Exploring ideological differences in online campaigning', *Political Communication* 30 (3): 434–455.

Baker S E and Edwards R (2012) *How Many Qualitative Interviews Is Enough? Expert Voices and Early Career Reflections on Sampling and Cases in Qualitative Research* (Southampton, National Centre for Research Methods).

Bang H (2005) 'Among everyday makers and expert citizens', in Newman J (ed) *Remaking Governance: Peoples, Politics, and the Public Sphere* (Bristol, Policy Press) pp159–179.

Barber B (2013) *If Mayors Ruled the World* (New Haven, CT, Yale University Press).

Barnett C and Bridge G (2013) 'Geographies of radical democracy: Agonistic pragmatism and the formation of affected interests', *Annals of the Association of American Geographers* 103(4): 1022–1040.

Barnett C, Cloke P, Clarke N, and Malpass A (2011) *Globalising Responsibility: The Political Rationalities of Ethical Consumption* (Oxford, Wiley Blackwell).

Bartle J, Dellepiane-Avellaneda S, and Stimson J A (2011) 'The moving centre: Preferences for government activity in Britain, 1950–2005', *British Journal of Political Science* 41(2): 259–285.

Baumgartner F R and Bonafont C (2015) 'All news is bad news: Newspaper coverage of political parties in Spain', *Political Communication* 32(2): 268–291.

Beck U (1992) *Risk Society: Towards a New Modernity* (London, Sage).

Bell D (1960) *The End of Ideology: On the Exhaustion of Political Ideas in the Fifties* (New York, NY, The Free Press).

Berger S (1979) 'Politics and antipolitics in Western Europe in the seventies', *Daedalus* 108(1): 27–50.

Best H and Cotta M (2000) *Parliamentary Elites in Europe, 1848–2000: Legislative Recruitment and Careers in 11 European Countries* (Oxford, Oxford University Press).

Bettles C (2016) 'McGowan's magic demystifies Canberra by empowering Indi's people', *Stock & Land*, 8 June.

Bevir M and Rhodes R (2005) 'Interpretation and its others', *Australian Journal of Political Science* 40(2): 169–187.

Black L (2005) 'Whose finger on the button? British television and the politics of cultural control', *Historical Journal of Film, Radio and Television* 25(4): 547–575.

Black L (2010) *Redefining British Politics: Culture, Consumerism, and Participation, 1954–70* (Basingstoke, Palgrave Macmillan).

Blumenthal S (1982) *The Permanent Campaign* (New York, NY, Simon and Schuster).

Blumler J G and Kavanagh D (1999) 'The third age of political communication: Influences and features', *Political Communication* 16(3): 209–230.

Bogdanor V (2009) *The New British Constitution* (London, Bloomsbury).

Bonnett A (2009) 'Radicalism is nostalgia', in Pugh J (ed) *What Is Radical Politics Today?* (Basingstoke, Palgrave Macmillan) pp179–187.

Borchert J and Zeiss J (2003) *The Political Class in Advanced Democracies: A Comparative Handbook* (Oxford, Oxford University Press).

Boswell J and Corbett J (2015) 'Stoic democrats? Anti-politics, elite cynicism, and the policy process', *Journal of European Public Policy* 22(10): 1388–1405.

Bowler S and Donovan T (2013) *The Limits to Electoral Reform* (Oxford, Oxford University Press).

Burnham P (2001) 'New Labour and the politics of depoliticisation', *British Journal of Politics and International Relations* 3(2): 127–149.

Butler D and Kavanagh D (2002) *The British General Election of 2001* (Basingstoke, Macmillan).

Butler D and Stokes D (1969) *Political Change in Britain: Forces Shaping Electoral Choice* (New York, NY, St. Martin's Press).

Cairney P (2007) 'The professionalisation of MPs: Refining the "PoliticsFacilitating" explanation', *Parliamentary Affairs* 60(2): 212–233.

Cantril H (1951) *Public Opinion: 1935–1946* (Princeton, NJ, Princeton University Press).

Cappella J N and Hall Jamieson K (1997) *Spiral of Cynicism: The Press and the Public Good* (Oxford, Oxford University Press).

Chanley V A, Rudolph T J, and Rahn W M (2000) 'The origins and consequences of public trust in government: A time series analysis', *The Public Opinion Quarterly* 64(3): 239–256.

Childers J P (2012) *The Evolving Citizen: American Youth and the Changing Norms of Democratic Engagement* (University Park, PA, Penn State University Press).

Chwalisz C (2017) *The People's Verdict* (London, Rowan & Littlefield).

Citrin J, McClosky H, Shanks J M, and Sniderman P M (1975) 'Personal and political sources of political alienation', *British Journal of Political Science* 5 (1): 1–31.

Clarke H D, Sanders D, Stewart M C, and Whiteley P (2004) *Political Choice in Britain* (Oxford, Oxford University Press).

(2009) *Performance Politics and the British Voter* (Cambridge, Cambridge University Press).

Clarke N (2012) 'Urban policy mobility, anti-politics, and histories of the transnational municipal movement', *Progress in Human Geography* 36(1): 25–43.

Clarke N and Cochrane A (2013) 'Geographies and politics of localism: The localism of the United Kingdom's Coalition Government', *Political Geography* 34: 10–23.

Clarke N, Jennings W, Moss J, and Stoker G (2016) 'Anti-politics and the Left', *Renewal* 24(2): 9–26.

(2017) 'Changing spaces of political encounter and the rise of anti-politics: Evidence from Mass Observation's general election diaries', *Political Geography* 56: 13–23.

Converse P (1964) 'The nature of belief systems in mass publics', *Critical Review: A Journal of Politics and Society* 18(1–3): 1–74.

Corbett J (2014) 'But why do we need politicians? A critical review', *Policy Studies* 35(5): 498–512.

Cotta M and Best H (2007) *Democratic Representation in Europe* (Oxford, Oxford University Press).

Cowley P and Kavanagh D (2016) *The British General Election of 2015* (Basingstoke, Palgrave Macmillan).

Crewe E (2015) *The House of Commons: An Anthropology of MPs at Work* (London, Bloomsbury).

Crewe I and Harrop M (1989) *Political Communications* (Cambridge, Cambridge University Press).

Crewe I, Särlvik B, and Alt J (1977) 'Partisan dealignment in Britain, 1964–1974', *British Journal of Political Science* 7(2): 129–190.

Crick B (1962) *In Defence of Politics* (London, Weidenfeld and Nicolson).

(2005) 'Populism, politics, and democracy', *Democratization* 12(5): 625–632.

Criddle B (2010) 'More diverse, yet more uniform: MPs and candidates', in Kavanagh D and Cowley P (eds) *The British General Election of 2010* (Basingstoke, Palgrave Macmillan) pp306–329.

(2016) 'Variable diversity: MPs and candidates', in Cowley P and Kavanagh D (eds) *The British General Election of 2015* (Basingstoke, Palgrave Macmillan) pp336–360.

Crouch C (2004) *Post-Democracy* (Cambridge, Polity).

Crozier M, Huntington S P, and Watanuki J (1975) *The Crisis of Democracy* (New York, NY, New York University Press).

Dalton R J (1984) 'Cognitive mobilisation and partisan dealignment in advanced industrial democracies', *Journal of Politics* 46: 264–284.

(2000) 'Value change and democracy', in Pharr S J and Putnam R D (eds) *Disaffected Democracies: What's Troubling the Tri-Lateral Countries?* (Princeton, NJ, Princeton University Press) pp252–269.

(2004) *Democratic Challenges, Democratic Choices: The Erosion of Political Support in Advanced Industrial Democracies* (Washington, DC, CQ Press).

(2009) *The Good Citizen: How a Younger Generation Is Reshaping American Politics, Revised Edition* (Washington, DC, CQ Press).

Dalton R and Welzel C (eds) (2014) *The Civic Culture Revisited: From Allegiant to Assertive Citizens* (Cambridge, Cambridge University Press).

D'Ancona M (2016) 'Voting Brexit to punish the PM would be self-defeating: Cameron's big challenge is to persuade people that the 23 June should not be a referendum on his job', *The Guardian*, 31 May.

Della Porta D (2013) *Can Democracy Be Saved? Participation, Deliberation, and Social Movements* (Cambridge, Polity).

Delli Carpini M and Keeter S (1996) *What Americans Know about Politics and Why It Matters* (New Haven, CT, Yale University Press).

Denver D, Carman C, and Johns R (2012) *Elections and Voters in Britain, Third Edition* (Basingstoke, Palgrave Macmillan).

Dobson A (2014) *Listening for Democracy: Recognition, Representation, Reconciliation* (Oxford, Oxford University Press).

Durr R H, Gilmour J B, and Wolbrecht C (1997) 'Explaining congressional approval', *American Journal of Political Science* 41(1): 175–207.

Durr R H, Martin A D, and Wolbrecht C (2000) 'Ideological divergence and public support for the Supreme Court', *American Journal of Political Science* 44(4): 768–776.

Easton D (1965) *A Systems Analysis of Political Life* (New York, Wiley).

(1975) 'A re-assessment of the concept of political support', *British Journal of Political Science* 5(4): 435–457.

Enns P (2014) 'The public's increasing punitiveness and its influence on mass incarceration in the United States', *American Journal of Political Science* 55(4): 857–872.

Ercan S A and Gagnon J-P (2014) 'The crisis of democracy: Which crisis? Which democracy?', *Democratic Theory* 1(2): 1–10.

Eslami M, Karahalios K, Sandvig C, Vaccaro K, Rickman A, Hamilton K, and Kirlik A (2016) 'First I "like" it, then I hide it: Folk theories of social feeds', *Proceedings of the 2016 CHI Conference on Human Factors in Computing Systems* pp2371–2382.

Evans J St B T (2012) 'Questions and challenges for the new psychology of reasoning', *Thinking & Reasoning* 18(1): 5–31.

Evans M and Stoker G (2016) 'Political participation in Australia: Contingency in the behaviour and attitudes of citizens', *Australian Journal of Political Science* 51(2): 272–287.

Fairclough N (2002) *Discourse and Social Change* (Cambridge, Polity).

Farrell D M (2014) 'Stripped down or reconfigured democracy', *West European Politics* 37(2): 439–455.

Ferguson J (1994) *The Anti-Politics Machine: Development, Depoliticisation, and Bureaucratic Power in Lesotho* (Minneapolis, MN, University of Minnesota Press).

Fielding S (1992) 'What did "the people" want? The meaning of the 1945 General Election', *The Historical Journal* 35: 623–639.

(2008) 'A mirror for England? Cinematic representations of politicians and party politics, circa 1944–1964', *The Journal of British Studies* 47(1): 107–128.

(2014) *A State of Play: British Politics on Screen, Stage, and Page, from Anthony Trollope to The Thick of It* (London, Bloomsbury).

Fielding S, Thompson P, and Tiratsoo N (1995) *'England Arise!' The Labour Party and Popular Politics in 1940s Britain* (Manchester, Manchester University Press).

Finifter A (1970) 'Dimensions of political alienation', *American Political Science Review* 64(2): 389–410.

Fischer F and Forester J (eds) (1993) *The Argumentative Turn in Policy Analysis and Planning* (London, UCL Press).

Foa R S and Mounk Y (2016) 'The democratic disconnect', *Journal of Democracy* 27(3): 5–17.

Ford R and Goodwin M (2014) *Revolt on the Right* (London, Routledge).

Ford R, Jennings W, and Somerville W (2015) 'Public opinion, responsiveness, and constraint: Britain's three immigration policy regimes', *Journal of Ethnic and Migration Studies* 41(9): 1391–1411.

Forestal J (2017) 'The architecture of political spaces: Trolls, digital media, and Deweyan democracy', *American Political Science Review* 111(1): 149–161.

Foucault M (1991) 'Politics and the study of discourse', in Burchell G, Gorden C, and Miller P (eds) *The Foucault Effect: Studies in Governmentality* (London, Harvester Wheatsheaf) pp53–72.

Franklin B (2004) *Packaging Politics: Political Communications in Britain's Media Democracy, Second Edition* (London, Bloomsbury).

Fukuyama F (1992) *The End of History and the Last Man* (London, Hamish Hamilton).

Fung A and Wright E O (2003) *Deepening Democracy: Institutional Innovations in Empowered Participatory Governance* (London, Verso).

Gallup G H (1976) *The Gallup International Public Opinion Polls, Great Britain: 1937–1975* (New York, NY, Random House).

Gamson W A (1992) *Talking Politics* (Cambridge, Cambridge University Press).

Gazeley I and Langhamer C (2013) 'The meanings of happiness in Mass Observation's Bolton', *History Workshop Journal* 75(1): 159–189.

Geissel B and Newton K (2012) *Evaluating Democratic Innovations* (London, Routledge).

Giddens A (1984) *The Constitution of Society: Outline of the Theory of Structuration* (London, Polity Press).

(1991) *Modernity and Self-Identity: Self and Society in the Late Modern Age* (Cambridge, Polity).

(1998) *The Third Way: The Renewal of Social Democracy* (Cambridge, Polity Press).

Goffman E (1961) *Encounters: Two Studies in the Sociology of Interaction* (Indianapolis, IN, Bobbs-Merrill).

Goot M (2002) 'Distrustful, disenchanted, and disengaged? Public opinion on politics, politicians, and the parties: An historical perspective', in Burchell D and Leigh A (eds) *Why Do Australians Dislike Their Politicians?* (Sydney, University of South Wales Press) pp9–46.

Goot M (2008) 'Mass-Observation and Modern Public Opinion Research', in Donsbach W and Traugott M W (eds) *Handbook of Public Opinion Research* (London, Sage) pp93–103.

Grasso M T, Farrall S, Gray E, Hay C, and Jennings W (2017) 'Thatcher's children, Blair's babies, political socialisation and trickle-down value change: An age, period, and cohort analysis', *British Journal of Political Science First View*.

Greasley S and Stoker G (2008) 'Mayors and urban governance: Developing a facilitative leadership style', *Public Administration Review* 68: 722–730.

Green J and Jennings W (2012) 'Valence as macro-competence: An analysis of mood in party competence evaluations in the UK', *British Journal of Political Science* 42(2): 311–343.

(2017) *The Politics of Competence: Parties, Public Opinion, and Voters* (Cambridge, Cambridge University Press).

Guttsman W L (1963) *The British Political Elite* (London, MacGibbon and Kee).

Hajer M A (2009) *Authoritative Governance: Policy-Making in the Age of Mediatisation* (Oxford, Oxford University Press).

Hay C (2002) *Political Analysis: A Critical Introduction* (Basingstoke, Palgrave Macmillan).

(2007) *Why We Hate Politics* (Cambridge, Polity Press).

Heath A, Curtice J, Jowell R, Evans G, Field J, and Witherspoon S (1991) *Understanding Political Change: The British Voter, 1964–1987* (Oxford, Pergamon Press).

Heath A, Jowell R, and Curtice J (1985) *How Britain Votes* (Oxford, Pergamon Press).

(2001) *The Rise of New Labour* (Oxford, Oxford University Press).

Held D (2006) *Models of Democracy, Third Edition* (Cambridge, Polity).

Held D, McGrew A, Goldblatt D, and Perraton J (1999) *Global Transformations: Politics, Economics, Culture* (Cambridge, Polity Press).

Hendriks C M (2017) 'Citizen-led democratic reform: Innovations in Indi', *Australian Journal of Political Science* 52(4): 481–499.

Hetherington M (2005) *Why Trust Matters: Declining Political Trust and the Demise of American Liberalism* (Princeton, NJ, Princeton University Press).

Hetherington M J and Rudolph T J (2008) 'Priming, performance, and the dynamics of political trust', *Journal of Politics* 70(2): 498–512.

Hibbing J R and Theiss-Morse E (1995) *Congress as Public Enemy: Public Attitudes toward American Political Institutions* (Cambridge, Cambridge University Press).

Hibbing J and Theiss-Morse E (2002) *Stealth Democracy: Americans' Beliefs about How Government Should Work* (Cambridge, Cambridge University Press).

Hilton M, McKay J, Crowson N, and Mouhot J (2013) *The Politics of Expertise: How NGOs Shaped Modern Britain* (Oxford, Oxford University Press).

Hinton J (1997) '1945 and the Apathy School', *History Workshop Journal* 43: 266–273.

Hinton J (2010) *Nine Wartime Lives* (Oxford, Oxford University Press).

(2013a) *The Mass Observers: A History, 1937–1949* (Oxford, Oxford University Press).

(2013b) 'Self reflections in the mass', *History Workshop Journal* 75(1): 251–259.

Hobsbawm E (1990) *Nations and Nationalism since 1970: Programme, Myth, Reality* (Cambridge, Cambridge University Press).

(1994) *Age of Extremes: The Short Twentieth Century, 1914–1991* (London, Penguin).

Hoggart R (1957) *The Uses of Literacy* (London, Chatto and Windus).

Holmberg S (1999) 'Down and down we go: Political trust in Sweden', in Norris P (ed) *Critical Citizens: Global Support for Democratic Governance* (Oxford, Oxford University Press) pp103–122.

Holland D and Quinn N (eds) (1987) *Cultural Models in Language and Thought* (Cambridge, Cambridge University Press).

Hörschelmann K and El Refaie E (2013) 'Transnational citizenship, dissent, and the political geographies of youth', *Transactions of the Institute of British Geographers* 39(3): 444–456.

Inglehart R (1977) *The Silent Revolution* (Princeton, NJ, Princeton University Press).

(1985) 'Aggregate stability and individual-level flux in mass belief systems: The level of analysis paradox', *American Political Science Review* 79(1): 97–116.

(1997) *Modernisation and Postmodernisation: Cultural, Economic, and Political Change in 43 Countries* (Princeton, NJ, Princeton University Press).

(1999) 'Postmodernisation erodes respect for authority, but increases support for democracy', in Norris P (ed) *Critical Citizens: Global Support for Democratic Governance* (Oxford, Oxford University Press) pp236–256.

Iyengar S (1991) *Is Anyone Responsible? How Television Frames Political Issues* (Chicago, IL, University of Chicago Press).

Jacquet V (2017) 'Explaining non-participation in deliberative mini-publics', *European Journal of Political Research* 56(3): 640–659.

Jefferys K (2007) *Politics and the People: A History of British Democracy since 1918* (London, Atlantic Books).

Jeffrey T (1978) *Mass Observation – A Short History* (Birmingham, University of Birmingham).

Jennings W and Stoker G (2016) 'The bifurcation of politics: Two Englands', *Political Quarterly* 87(3): 372–382.

Jennings W, Clarke N, Moss J, and Stoker G (2017a) 'The decline in diffuse support for national politics: The long view on political discontent in Britain', *Public Opinion Quarterly*, nfx020, https://doi.org/10.1093/poq/nfx020.

Jennings W, Stoker G, and Twyman J (2016) 'The dimensions and impact of political discontent in Britain', *Parliamentary Affairs* 69(4): 876–900.

Jennings W, Farrall S, Gray E, and Hay C (2017b) 'Penal populism and the public thermostat: Crime, public punitiveness, and public policy', *Governance* 30 (3): 463–481.

Jun U (2003) 'Great Britain: From the prevalence of the amateur to the dominance of the professional politician', in Borchert J and Zeiss J (eds) *The Political Class in Advanced Democracies* (Oxford, Oxford University Press), pp164–186.

Kahneman D (2011) *Thinking, Fast and Slow* (London, Penguin).

Kandiah M D (1995) 'Television enters British politics', *Historical Journal of Film, Radio, and Television* 15(2): 265–284.

Kane J and Patapan H (2012) *The Democratic Leader: How Democracy Defines, Empowers, and Limits Its Leaders* (Oxford, Oxford University Press).

Kavanagh D (1995) *Election Campaigning: The New Marketing of Politics* (Oxford, Blackwell).

Kavanagh D and Cowley P (2010) *The British General Election of 2010* (Basingstoke, Palgrave Macmillan).

Keele L (2007) 'Social capital and the dynamics of trust in government', *American Journal of Political Science* 51(2): 241–254.

Keesing R M (1987) 'Models, "folk" and "cultural": Paradigms regained?', in Holland D and Quinn N (eds) *Cultural Models in Language and Thought* (Cambridge, Cambridge University Press) pp369–394.

Kempton W (1986) 'Two theories of home heat control', in Holland D and Quinn N (eds) (1987) *Cultural Models in Language and Thought* (Cambridge, Cambridge University Press) pp222–241.

Kepplinger M (2000) 'The decline of the image of the political elite in Germany', *The Harvard International Journal of Press/Politics* 5(4): 71–80.

King A (1975) 'Overload: Problems of governing in the 1970s', *Political Studies* 23 (2–3): 284–296.

King A and Wybrow R (2001) *British Political Opinion 1937–2000* (London, Politicos).

King D C (1997) 'The polarisation of American parties and mistrust of government', in Nye J S, Zelikow P D, and King D C (eds) *Why People Don't Trust Government* (Cambridge, MA, Harvard University Press) pp155–178.

Kuklinski J H and Quirk P J (2000) 'Reconsidering the rational public: Cognition, heuristics, and mass opinion', in Lupia A, McCubbins M D, and Popkin S L (eds) *Elements of Reason: Cognition, Choice, and the Bounds of Rationality* (Cambridge, Cambridge University Press) pp153–182.

Kushner T (2004) *We Europeans? Mass Observation, Race, and British Identity in the Twentieth Century* (Aldershot, Ashgate).

Kynaston D (2007) *Austerity Britain 1945–51* (London, Bloomsbury).

Laclau E and Mouffe C (1985) *Hegemony and Socialist Strategy: Towards a Radical Democratic Politics* (London, Verso).

Lakoff G (1996) *Moral Politics: What Conservatives Know That Liberals Don't* (Chicago, IL, University of Chicago Press).

(2002) *Moral Politics, Second Edition: How Liberals and Conservatives Think* (Chicago, IL, University of Chicago Press).

(2009) *The Political Mind* (New York, NY, Penguin Books).

Lakoff G and Johnson M (2003) *Metaphors We Live By* (Chicago, IL, University of Chicago Press).

Langhamer C (2013) *The English in Love: The Intimate Story of an Emotional Revolution* (Oxford, Oxford University Press).

Lawless J and Fox R (2015) *Running from Office: Why Young Americans Are Turned Off to Politics* (Oxford, Oxford University Press).

Lawrence J (2006) 'The transformation of British public politics after the First World War', *Past and Present* 190: 185–216.

(2009) *Electing Our Masters: The Hustings in British Politics from Hogarth to Blair* (Oxford, Oxford University Press).

Lazer D M, Sokhey A E, Neblo M A, Esterling K M, and Kennedy R (2015) 'Expanding the conversation: Multiplier effects from a deliberative field experiment', *Political Communication* 32(4): 552–573.

LeMahieu D L (1988) *A Culture for Democracy: Mass Communication and the Cultivated Mind in Britain between the Wars* (Oxford, Clarendon Press).

Lichfield J (2016) 'There's a case to be made for Leave – but we're not hearing it', *The Independent*, 24 April.

Lijphart A (1996) *Institutional Design in New Democracies: Eastern Europe and Latin America* (Boulder, CO, Westview Press).

(2004) 'Constitutional design for divided societies', *Journal of Democracy* 15(2): 96–109.

Listhaug O (2006) 'Political disaffection and political performance: Norway, 1957–2001', in Torcal M and Montero J R (eds) *Political Disaffection in Contemporary Democracies* (London, Routledge) pp215–243.

Lupia A and McCubbins M D (2000) 'The institutional foundations of political competence: How citizens learn what they need to know', in Lupia A, McCubbins M D, and Popkin S (eds) *Elements of Reason: Cognition, Choice, and the Bounds of Rationality* (Cambridge, Cambridge University Press) pp47–66.

Lupia A, McCubbins M D, and Popkin S (2000) *Elements of Reason: Cognition, Choice, and the Bounds of Rationality* (Cambridge, Cambridge University Press).

MacClancy J (1995) 'Brief encounter: The meeting, in Mass-Observation, of British surrealism and popular anthropology', *The Journal of the Royal Anthropological Institute* 1(3): 495–512.

Macedo S et al. (2005) *Democracy at Risk: How Political Choices Undermine Citizen Participation, and What We Can Do about It* (Washington, DC, Brookings Institution Press).

Machiavelli N (2003) *The Prince* (London, Penguin).

Mair P (2013) *Ruling the Void: The Hollowing Out of Western Democracy* (London, Verso).

Majone G (1992) *Evidence, Argument, and Persuasion in the Policy Process* (New Haven, CT, Yale University Press).

Malle B F (2000) *How the Mind Explains Behaviour: Folk Explanations, Meaning, and Social Interaction* (Cambridge, MA, Massachusetts Institute of Technology Press).

Manning N and Holmes M (2013) '"He's snooty 'im": Exploring "white working class" political engagement', *Citizenship Studies* 17(3–4): 479–490.

Marcus G E, Neuman W R, and MacKuen M (2000) *Affective Intelligence and Political Judgment* (Chicago, IL, University of Chicago Press).

Marcuse P (1964) *One-Dimensional Man: Studies in the Ideology of Advanced Industrial Society* (London, Routledge and Kegan Paul).

Marien S and Hooghe M (2011) 'Does political trust matter? An empirical investigation into the relation between political trust and support for law compliance', *European Journal of Political Research* 50: 267–291.

Marquand D (2004) *Decline of the Public* (Cambridge, Polity Press).

Marshall T H (1950) *Citizenship and Social Class* (Cambridge, Cambridge University Press).

Mazzoleni G and Schulz W (1999) '"Mediatisation" of politics: A challenge for democracy?', *Political Communication* 16(3): 247–261.

McCallum R B and Readman A (1947) *The British General Election of 1945* (London, Oxford University Press).

McDowell L, Rootham E, and Hardgrove A (2014) 'Politics, anti-politics, quiescence, and radical unpolitics: Young men's political participation in an "ordinary" English town', *Journal of Youth Studies* 17(1): 42–62.

McLean I (2010) *What's Wrong with the British Constitution?* (Oxford, Oxford University Press).

Medvic S K (2013) *In Defence of Politicians: The Expectations Trap and Its Threat to Democracy* (London, Routledge).

Mellors C (1978) *The British MP: A Socio-Economic Study of the House of Commons* (Farnborough, Saxon House).

Micheletti M (2003) *Political Virtue and Shopping: Individuals, Consumerism, and Collective Action* (Basingstoke, Palgrave Macmillan).

Miller A H (1974) 'Political issues and trust in government', *American Political Science Review* 68(3): 951–972.

Mishra P (2017) *Age of Anger: A History of the Present* (London, Allen Lane).

Moon N (1999) *Opinion Polls: History, Theory, and Practice* (Manchester, Manchester University Press).

Moshman D (2000) 'Diversity in reasoning and rationality: Metacognitive and developmental considerations', *Behavioural and Brain Sciences* 23: 689–690.

Moss J, Clarke N, Jennings W, and Stoker G (2016) 'Golden age, apathy, or stealth? Democratic engagement in Britain, 1945–1950', *Contemporary British History* 30(4): 441–462.

Mouffe C (2005) *On the Political* (London, Routledge).

Mulgan G J (1994) *Politics in an Antipolitical Age* (Cambridge, Polity).

Mycock A and Tonge J (2014) *Beyond the Youth Citizenship Commission: Young People and Politics* (London, Political Studies Association).

Neblo M A, Esterling K M, Kennedy R P, Lazer D M J, and Sokhey A E (2010) 'Who wants to deliberate and why?', *American Political Science Review* 104(3): 566–583.

Nettleton S and Uprichard E (2011) '"A slice of life": Food narratives and menus from mass-observers in 1982 and 1945', *Sociological Research Online* 16(2).

Neustadt R E (1997) 'The politics of mistrust', in Nye J S, Zelikow P D, and King D C (eds) *Why People Don't Trust Government* (Cambridge, MA, Harvard University Press) pp179–201.

Nevitte N (1996) *The Decline of Deference: Canadian Value Change in Cross-Cultural Perspective* (Peterborough, Broadview).

Newton K (2012) 'Making better citizens', in Geissel B and Newton K (eds) *Evaluating Democratic Innovations* (London, Routledge) pp137–162.

Nicholas H G (1951) *The British General Election of 1950* (London, Macmillan).

Norris P (1997a) *Passages to Power: Legislative Recruitment in Advanced Democracies* (Cambridge, Cambridge University Press).

(1997b) *Electoral Change since 1945* (Oxford, Blackwell).

(ed) (1999) *Critical Citizens: Global Support for Democratic Governance* (Oxford, Oxford University Press).

(2002) *Democratic Phoenix: Reinventing Political Activism* (Cambridge, Cambridge University Press).

(2011) *Democratic Deficit: Critical Citizens Revisited* (Cambridge, Cambridge University Press).

Norris P and Lovenduski J (1995) *Political Recruitment: Gender, Race, and Class in the British Parliament* (Cambridge, Cambridge University Press).

Norris P, Walgrave S, and Van Aelst P (2006) 'Does protest signify disaffection? Demonstrators in a postindustrial democracy', in Torcal M and Montero J R (eds) *Political Disaffection in Contemporary Democracies* (London, Routledge) pp279–307.

Nye J S, Zelikow P D, and King D C (1997) *Why People Don't Trust Government* (Cambridge, MA, Harvard University Press).

OECD (2011) 'Society at a glance 2011', *OECD Social Indicators* (Paris, OECD).

Offe C (2006) 'Political disaffection as an outcome of institutional practices? Some post-Tocquevillean speculations', in Torcal M and Montero J R (eds) *Political Disaffection in Contemporary Democracies* (London, Routledge) pp23–45.

Olsen M (1969) 'Two categories of political alienation', *Social Forces* 47(3): 288–299.

Osman M (2004) 'An evaluation of dual-process theories of reasoning', *Psychonomic Bulletin & Review* 11(6): 988–1010.

O'Toole T, Marsh D, and Jones S (2003) 'Political literacy cuts both ways: The politics of non-participation among young people', *The Political Quarterly* 74(3): 349–360.

Pattie C, Seyd P, and Whiteley P (2004) *Citizenship in Britain: Values, Participation, and Democracy* (Cambridge, Cambridge University Press).

Peterson A, Hattam R, Zembylas M, and Arthur J (eds) (2016) *The Palgrave International Handbook of Education for Citizenship and Social Justice* (London, Palgrave Macmillan/Springer).

Pew Research Center (2015) *Beyond Distrust: How Americans View Their Government* (Washington, DC, Pew Research Center).

Pharr S J and Putnam R (2000) *Disaffected Democracies: What's Troubling the Trilateral Countries?* (Princeton, NJ, Princeton University Press).

Philo G (1990) *Seeing and Believing: The Influence of Television* (London, Routledge).

Pierce A (2005) 'Horror as Cameron brandishes the B-word', *The Times*, 5 October.

Piven F F (2006) *Challenging Authority: How Ordinary People Change America* (Lanham, Rowman and Littlefield).

Popkin S L (1991) *The Reasoning Voter* (Chicago, IL, Chicago University Press).

Propp V I (1968) *Morphology of the Folktale, Second Edition* (Austin, TX, University of Texas Press).

Pugh M (1982) *The Making of Modern British Politics, 1867–1945* (Oxford, Blackwell).

Putnam R D, Pharr S J, and Dalton R J (2000) 'Introduction: What's troubling the trilateral democracies?', in Pharr S J and Putnam R D (eds) *Disaffected Democracies: What's Troubling the Trilateral Countries?* (Princeton, NJ, Princeton University Press) pp3–30.

Quinn N and Holland D (1987) 'Culture and cognition', in Holland D and Quinn N (eds) *Cultural Models in Language and Thought* (Cambridge, Cambridge University Press) pp3–40.

Rahn W M (2000) 'Affect as information: The role of public mood in political reasoning', in Lupia A, McCubbins M D, and Popkin S (eds) *Elements of Reason: Cognition, Choice, and the Bounds of Rationality* (Cambridge, Cambridge University Press) pp130–150.

Rancière J (1999) *Disagreement* (Minneapolis, MN, University of Minnesota Press).

Rawnsley A (2016) 'Will politicians use this time to swap poison for serious debate?' *The Observer*, 19 June.

Rentoul J (2014) 'The fun has gone out of my referendum sweepstake; or why I plead guilty to being no good at election predictions, and living in the Westminster bubble', *The Independent*, 14 September.

Reynolds A (2011) *Designing Democracy in a Dangerous World* (Oxford, Oxford University Press).

Richey S and Zhu J (2015) 'Internet access does not improve political interest, efficacy, and knowledge for late adopters', *Political Communication* 32(3): 396–413.

Riddell P (1993) *Honest Opportunism* (London, Phoenix).

Robinson M J (1976) 'Public affairs television and the growth of political malaise: The case of "The Selling of the Pentagon"', *American Political Science Review* 70(2): 409–432.

Roodhouse M (2012) '"Fish-and-chip intelligence": Henry Durant and the British Institute of Public Opinion, 1936–63', *Twentieth Century British History* 24(2): 224–248.

Rosenbaum M (1997) *From Soapbox to Soundbite: Party Political Campaigning in Britain since 1945* (Basingstoke, Macmillan).

Rubinstein W D (2003) *Twentieth-Century Britain: A Political History* (Basingstoke, Palgrave Macmillan).

Rush M (1969) *The Selection of Parliamentary Candidates* (London, Nelson).

Salter A (2010) 'Filling the silences? Mass-Observation's wartime diaries, interpretive work, and indexicality', *Life Writing* 7(1): 53–65.

Särlvik B and Crewe I (1983) *Decade of Dealignment: The Conservative Victory of 1979 and Electoral Trends in the 1970s* (Cambridge, Cambridge University Press).

Saunders C (2014) 'Anti-politics in action? Measurement dilemmas in the study of unconventional political participation', *Political Research Quarterly* 67(3): 574–588.

Savage M (2008) 'Affluence and social change in the making of technocratic middle-class identities: Britain, 1939–55', *Contemporary British History* 22 (4): 457–476.

——— (2010) *Identities and Social Change in Britain since 1940: The Politics of Method* (Oxford, Oxford University Press).

Scharpf F W (2000) 'Interdependence and democratic legitimacy', in Pharr S J and Putnam R D (eds) *Disaffected Democracies: What's Troubling the Trilateral Countries?* (Princeton, NJ, Princeton University Press) pp101–120.

Schedler A (1997) *The End of Politics? Explorations in Modern Antipolitics* (Basingstoke, Macmillan).

Schumpeter J (1942) *Capitalism, Socialism, and Democracy* (New York, Harper and Brothers).

Searle G R (1995) *Country before Party: Coalition and the Idea of "National Government" in Modern Britain, 1885–1987* (London, Longman).

Seeman M (1959) 'On the meaning of alienation', *American Sociological Review* 24: 783–791.

Segatti P (2006) 'Italy, forty years of political disaffection: A longitudinal exploration', in Torcal M and Montero J R (eds) *Political Disaffection in Contemporary Democracies* (London, Routledge) pp244–276.

Sennett R (1977) *The Fall of Public Man* (New York, NY, Knopf).

Shanks M (1961) *The Stagnant Society: A Warning* (London, Penguin).

Sheridan D (1993) 'Writing to the archive: Mass Observation as autobiography', *Sociology* 27(1).

——— (1994) 'Using the Mass-Observation Archive as a source for women's studies', *Women's History Review* 3(1): 101–113.

——— (1996) *Damned Anecdotes and Dangerous Confabulations: Mass Observation as Life History* (Brighton, Mass Observation Archive).

Simon H (1985) 'Human nature in politics: The dialogue of Psychology with political Science', *American Political Science Review* 79(2): 293–304.

Smith G (2009) *Democratic Innovations: Designing Institutions for Citizen Participation* (Cambridge: Cambridge University Press).

Smith T (1972) *Anti-Politics: Consensus, Reform, and Protest in Britain* (London, Charles Knight).

Sniderman P (1981) *A Question of Loyalty* (Berkeley, CA, University of California Press).

Sniderman P M, Brody R A, and Tetlock P E (1993) *Reasoning and Choice: Explorations in Political Psychology* (Cambridge, Cambridge University Press).

Soroka S and McAdams S (2015) 'News, politics, and negativity', *Political Communication* 32(1): 1–22.

Spada P, Jennings W, Smith G, Stoker G, Flinders M, Ghose K, Prosser B, and Renwick A (2017) 'Deliberation and anti-politics', working paper available from the authors.

Stanovich K and Toplak M E (2012) 'Defining features versus incidental correlates of Type 1 and Type 2 processing', *Mind and Society* 11: 3–13.

Stanovich K E and West R F (2000) 'Individual difference in reasoning: Implications for the rationality debate?', *Behavioural and Brain Sciences* 23: 645–726.

Stimson J A (1991) *Public Opinion in America: Moods, Cycles, and Swings* (Boulder, CO, Westview).

Stimson J A, Thiébaut C, and Tiberj V (2012) 'The evolution of policy attitudes in France', *European Union Politics* 13(2): 293–316.

Stoker G (2006) *Why Politics Matters: Making Democracy Work* (Basingstoke, Palgrave Macmillan).

——— (2017) *Why Politics Matters: Making Democracy Work, Second edition* (London, Palgrave Macmillan).

Stoker G et al. (2011) *Prospects for Citizenship* (London, Bloomsbury).

Stoker G and Hay C (2017) 'Understanding and challenging populist negativity towards politics: The perspectives of British citizens', *Political Studies* 65 (1): 4–23.

Stoker G, Hay C, and Barr M (2016) 'Fast thinking: Implications for democratic politics', *European Journal of Political Research* 55(1): 3–21.

Stoycheff E and Nisbet E C (2014) 'What's the bandwidth for democracy? Deconstructing internet penetration and citizen attitudes about governance', *Political Communication* 31(4): 628–646.

Strömbäck J (2008) 'Four phases of mediatisation: An analysis of the mediatisation of politics', *Press/Politics* 13(3): 228–246.

Sturgis P, Baker N, Callegaro M, Fisher S, Green J, Jennings W, Kuha J, Lauderdale B, and Smith P (2016) *Report of the Inquiry into the 2015 British General Election Opinion Polls* (London, Market Research Society/British Polling Council).

Sylvester R (2014) 'UKIP is cashing in on our obsession with class: British society remains as stratified as ever, but the political loyalties that went with it have been shattered', *The Times*, 25 November.

Swyngedouw E (2005) 'Governance innovation and the citizen: The Janus face of governance-beyond-the-state', *Urban Studies* 42(11): 1991–2006.

Tarrow S (1998) *Power in Movement: Social Movements and Contentious Politics* (Cambridge, Cambridge University Press).

Thompson M (2016) *Enough Said: What's Gone Wrong with the Language of Politics?* (London, Bodley Head).

Thrift N (1983) 'On the determination of social action in space and time', *Environment and Planning D: Society and Space* 1: 23–57.

——— (1996) *Spatial Formations* (London, Sage).

Tilly C (2004) *Social Movements, 1768–2004* (Boulder, CO, Paradigm).

Todd S (2014) *The People: The Rise and Fall of the Working Class* (London, John Murray).

Tonge J, Mycock A, and Jeffery B (2012) 'Does citizenship education make young people better-engaged citizens?', *Political Studies* 60(3): 578–602.

Torcal M and Lago I (2006) 'Political participation, information, and accountability: Some consequences of political disaffection in new democracies', in Torcal M and Montero J R (eds) *Political Disaffection in Contemporary Democracies* (London, Routledge) pp308–332.

Torcal M and Montero J R (2006) *Political Disaffection in Contemporary Democracies: Social Capital, Institutions, and Politics* (London, Routledge).

Toynbee P (2015) 'This leadership race is bigger than Labour: If Corbyn wins, Britain could be out of Europe', *The Guardian*, 25 August.

Van Wessel M (2010) 'Political disaffection: What can we learn from asking the people?', *Parliamentary Affairs* 63(3): 504–523.

Walker J L (1966) 'A critique of the elitist theory of democracy', *American Political Science Review* 60(2): 285–295.

Walters W (2004) 'Some critical notes on "governance"', *Studies in Political Economy* 73: 27–46.

Webb P (2013) 'Who is willing to participate? Dissatisfied democrats, stealth democrats, and populists in the United Kingdom', *European Journal of Political Research* 52: 747–772.

Weber M (1984) 'Politics as a vocation', in Owen D and Strong T B (eds) *Max Weber: The Vocation Lectures* (Cambridge, Hackett), pp32–94.

Weltman D and Billig M (2001) 'The political psychology of contemporary anti-politics: A discursive approach to the end-of-ideology era', *Political Psychology* 22(2): 267–382.

Whiteley P (2012) *Political Participation in the UK: The Decline and Revival of Civic Culture* (Basingstoke, Palgrave Macmillan).

Whiteley P, Clarke H D, Sanders D, and Stewart M C (2013) *Affluence, Austerity, and Electoral Change in Britain* (Cambridge, Cambridge University Press).

(2016) 'Why do voters lose trust in governments? Public perceptions of government honesty and trustworthiness in Britain, 2000–2013', *British Journal of Politics and International Relations* 18(1): 234–254.

Wilson J and Swyngedouw E (2014) *The Post-Political and Its Discontents: Spaces of Depoliticisation, Spectres of Radical Politics* (Edinburgh, Edinburgh University Press).

Wood M, Corbett J, and Flinders M (2016) 'Just like us: Everyday celebrity politicians and the pursuit of popularity in an age of anti-politics', *The British Journal of Political Science and International Relations* 18(3): 581–598.

Worcester R (1991) *British Public Opinion: A Guide to the History and Methodology of Political Opinion Polling* (Oxford, Wiley-Blackwell).

Wring D (1995) 'From mass propaganda to political marketing: The transformation of Labour Party election campaigning', *British Elections and Parties Yearbook* 5(1): 105–124.

Zaller J (1992) *The Nature and Origins of Mass Opinion* (New York, NY, Cambridge University Press).

Žižek S (1999) *The Ticklish Subject: The Absent Centre of Political Ontology* (London, Verso).

Index